GUNG HO!

Other Tactics/Intelligence Supplements from Posterity Press:

Global Warrior: Averting WWIII
Expeditionary Eagles: Outmaneuvering the Taliban
Homeland Siege: Tactics for Police and Military
Tequila Junction: 4th-Generation Counterinsurgency
Dragon Days: Time for "Unconventional" Tactics
Terrorist Trail: Backtracking the Foreign Fighter
Militant Tricks: Battlefield Ruses of the Islamic Militant
Tactics of the Crescent Moon: Militant Muslim Combat Methods
The Tiger's Way: A U.S. Private's Best Chance for Survival
Phantom Soldier: The Enemy's Answer to U.S. Firepower
One More Bridge to Cross: Lowering the Cost of War
The Last Hundred Yards: The NCO's Contribution to Warfare

GUNG HO!

THE CORPS' MOST PROGRESSIVE TRADITION

ILLUSTRATED

H. JOHN POOLE
FOREWORD BY
GEN. ANTHONY C. ZINNI USMC (RET.)

POSTERITY
PRESS

Published by Posterity Press
P.O. Box 5360, Emerald Isle, NC 28594
(www.posteritypress.org)

Cataloging-in-Publication Data

Poole, H. John, 1943-
Gung Ho!
Includes bibliography and index.
1. Infantry drill and tactics.
2. Military art and science.
3. Military history.
I. Title. ISBN: 978-0-9818659-4-2 2012 355'.42
Library of Congress Control Number: 2012908210

Cover art © 2012 by Edward Molina
Edited by Dr. Mary Beth Poole
Proofread by William E. Harris

First printing, United States of America, August 2012

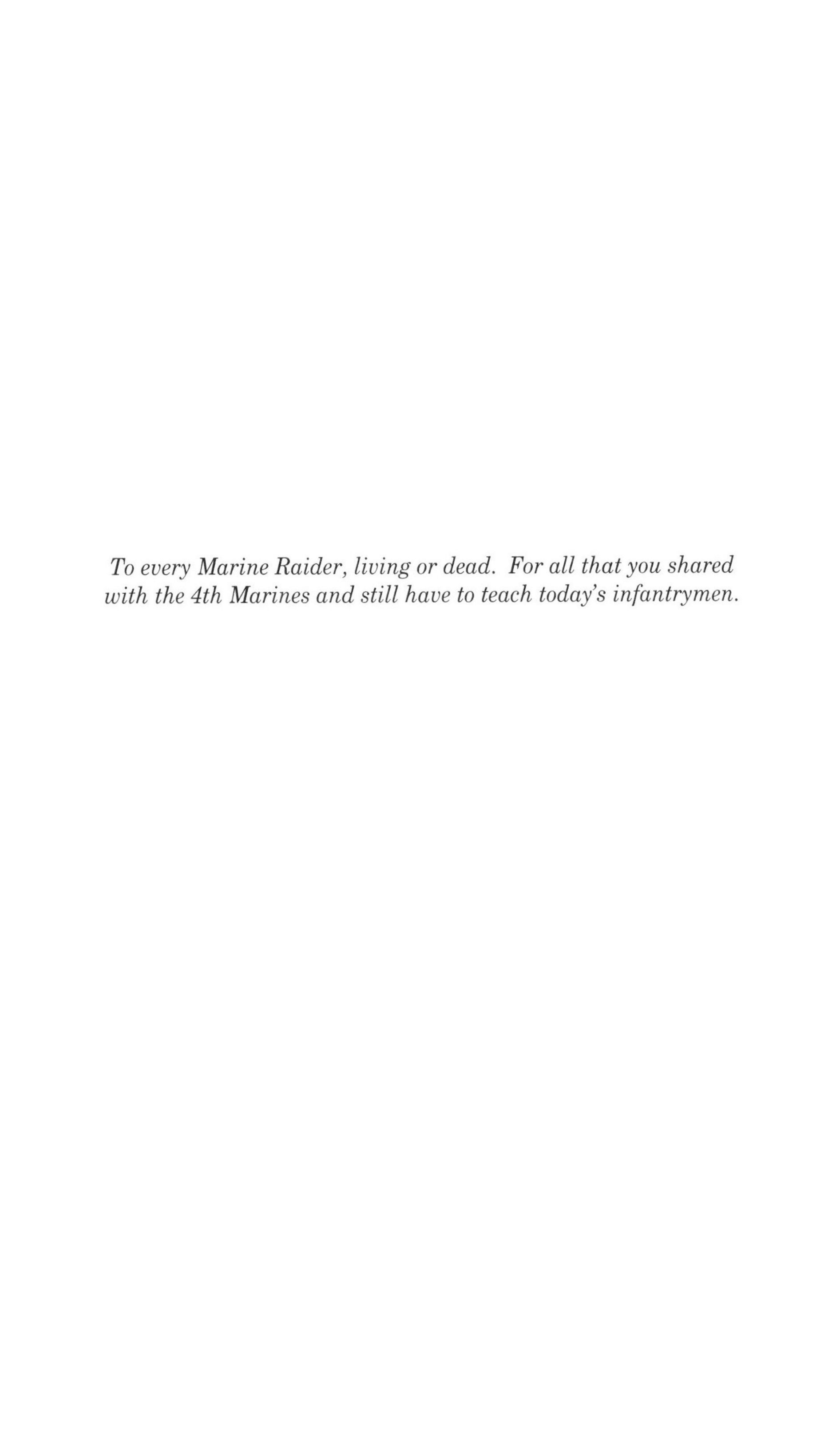

To every Marine Raider, living or dead. For all that you shared with the 4th Marines and still have to teach today's infantrymen.

The Marine Raiders of WWII

(Source: Official recruiting poster, image designator "post_usmc_168th-birthday_ww2.jpg," retrieved from U.S. Nat. Archives and Records Admin., by www.bluejacket.com)

DISCLAIMER: *WHILE ATTEMPTING TO ASSIST THE CURRENT GENERATION OF U.S. INFANTRYMEN, THE AUTHOR MAY HAVE INSUFFICIENTLY CREDITED THEIR PREDECESSORS. IF ANY MARINE RAIDER OR 4TH MARINE REGIMENT ACCOMPLISHMENT IS IN ANY WAY UNDERSTATED, THE AUTHOR IS SORRY.*

Contents

Illustrations

Maps:

Figures:

Tables

Foreword

During my tour of duty in 1983 as the head of a section at Headquarters Marine Corps responsible for counter terrorism, low intensity, and special operations, I was directed to conduct a study on the Marine Corps' potential creation of a special operations capability. That study and one conducted by one of our Marine Expeditionary Forces, resulted in the development of our Marine Expeditionary Unit (Special Operations Capable). Years later the Marine Corps, like the other services, created a Marine Corps Special Operations Command. As part of our study, we researched the Corps' past experiences with the World War II Marine Raider Battalions. I was struck with the focus of those involved in creating the Raiders on small unit tactics, organization, and equipment. Much of what they developed was incorporated into the structure of our infantry battalions. That legacy gave us a dynamic small unit organization that proved highly effective in the conflicts that followed.

One aspect of the Raider development that is well known but rarely examined is the concept of *Gung Ho*. Evans Carlson, commander of the Second Raider Battalion, brought the concept to the Raiders from his experiences with the Chinese forces. The importance of analyzing this concept is timely given the nature and form of current conflicts. It also encourages examination of the psychology and mindset required to conduct small unit independent operations. Our Special Operations Forces such as the U.S. Army's Special Forces have done significant studies in these areas and a look back at the Carlson approach and its applicability today is valuable.

John Poole's *GUNG HO!* is a superb and fascinating study. Like all his works, it demonstrates a deep level of understanding of the battlefield and its dynamics. This book goes beyond the mechanics of the weapons, tactics, and formations and brings out the thinking and attitude required to succeed in the most stressful environment of war a Marine could face. It is a great addition to the prolific and creative books John has given us.

GEN. ANTHONY C. ZINNI USMC (RET.)
FORMER HEAD OF CENTCOM

Preface

Writing about the United States Marine Corps (USMC) is no easy matter for a former member. That's because so many extraordinary people have passed through its ranks. For them, there can be only admiration. Tens of thousands have been cited for bravery in combat. As many others have displayed courage in peacetime, only to be met with a rebuke. But, whatever the outcome, almost all will admit to being "a better man" for the experience. Such is the bond that holds all Leathernecks together. Within their collective past learning lies the solution to all future challenges. This book is about how a little understood (and somewhat suppressed) portion of Marine Corps history could still be of use to all U.S. service branches.

Since 1775, U.S. Marines have faced all foes under every circumstance. With their nation and world again in grave danger, they must now draw on that diverse heritage to more effectively practice 3rd- and 4th-Generation Warfare (3GW and 4GW). It is with 3GW and 4GW that one can sidestep an enemy's strengths to more easily get at his weaknesses. At less cost in lives and wherewithal, that in turn leads to a more decisive victory.

One of the Corps' more obscure traditions is as much loyalty down the chain of command as up it (support for lower echelons). After going to the I MEF commander for career assistance in 1983, a reserve Major improbably declared: "General, you owe me." Just because the General had been his battalion commander in Vietnam, that Marine—after only marginal service—still felt comfortable in saying that to someone many pay grades his senior.[1] How was this possible? Mid-level infantry leaders of the period must have attributed all battlefield success to subordinates—however average—and considered themselves to be only facilitators. This was the inclination then, and it may again prove useful. Perhaps, that's also the most productive relationship between an infantry Captain and his Corporals.

Whenever possible, what the rank and file collectively know to be true should be incorporated into every leadership decision. Nothing but "unquestioning" loyalty up the chain might lead to a few tactical miscues. Lt.Col. Evans Fordyce Carlson was able to utilize the advice of his lowest-ranking Marine Raiders during World War II (WWII), Within that legend may lie more battlefield prowess for today's infantrymen and special operators.

LT.COL. H. JOHN POOLE USMC (RET.)
FORMER GY.SGT. FMCR

Acknowledgments

Heaven's halls are guarded by United States Marines. Most have made the ultimate sacrifice while still in their teens. They never got the chance to marry their high school sweetheart or grow old with their fishing pal. Yet, it is largely they who have given every American the freedom to think, believe, and speak as they wish. To them is owed every U.S. citizen's duty to preserve this experiment in democracy. Only with everyone now "working together" will those countless thousands of observant souls remain content with their sacrifice.

Part One

The Extent of "Working Together"

"Those whose upper and lower ranks
have the same desire are victorious." — Sun Tzu

(Source: "The Art of War," by Sun Tzu, translated by Thomas Cleary, pp. 80, 81)

1 Historical Backdrop

- To what extent have GIs been exposed to Chinese tactics?
- Have they ever tried those tactics at the small-unit level?

One U.S. Marine major had the president for his father.

(Source: Corel Gallery Clipart, Portraits Historical, #01C035)

The Roots of Nontraditional Wisdom

Literally translated, *"gung ho"* means "working together" in Chinese. While the term did not become an official part of USMC jargon until 1942, its message was far from new to its members. After helping to defend Peking's diplomatic enclave in 1900, Leathernecks routinely served in China for 40 years. (See Table 1.1 and Figure 1.1.) Of course, the tradition of working together was not uniquely Asian. While fighting the World War I (WWI) Germans, Devil Dog infantrymen had painfully witnessed the power of decentralized control and "bottom-up" thinking.[1] (See Figure 1.2.)

1843 China: Sailors and Marines from the St. Louis landed after clash with locals at the trading post in Canton.

1854 China: U.S. ships landed forces to protect American interests in and near Shanghai during Chinese civil strife.

1855 China: U.S. forces protected American interests in Shanghai and fought pirates near Hong Kong.

1856 China: U.S. forces landed to protect U.S. interests at Canton and to avenge an assault upon an unarmed U.S. boat.

1859 China: Naval force landed to protect U.S. assets in Shanghai.

1866 China: U.S. forces punished an assault on the American consul at Newchwang.

1894-95 China: Marines stationed at Tientsin and penetrated to Peking to protect U.S. assets during Sino-Japanese War.

1894-95 China: A naval vessel was beached and used as a fort at Newchwang for protection of American nationals.

1898-99 China: U.S. forces provided a guard for the legation at Peking and the consulate at Tientsin during contest between the Dowager Empress and her son.

1900 China: U.S. troops protect foreign lives during the Boxer Uprising, particularly at Peking. Then, permanent legation guard maintained in Peking, and periodically strengthened.

1911 China: As Nationalist Revolution approached, a small naval party unsuccessfully tried to enter Wuchang to rescue missionaries, and a small landing force guarded U.S. property and consulate at Hankow. Marines deployed to guard the cable stations at Shanghai; landing forces sent for protection to Nanking, Chinkiang, Taku and elsewhere.

1912 China: On Kentucky Island and at Camp Nicholson, U.S. forces protected Americans and U.S. interests during revolutionary activity.

Table 1.1: U.S. Military's Exposure to Chinese Ways

(Source: "Instances of Use of United States Armed Forces Abroad, 1798-2010," by Richard F. Grimmett, CRS #R41677, 10 March 2011)

1912-41 China: The dynasty overthrow during the Kuomintang Rebellion in 1912, and the invasion of China by Japan, led to many local demonstrations and protective U.S. landings from 1912 on to 1941. The guard at Peking and along the route to the sea was maintained until 1941. In 1927, the U.S. had 5,670 troops ashore and 44 naval vessels in Chinese waters. In 1933 the U.S. had 3,027 men ashore.

1916 China: American forces landed to quell a riot taking place on American property in Nanking.

1917 China: American troops were landed at Chungking to protect American lives during a political crisis.

1920 China: A landing force was sent ashore for a few hours to protect lives during a disturbance at Kiukiang.

1922-23 China: Marines were landed five times to protect Americans during periods of unrest.

1924 China: Marines were landed to protect Americans and other foreigners in Shanghai during Chinese factional hostilities.

1925 China: Riots and demonstrations in Shanghai brought the landing of American forces to protect lives and property in the International Settlement.

1926 China: Nationalist attack on Hankow brought the landing of American naval forces to protect American citizens. A small guard was maintained at consulate general when the rest of the forces were withdrawn. Likewise, when Nationalist forces captured Kiukiang, naval forces were landed for the protection of foreigners.

1927 China: Fighting at Shanghai caused American naval forces and Marines to be increased. A naval guard was stationed at the U.S. consulate at Nanking after Nationalist forces captured the city. American destroyers later used shell fire to protect Americans and other foreigners. Subsequently additional forces of Marines and naval vessels were stationed in the vicinity of Shanghai and Tientsin.

Table 1.1: U.S. Military's Exposure to Chinese Ways (cont.)

(Source: "Instances of Use of United States Armed Forces Abroad, 1798-2010," by Richard F. Grimmett, CRS #R41677, 10 March 2011)

1932 China: American forces were landed to protect American interests during the Japanese occupation of Shanghai.

1934 China: Marines landed at Foochow to protect U.S. Consulate.

1941-45 World War II: The United States goes to war with Japan, Germany, Italy, Bulgaria, Hungary and Rumania. Marine Raider battalions patterned after Mao's 8th Route Army operate in the South Pacific. and Gen. Stilwell's "Chindits" in Burma.

1945 China: 50,000 U.S. Marines were sent to North China to assist Chinese Nationalist authorities in disarming and repatriating the Japanese in China and in controlling ports, railroads, and airfields. This was in addition to approximately 60,000 U.S. forces remaining in China at the end of World War II.

1948-49 China: Marines were dispatched to Nanking to protect the American Embassy when the city fell to Communist troops, and to Shanghai to aid in the protection and evacuation of Americans.

1950-53 Korean War: The United States responded to North Korean invasion of South Korea by going to its assistance, pursuant to United Nations Security Council resolutions. U.S. forces deployed in Korea exceeded 300,000 during the last year of the conflict. In October 1950, upwards of 130,000 Chinese "volunteers" had come to the assistance of the North Koreans (Hastings, "The Korean War," New York: Simon & Schuster, p. 137)

1964-73 Vietnam War: U.S. military advisers had been in South Vietnam for a decade, and their numbers had been increased as the military position of the Saigon government became weaker. After the Tonkin Gulf Resolution and a Communist attack on a U.S. installation in central Vietnam, the United States escalated its participation in the war to a peak of 543,000 military personnel by April 1969. Throughout the war, many thousands of Chinese "volunteers" had manned the air and ground defenses around Hanoi and Haiphong (Tourison, "Talking with Victor Charlie," New York: Ivy, pp. 234, 235).

Table 1.1: U.S. Military's Exposure to Chinese Ways (cont.)

(Source: "Instances of Use of United States Armed Forces Abroad, 1798-2010," by Richard F. Grimmett, CRS #R41677, 10 March 2011)

Figure 1.1: Deployed U.S. Military Contingent
(Source: U.S. Army Ctr. of Mil. Hist., artphoto archives, illustration designator "avop03-98_1.jpg," Thank God for the Soldiers—U.S. Army ... in San Francisco, 1906)

From whatever source, the idea of jointly supporting each other has had a pronounced effect on USMC history. In fact, it may be what still sets the Corps apart from other U.S. service branches.

Enter Evans Fordyce Carlson

In 1927, Lieutenant Evans Carlson deployed to Shanghai with the 4th Marines. As regimental intelligence officer, he developed

Figure 1.2: WWI Had Not Been Won by Allied Artillery
(Source: U.S. Army Center of Military History, posters, illustration designator "couldnt_fight.jpg," by Clyde Forsythe, 1918)

a deep interest in the Chinese version of guerrilla warfare. After a brief stint with the Nicaraguan Guardia National (in which he led a daring night attack), he returned to Peking's Legation Guard. Then, in 1937, Captain Carlson came back to Shanghai for a third China tour. After watching the Japanese take over the city, he got permission to briefly accompany Mao Tse-tung's 8th Route Army. During this physically demanding period, he refined his ideas on guerrilla warfare and the "emphasis on individual effort" that it seemed to entail. Censured after talking to the press, he resigned his commission and returned to the States to speak out on how best to help the Chinese evict the Japanese. Among his literary contributions were *The Chinese Army* and *Twin Stars of China*. After another trip to China as a civilian, he rejoined the U.S. Marine Corps in April 1941. Through his friendship with President Roosevelt's son James, Carlson was soon asked to establish the 2nd Raider Battalion. ("Red Mike" Edson had already formed the 1st.[2])

While the Raiders were mainly intended to prepare shorelines for invasion during WWII, the 2nd Battalion would become the first U.S. force to practice the Guerrilla aspect of Unconventional Warfare (UW).[3] (See Map 1.1.) Thus, they were the forerunners of all U.S. special operators. Unlike Edson, Carlson and his Executive Officer (XO) Roosevelt were to instill within the 2nd Battalion a "mixture of Chinese culture, Communist egalitarianism [equal rights], and New England town hall democracy."[4]

> Every man would have the right to say what he thought, and their battle cry would be "*Gung Ho!*" . . . Officers would have no greater privileges than the men, and would *lead by consensus rather than rank*. There would also be "Ethical Indoctrination." . . . [It] supposedly ensured that each man knew what he was fighting for and why. [Italics added.] [5]
>
> — History and Museums Division, HQMC, 1995

How the Chinese 8th Route Army Operated

From 1934 to 1935, Mao Tse-tung and the entire Red Army had retreated some 6,000 miles across China to escape annihilation by the Nationalist Kuomintang Army of Chiang Kai-shek. Of the 80,000 soldiers who began this withdrawal, only one-tenth may have completed it.[6] From this episode and previous guerrilla activity, Mao had necessarily learned how to get the most out of his individual fighters. How he then operated will be hard for Americans to believe.

> [T]he reason why the Red Army can sustain itself . . . in spite of such a poor standard of material life and such incessant engagements, is its practice of *democracy*. . . . [O]fficers and men receive equal treatment; soldiers enjoy freedom of assembly and speech; cumbersome ceremonies are done away with; and the books are open to the inspection of all. [Italics added.] [7]
>
> — Mao Tse-tung

This purported use of democracy within the army of a totalitarian regime was of great interest to Carlson. Having watched the grinding inertia of a "top-down" military for almost 30 years, he thought more input from the bottom might do it good.

The Original Dispute over the Raiders' Role

During the early days of WWII, President Roosevelt needed forces to harass and delay a much stronger foe in the Pacific. He soon seized upon a commando model for maritime raiders and guerrilla fighters. Unfortunately, Headquarters Marine Corps (HQMC) wanted no part of the guerrilla role.[8] This internal squabble over mission was eventually to doom the whole Raider concept. Carlson's guerrilla training came to a roaring halt in 1943 on New Caledonia, when Lt.Col. Alan Shapely took over 2nd Battalion. According to the official Raider chronicle, this "put an end to Carlson's *'Gung Ho'* experiments."[9] Because 2nd Battalion was to do things so extraordinary during its short tenure, the exact nature of those "experiments" will be the goal of Part One. Of course, 1st Raider Battalion also fought hard and earned its own niche in history. Yet, the full combat potential of the both Raider units would never be realized.

All Raider battalions (to include the sequels to 1st and 2nd) were more often utilized as elite jungle infantry than either of their intended roles.[10] Right up to the time they became part of the reconstituted 4th Marine Regiment, they were given the most uninhabitable South Pacific islands to work. Carlson's men may have been able to more

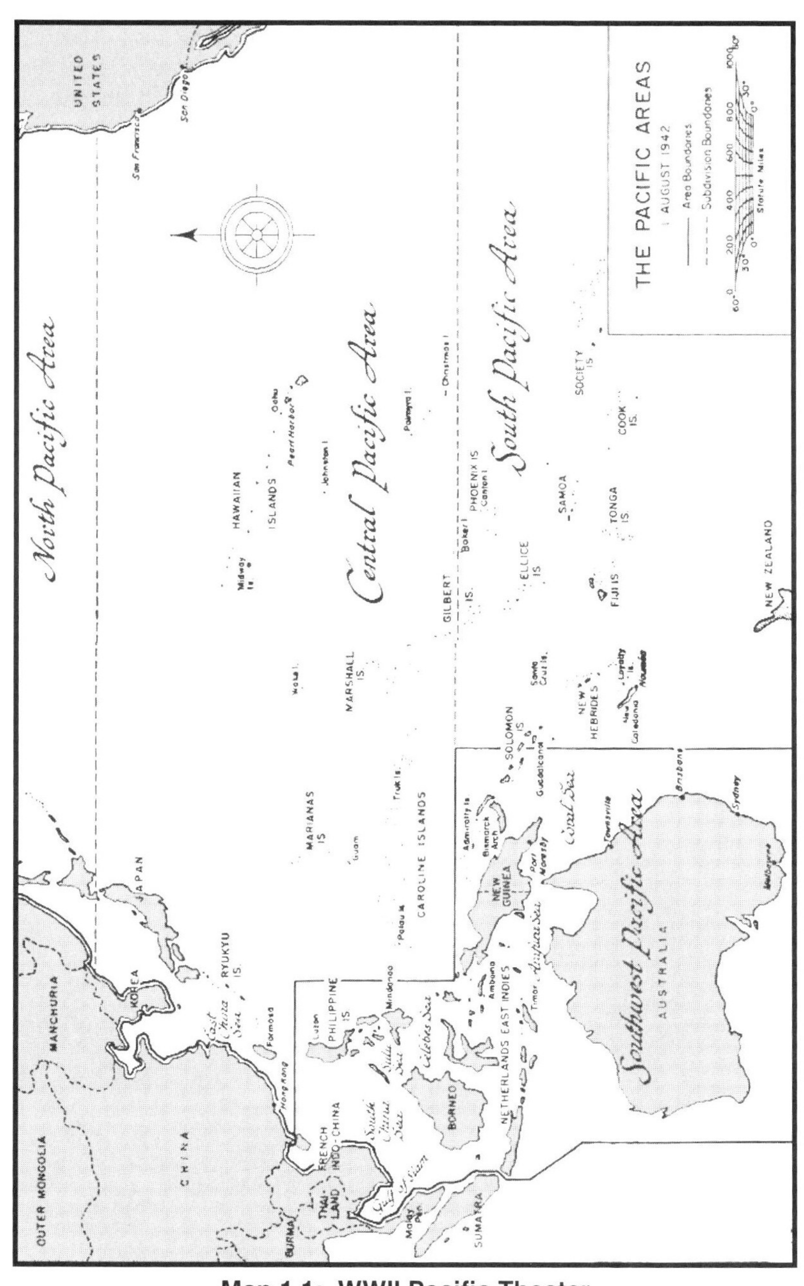

Map 1.1: WWII Pacific Theater

(Source: "First Offensive: The Marine Campaign for Guadalcanal," by Henry I. Shaw, Marines in WWII Commemorative Series, HQMC, 1992, p. 2)

secretly approach an enemy strongpoint than regular U.S. infantry. But, like that infantry, they never acquired enough attack expertise to capture a "prepared enemy position"—one protected by barbed wire, mines, and interlocking machinegun fire—by surprise. Only through trial and error, did their sequel—the 4th Battalion Raiders—do well against a strongpoint matrix in their last desperate struggle on New Georgia. With some advanced assault technique, they might have punched all the way through it. Still, the experience was to pay big dividends. As part of the 4th Marines, the same group would have more success than other battalions with the mutually supporting bunker complexes of WWII's greatest test—Okinawa's Sugar Loaf Complex. (See Figure 1.3.)

Figure 1.3: Former Raiders Were to Face Okinawa Meat Grinder
(Source: "Closing In: Marines in the Seizure of Iwo Jima," by J.H. Alexander, Marines in WWII Commemorative Series, HQMC, 1994, drawing by Charles H. Waterhouse, p. 22)

Out of Seeming Defeat May Have Sprung Great Potential

Lt.Col. Evans Carlson soon suffered all the torment of any reformer to the bureaucratic *status quo*. His attempts to infuse a Western military with a little Eastern culture had made him minimally eccentric in the eyes of most. Surviving members of the sequel battalions still describe both him and Edson as "crazy."[11] After the war, Carlson's ideas then had to contend with all the anti-Communist paranoia of the pre-McCarthy era. Before dying penniless (and possibly of a broken heart) in 1947, he was considered by his monocultural detractors to be more than just a little "pink."

Because of the good Colonel's famous aversion to rank, most modern-day infantrymen assume he made no other contribution to their heritage (or small-unit tactics). Yet, most of his ideas were more counter-cultural than impractical. Junior enlisted personnel should be able to come up with the most surprise-oriented squad, fire team, and individual maneuvers. It is they, after all, who must pay the ultimate price for premature detection. So, within the extent of his experiments may lie the seeds to combat's Holy Grail—more flexibility and momentum through sub-element cooperation than through direct supervision.

Only squads and below can operate "on auto-pilot"—move around a battlefield using rehearsed maneuvers based on anticipated circumstances. (All larger contingents require some headquarters coordination.) Thus, only squads and below have "tactical techniques." Because the 8th Route Army relied so heavily on small-unit autonomy for its Guerrilla phase, it would have wanted equally powerful techniques for its Mobile and Positional phases.[12] During the stint with this Communist army, Carlson may have witnessed how each unit was able to adapt its guerrilla methods to more conventional purposes. With a similar procedure, Americans might develop—from scratch—the most appropriate moves for common scenarios. When rehearsed, those moves would then allow squads and below to more quickly adapt to battlefield circumstances (and thus win their engagements).

It is known that "*Gung Ho*" applied to more than just individual attitude. It included the collective opinions of all lower ranks. (2nd Battalion Raiders still had ranks; the recipients just didn't wear them.) If field trials were following technique proposals on New Caledonia, Carlson may have been developing tactical methods far superior to anything from HQMC. Such an accomplishment would have had repercussions. That much "in-unit" democracy did not sit well with traditional leaders. Standardized training better insured their control.

Not Everyone Thought Squad Autonomy an Asset

For military groups of highly spirited and individualistic Americans, leadership can be the most elusive ingredient. With better (self-generated) maneuvers, those Raider squads would have provided their company commanders with more tactical options—like how to do the same job with fewer people. But, already subject to troop criticism, those Raider officers may not have completely welcomed this way of influencing their battlefield decisions.

Why the disdain for something so logical? It has mostly to do with cultural heritage. While the Asian officer studies his troops' capabilities and then looks for conducive battlefield circumstances,[13] his Western counterpart trains his troops and then marches to the sound of the guns. Both approaches will work, but only within their own cultural context. In effect, the Asians have had to make do with much less technological wherewithal. Still, no present-day U.S. military commander would pass up a way to more consistently win engagements. That's how momentum is established. If so doing takes borrowing an idea from someone else, then the consummate professional will still jump at the chance. Thus, Carlson's ideas deserve a second, more extensive look. As long as the U.S. rank system remains intact, what's the harm? Those ideas may now help the cash-strapped (and firepower-reduced) Pentagon to keep more Government Issues (GIs) alive.

The Marine Raiders' Initial Contribution

- What was the difference between Raider battalions?
- Would their separate visions ever combine?

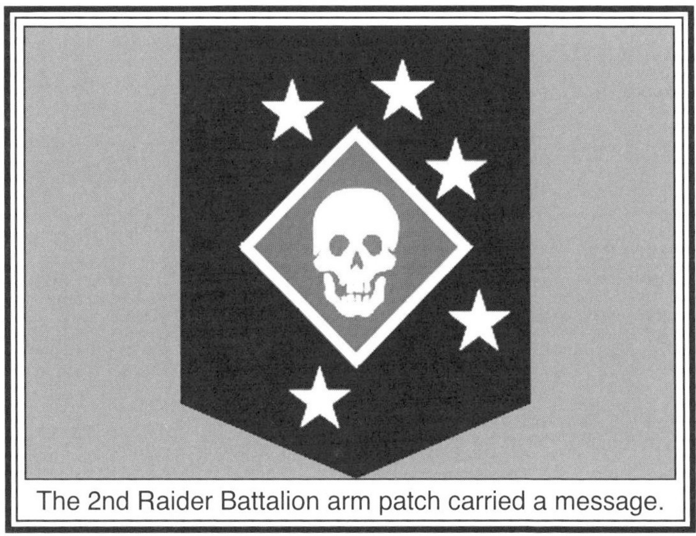

The 2nd Raider Battalion arm patch carried a message.

(Source: Wikipedia Encyclopedia, s.v. "Carlson's Raiders")

Not All Raider Units Patterned after Mao

Carlson formed the 2nd Raider Battalion, after Edson had already established the 1st Raider Battalion from a redesignated infantry unit—1st Battalion, 5th Marines (1/5).[1]

Intent on copying 8th Route Army methods, Carlson and his XO— James Roosevelt—then spurned a HQMC attempt to use Edson Raider personnel as the nucleus for their new Raider battalion. Thus, only the 2nd and 4th (later to be formed by Roosevelt) Battalions were the product of a direct Chinese influence.[2] Of course, some of that influence would eventually rub off on 1st Battalion and its sequel (the 3rd). However, that part would have more to do with subunit breakdown than subunit utilization and overall leadership style.

The First Change Would Be to Unit Structure

Carlson soon became the first American military commander to adopt a three-fire-team squad. Each of those fire teams, in turn, had three members. So, in all, the new Raider squads were comprised of 10 men. In his book *Edson's Raiders,* Col. Joseph Alexander confirms that other Marine squads of the period were still unitary in nature—with only eight men and no subdivisions. That means the squad leader personally directed all seven members.[3]

Carlson's three-element breakdown is still in effect at almost every echelon within Asia's Communist armies.[4] Not only are their squads composed of three fire teams, but each of those fire teams has a veteran and two inductees.

At first, Edson stayed with the standard eight-man squad, but with two Browning Automatic Rifle (BAR) men instead of one, and a sniper. On the advice of his XO, he would later champion the four-man fire team.[5] (That XO—Samuel Griffith—had studied Chinese in Peking in 1937 and then seen Carlson's training,[6] so he most likely helped Edson to realize the fire team's value.)

Because the U.S. Army still utilizes a two-fire-team (nine-man) squad, the significance of Carlson's three-team arrangement has been largely lost to history. Only those who have experimented extensively with squad tactics realize how much more potential the "triple combo" has for maneuver. Instead of the predictable "bounding" of a two-element team, it allows for a third diversionary or augmentation element. The first would distract the defenders during a hasty attack, while the second would allow for a "beefed-up" base-of-fire or assault element during a deliberate attack. Though a double-envelopment around the perimeter trench of a fortified position is strictly forbidden by U.S. doctrine, two fire teams in the assault make possible a series of lifesaving feints. One team can be moving while the other draws the defenders' fire; and then they alternate roles. That way, all enemy eyes need not be riveted on the advancing party. However, three fire teams are not just useful in the offense. During any squad-sized patrol, they enable one team to stay with the squad leader as a ready reaction force while the other two are deployed as security. On defense, the three teams allow for an additional strongpoint or sentry post.

Thanks largely to Carlson, present-day Marines still enjoy a three-fire-team setup. Its most important advantage is flexibility. With three teams, the Marine squad leader enjoys more tactical options, to include a little deception. The extent to which he can outmaneuver his opponent will then dictate platoon and company momentum.

The Difference in Tactics between Battalions

While Carlson was primarily interested in the guerrilla tactics of UW, he never got the time to fully develop them. The system he had borrowed from the 8th Route Army was to create a force suited "for infiltration and the attainment of objectives by unorthodox and unexpected methods."[7] The unexpected can be achieved through impulsive behavior, but the unorthodox requires that habits be broken. His first deployment had been a fairly conventional raid on Makin Island in which his troops got little chance to apply their guerrilla methods. Not until their month-long patrol behind enemy lines on Guadalcanal, did those new methods come into play. (See Figure 2.1 and Map 2.1.) Late in that patrol, the Raiders did finally encounter a prepared enemy position on Mount Austin. But, because that position was not being actively manned at the time, they required no advanced assault technique to take it. This was just as well, because the Raiders had become skilled at sneaking up on enemy lines, not through them.

During that Long Patrol, Carlson felt most comfortable with sending his small, highly mobile contingents after enemy units withdrawing from Henderson Field. Like hounds nipping at a fox's heels, they would creep up on the Japanese, strike swiftly, and then quickly retire guerrilla fashion.[8] Such tactics were purely Maoist.

> Enemy advances, we retreat.
> Enemy halts, we harass.
> Enemy tires, we attack.
> Enemy retreats, we pursue.[9]
> — Mao's guerrilla guidance

Therefore, Carlson must have ultimately sought the "swarming" capabilities of loosely controlled guerrilla bands. Yet, as he had professed in Nicaragua (and subsequent engagements would

Figure 2.1: How Guadalcanal Looked at Ground Level
(Source: U.S. Army Center of Military History, artphoto archives, illustration designator "0806-1.jpg," Still Life—Guadalcanal, by Aaron Bohrod, 1943)

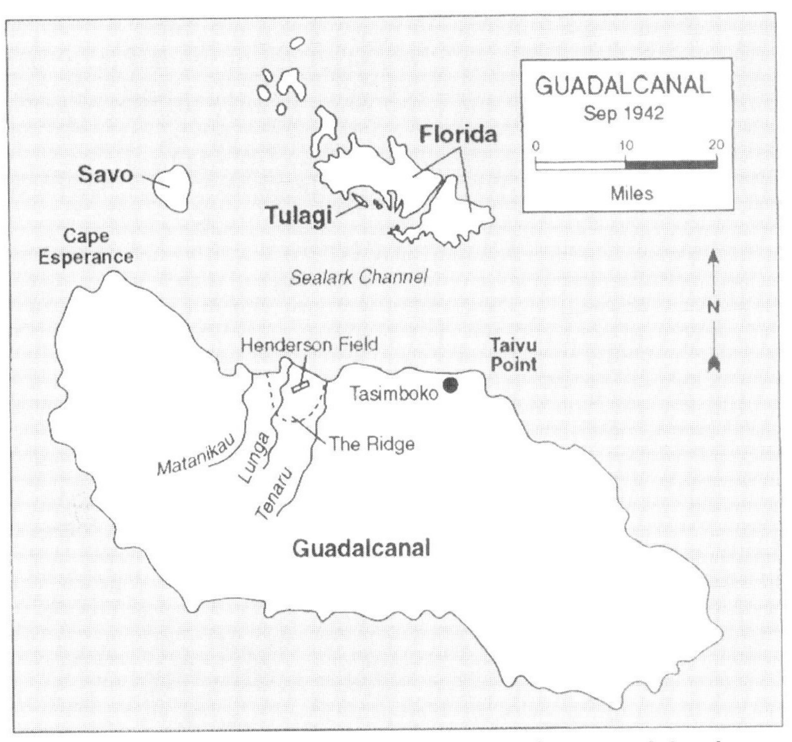

Map 2.1: Guadalcanal in the Southern Solomon Islands
(Source: "From Makin to Bouganville: Marine Raiders in the Pacific War," by Maj. Jon T. Hoffman, Marines in WWII Commemorative Series, HQMC, 1995, p. 12)

prove),[10] he was only interested in surprise during the movement to contact. Then, his tiny units were to overwhelm their immediate foe with small-arms fire. In other words, they would make no attempt at secrecy during the assault itself. To help in this regard, he had added five additional automatic weapons to the Marine squad—two BARs and three Thompson submachineguns. (See Figure 2.2.) There were also three semi-automatic rifles where before had been only the single-shot variety. His men each carried 80 pounds, of which too little was food.[11] So, the rest must have been ammunition.

All Asian Communist soldiers are shown how to overcome unhealthy odds,[12] so Carlson's less-than-secretive assault may have been fairly consistent with the period. Nearly invisible approach marches before totally silent "sapper" attacks would not become common practice until the Vietnam era. Short periods of highly intense fire have always been part of the Communists' defensive scheme.

Red Mike Edson, on the other hand, wanted the increased mobility of light infantry, but without as much emphasis on surprise.

Figure 2.2: Each Carlson Squad Had Two "Tommy Gunners"
(Source: U.S. Army Center of Military History, posters, illustration designator, "1-36-49.jpg," Soldier with Sub Machine Gun, by Harry M. Meyers)

Figure 2.3: Edson's Men Carried Lighter But Conventional Loads
(Source: "Up the Slot: Marines in the Central Solomons," by Maj. Charles D. Melson, Marines in WWII Commemorative Series, HQMC, 1993, drawing by Kerr Eby, p. 6)

While permitting his troops lighter ordnance loads so they could march faster, he still mostly relied during his raids on conventional (heavy infantry) maneuvers.[13] (See Figure 2.3.) His battalion was trained for single-company outings by specially outfitted boat. At Guadalcanal it ran several by APD (Auxiliary Personnel [Transport] Destroyer). Edson's troops were also extremely aggressive in combat.

After seizing one of Guadalcanal's offshore islands, his battalion raided one of the enemy's debarkation points at Tasimboko. Then, his men helped to thwart the main Japanese attack on Henderson Field. On Tulagi, it had shown an affinity for tiny, secretive envelopments. At Bloody Ridge, it had repelled repeated enemy assaults from a linear defense in depth that at times resembled separate strongpoints. (See Figure 2.4 and Map 2.2.) Yet, Edson was clearly committed to conventional methods. On a later reconnaissance foray beyond Bloody Ridge, his troops applied liberal amounts of artillery and crew-served weapons fire to any hint of enemy resistance.[14]

Figure 2.4: 1st Battalion Raiders at Bloody Ridge
(Source: "First Offensive: The Marine Campaign for Guadalcanal," by Henry I. Shaw, Marines in WWII Commemorative Series, HQMC, 1992, drawing by Donard L. Dixon, p. 25)

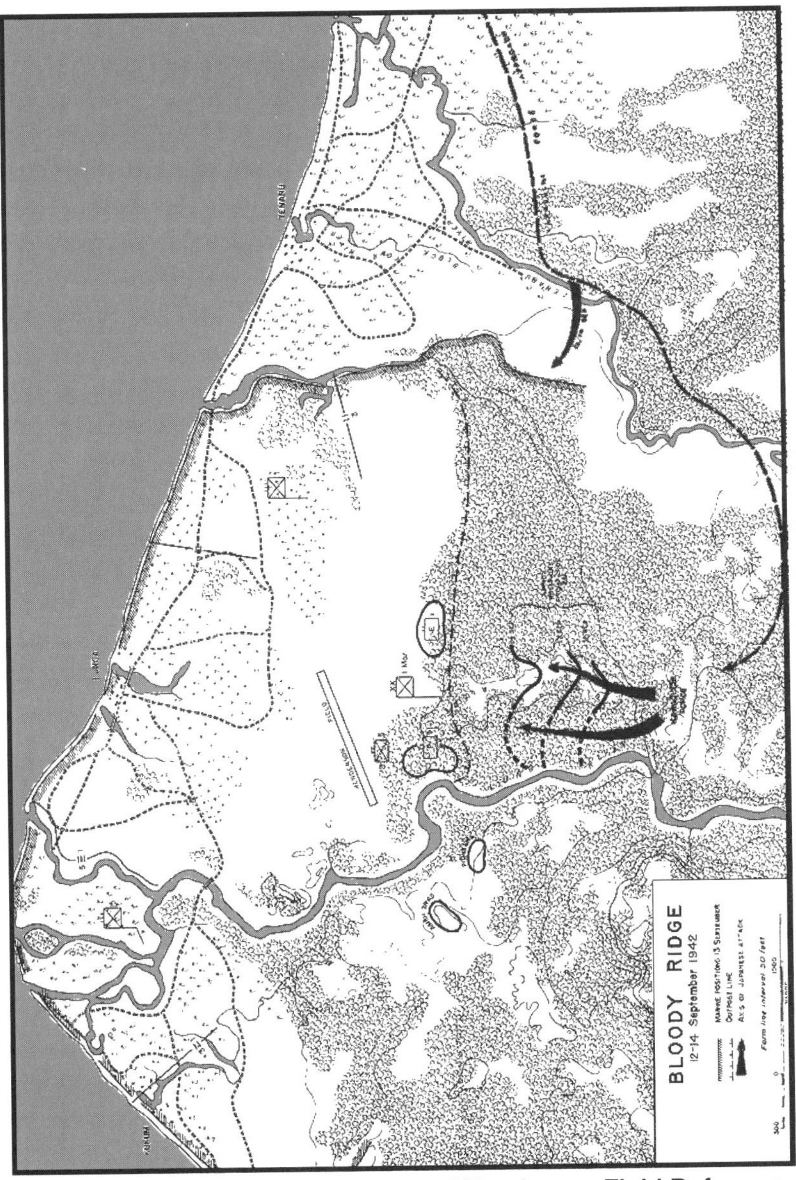

Map 2.2: Bloody Ridge Segment of Henderson Field Defenses

(Source: U.S. Army Center of Military History, The Green Books, Guadalcanal: The First Offensive, illustration designator "lmap-vi.jpg.")

Why 2nd Battalion May Have Gotten More from Its Squads

Both commanders had wished to increase their "mobility." By this, they mostly meant foot-marching more quickly along trails. Both were also interested in small-unit tactical proficiency. Because so much attention had been paid to the accidental discharge on Makin, 2nd Battalion may have been slightly more surprise oriented than the 1st. Carlson is known to have trained for night combat (when surprise is more easily achieved).[15] The battle chronicles further suggest his men crept closer to the Japanese before opening fire. But, surprise can be attained three ways—through speed, stealth, and deception. Even 2nd Battalion underutilized the latter. While "Carlson's system . . . was . . . for . . . the attainment of objectives by unorthodox and unexpected methods,"[16] there is no evidence of it ever developing highly deceptive small-unit maneuvers. So, that aspect of surprise may have been limited to the self-defense training. A few fairly tricky fire team and squad maneuvers may have cropped up on their own and even been tried in combat. Such are the fruits of loosely controlled units. But those maneuvers were never institutionalized (endorsed, disseminated, recorded, and then universally practiced).

Carlson's little group "get-togethers" had certainly helped in this regard. When under no fear of retribution, troops will readily criticize any tactic that promises to get them killed. Who is better qualified to judge? That's the rough equivalent of field testing a procedure with MILES [Multiple Integrated Laser Engagement System] or more modern casualty-assessment gear. So, within the 2nd Battalion, peer pressure alone may have limited the number of poorly advised small-unit maneuvers. The same principle applies either way—tactical worth is inversely proportional to casualties expected or suffered.

Of course, neither did Edson appear to make any particular contribution to the evolution of small-unit tactics, with the possible exception of the four-man fire team. By permitting its further subdivision into buddy teams, it had helped the commander to distribute his work. Much of what goes on in infantry combat, as in police work, takes two people to perform safely. But, in terms of any advanced fire team or squad maneuvers, there were none in 1st Battalion, or they would have been dutifully recorded and universally practiced. Within a world-class light-infantry portfolio would have been quiet sapper-style penetrations and ways for whole squads to enter a prepared enemy position without the majority of defenders ever realizing they were under ground assault. Also included would have been how self-sufficient squads could function as the strongpoints of a rearward-moving defense.

Still, the joint contribution of these two Marine giants—with somewhat differing visions—cannot be overstated. As Part's Two and Three will confirm, it has not only shaped the present-day Corps, but may also point toward a brighter future. First, some of the more controversial aspects of Carlson's program must be examined.

3 The Counter-Cultural "*Gung Ho* Session"

- How really democratic is a U.S. infantry unit?
- Which armies have relied on consensus opinions?

Carlson had also borrowed the Red's "*Gung Ho* Session."

(Source: Cassell PLC, from "World Army Uniforms since 1939," © 1975, 1980, 1981, 1983 by Blandford Press Ltd., Part II, plate 80; FM 21-76 [1957], p. 95)

"*Gung Ho!*" Has Changed Twice in Meaning over the Years

After the Raiders went away in 1943, the term "*Gung Ho*" first came to mean "spirit" and "can-do attitude" (as applied to each separate Marine).[1] Within this second ability was the confidence to individually make a difference. That's the same as initiative—one of the most sought-after combat attributes. At some point, the expression "*Gung Ho*" was watered down to infer "enthusiastic" or "dedicated."[2] Then, personal initiative, self-discipline, integrity, and any number of other East Asian qualities were no longer required of its recipient.

The Root Connotation

According to *Webster Dictionary,* "*gung ho*" had come from "*gonghé,*" which was short for Zhongguó Gongyè Hézuò Shè (Chinese Industrial Cooperative Society).[3] At least part of its original meaning was thus linked to the inner workings of Communist cooperatives. An agricultural cooperative, for example, was a farm owned and managed by its workers. Through their mutual effort, those workers had removed any need for a coordinator or leader. Within the highly hierarchical U.S. military, the necessity of a boss at all echelons was never questioned in 1941. Every element, however large, was thought to require someone's continual oversight. Yet, there had been plenty of examples to the contrary—like when squad leaders decided a platoon's next move after its lieutenant died. Group decisions are nothing new, and "management by exception" has long been a way to evoke more commitment from one's subordinates. Yet, some Western traditionalists may still consider such a leaderless arrangement to be Communist in origin. Actually, it predates all the "ism's."

> "I was trying to build up the same sort of working spirit I had seen in China. . . . I told them [the men] of the motto of the Chinese Cooperatives, '*Gung Ho*'."[4]
>
> — Carlson quote in *Life Magazine*, 1943

What Had Been Intended with the "Ethical Indoctrination"

In the 1947 biography—*The Big Yankee*—is Evans Carlson's explanation of the Ethical Indoctrination to which all Raiders were continually exposed. For Chinese soldiers, it had been "giving conviction through persuasion" to holistic thinkers.[5] For American troops, it may have been a way to encourage cooperation between individuals who were more culturally disposed toward separation of responsibilities.

> In the Eastern way of thinking, one starts with the whole, takes everything as a whole and proceeds with a comprehensive and intuitive synthesization [combination]. In the Western way of thinking . . . , one starts with the parts,

> takes [divides] a complex matter into compound parts and then deals with them one by one.[6]
>
> — Cao Shan, *The Strategic Advantage*

All members of the 8th Route Army had understood why every man's efforts were so crucial to the Chinese cause as a whole. Out of the Ethical Indoctrination, Carlson had hoped to give his men more confidence in themselves, their leaders, and their peers. Each man was continually reminded that his efforts counted, so that none would think of himself or his job as more or less important than another. Out of this mutual respect and confidence would supposedly come the ability of men "to work together wholeheartedly, without fear or favor or envy or contempt."[7] From this Raider tradition may have sprung the leadership axiom to never play favorites.

Why Carlson Placed So Much Emphasis on the Individual

As with 8th Route Army soldiers, always knowing the reason for fighting helped the Raiders to overcome difficult conditions. Over the years, Chinese soldiers have also been kept regularly apprised of the strategic and tactical "intents" of all leaders.[8] That's so they can either make a strategic contribution or get the hell out of the way. Yet, this part of the Asian tradition seems inconceivable to most Americans. They know of the poor human rights record of China's Communist regime. It clearly has less regard for human life than their own. That was evident in Korea. (See Figure 3.1.) But, this in no way restricts its use of infantrymen. Each soldier's life may not be held in particularly high regard, but his combat potential is. In fact, a detailed study of the subject shows the average Asian infantryman to be better prepared for the rigors of close combat than his Western counterpart.[9]

Because there are so many Orientals on the planet, most Americans think they do everything *en masse*. That would be very far from the truth.

> Whether in guerrilla . . . or limited regular warfare, . . . it [armed Communist struggle] is fully capable of . . . getting the better of a modern [high-tech] army. . . . This is the development of the . . . military art, the main content of

Figure 3.1: The North Koreans Had Been Hard to Stop
(Source: U.S. Army Center of Military History, artphoto archives, illustration designator "avop05-98_2.jpg," The American Soldier, 1950)

which is *to rely chiefly on [the] man, on his patriotism and . . . [individual] spirit.* [Italics added.] [10]
— Gen. Vo Nguyen Giap

With more emphasis on the lone fighter, an Asian army is also capable of very proficient small groups of fighters. China's political model may be top-down (with one party in charge), but its cultural orientation is still bottom-up. Thus, the People's Liberation Army (PLA) can turn to this aspect of its civilian culture to more easily accomplish grassroots strategies.

Meanwhile, most Western armies have had to operate within a top-down civilian culture. That's far too autocratic an environment. It makes them vulnerable to three syndromes: (1) over-attention to orders; (2) subdivision of responsibilities; and (3) exaggerated security. Because their top-ranking officers must follow—to the letter—the orders of their civilian bosses, they expect all subordinates to do likewise. To better distribute the work, they subdivide responsibilities. And, for security reasons, they keep battlefield plans from the troops. As a result, many of their personnel work at cross purposes or with no clear focus. To make matters worse, most Western commanders are "spared" (by their subunit leaders) from the day-to-day problems (and discoveries) of their lowest-echelon personnel. Thus, they are little good at either countering or generating a grassroots strategy. That's why Carlson's emphasis on the lone fighter was so unusual in 1941 and still so useful today. It constituted a new way of not only exercising control, but of also amassing knowledge. (See Figures 3.2 and 3.3.) If the loss of Vietnam is any indication, this new operational focus can be very powerful.

How Eastern Armies Operate

In Western military outfits, task forces execute strategy, regiments or battalions handle operations, and companies or platoons perform tactics. Each member within this strict hierarchy must fully support all parent-unit goals. While all three American squads most certainly contributed to their platoon's mission in 1941, their individual members were mostly restricted to following orders. Eastern-style military organizations are not like that. More often than not, they operate from the bottom up. A squad scout first locates an enemy weakness. Then, if his chain of command deems it an opportunity, squads either spearhead the offensive or anchor the defense. Thus, the Asian rifleman plays a much more significant role. That's what Carlson had been attempting to mimic. He first told each Raider how important his contribution would be, then kept him continually informed of all battlefield plans (whether strategic, operational, or tactical), and finally encouraged him to assess the progress.

Most illuminating in this regard was the 1943 moving picture about Carlson's Raiders—"Gung Ho." If it had not been historically accurate, the U.S. War Department would never have permitted its release. Therein the Carlson role player makes several revealing statements. He first wants each man to fully understand his duty so that he can better perform it. (In a normal Western outfit, one's "duty" is normally left up to the platoon or squad leader. That's

Figure 3.2: WWII Had Required a Lot of Individual Effort
(Source: U.S. Army Center of Military History, posters, illustration designator "1-18-49.jpg," Infantry under Fire, unknown artist)

Figure 3.3: Carlson's Raider with Soon-to-Be-Replaced Reising
(Source: "First Offensive: The Marine Campaign for Guadalcanal," by Henry I. Shaw, Marines in WWII Commemorative Series, HQMC, 1992, drawing by Donald Dixon, p. 37)

because it tends to vary with the subunit's mission. Carlson's double goes on to say that each man's job is important.[11] In a Communist army of the period, there were no ranks but only leadership billets—ergo, each rifleman worked for a squad leader (instead of a Corporal) and platoon leader (instead of a Lieutenant). By copying this system, Carlson was able to remove the barriers between him and his men that rank creates. Then, with the constant get-togethers, he even superseded the subunit structure. In a sense, all Raiders worked directly for him. He had become the Confucian father image.

According to the movie, all Raiders were briefed by their commander on the battalion's "plans and objectives" before every operation and then asked to critique its success in open forum. While fewer errors would have been "swept under the rug" this way, the company, platoon, and squad leaders may have also felt their authority diminished.

In the movie, Carlson defines *Gung* as work, and then *Ho* as harmony. What he apparently sought was a smooth running machine in which each man helped—as opposed to competing with—his peers. But, this was to be a different kind of a machine—one that operated mostly from the bottom up. It was not the first time that Marines had looked out for each other. Men fight more for each other than glorious reasons. However, being the collective managers of their own battalion was something quite new to them. Because such a thing meshed poorly with their cultural background, it was to pay dividends in some ways and not in others.

The Chinese Structural Model at the Time

The Chinese Army's emphasis on billet assignment over rank may have been to more completely focus on the mission. Because the PLA has since vacillated several times between having and not having rank, the latter may entail too big a loss in unit cohesion. At present, the PLA does enjoy a rank system.[12] But as late as 1984, PLA Ground Force platoons had three squads of 12 men each. As those squads had "deputy squad leaders," one can assume three fire teams of three men each (a veteran fighter and two recent conscripts).[13] (See Table 3.1.) According to the Defense Information Agency's (DIA's) Table of Equipment, the tenth man in the squad carried a light machinegun.[14] This should come as no surprise, as the Japanese, Soviets, and Germans had all married their infantry squads to a machinegun by WWII.[15] On defense, the squad could then function as a strongpoint. On offense, it could create its own base of fire.

Carlson's Tactical Focus Was on the Very Bottom Echelon

Carlson was clearly interested in how Mao's 8th Route Army—though now mostly conventional in format—had managed to retain many of its guerrilla methods during the Nipponese resistance. At the start of the 1943 movie, Carlson's character claims that poorly fed peasants had outmaneuvered, outmarched, and outfought the Japanese. He attributes this feat to a mutual belief in certain causes and obligation to associated duties.[16] Thus, for Carlson, what his

Years in Service	Monthly PositionPay	Basic	(US $ Equivalent)
1	Conscript	7 yuan	($3.42)
2	Fighter	8 yuan	($3.51)
3	Deputy Squad Leader	9 yuan	($4.40)
4	Squad Leader	11 yuan	($5.38)
4 +	Deputy Platoon Leader	Increased by 5 yuan each year after 4 years in service	($2.45)

Table 3.1: Enlisted Echelons within the PLA Platoon

individual fighters could manage was vastly more important than what his fire teams or squads might do through tactical techniques (rehearsed maneuvers).

That may help to explain why Carlson's initial training emphasis had been on how to win every one-on-one encounter between individuals. He wanted only those Marines who were prepared to kill or be killed at close range with a knife. Then, he gave them close-combat skills and endurance. His troops learned to watch for an attack against their person from any direction and—through various ruses—instantly to gain the upper hand against an onrushing assailant. While the command guidance was "always to expect the unexpected,"[17] most Raider deception appears limited to the micro-defense.

Though the 2nd Battalion had just created fire teams, there is no evidence of any maneuvers being designed for them or with them. It may have been Carlson's belief that only highly motivated troops could come up with good fire and movement schemes anyway. He may have further thought that such schemes would naturally evolve without any particular inducement.

Squads Not Earmarked for Better Maneuvers

2nd Raider Battalion's commander is known to have attested to three things about his fire teams: (1) their primary emphasis in his agenda; (2) their maneuver improvement through *"Gung Ho* Session" input; and (3) their outstanding performance.[18] However,

Figure 3.4: GIs Have Never Used Many Concussion Grenades
(Source: U.S. Army Center of Military History, artphoto archives, illustration designator "0107-4.jpg," Grenade, by Joseph W. McDermott, 1942)

he was much less vocal about his squads. Thus, it is doubtful that any sophisticated squad assault technique was ever developed by the Raiders or even borrowed from someone else. The best example to date had been that of the WWI German Stormtroopers, and the Pentagon has never liked admitting it. The Raiders did receive training on how to cross man-made barriers—an essential part of any assault on a prepared enemy position. Among the methods were wall scaling, barbed-wire crushing, and invisible-obstacle vaulting (like over a stream of machinegun bullets).[19] Though much of the maneuver instruction was then left up to the squad leaders,[20] never to emerge were any of the deceptions that had defined the magnificent German procedure.[21] (See Figure 3.4.) No one considered the value to surprise of "not firing any small arms" or of "simulating standoff mortar fire with concussion grenades."

Of course, one can also secretly attack a fortified objective by short-range infiltration. Its roots are more universal, with China's *moshuh nanren* precursor to *ninjutsu* very near the top of the list.[22] The WWI German infiltration attacks are more correctly classified as the long-range variety. They circumvented strongpoints. That's quite different than secretly penetrating a line of closely arrayed fighting holes. Within the Chinese guerrilla capabilities were many skills applicable to short-range infiltration. Some, like the stalking of an opposition sentry, may have helped 8th Route Army sappers to breach an enemy line. Others, like the looser control by headquarters, would have given 8th Route Army infiltration teams the confidence to work alone. However, there is no record of 2nd Raider Battalion personnel ever attempting silently to enter a Japanese bastion.

Carlson May Have Only Partially Understood Mao's Method

Carlson's claim that 8th Route Army fighters were under no command pressure during their unit analyses doesn't correlate well with subsequent observations of Communist armies. During the Vietnam War, one American Marine reported seeing two North Vietnamese Army (NVA) regulars chained to their machinegun position.[23] At one point, Mao had been lenient with Nationalist Chinese prisoners. But, this was not because of any innate respect for human life. He did so as a psychological ploy.[24] Most U.S. students of the region would agree that 8th Route Army leaders had the power of life and death over their men.

Chinese tactics are as different as night and day from the Western variety. When they appear similar, it's generally a feint of some kind.[25] Carlson may not have fully understood this. Most Western military thinkers have difficulty envisioning how a conventional army could quickly switch to guerrilla warfare. After dispersing, wouldn't all of its parts be destroyed piecemeal? Not necessarily. Chinese units have had the "Cloud Battle Array" with which to spread out for centuries. Tiny elements can more easily move out of the way than big ones.[26]

Far from the average Yank, Evans Carlson must have sensed the potential of this alternative way of fighting. He had worked and studied in the Far East long enough to see how bottom-up opportunism could out-perform top-down planning. Yet, he may not have fully realized why. There had been no hint during his troop meetings that rehearsed subunit procedure made looser overall control possible. He knew only that his men could spread out and come together, just as the Chinese had.

Implicit in any shift from Positional to Guerrilla Warfare would have been the decentralization of control. His new fire team breakdown would help. Then, to achieve a more universal display of initiative, he would need something in the place of continual orders. Part of that something would be the Ethical Indoctrination. The remainder was the precursor to North Vietnam's "*Kiem Thao* Session"—a mixture of past assessment and future design.

> Borrowing an idea from China, Carlson frequently has what he calls 'kung-hou' meetings. . . . Problems are threshed out and orders explained.[27]
>
> — *New York Times,* 1942

> During World War II, Lt.Col. Evans F. Carlson's 2nd Raider Battalion held regular *"Gung Ho* meetings" in which all Marines and sailors had an equal voice in working out issues.[28]
>
> — *Marine Corps Gazette,* 2003

Only missing were any nuances to China's tactical tradition. For the country that invented deception, some should have been expected.

What Carlson May Have Finally Realized

- How popular was Carlson's aversion to rank?
- Might he have still made a tactical contribution?

One had to be opportunistic to catch the Japanese offguard.

(Source: "Handbook on Japanese Military Forces," TM-E 30-480 [1944], U.S. War Dept., plate II; FM 21-76 [1957], p. 61; FM 21-76 [1992], p. 6-7)

The *Gung Ho* Session as a Management Tool

As a former enlisted man (five years in the Army and one more in the Marines), Carlson knew what junior enlisted personnel could accomplish.[1] He respected their opinions and was not the least bit hesitant about asking for them. Still, no one individual—however near to the action—will be right about all its details, and groups of frontline fighters still need some way to compare notes. So, as in the Chinese 8th Route Army, Carlson wanted a regularly occurring forum at which his young Raiders could recount their experiences. Those not too different from the group perception could then be used to refine strategies and procedures. As such, the get-togethers were not only an outlet for grievances, but also a source of new knowledge.

By arriving—through open discussion—at battlefield plans that drew no active complaint, Carlson was additionally able to obligate his men to certain "tactical guidelines." In a loosely controlled organization, such guidelines can largely take the place of both direction and supervision. It is a leadership trick of sorts, but very effective in arriving at an all-hands effort. That to which the young fighters did not object during the "official briefing" would have to be closely obeyed later.

He was also seeking a change in attitude. With almost 30 years under his belt in the U.S. military,[2] he knew how often Privates were solicited for their opinions. He thought participating in the discussions would give them more confidence. Open forums have other benefits. For example, people's combat mistakes can lead to debilitating guilt. Given the chance, they will publicly admit to them in the hopes that others will empathize. Either way, the guilt is lessened and combat efficiency enhanced. While describing the North Vietnamese equivalent to a *Gung Ho* Session, one author points to Carlson's most likely goal.

> Each [NVA] soldier and officer criticized his own actions and the other members of the company regardless of rank. After each confession or criticism, a general [group] discussion ensued. . . . [I]t gave the soldiers a sense of participation in the unit's decision-making process. They viewed themselves, therefore, not as witless cannon fodder, but as thinking members of a team.[3]
>
> — *Vietnam at War—The History: 1946-1975*

The Session's Leadership Ramifications

Within Mao Tse-tung's 8th Route Army method was the bottom-up way of problem solving for which the Orient is so unique. The Communist Chinese troops were not just doing what they were told, but rather generating many of their own solutions. This took a better understanding of their foe, leaders' goals, and personal capabilities. Those three things are what Carlson was attempting in the 2nd Raider Battalion. He thought he could win more close encounters that way. In his own book, he wrote the following in 1940:

> The superb fighters of the Chinese Eighth Route Army had studied the Japanese methods, tactics, and psychology for years. . . . Surprise was the Eighth's heaviest weapon against the invaders. . . . But there was another and even more important element which made the success of the Eighth Route Army. . . . It could be nothing but the Desire and Will of each individual to complete the task. Here was the secret weapon of the Eighth Route Army. . . . So, if men have confidence in their leaders, if they are convinced that the things for which they endure and fight are worthwhile, if they believe the effort they are making contributes definitely to the realization of their objectives, then their efforts will be voluntary, spontaneous, and persistent.[4]
>
> — Evans Fordyce Carlson, *Twin Stars of China*

Within the Communist unit structure were assistant platoon leaders—a rough equivalent to the Staff Noncommissioned Officer (SNCO) hierarchy on which Western militaries so heavily depend for discipline.[5] (Refer back to Table 3.1.) Yet, these older enlisted men were not suppressing troop complaints. As was their goal within the lowest echelons, displays of initiative had replaced unquestioning compliance. Thus, it is safe to say that Carlson was attempting a fairly non-Western approach to leadership.

For 2nd Raider Battalion's commander so often to discuss things with his fighters may have helped them to understand, but it also had its downside. It impugned the authority of intermediate leaders and made their ingenuity far less likely during the execution of an order. In essence, he had sacrificed higher-rank expertise for organizational continuity. (See Figure 4.1.)

As with Mao, Carlson's whole combat methodology became bottom-up—with the low-ranking scout first spotting an enemy weakness and then his parent echelons deciding whether or not to exploit that weakness. More often than not, the first few Raiders on the scene did all the exploiting with their automatic weapons and then quickly withdrew into the jungle before any counterattack could be launched.

Figure 4.1: Carlson Didn't Soley Rely on His Officers' Wisdom
(Source: "First Offensive: The Marine Campaign for Guadalcanal," by Henry I. Shaw, Marines in WWII Commemorative Series, HQMC, 1992, drawing by Donard L. Dixon, p. 16)

The *Gung Ho* Session as a Way to Learn from One's Mistakes

Though most Americans still do not believe it, a firsthand observer has described Mao's soldiers as "constantly studying their mistakes, and improvising methods to . . . offset modernized equipment."[6] Always on the verge of annihilation, they had little choice.

In a lesser-known aspect of *"Gung Ho,"* each 2nd Battalion enlisted fighter had a responsibility in this regard. He was not only to study and correct his own errors, but also to monitor the overall progress of all units to which he belonged. (Asians are more holistic in their thought processes, instead of mostly concentrating on one field of study.) That individual Raider was supposed to remember what went wrong around him, make sure it was accurately recorded, and then suggest ways to fix it. Unfortunately, the officers—who most often made the tactical decisions—then came under a lot of emotional duress. "[T]he *Gung Ho* sessions featured open criticism of officers without fear of retribution."[7] In contrast, the 8th Route Army soldiers had probably been in so much fear of their leaders as to mostly criticize each other.[8]

"Gung Ho's" Forgotten Prerequisite

Evans Carlson had grown to dislike the military careerism that overemphasis on rank tended to evoke.[9] He believed that all Marines should work only for the good of the country. Because 2nd Battalion leaders could not apply the "Silent Contempt" rule that was keeping other enlisted populations in check, many came under severe psychological pressure from below. This ability of the fighters to impugn their leader's very existence (as opposed to just his ideas) is what eventually led to the Raiders' demise. Carlson is known to have personally relieved several company commanders (one at Makin and two more on the Long Patrol) after listening to the complaints of their subordinates.

That many of the leaders' tactical plans seemed illogical to the fighters had more to do with a Western tactical tradition than officer ineptitude. The Marine standard at the time was to attack as many enemy soldiers as one could with as much firepower as one could. For the fighters to now want surprise added to the equation posed somewhat of a threat to a time-honored system. It was to prove as counterproductive to leader-follower relations as it was helpful to maneuver. In contemporary U.S. military circles, that much self-determination among the lowest ranks is still unacceptable. Yet, some objective thinking at every organizational level is always necessary. One of the best ways to get beaten by an opportunistic opponent is for those at any echelon to blindly follow orders. That's why Carlson's reminder to the lowly grunts to always keep thinking was of such a help later in the war—like when they were facing the mutually supporting bunkers on Iwo Jima.[10]

Very Few *Gung Ho* Suggestions While on an Operation

Carlson still understood the need for battlefield discipline. Orders were orders, and he expected all to be followed in combat. He wanted his fighters to make recommendations before, and not during, an operation. He was looking for how—not whether—things would be done; and his enlisted advice seems mostly restricted to fire team and squad method. If a fire team was to attack a pillbox,

Figure 4.2: First Raiders Had Little Deliberate Assault Technique
(Source: "Closing In: Marines in the Seizure of Iwo Jima," by J.H. Alexander, Marines in WWII Commemorative Series, HQMC, 1994, drawing by Charles H. Waterhouse, p. 31)

he wanted input on how to best take it.[11] Unfortunately, the 2nd Raider Battalion was to face too few Japanese machinegun bunkers to develop any truly advanced assault technique. (See Figure 4.2.) Not even the famous "Blind 'em, Burn 'em, and Blast 'em" was probably any of their doing.

During one *Gung Ho* Session, a Raider was heard to disagree with his company commander over the maneuvers they had just practiced.[12] Such interactions may be good for the learning dynamic, but they also spawn animosity. Like most enlisted men, that fighter may have considered his officer somewhat naive about close-quarters combat. And like most officers, that leader may have lacked the in-squad experience to understand what his fighter meant. The "basics," after all, do possess hundreds of subcategories. But, Carlson was to stick with this organized introspection to supposedly develop a willingness, resourcefulness, and initiative among his enlisted personnel.[13] As a former E-8 or E-9,[14] he may have also wanted his officers to better understand "where the rubber meets the road." In true Chinese fashion, he considered his lowest-ranks—and not his highest—to be the most essential ingredient of a successful unit. The Eastern bottom-up way of war depends more on the initiative of the frontline fighter than any amount of headquarters intellect. That whole counter-cultural subject will be more completely addressed in Part Two.

The Extent of Bottom-Up Input in Combat

Carlson did hold a single *Gung Ho* Session near the end of the Long Patrol,[15] but it was only to shore up his Raiders' flagging morale. He probably asked for no input on how tactically to improve. There was one way that had undoubtedly occurred to his fighters, but he would not hear about it until the Raiders had left Guadalcanal.

Each trio of fire team leaders might have helped their squad leader pick the best battlefield moves. But Carlson seemingly had no interest in applying his democratic model to active combat so as to more quickly adapt to changing circumstances. Yet, he may still have realized this rather amazing possibility near the end of his tenure. This could have been one of his last *Gung Ho* experiments.

Whether Small-Unit Maneuver Experiments Ever Ensued

According to one historian, *Gung Ho* discussions specifically included ways to improve the training. A former member of 3rd Battalion (who only served under Roosevelt for a month at school) remembers hearing about tactical experimentation by both Carlson and Edson.[16] More likely, Edson was looking for ways to more quickly move inland from the destroyers; and Carlson was interested in how better to concentrate small-unit firepower.

Yet, this member of 3rd Battalion remembers only a few battle-drills—those involving his whole company. "Canned" company-size maneuvers (as controlled by whistle blasts) were still being used by the Chinese at the Chosin Reservoir in 1950.[17] They were not "techniques" *per se* (performable on auto-pilot), because that many people cannot move around in unison without constant supervision.

Still, something had enthralled Major Samuel Griffith during his two week visit to 2nd Battalion before assuming command of the 1st, and it probably wasn't the avoidance of rank. Instead of being regularly assessed in training, promising Raider maneuver proposals had been occasionally tried in combat. Mao was, after all, more interested in on-the-job training (OJT).

> Reading books is learning, but application is also learning and the more important form of learning. To learn warfare through warfare—this is our chief method.[18]
>
> — Mao Tse-tung

There Is More Than One Way to Improve Technique

That former Raider says much of his tactical instruction had been by squad leader. It may have deviated from the published procedures very little. But, even when stuck with a headquarters' maneuver, a squad leader will still want to practice it—just as a football coach does with an old play. While so doing, that squad leader might even risk a few minor changes to make things go a little smoother. What results is a rather elementary form of scientific inquiry. With so much emphasis on surprise in the 2nd Battalion, the most likely modifications would have been to how the foe was approached and his sentries handled. While some good long-range infiltration technique may have resulted, more would have been possible with simulated casualty comparisons.

Sadly, there is no direct evidence of Carlson ever getting a show of hands with regard to someone's maneuver proposal, or of it being subsequently tested in a mock-combat setting. Yet, something similar does automatically result when lessons learned are continually disseminated to engaged fighters. A promising method gets tried by someone. The word gets around, and soon others are doing it. But, the welfare of a unit cannot be left to luck. That's why it is so important for every U.S. infantry headquarters to allow their units to experiment with squad tactics.

Evans Carlson had mentioned physical conditioning, Ethical Indoctrination, and "use of the fire team" as his main focus.[19] So, everyone's attention would have been on fire team member interactions. But, how the composite teams could then assist the squad may have been less important to them. Still, in such a learning environment, increasingly useful fire team movements would have ensued. What precisely they were has been has been largely lost to history. They most probably maximized firepower, as there is evidence of a squad technique in which all member weapons could be brought to bear on the foe within 15 seconds of a head-on chance contact.[20]

Carlson Was Also Preparing Guerrilla Trainers

Having worked with the Guardia National in Nicaragua, Carlson knew how to get the most out of indigenous fighters.[21] As guerrillas also rely on the public for much of their strength, he wanted all Raiders to be able to train and lead others. Being at the head of every charge was part of the equation, but so too was building up (as opposed to the tearing down) each indigenous member's self-confidence. This was more likely to occur from exploiting his cultural strengths than correcting his personal weaknesses.

With guerrilla war as a mandatory format, all Communist special operators double as light-infantry instructors. North Korea's commandos have—for their headquarters—the "Light Infantry Training Guidance Bureau."[22] With the extra ability and how to teach it, they become better force multipliers for local units.

During the Vietnam War, every NVA soldier was required to train local militiamen before heading south.[23] This initial teaching assignment was important because of the critical role that southern guerrillas would play in the NVA's overall effort. They would be its early warning sentinels, intelligence gatherers, infiltration/resupply route protectors, local guides, and penetration sappers. Thus, all NVA soldiers required the ability to train—or at least work with—Viet Cong (VC). As any long-time instructor will attest, the teaching experience creates a much deeper level of understanding and commitment.

Did the Communists Engage in Tactical Experimentation?

By institutionalizing a Guerrilla phase, the Chinese PLA had made three things possible during its Mobile and Positional phases: (1) decentralized control; (2) dispersed operations; and (3) technique variations between units. Of all the Western armies, only the Germans have so far matched this feat. So doing has paid them huge dividends—with regard to small-unit tactics—in both World Wars. In fact, it is they—and not the Asians—who are generally credited with the latest advances in squad offensive and defensive methods. While German Noncommissioned Officers (NCOs) are known to have helped to develop those methods, so implicitly did German Privates.

> [T]he social relations between officers, noncommissioned officers, and men . . . were the essence of Stormtroop tactics.[24]
> — Gudmundsson, *Stormtroop Tactics*

Those German tactical advances were probably as a result of trial runs by Capt. Rohr while head of the NCO school.[25] All armies strive to improve, and many of those that are Asian have similarly discovered their lowest ranks to be the key to world-class technique.

The Asian version of the *Gung Ho* Session focuses more on the performance of oneself and one's peers than on that of unit leaders. When a private or NCO gets criticized for what he did in combat, he will often say that it made more sense than the standard. Within such a claim is always the seed of better technique.

> In *Kiem Thao* [S]essions, the [NVA] soldiers offered judgments of their comrades and listened to evaluations of their own performances. The meetings sometimes featured discussions of tactics from the unit's recent engagements or [various] suggestions . . . sent from the army command.[26]
>
> — Maitland and McInerney, *Vietnam Experience*

Communist Asian armies are very secretive about how they prepare the junior enlisted personnel for close-quarters combat, because they more heavily depend on them. Thus, even if formal experimentation with squad, fire team, and individual movements had happened in the Orient, there may be no hard evidence of it. Yet, there are less certain ways of improving tactical technique. Perhaps one of those was used.

A Good Training Alternative to Field Experimentation

Instead of conducting progressively better versions of the same maneuver against simulated casualty assessment, the Communists may have just kept improving their battledrills until the troops felt comfortable with them. The rank and file know when something is about to get them killed, and even in training they can sense which battlefield movements are feasible. The NVA *Kiem Thao* Session, and its Chinese and North Korean equivalents would have given them the chance to continually reassess those drills. As long as the Communist drills were not set in doctrinal cement, they would gradually improve.

Before any attack, NVA squads could comment on the maneuver they were asked to run through a life-size mockup. In this way, they helped to develop unique battledrills for each objective. When everyone stopped complaining about those drills would be the rough equivalent of field testing them against simulated casualty assessment. Over time, all of their small-unit maneuvers would have improved. A captured NVA soldier has confirmed this conclusion.

> Yes, they [he and his buddies] were given the chance to discuss and criticize [most tactical plans]. The idea was to get unity of command and action during the operation. Before any operation, a few among us would be sent out to make a study and survey of the battlefield, and then a

> plan of operation would be drawn up and presented to all the men in the unit. Each would then be given a chance to contribute ideas and suggestions. Each squad, [and then] each man, would be told what action to take if the enemy was to take such-and-such a [defensive] position . . . but it was also the fighters' duty to contribute to the plan by advancing suggestions or criticizing what had been put forward. Thus, the final decision concerning an operation or attack was very often the result of a collective discussion in which each member had contributed his opinion or suggestion.[27]
>
> — U.S. defense agency study

North Korean,[28] North Vietnamese,[29] and Chinese troops all regularly practice "small-unit battledrills." The North Vietnamese are known to have had some for squad assault during the 1960's and 70's.[30] So, it should come as no surprise that one of them was for the virtual equivalent of German Stormtrooper technique (still the state of the art for unsilenced weapons).[31] Between those drills and that advanced result had been a way to improve. According to one source, the agent of change had not been systematic experimentation *per se,* but rather a constant attempt by sapper units to perform those drills "better" than regular infantry units could.[32] In a bottom-up army, there wouldn't have been any tactical doctrine to inhibit a little drill modification. With only guidelines to follow, some sapper units would have combined a few ruses to arrive at more surprise-oriented technique. Then, such competition between units would have eventually led to advanced assault methods. There was also a lot of competition between units in the pre-WWII Japanese Army.[33]

What Carlson May Have Begun to Suspect after Guadalcanal

At some point, a "smart-ass" Private must have stood up in one of Carlson's *Gung Ho* Sessions to ask why more of the fire team and squad maneuvers they had refined through group discussion had not been tried in combat. That would have gotten the Colonel thinking about how more frequently to incorporate such methods. Why settle for happenstance application of something that valuable? Carlson knew the Chinese held small-unit maneuvers in high regard and possibly wondered why he had seen the same ones over and over.

> Those who understand big and small units will be victorious.[34]
>
> — Sun Tzu

During the 2nd Battalion's refitting period, Carlson may have finally come to grips with an answer to that Raider's question—how more directly to harness troop wisdom in combat. He had, after all, held one *Gung Ho* meeting near the end of the Long Patrol, just to motivate his men.[35] So, there had been a precedent, of sorts, for collective thinking in combat. Instead of allowing subunit leaders to occasionally follow past suggestions, he could encourage them to choose between refined procedures. The Chinese volunteers who deployed to Korea in 1950 practiced small-unit drills,[36] so the 8th Route Army probably did as well. With a tiny portfolio of numbered maneuvers, each Raider squad leader could let his fire team leaders help him decide which one to use. Because each team leader had a slightly different view of the battlefield, their input would be like an impromptu reconnaissance. The maneuvers had already been practiced, so a "deliberate attack" was now possible (with better chances than a "hasty" one). By polling team leaders, the squad leader even ensured their cooperation.

Part One Has Only Led to a Deeper Mystery

Lt.Col. Carlson's New Caledonia experiments may have been on how more effectively to fight using a portfolio of constantly refined techniques. Or, they may have just been to assess existing methods. To speed up any maneuver refinement, he may have even resorted to a few "shows of hands." That and "polling one's team leaders" look too much like "voting" to be very popular in an organization that had previously prided itself on instant compliance of lowest-echelon orders. The impending traditionalists would not have appreciated it. In their defense, the most stubborn emplacements of 1944 and 1945 were to be mostly taken "by the numbers" (where squad members closely obeyed every instruction in the established sequence). But, Carlson's Chinese ideas were still valid—where the foe was less prepared, farther away, or emerging to one's rear. Everyone would soon be searching for a way to deal with mutually supporting bunkers. There, precision execution is virtually impossible.

The Chinese Communists had developed a very powerful yet still

"small" way of fighting. Parts Two and Three will assess its potential—through the exploits of the Mao-emulating Raiders and their Regular Establishment successors.

Part Two

The Asian Influence on U.S. Doctrine

"Those who discern when to use many or few troops are victorious." — Sun Tzu

(Source: "The Art of War," by Sun Tzu, translated by Thomas Cleary, pp. 80, 81)

Modern War Precepts from Ancient China?

- What are the main "Maneuver Warfare" precepts?
- Which had been conceptualized by 400 B.C. in Asia?

Might the Asians also have learned something of war?

(Source: Courtesy of Stefan H. Verstappen, "The Thirty-Six Strategies of Ancient China," © 1999)

Modern Conflict Theory Does Have a Few Asian Roots

There have been a number of evolutionary changes to tactical procedure over the years. Many of the most recent are German, but a few are uniquely Asian. Within this latter category are the following: (1) battlefield deception; (2) short-range infiltration; and (3) non-martial alternatives.

The U.S. Marine Corps switched from Attrition to Maneuver Warfare (MW) doctrine in 1986. Of late, 4GW—war fought in the martial, economic, political, and psychological arenas simultaneously—has been proposed as the sequel to MW. While the WWI

Figure 5.1: Doughboy Defenses Couldn't Stop the Hun Squads
(Source: U.S. Army Center of Military History, artphoto archives, illustration designator "avop05-98_1.jpg," American Troops Advancing, by Harold Brett)

Germans have been credited with the Marines' new application parameters for MW, a very insightful American—William S. Lind—has helped them to understand 4GW.[1] (See Figure 5.1.) Yet, by cultural orientation, Asian armies are more likely to practice the comprehensive sequel. Washington has always preferred that its generals leave foreign politics to the State Department and foreign economics to the Commerce Department. In fact, this separation of duties has become so much a part of U.S. society that the term 4GW is no longer encouraged aboard any Stateside Marine base.

Figure 5.2: Sun Tzu Appears to Have Understood MW Theory
(Source: Courtesy of Stefan H. Verstappen, "The Thirty-Six Strategies of Ancient China," © 1999)

The Probability of an Oriental Equivalent to MW

Asians are not stupid, nor are they solely dependent on Eastern ideas. Thus, they could have come up with something quite similar to MW on their own, or simply copied the Germans. Ancient Chinese literature suggests the former.

With MW, one tries to bypass an adversary's manpower concentrations (battlefield strongpoints) to more easily get at his logistic and control apparatus (strategic assets). Among its main precepts are the following: (1) surfaces and gaps; (2) focus of effort; (3) centers of gravity; and (4) speed and surprise.[2] While somewhat disconcerting to WWI Stormtrooper enthusiasts, Sun Tzu (and his disciples) have been pushing these same principles since 400 B.C. In many instances, even the words are the same. (See Figure 5.2.)

> To advance irresistibly, push through their *gaps*. [Italics added.][3]
>
> — Sun Tzu

> An army may be likened to water: water leaves dry the high places and attacks hollows; an army *turns from strength and attacks emptiness.* [Italics added.] [4]
>
> — Sun Tzu

> Try to grasp the *crux of the battle* and attack where the enemy feels invulnerable, thus bringing about a decisive change. [Italics added.] [5]
>
> — Sun Tzu

> Wise commanders actively consume [or destroy] the enemy's *supplies.* . . . [S]natch the enemy's advantages by means of valuable goods. [Italics added.] [6]
>
> — Sun Tzu

> *Speed* is the essence of war. Take advantage of the enemy's unpreparedness; travel by unexpected routes and strike him where he has taken no precautions. [Italics added.] [7]
>
> — Sun Tzu

> All warfare is based on *deception.* Therefore, when capable of attacking, feign incapacity; when active in moving troops, feign inactivity. When near the enemy, make it seem that you are far way; when far away, make it seem that you are near. [Italics added.] [8]
>
> —Sun Tzu

Thus, while the WWI Germans may have come up with the most definitive array of parameters with which to practice MW,[9] the Chinese were previously aware of its theories. Unfortunately, the Asian Communists have been so secretive about the design of their short-range battlefield methods that many of their own MW parameters may have been obscured.

The Oriental Origins of 4GW

Because MW is more about demoralizing a foe than destroying him, 4GW can be viewed as an advanced version of it.

The object of "maneuver" is not so much to destroy physi-

> cally as it is to shatter the enemy's cohesion, organization, command, and psychological balance.[10]
> — FMFM 1, *Warfighting*

As for the possibility that 4GW theory originated in the West, there is much evidence to suggest that the Chinese have been fighting their wars in all four arenas for centuries. As the masters of deception, wouldn't they also be good at non-martial conflict? Western examples of mostly bloodless conflict are much harder to identify.

> The supreme art of war is to subdue the enemy without fighting.[11]
> — Sun Tzu

> Sun Zi [Tzu] grasped the quintessence of war and the relationship between the outcome of war and the political, economic, and diplomatic factors of a society.[12]
> — Beijing's New World Press, 1997

How Red Army May Have Developed Chinese Version of MW

Mao Tse-tung did not come up with all of his military insights from scratch. They largely mirrored Sun Tzu's teachings.

> [Sun Tzu's] *The Art of War* has had a profound influence throughout Chinese history and on Japanese thought; it is the source of Mao Tse-tung's strategic theories and of the tactical doctrine [guidelines] of the Chinese armies.[13]
> — B.Gen. Sam Griffith, former Raider commander

The main source of Mao's ideas is obvious from his personal writings and recorded comments. In the following description, he applies Sun-Tzu-like rhetoric to a MW thought.

> In guerrilla warfare, select the tactic of seeming to come from the east and attacking from the west; avoid the solid, attack the hollow; attack; withdraw; deliver a lightning blow; seek a lightning decision.[14]
> — Mao Tse-tung quote in *Marine Corps Gazette,* 1941

Any size of unit within Mao's Red Army could alternate between Positional, Mobile, and Guerrilla Warfare.[15] That, in itself, would suggest that his Mobile Warfare is the Chinese equivalent to MW. The multiple-style capability would make MW much easier to practice. The decentralized control that is so important to MW is also a prerequisite of Guerrilla Warfare.[16] Thus, Mao's troops would already have what it takes to quickly maneuver as tiny semi-autonomous elements.

During the Long March of 1934 and 1935, Mao Tse-tung and his fledgling Red Army retreated under pressure all the way from Jiangxi Province in the South to Yunan Province in the North. That's about 6,000 miles.[17] Such an ordeal would have developed a real appreciation for the MW concepts of flexible defense and tactical withdrawal.

Finally, to move quickly enough to escape entrapment, the Red Army would have also found the MW concept of "recon pull" to be much more reliable than "command push."[18]

The Chinese Version of MW May Even Have an Edge

A former guerrilla army from the East may be able to practice a more "complete" version of MW—one also capable of application to the lowest echelons. Western armies have had difficulty practicing MW below company level because of the strictness of their control. Their lower-ranking members are not allowed enough self-confidence, individual technique, and personal initiative to safely operate alone. That's why Evans Carlson felt it so necessary to instill his men with self-discipline.

> [T]he basis for guerrilla discipline must be individual conscience. With guerrillas, a discipline of compulsion is ineffective.[19]
>
> — Mao Tse-tung quote in *Marine Corps Gazette,* 1941

Problems U.S. MW Has Faced

In modern America, war is the product of three hierarchically descending processes: (1) strategic; (2) operational; and (3) tactical. Strategy is considered to be a manifestation of national policy. So, each of the others must be a little less important than the one preceding.

> Activities at the strategic level focus directly on national policy objectives. . . .
> Activities at the tactical level of war focus on the application of combat power to defeat the enemy in combat (JCS Pub. 1-02). . . .
> . . . The operational level of war links the strategic and tactical levels (JCS Pub. 1-02). . . . Actions at this level imply a broader dimension of time and space than do tactics. As strategy deals with wars, and tactics with battles and engagements, the operational level . . . is the art of winning campaigns.[20]
>
> — FMFM 1, *Warfighting*

Most Americans assume these embedded stages of military mission will be assigned to successive levels in the same chain of command. Ergo, an expeditionary army would work on strategy, while its divisions and regiments take care of campaigning, and the battalions on down conduct tactics. That is fairly close to what routinely happens throughout America's far-flung defense establishment. Yet, nowhere in the military literature does it say that lone squads or simply sappers—in enough quantity—could not single-handedly accomplish a strategy. There are historians who feel it was half-naked saboteurs who ultimately defeated the U.S. phalanx in Vietnam.[21] If that were true, intermediate headquarters would have much less utility. Perhaps that's why German division commanders dealt directly with company commanders during the Spring Offensives of 1918.[22]

Mao's Circumstances Were Perfect for MW

With a bottom-up culture and chronic shortage of equipment, the Chinese Communists decided to pursue many wartime strategies through tiny units. Through deceptive maneuver, those tiny units could more easily dodge the enemy's firepower.

> I'm afraid we [the Marines] haven't recognized the most

> important lesson from Korea. The Communists have developed a totally new kind of warfare. . . . This is a total warfare, yet small in scope, and it's designed to neutralize our big . . . weapons.[23]
>
> — B.Gen. Lewis B. "Chesty" Puller USMC (Ret.)

Such a grassroots scheme is also the essence of guerrilla warfare. Enough winning of skirmishes can be every bit as powerful as a massive invasion. The mosquito is only insignificant until he and several thousand of his buddies swarm.

> The strategy of guerrilla war is to pit one man against ten, but the tactics are to pit ten against one.[24]
>
> — Maxim from Mao Tse-tung

Was Carlson Practicing this Chinese Version of MW?

Carlson was attempting the "egalitarian" and team-building procedures he had learned from the Chinese Communist Army. The way he operated on Guadalcanal could therefore be viewed as how that army fought. He had only two categories of personnel—leaders and fighters. To all, he gave an Ethical Indoctrination—explaining why each man was important. Within his subsequent *Gung Ho* Sessions were regular updates on future battle plans [25]—just like the MW concept of "commander's intent."[26]

The conglomeration of random and quickly withdrawn Raider jabs on Guadalcanal was also a perfect example of what MW would look like at the lowest echelons of an infantry unit. It is one of the very few in modern U.S. history.

What Has Happened Since

Some 70 years have passed since Mao and Carlson. Yet, in the history of warfare, this is little more than a millennial minute. While technology may influence small-unit maneuver (as when the machinegun dictating more surprise in the assault), it can never take the place of maneuver. Having lately operated with almost unlimited firepower, American infantry commanders have been slow to realize this. Just by trying to copy Western mechanization of forces, the Chinese Army got badly embarrassed by North Vietnamese border militia in 1979.[27] But the victors of that particular "dust up" were also following Maoist methods, so perhaps the PLA—in its haste to modernize—had simply violated too many of Mao's original principles. Through a bottom-up system of checks and balances, the PLA can more easily learn from its mistakes than most Western armies,[28] so there is no telling how good it is now.

Technology, in itself, is not bad as long as it supports, rather than inhibits maneuver. *Hezbollah* may have used a little Chinese technical advice to block the fully supported Israeli mechanized force that swept into Southern Lebanon in 2006.[29] Chinese-manufactured missiles were certainly part of that remotely controlled armor-killing network.[30] In other parts of the world, China has been less secretive in its expansion. That only five rightist regimes now remain in the entire Western Hemisphere may signal a 4GW sequel to Mao's original plan.[31]

Mao's Influence on Raider Tactics

- To what extent did Raider tactics look like those of Mao?
- What are the present-day ramifications of this?

Mao Tse-tung became adept at more than just guerrilla warfare.

(Source: Corel Gallery Clipart, Portraits Historical, #01C100)

Whether a Chinese Version of MW Really Existed

Overall precepts don't a warfare style make. Also required are their various "application parameters." After shifting to MW doctrine in 1986, the U.S. Marines adopted the same application criteria that had been pioneered by the Germans in 1917. While the Marines' MW precepts closely resemble Sun Tzu's teachings, Mao's usage guidelines may not be the same. If too many are missing, then Mao's interpretation of Mobile Warfare cannot be called MW. One of the easiest ways to tell is through an in-depth look at Carlson's imitation of the 8th Route Army.

Central to Maoist Thinking

Dispersal to escape annihilation and then reassembly to strike back seems a recurring theme in Mao's writings, so it would have been a part of his Mobile Warfare interpretation as well.

> Disperse or concentrate one's own forces swiftly on a wide and flexible battlefield. . . . One's own forces must be assembled in secrecy and must attack at the time and place which the enemy least expects.[1]
>
> — Mao

Marine MW includes both "decentralization of control" and "convergence of effort,"[2] but no particular emphasis on rapid dispersion or reassembly. The WWI Germans' best example of dispersal was their defensive "squad strongpoint matrix."[3] But, they lacked the reassembly criteria to resume the attack with the same people. While some forward squads were designated for counterattack, that maneuver was mostly accomplished by large rearward elements.[4] For a dispersed Chinese unit, any reassembly would have had to be carefully located and secretly executed. Until 1960, it was sometimes accomplished by subunits rendezvousing after separate long-range

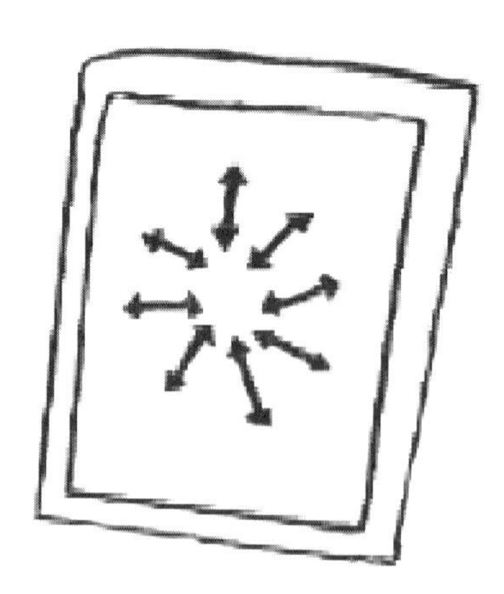

Figure 6.1: The "Cloud Battle Array"
(Source: "Phantom Soldier: The Enemy's Answer to U.S. Firepower," © 2001 by H. John Poole, p. 37)

infiltrations.[5] The Chinese dispersal and reassembly regimen would have normally followed the Cloud Battle Array—where a whole unit scatters in every direction and then comes together the same way.[6] (See Figure 6.1.) Within the following manual excerpt may lie the most likely application parameters for any Chinese version of MW.

What the Chinese Manuals Say

As of 1960, four criteria defined Chinese offensive action. The first was how speed was applied; the second about attacking from several sides; the third on how to divide and destroy a strongpoint; and the fourth about penetrating enemy lines.

a. . . . *Four Fast—One Slow.* The *"One Slow"* . . . refers to the commander's responsibility for careful evaluation, planning, and inspection prior to the attack. The *"Four Fast"* . . . relates to the speed in execution of the attack:
   (1) Speed in preparation, including reconnaissance.
   (2) Speed in the advance, to flank or encircle the enemy.
   (3) Speed in exploitation of gains, to prevent enemy regrouping.
   (4) Speed in pursuit, to overtake and destroy a retreating enemy.

b. The *One Point—Two Sides* tactical technique is the launching of a number of separate attacks against one objective. . . .
   (1) *One Point* means to concentrate overwhelmingly superior strength and attack a selected weak point.
   (2) *Two Sides* means that when making an attack, two or more efforts of attacking forces are necessary, but it does not mean the attack is limited to only two sides.

c. The isolation and subsequent detailed reduction of individual strong points of a defensive zone are called the *Divide-and-Destroy* tactical method. It is based on the theory that no defensive system can be equally strong everywhere and that weak spots exist which, if captured, will permit an attack from the flank or rear on adjacent strong points.

d. *Strategic penetration* is defined as a massive frontal attack against an enemy in a fixed defense line, the flanks of which are secure. The operation is designed to breach the defense at selected locations, create flanks, and permit passage of mobile forces deep into the enemy rear, to envelop and destroy him.[7]

— *Handbook of the Chinese Communist Army*
DA Pamphlet 30-51, 7 December 1960

How Much Like Marine MW Was this Chinese Guidance?

Notice the potential conflict between the first Chinese axiom and Boyd's decision cycle.[8] The initial "slow" was for spotting an enemy's tricks and adjusting to his alignment. Asians routinely attempt the "False Face and Art of Delay" and "Winning Battles before They Are Fought." Thinking more rapidly than one's foe only works when his last Western-style action was not a sucker move. Therefore, any Chinese version of MW would be more heavily focused on deception.

> [A] victorious army first wins [during its preparation phase] and then seeks battle; a defeated army first battles and then seeks victory.[9]
>
> — Sun Tzu

With some deception and reassembly parameters, the Chinese system might be almost as comprehensive as the German model. But would it contain all of the German application criteria as well? Figures 6.2 and 6.3 appear to show strongpoints being reduced (instead of bypassed) before the attackers move forward. The Stormtrooper squads of 1918 would secretly penetrate an Allied position and then sometimes go on to the next one before follow-on forces had completely consolidated the first. So, there may be slight differences in the attack criteria. Carlson's efforts on Guadalcanal could help to solve this mystery. Unfortunately, he had more than one thing on his mind at the time.

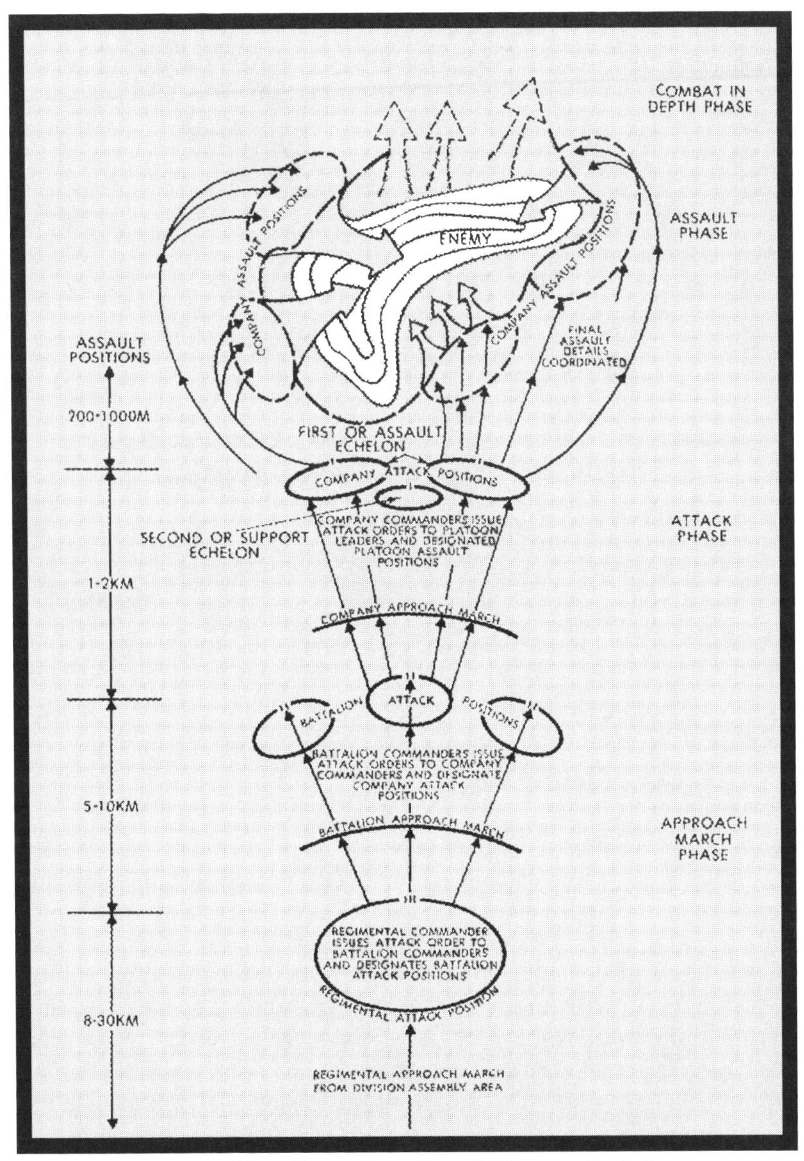

Figure 6.2: How Battalion Attack Elements Advance

(Source: "Handbook on the Chinese People's Liberation Army," DDB-2680-32-84 [November 1984], DIA, fig. 5, p. 29)

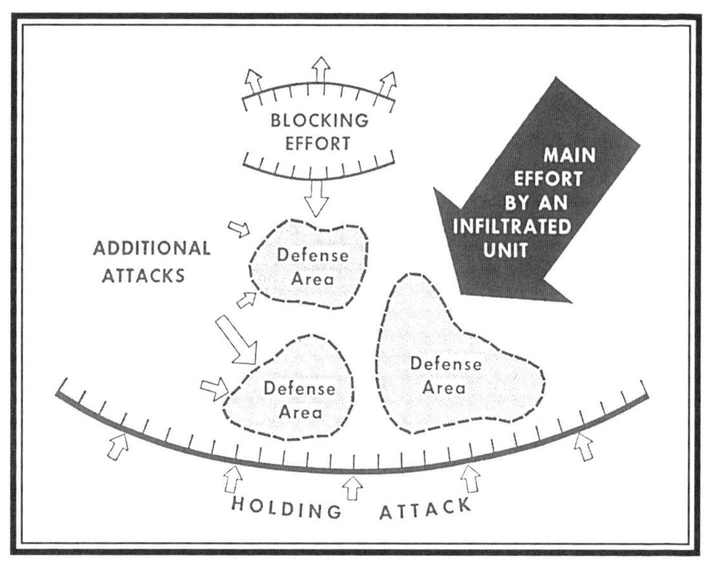

Figure 6.3: One-Point, Two-Sides Attack
(Source: "Handbook on the Chinese Communitst Army," DA Pamphlet 30-51 [1960], p. 24)

Carlson's Conflicting Goals

Though an enthusiastic proponent of Maoist tactics, Carlson was still from a Puritan background. The two philosophies did not always mesh. Having personally witnessed the finality with which Asians fight, he wished to decisively disrupt the Japanese rear. His Raiders' skull head patch left little doubt as to their intent. It was to close with and destroy as many enemy soldiers as they could—commando fashion (with a knives, if necessary). Fast-moving guerrillas can't afford many prisoners. Carlson was nonetheless attempting—through his indoctrination sessions—to seize the moral high ground.

Also implicit in Carlson's mission was the formation of local insurgent forces. At least, that was the agenda being pushed to

President Roosevelt by legendary William J. Donovan.[10] James Roosevelt had suggested a like arrangement in the Marshalls, Marianas, Carolines, and northern Japan as existed between British commandos and Chinese guerrillas.[11] But, Carlson would only use indigenous personnel for scouting. While how to train others may have been part of the 2nd Raider curriculum, there is no indication of battlefield locals ever receiving much instruction.

Understandably, Marine Commandant Holcomb was more interested in hit and run raids and diversions during amphibious operations. Later, his goals would include spearhead attacks to make each landing safer. Never a fan of elitist units, Gen. Holcomb constantly insisted that—with sufficient workup—regular infantry battalions could perform the same function as British commandos had with the Chinese guerrillas.[12]

Thus, Carlson's thought processes must have been somewhat conflicted on Guadalcanal, much as Lt.Col. David Hackworth's would be in Vietnam. Both were completely enthralled with Guerrilla Warfare, with Hackworth actually interested in "out-G'ing the G."[13]

Carlson's Take on Guerrilla Warfare

In a 1937 article describing the Nicaragua tour, Carlson revealed his five priorities with regard to counterguerrilla warfare. Within each was implicitly his view on how best to operate as a guerrilla. First came the reminder that small units which "speedily strike and then disappear into the countryside" can better confront guerrilla bands. Then came the emphasis on patrols so mobile they can "live off the land and follow the bandits home." Next was the importance of immediately establishing fire superiority and then cutting off "the rebels' means of escape." Fourth was the continual application by all hands of unrestricted initiative to counter "guerrilla opportunism." The fifth and last was enough "mobility to always achieve surprise and then extricate oneself from unfavorable circumstances," if necessary.[14]

Thus, the good Colonel possessed a strange mix of American boldness and Eastern caution. Though thoroughly aggressive, he never bit off more than he could chew. Two Chinese proverbs may help to explain the second part of this strange dichotomy.

Figure 6.4: Lead Element on Carlson's Long Patrol
(Source: U.S. Army Center of Military History, artphoto archives, illustration designator "jungle.jpg," Patrol in the Jungle, by Roger Blum)

> The expert commander strikes only when victory is certain.[15]
>
> — Sun Tzu

> He who knows when he can fight and when he cannot will be victorious.[16]
>
> — Sun Tzu

A Closer Look at the Long Patrol

Carlson's Long Patrol on Guadalcanal happened almost by accident, so it is frequently viewed as a headquarters afterthought or guerrilla experiment. (See Figure 6.4 and Map 6.1.) Yet, it was

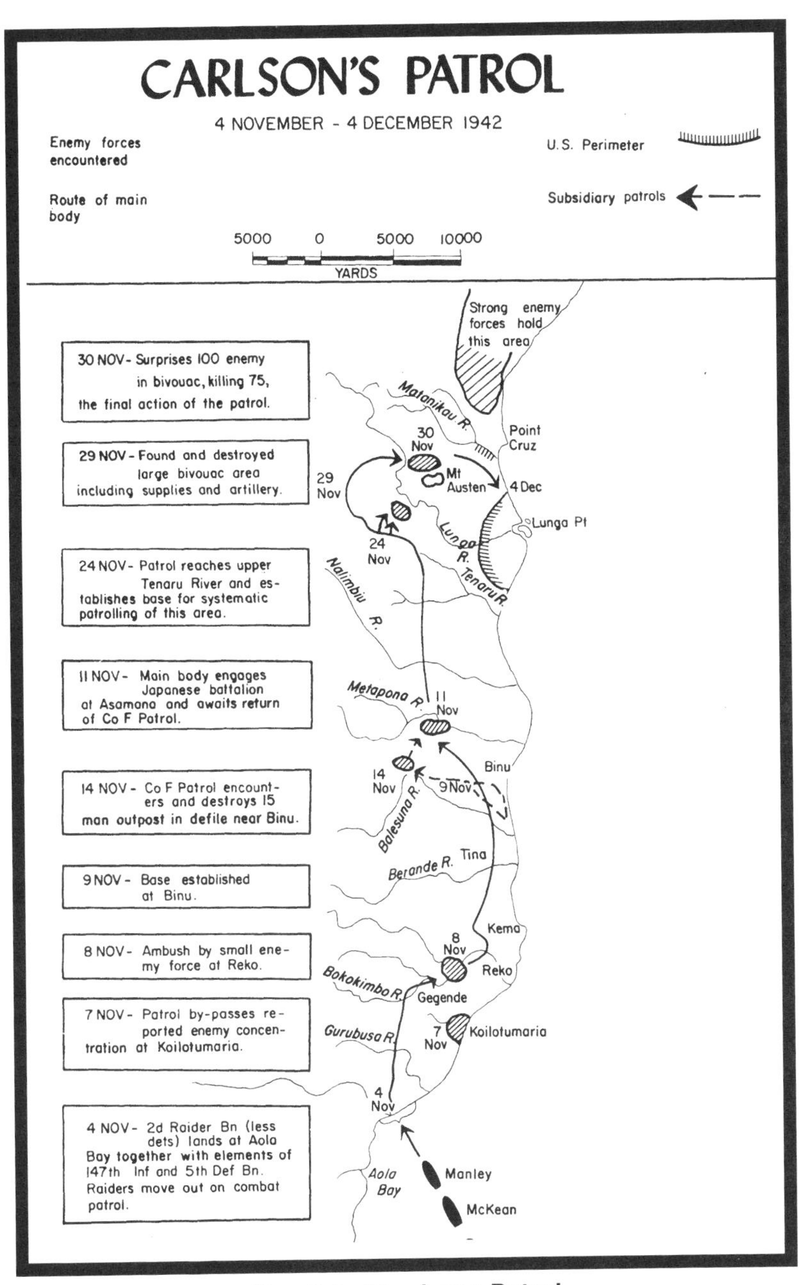

Map 6.1: The Long Patrol

(Source: "From Makin to Bouganville: Marine Raiders in the Pacific War," by Maj. Jon T. Hoffman, Marines in WWII Commemorative Series, HQMC, 1995, p. 20)

much more than that. What happened on that 30-day patrol would become the only historical example of how Maoist tactics might work for U.S. troops. Merrill's Marauders only occasionally fought alongside Nationalist Chinese "X-Force" personnel. While the Marauders were partially modeled after Orde Wingate's "Chindits," those Chindits were exclusively Indian.[17]

After being sent to Aola Bay on the northeast coast to help with a new airstrip, 2nd Raider Battalion was ordered to disrupt a force of 3,000 Japanese withdrawing from a battle at Henderson Field.[18] Aola Bay was just east of Tasimboko—the same Japanese debarkation point that had been attacked earlier by 1st Raider Battalion. Carlson's patrol route entailed considerable risk by blocking the enemy's most likely escape route. In fact, three of his companies were landed at Tasimboko on 10 November 1942 to more easily catch up with the patrol.[19] Using native scouts and partial resupply by airdrop, Carlson and the other companies had four days earlier moved westward along inland trails. (See Figure 6.5.)

Then came a unique combination of Positional Warfare outposts and Guerrilla Warfare maneuvers. To more easily locate the retreating Japanese, those outposts functioned as patrol bases. Every time one of their resident patrols made contact with the quarry, others would converge on that quarry as if independent guerrilla bands.

The Extent of Guerrilla Warfare on the Patrol

While creating indigenous militia is an important aspect of guerrilla warfare, there is no evidence of Carlson ever mobilizing Guadalcanal's inhabitants for their own campaign against the Japanese. He only used them as scouts and porters. Assisted by "150 native scouts,"[20] 2nd Raider Battalion set up a succession of patrol bases from which to look for the retreating Japanese.[21] Once those Japanese were located, the Raiders attacked them guerrilla fashion—through a partial encirclement by tiny elements that struck quickly and then disappeared back into the jungle. Such swarm tactics are mostly Eastern in origin. Because of the potential for fratricide, U.S. doctrine has never permitted assaulting an objective from more than one direction at once. Whether terrain or other obstructions might preclude stray rounds is never considered. Carlson did no more to encourage encirclement than occasionally "vectoring" units in the right direction.[22]

When 2nd Raider Battalion Switched to Mobile Warfare

At first, Carlson moved forward through a series of village base camps. While a single company guarded that camp, the others patrolled forward. If one made contact, it acted as a holding force while its sisters outflanked the quarry. In one such instance on 11 November (when a bivouacking Japanese battalion was disturbed at Asamana), the holding company was forced to extricate itself when Carlson's enveloping force met resistance. Its orders had been to move around the Japanese force and secretly attack it from the flank and rear, just as the 8th Route Army had done.[23] After regrouping, the good Colonel then occupied the now empty bivouac site to apply ambushes and artillery (combined arms) to returning enemy patrols.[24] Throughout this period, his supplies had been ferried along the coast by Higgins Boat and delivered by native porters.[25] An American Army unit had been concurrently occupying the Guadalcanal beachfront.[26]

When 2nd Battalion was later to look for "Pistol Pete" (the long-range gun) on Mount Austin, its commander switched to a more deliberate (but similar) attack mode on 25 November. From his now six companies, he created three two-company task forces. Each task force was to operate from its own patrol base, and the three bases daily move (roughly on line) a little farther inland. This staggered patrol base formation was tantamount to a strongpoint matrix. Should the enemy counterattack, it had more defensive power than the linear alignment of a standard sweep. Each base enjoyed not only its own perimeter security, but also interlocking protective fires—in any direction—from sister bases. All the while, the three faced the most probable Japanese concentration. When a nearly abandoned Japanese bastion was finally discovered atop Mount Austin, Carlson used a double-envelopment to capture it.[27] Note how similar this and the Asamana evolution are to the Chinese attack model in Figure 6.2.

The Raiders' Encircling Attacks

Central to Mao's writings are the twin concepts of encirclement and annihilation.[28] Throughout the Long Patrol, almost every Raider contact resulted in freewheeling elements moving in to hit the enemy's rear and flanks. While the U.S. military has never encouraged either encirclement or autonomous subunits, both were allowed by the Chinese Army.

The Raiders' Double-Envelopments

The WWII Japanese liked both encirclements and double-envelopments, but clearly differentiated between the two. During the hasty double-envelopment associated with a chance contact, they made little provision for opposing-unit size.[29] As possibly in 8th Route Army contact, Carlson's patrols routinely sent people around both flanks through a wider loop than the Japanese were expected to use.[30]

Figure 6.5: Carlson's Men Were Beset by Illness
(Source: Drawing by F. Boggs, "Top of the Ladder: Marine Operations in the Northern Solomons," by J.C. Chapin, Marines in WWII Commemorative Series, HQMC, 1997, p. 19)

Finally to take a poorly manned enemy bastion on Mount Austin, Carlson had to run two consecutive double-envelopments.[31] If conducted on a wide enough loop to be obscured from the defender, such a maneuver would have been like an encirclement.

The Raiders' Dual-Purpose Attack Formation

Where the foe was thought to be well dug-in behind Henderson Field, Carlson moved in a staggered row of two-company patrol bases. While possibly intended to more easily detect the Japanese, such an attack formation was for all practical purposes a forward-moving defense. In Korea, the Chinese had often used rearward moving mobile defenses.[32] Why couldn't the same formation work almost as well moving forward? While deployed along the same trench, troops are ready to switch over to the offense. However, the idea of a dual purpose formation in regular terrain sounds very Sun-Tzu-like. As part of Chinese MW, it would have required its own usage criteria.

> Before defensive lines became fixed in Korea, the CCF [Chinese Communist Forces] did not employ . . . position defense. Instead, they employed a basic defensive scheme of "one up and two back." In this scheme, the "up" group operated as a screening and delaying force. The two "back units" . . . [were prepared] for [either a counteroffensive or the defense.[33]
>
> — U.S. Army, *Leavenworth Research Survey No. 6*

It's not clear whether Mao ever attacked with patrol bases on line in the flatlands of China. That may just have been the easiest jungle format. But Carlson's advancing screen had both detected the foe and removed any need for a prearranged maneuver scheme. While he occasionally vectored units in to help the one in contact (and even suggested their route), detailed assault instructions were never issued. How those units closed with their target (after conferring with the holding unit) was up to them. This is tantamount to swarm tactics. It takes strength from the lack of bureaucratic inertia and abundance of small-unit initiative. It was, quite simply, a good example of MW.

The Raiders' Asian Approach to Short-Range Combat

While staying aggressive in spirit, Carlson's men never tried to move forward through intense small-arms fire. This is one of the biggest differences between the Eastern and Western thought processes. The Eastern unit will wait for a natural opportunity to advance, whereas the Western unit will routinely force the issue. Of course, this way of operating is also consistent with the "gaps and surfaces" philosophy of German MW. Yet, that philosophy was not Marine doctrine in 1942.

There was another event near the end of the Long Patrol that was quite out of character for an American unit. Shortly after 30 November, another Nipponese bivouac site was mistakenly entered by a Raider patrol's lead element. Within a few minutes, 75 of its 100 occupants had been summarily dispatched by just a few individuals.[34] At the doctrinal level, "a few taking on many" is again an Oriental concept with its roots in the guerrilla experience.

How Productive Were Such Nontraditional Maneuvers?

From a tactical standpoint, the Long Patrol had been a great success. According to one author, 2nd Battalion Raiders even found Pistol Pete on the South Bank of the Lunga.[35] They had killed 488 enemy soldiers at a loss of 16 dead and 18 wounded. In the after-action report, Carlson credited his "guerrilla tactics" for the lopsided casualty ratio. Of course, not everyone agreed with his assessment. There had also been problems on the patrol. Undernourished (as the Chinese had also been), many of Carlson's men had to be "medivaced" *en route* for some jungle disease. Upon reentering the Henderson Field perimeter on 4 December, they were only at one fifth of the original number.[36] (Refer back to Figure 6.5.)

In a hurry to withdraw from the island (so the conventional wisdom went), the Japanese had become careless and easy for Raider artillery spotters to target. This is highly doubtful. These soldiers of Nippon were some of the best light infantrymen in the world and expert at camouflage. (See Figures 6.6 and 6.7.) Many had just come from the Malaysian jungles and taking of Singapore. Marine artillery rounds of the period would have had limited affect in this much vegetation. More likely, Carlson's low-ranking fighters had simply been given enough skill to sneak up on someone and then enough authority to exercise a little initiative. Able to attack or withdraw at will, their automatic-weapon-carrying point men didn't need a manpower advantage. To this day, Chinese and North Korean troops are trained—mostly through maneuver—to handle many times their number of enemy personnel.

Still, the opening question persists. Was Carlson using enough of the contemporary usage criteria to make this MW? (Look ahead at Tables 6.1 and 6.2.) If so, the Chinese version may be slightly more comprehensive, as it would include criteria for reassembly, deception, dual-purpose formations, and short-range infiltration.

Whether These Raider Tactics Qualified As MW

As demonstrated by the last chapter, Chinese Mobile Warfare shared the MW precepts. But, did it have enough of the same application criteria? Carlson was obviously using a combination of Chinese Mobile and Guerrilla Warfare during his Long Patrol on Guadalcanal. Considering Mao's guerrilla guidance, the Mobile style would have been more likely during the Asamana and Mount Austin offensives.

> Enemy advances, we retreat.
> Enemy halts, we harass.
> Enemy tires, we attack.
> Enemy retreats, we pursue.[37]
> — Mao's guerrilla guidance

Whether the Colonel's imitation of Chinese Mobile Warfare at those locations can qualify as MW will depend upon its correlation with Tables 6.1 and 6.2. His patrolling screen should count as a type of "reconnaissance pull." His encircling maneuvers could be viewed as "moving through gaps" and "bypassing enemy concentrations." He had also been issuing mission-type (uncomplicated) orders. Only really missing from his effort is the night attack. Yet, the Chinese Communists are well known for their night-fighting ability.[38] A look back at Figure 6.3 shows the main attack by short-range infiltration, and even the U.S. Army admits that most of this happened at night.[39] Thus, one could reasonably conclude that the Chinese had their own fully operational (and possibly enhanced) version of MW by 1940. This should come as no particular surprise, as the Germans had already developed all of their parameters by 1917.[40]

Traditional U.S. Attrition War	New U.S. MW (Commonsense War)
Tries to Kill Enemy	Tries to Bypass/Demoralize Foe
Depends On Firepower	Depends on Surprise
Takes Centralized Control	Takes Decentralized Control
Focus Is Inward on Self	Focus Is Outward on Enemy
Hits Foe Concentrations	Moves through Gaps
Objectives Are Hilltops	Objectives Are "Centers of Gravity"
Biggest Weapon Used	Combined Arms Employed
Methodical	High Tempo
Command Push	Reconnaissance Pull
Attacks All Along a Line	Exploits Breakthroughs
Day Attacks Only	Mostly Night Attacks
Never Retreats	Sometimes Backs Up
Defends Often	Defends Only As a Trap
War Takes a Long Time	War Won Quickly

Table 6.1: The Two Styles Are Largely Opposite
(Source: "One More Bridge to Cross: Lowering the Cost of War," © 1999 by H. John Poole, table 10.1, p. 67)

Traditional U.S. Attrition Style	New U.S. MW (Commonsense) Style
All Do What They're Told	Initiative Encouraged
Unit Asks Permission	Unit Informs Commander
Detailed Orders	Mission Type Orders
Control through Orders	Control through Training
Train to a Standard	Train As They Want
Train As Always	Train to the Threat
Complicated Signaling	Not Much Signaling Necessary

Table 6.2: Different Control Parameters
(Source: "One More Bridge to Cross: Lowering the Cost of War," © 1999 by H. John Poole, table 10.2, p. 68)

Figure 6.6: Guadalcanal Japanese Were Expert Jungle Fighters
(Source: "A Concise History of the Unites States Marine Corps 1775-1969," by Capt. William D. Parker, Hist. Div., HQMC, 1970, sketch by Capt. Donald L. Dickson, p. 62)

Implied Is a Great Opportunity for the Pentagon

From Table 6.1, one can also conclude that Chinese Positional

Figure 6.7: Marine Artillery of the Period
(Source: "First Offensive: The Marine Campaign for Guadalcanal," by Henry I. Shaw, Marines in WWII Commemorative Series, HQMC, 1992, p. 12)

Warfare is about the same as American Attrition Warfare. Instead of encouraging more maneuver through a modification of doctrine, the Chinese Communists had merely required all units to be able to quickly alternate between styles. With a few Guerrilla Warfare techniques, present-day U.S. infantry commanders might be able to match the feat of 2nd Raider Battalion—conducting MW at the squad level.

"*Gung Ho's*" Gift to Combat Momentum

- Do sister units always need coordinating instructions?
- Why couldn't small ones just cooperate on a mutual goal?

The WWII Japanese were expert light infantrymen.

(Source: Courtesy of Cassell PLC, from "World Army Uniforms since 1939," © 1975, 1980, 1981, 1983 by Blandford Press Ltd., Part I, plate 155; FM 21-76 [1957], p. 112)

Chinese Influence at the Raider Training Center

This Marine Raider Training Center became operational at Camp Pendleton, California, in early February 1943. Because of Lt.Col. James Roosevelt's help in setting it up, Carlson's vision initially influenced the curriculum—with guerrilla warfare classes supplementing those on more traditional individual skills.[1] Free-wheeling aggressor duty also took the place of "canned" exercise participation. But, giving more autonomy to the rifleman and his fire team conflicted with the U.S. rank system and was therefore on borrowed time.

Chinese Influence on Small-Unit Maneuver

When Lt.Col. Alan Shapley—an orthodox line officer—took over 2nd Raider Battalion in March of 1943 and Lt.Col. Michael S. Currin the 4th Raider Battalion a month later, the *Gung Ho* experiment was officially over.[2] Still, the whole idea of allowing one's frontline fighters to help with the decision making had captured the enlisted Marines' imagination. Thus, the *Gung Ho* spirit and many of Carlson's ideas were to become part of the Corps' magnificent heritage. Premier among those ideas was the three-fire-team squad. Through structural subdivision, he had encouraged more maneuver. One fire team could establish a base of fire, while the other two took turns sneaking up on the squad leader's quarry. Meanwhile, Edson had also put more emphasis on the envelopment aspect of light-infantry tactics. Yet, neither Raider chieftain had completed all the steps for a deliberate assault against a prepared enemy position. They had worked on a stealthy approach and obstacle crossing but no way to deceive an alerted defender. As the Japanese began to heavily fortify their island bastions, this was to limit the Raiders' usefulness. (See Figure 7.1.)

Firepower Requires Coordination

As any firepower buff will admit, his favorite solution requires considerable coordination to keep friendlies from getting hit by their own munitions. Carlson was quite interested in overwhelming small-arms fire from his tiny contingents. Such things require all members to stay in column or on line. That's the equivalent of an elementary fire team technique.

PFC William J. Onstad later compared the three Raider fire teams to his high school football team (10 men per squad versus 12 men per team). He then talked about how all of his squad's firepower could be brought to bear within 15 seconds on a point target from a jungle trail at night.[3] If all squad members had been attached by six-foot-long toggle rope on a relatively straight path,[4] that might have been possible against a flank target. But, if the target were directly ahead (as was generally the case), all fire teams would have had quickly to align perpendicular to the trail. Big-picture thinkers don't have much interest in such things. Neither are they in any danger of being shot by an overzealous comrade. Onstad's comparison

Figure 7.1: It Would Soon Be about Taking Bunkers
(Source: U.S. Army Center of Military History, artphoto archives, illustration designator "avop05-99_1.jpg," Follow Me, by H. Charles McBarron, at Leyte, 1944)

means that Carlson's squads had a few "movement techniques" just as football teams have "plays." What those techniques specifically were has been largely lost to history, but they probably had more to do with massed firepower than surprising anyone.

The Maverick's Possible "Ah-Ha" Moment

Just as contemporary Chinese squads have three fire teams, so probably did those of the 8th Route Army. Both may have utilized these tiny groups of fighters in a fairly non-Western manner. Because of the bottom-up environment, their team members did not require constant direction and supervision.

Carlson called this new three-man contingent a "combat group." With a name like that, mutual cooperation was almost certainly intended to supplement squad leader guidance. From a tactical standpoint, this may be the most important aspect of "*Gung Ho.*" It may be the central essence of Asian tactics that rank-conscious Americans have so much trouble appreciating. War veterans and historians alike have often wondered how tiny Asian contingents can so cleverly proceed with so little management from above. For an attack objective, their run-throughs of full-scale mockups may be responsible. But how about this same syndrome during a chance contact in unfamiliar terrain? Might the sophistication of their techniques be allowing them to successfully interact without any leader? Then, they would be truly "working together" as opposed to "working for someone else."

The Spread of the Fire Team and Its Most Powerful Use

Griffith didn't share Edson's animosity toward Carlson. In fact, he had cordially visited with the 2nd Raider Battalion for two weeks before taking over the 1st, "to learn more of his [Carlson's] unique organizational and training ideas."[5] Among those ideas may have been how tiny Raider elements could mount a successful campaign—with very little guidance from any headquarters.

Then, within the 1st Battalion, Griffith created his own version of the squad subdivision (initially only three men per team). At first, he called them "fire groups." Instead of Carlson's Thompson submachinegunner, he added an assistant BAR man with his own rifle. In 1944, with Edson's blessing, the Corps would adopt four-man fire teams built around the BAR.[6] But, the days of semi-autonomous small-units working together without any leader whatsoever were just about over. Only by accident would they ever return to the Corps.

It takes time to coordinate the actions of subordinate units. Time is the enemy of momentum. With the gradual diminution of 2nd Raider Battalion's vision, the Corps became less capable of capturing the momentum during small-unit encounters. Each encounter had first to be reported to, and considered by, some headquarters. Then, the headquarters decision (albeit by a squad leader) had to be relayed to the action player. By that time, the enemy had either disappeared or put that player at a decided disadvantage.

Collective Wisdom or Headquarters Control

- Could many officers effectively function as riflemen?
- Who knows more about short-range combat?

Most U.S. leaders of this era were very much in charge.

(Source: Corel Gallery Clipart, Portraits Historical, #01C077)

Carlson's Nontraditional Leadership Paradigm

Lt.Col. Carlson was doing something completely contrary to American military procedure of the period. He was attempting troop-oriented democracy within the ranks of an organization that had always prided itself on total compliance with all lowest-echelon orders.

> [2nd Battalion] Officers would . . . lead by consensus rather than rank.[1]
>
> — Official Marine pamphlet on the Raiders

Figure 8.1: Over-Reliance on Any Commander Is Risky
(Source: U.S. Army Center of Military History, artphoto archives, illustration designator "avop07-98_3.jpg," The American Soldier, 1944)

According to *Webster's Dictionary*, "consensus" means unanimity, agreement of opinion, or general opinion.[2] Carlson's subunit commanders were to follow the general opinions of their fighters while making most decisions. In other words, they were to facilitate the combined wisdom of their subordinates. For a Western military organization, this kind of thing is almost unheard of. Its officers primarily ensure that all orders from above are followed. Whether or not those orders make any sense to the rank and file is never at issue. Thus, Carlson's attempt to lead by consensus was revolutionary to say the least, and possibly even detrimental to traditional discipline. Still, it obeys most of the rules of logic. It makes perfect sense to let those who are there determine the situation. It makes further sense to allow them collectively to decide how best to deal with that situation. As long as no headquarters initiatives are endangered, what's the harm? There is a limit to what any standoff commander can successfully imagine. (See Figure 8.1.)

Wrapping Oneself around a Completely Foreign Concept

For an American, "working together" evokes images of individuals cooperating, doing things side by side, or having the same overall goals. For the Asian, who must live next-door to half of the world's population, it means something quite different. For him, it connotes hordes of ordinary citizens successfully interacting without much structure to guide them. This mostly Asian syndrome is readily observable in India. Throughout New Delhi, Agra, Jaipur, Varanasi, Calcutta, and Chennai, there are very few stop signs or traffic lights. Yet, millions of vehicles successfully negotiate their congested streets daily.[3]

Thus, within the concept of "*Gung Ho,*" may be the same implied lack of central management. For the sake of momentum, Carlson may have being trying to supersede some of the procedural edicts that have so fully permeated the U.S. military establishment.

Tactical Precedents of Looser Control Still Working

It is now well known that the Chechen rebels were able to repel the first Soviet armored assault on Grozny in 1995 by simply allowing semi-independent and untrained bands to swarm around it.[4] After adopting more military structure in 1999, the rebels were unable to keep the Soviets out.[5] Their greater organization had made a true "urban swarm" impossible.

> They [the rebels occupying Grozny in 1999]. . . operated in a very centrally controlled fashion instead of the "defenseless defense" or "let the situation do the organizing" mode of 1995.[6]
>
> — *Marine Corps Gazette,* April 2000

When a patrol hastily assaults during a chance contact, it normally uses some "fire and movement" format. That's where subunits alternately move forward while others cover them by fire. Because of differences in microterrain and resistance, such an evolution is better accomplished randomly. That often equates to one buddy team member moving forward while all eyes are on another. Anyone who has witnessed—from the enemy's standpoint—a more structured version will know why unnecessary casualties occur.

The Power of Collective Thinking

While very patriotically applied by the Minutemen of 1776, collective thinking is still an Eastern concept and mostly practiced by Western revolts. That's because it flies in the face of established authority. But, what if that Western establishment has been trying unsuccessfully for years to solve some problem. Then, it has little choice but to look eastward.

Shared wisdom is not just useful during rebellions. It does not necessarily imply Communism, Socialism, or public discord. In fact, it is what makes participatory democracy work. It can be just as useful in a military organization. Periodic initiative and following of orders need not be mutually exclusive. The same person can accomplish either at the appropriate time. What several persons can mostly agree on is generally more valid than what any one thinks he knows. Thus, collective thinking holds great promise in the military. It has already proven its worth in the civilian sector. So too has the leaderless farm cooperative on which Carlson based his model. Some business cooperatives have been highly successful in Great Britain.[7] A recent training example should help to make the point.

It has been often said that an instructor learns more than his students. How could this be? At his disposal is the combined organizational wisdom of all who have come before. To see why, one must imagine "Situation Stations" during a "Round-Robin" training session for 12-man "sticks" (groups). Most informative are the scenarios with no official solution. Instead of rattling off the generally applicable axioms, the instructor pretends to know the answer and to lead his students toward it through a series of questions. That to which his students mostly agree becomes his working solution.

After about the third or fourth stick, he easily recognizes the "duty solution" to the scenario. Those students now consider him their best instructor ever.[8]

Because the word "training" has come to connote extreme boredom to most U.S. military personnel, another subject must be broached before any more examples of fun and productive instruction. That subject is the extent to which Carlson and Edson influenced subsequent Marine Corps history. The Raiders turned into the 4th Marine Regiment in 1943, so that's a good place to start.

Further Maoist Raider Participation in WWII

- When did Carlson lose command of 2nd Raider Battalion?
- Did 2nd and 4th Battalions see more action?

The Japanese also mostly relied on "non-Western" tactics.

(Source: Cassell PLC, from "World Army Uniforms since 1939," © 1975, 1980, 1981, 1983 by Blandford Press Ltd., Part I, plate 156; FM 21-76 [1957], p. 54)

A Formal End to the Chinese Ways

Except for the fire team concept, HQMC soon put a stop to Maoist philosophies within the Raider establishment. Carlson was replaced as Commanding Officer (CO) of 2nd Raider battalion on 21 March 1943 (three and a half months after the Long Patrol). Then, there was a succession of more traditional thinkers: (1) Lt.Col. Alan Shapley, 22 March to 30 August 1943; (2) Lt.Col. Joseph W. McCaffery, 1 September to 1 November 1943; (3) Maj. Richard T. Washburn, 1 November 1943 to 25 January 1944; and (4) Capt. Bernard W. Green, 26-31 January 1944.[1]

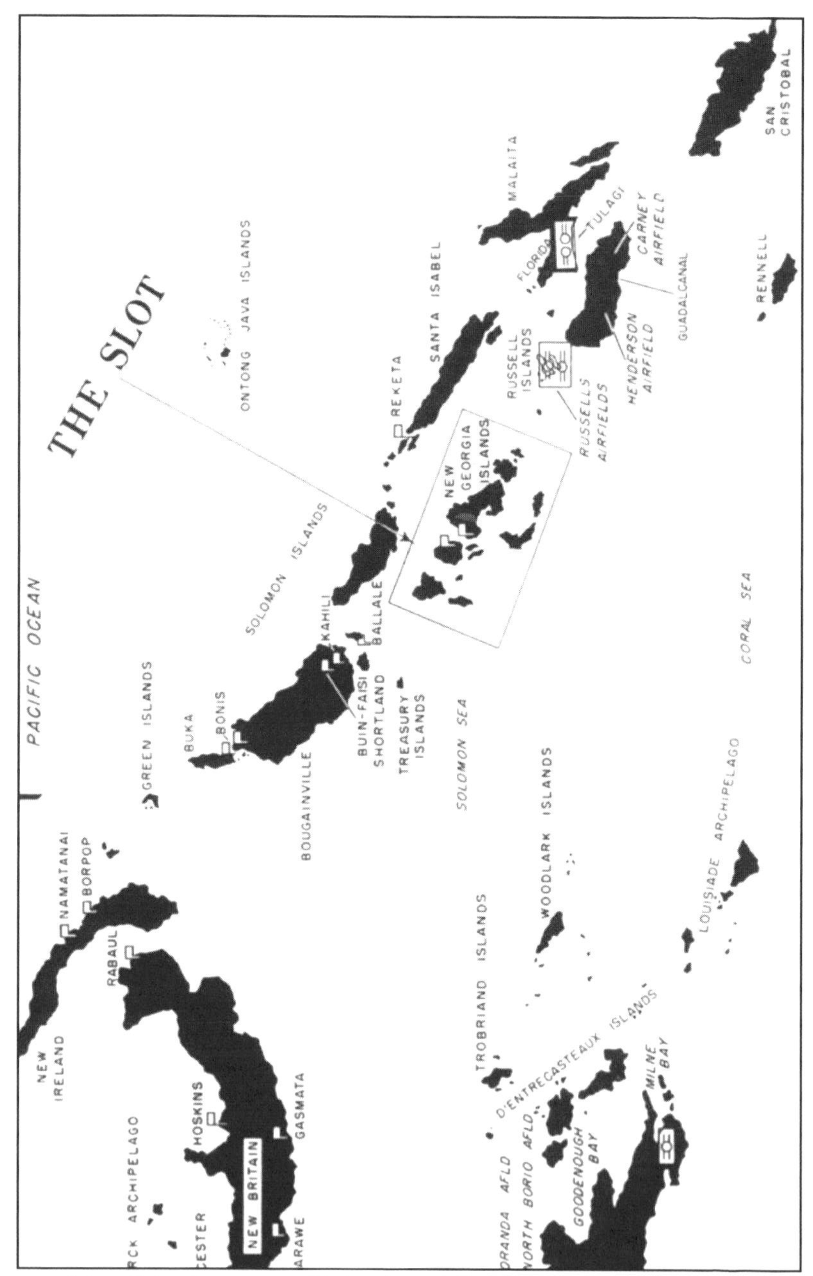

Map 9.1: Japanese Rabaul and the Solomons Approach

(Source: "Marines in the Central Solomons," by Maj. John N. Rentz, USMC Historical Monograph, HQMC, 1952, chapt. 1)

Similarly, James Roosevelt (the president's son) was replaced as CO of 4th Raider Battalion on 28 April 1943 (before it had seen any combat). Taking his place were the following more conventional leaders: (1) Maj. James R. Clark, 29 April to 3 May 1943; (2) Lt.Col. Michael S. Currin, 4 May to 14 September 1943; and (3) Maj. Robert H. Thomas, 15 September 1943 to 1 February 1944.[2] (Roosevelt's change of assignment also meant an end to the guerrilla warfare classes at Camp Pendleton's Raider Training Center.)

With the arrivals of Shapley and Clark, 2nd and 4th Raider Battalion personnel no longer participated in rankless subunits, *Gung Ho* Sessions, or any of Carlson's other experiments. His fire teams would persist, and some of his Oriental tactics; but—despite the continuation of special-operations-type missions—both battalions would return to a more conventional operating format. Under the command of old-China-hand Samuel Griffith, 1st Raider Battalion would retain some of Carlson's ways, but which ones are not completely clear.

2nd Raider Battalion Saw Action after Guadalcanal

After the Long March, 2nd Battalion went to New Zealand for rest and rehabilitation. In March 1943, it returned to the Solomons as part of a Marine Raider Regiment. Now composed of E, G, and H companies,[3] it would go on to fight in one of the most inhospitable places on the way to Rabaul—Bougainville. (See Maps 9.1 and 9.2.) Though in the Northern Solomons, Bougainville had been administered as part of the Australian Territory of New Guinea. It was closer to the Equator than Guadalcanal, heavily jungled, and beset by torrential rains. (See Figure 9.1.) In many places, the jungle came right down to the ocean's edge. Someone at Headquarters must have thought Carlson's men to be swamp experts.

On 1 November 1943, 2nd Battalion made an assault landing at Empress Augusta Bay on Bougainville as a part of 2nd Raider Regiment. Landing over Green beach #1 on Cape Torokina at 0730 hours, it encountered big trouble immediately.[4]

> The Raiders, led by Major Richard T. Washburn [Lt. Col. Joseph W. McCaffery by some accounts], went ashore in the face of heavy machine gun and rifle fire from two enemy bunkers and a number of supporting trenches about 30

yards inland. Japanese defenders were estimated at about a reinforced platoon. After the first savage resistance, the enemy fire slackened as the Raiders blasted the bunkers

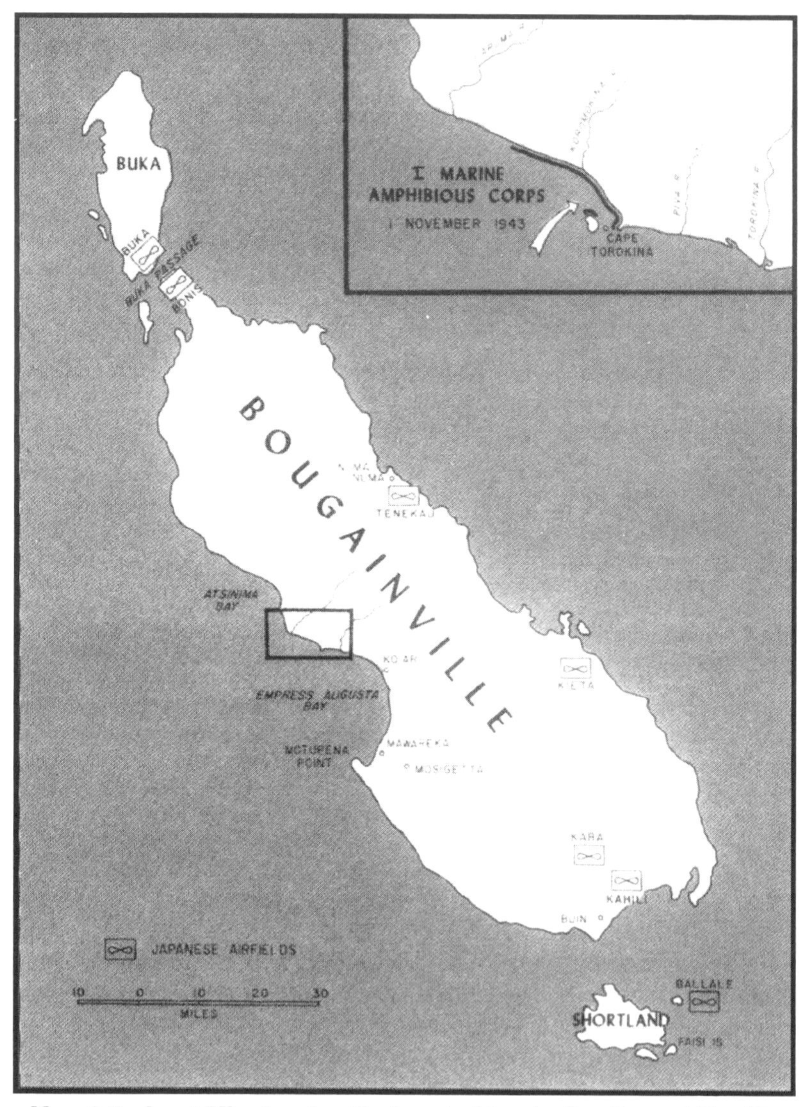

Map 9.2: Last Mission for Carlson's Men in Southwest Pacific
(Source: "Top of the Ladder: Marine Operations in the Northern Solomons," by Capt. John C. Chapin, Marines in WWII Commemorative Series, HQMC, 1997, p. 1)

Figure 9.1: The Muddy Morass of Bougainville
(Source: "Top of the Ladder: Marine Operations in the Northern Solomons," by J.C. Chapin, Marines in WWII Commemorative Series, HQMC, 1997, drawing by Kerr Eby, p. 19)

apart to kill the occupants. Other enemy soldiers retreated into the jungle. Only after the beach area was secured did the Raiders discover that . . . Lieutenant Colonel Joseph W. McCaffery, had been fatally wounded while coordinating the assault of combat units against the enemy dispositions.

Extensive lagoons and swampland backing the narrow beach limited reconnaissance efforts, and reorganization of the assault platoons and companies was hindered by constant sniper fire. Despite these handicaps, the Raiders pushed slowly into the jungle and, by 1100, had wiped out all remaining enemy resistance. Raider Company M, attached to the 2nd Raider Battalion for the job of setting up a trail block farther inland to stall any enemy attempt to reinforce the beachhead, moved out along the well-marked Mission Trail and was soon far out ahead of the Raider perimeter.[5]

— *History of USMC Operations in World War II*

The Piva Trail Experience

On 8 November 1943, 2nd Raider Battalion participated in the two-day Battle of Piva Trail. Safely to move up that trail, it had initially leapfrogged patrol bases (as on Guadalcanal). Then, its separate company perimeters were to work well near the assigned roadblock. That's because they now resembled a strongpoint defense.

> Since D-Day, the 2nd Raider Battalion with Company M of the 3rd Raider Battalion attached had slowly but steadily pressed inland astride the trail leading from the Buretoni Mission towards the Piva River. This trail, hardly more than a discernible pathway through the jungle, was the main link between the Cape Torokina area and the Numa Numa trail; and if the Japanese mounted a serious counterstroke, it would probably be aimed along this route.
>
> Advance defensive positions were pushed progressively deeper along this path by Raider companies, and, by 5 November, the Marines had established a strong trail block about 300 yards west of the junction of the Piva [and] Numa Numa trails.[6]
>
> — *History of USMC Operations in World War II*

Then came the Japanese push from the other direction. To stop it, the 2nd Raider Battalion had first to defend its roadblock and then to counterattack. (See Map 9.3.)

> That night [5 November], with Company E of the 2nd Raiders manning the defensive position, the Japanese struck twice in sharp attacks. . . .
>
> The following day was quiet, but anticipating further attempts by the Japanese to steamroller past the road block, the 2nd and 3rd Raider Battalions, . . . were moved into position to give ready support of the road block. . . .
>
> The first enemy thrust came during the early part of the afternoon of 7 November, shortly after Company H of the 2nd Raiders had moved up to the trail block to relieve Company F. . . . One platoon from Company E, 2nd Raiders, then rushed to the trail block to reinforce Company H until another Raider unit, Company G, was in position to help

defend the trail. The enemy, unable to penetrate the Marine position after several furious attacks, withdrew about 1530, and was observed digging in around Piva Village, some 1,000 yards east. The Japanese force was estimated at about battalion strength. . . .

Early the next morning, 8 November, Company M of the 3rd Raiders hurried forward to relieve Company H while Company G took over the responsibility for the trail block. Company M took up positions behind the trail block and deployed with two platoons on the left side of the trail and one platoon on the right. Before Company H could leave the area, however, enemy activity in front of Company G increased and returning patrols reported that a large-scale attack could be expected at any time. Reluctant to leave a fight, Company H remained at the trail block. The Japanese assault was not long in coming. Elements of two battalions, later identified as the 1st and 3rd Battalions of the 23rd Infantry from the Buin area, began pressing forward behind a heavy mortar barrage and machine gun fire. By 1100, the trail block was enveloped on all sides by a blaze of gunfire as the Marine units sought to push the attackers back. Company G, solidly astride the trail, bore the brunt of the enemy's assault. . . .

Flanking movements by either the attackers or the defending Marines were impossible because of the swampy ground on either side of the trail, and two attempts by enemy groups to envelop the flanks of the Marine position ended as near-frontal attacks with heavy casualties to the attacking troops. In each instance, the Japanese were exposed to the direct fire of a Marine company in defensive positions. Both attacks were beaten back.

At 1300, with the enemy assault perceptibly stalled, the 2nd Raiders attempted a counterattack. Company F, returned to the trail block from a reserve area, together with Company E began a flanking maneuver from the right. After struggling through the swamps for only 50 yards, the two Raider companies struck a large force of Japanese, and the fight for possession of the trail began once more.

The enemy soldiers, attempting another counterattack, ran full into the fire of Company G's machine guns and once again took heavy casualties. Half-tracks of the 9th Marines

Weapons Company, with two supporting tanks, moved forward to help the Marine attack gain impetus, but the thick jungle and the muddy swamps defeated the attempts of the machines to reinforce the front lines. Unable to help, the machines began evacuating wounded. By 1600, the fight at the trail block was a stalemate. The Marines were unable to move forward, and the enemy force had been effectively stalled. Another Japanese counterattack, noticeably less fierce than the first, was turned back with additional casualties to the enemy.

With darkness approaching, the Raider companies were ordered to return to their prepared lines, and the Marines began to withdraw through the trail block. Company F covered the disengagement and beat back one final enemy attempt before the withdrawal was completed. The Raider casualties were 8 killed and 27 wounded. The Marines estimated that at least 125 Japanese had been killed in the day's fighting. . . .

At 0620 the following morning, 9 November, the Raider units returned to the trail block area which had been held overnight by Company M and . . . Company I. The two assault companies deployed behind Company I with Company L taking positions on the left of the trail and Company F [2nd Raider Battalion] on the right side of the trail. At 0730, the artillery preparation by 1/12 began to pound into the Japanese positions ahead of the trail block. . . .

The Japanese, though, had not waited to be attacked. At first light, the enemy . . . moved to within 100 yards of the Marine position. There they had established a similar trail block with both flanks resting on an impassable swamp. Other enemy soldiers, who had crept up to within 25 yards of the front lines during the night, remained hidden until the artillery fires ceased and the Raider companies began the attack. Then the Japanese opened up with short-range machine gun fire and automatic rifle fire.

The enemy's action delayed part of Company F, with the result that, when Company L began the attack at 0800, only half of Company F moved forward. Coordination between the two attacking units was not regained, and, by 0930, the Raider attack had covered only a few yards. The two compa-

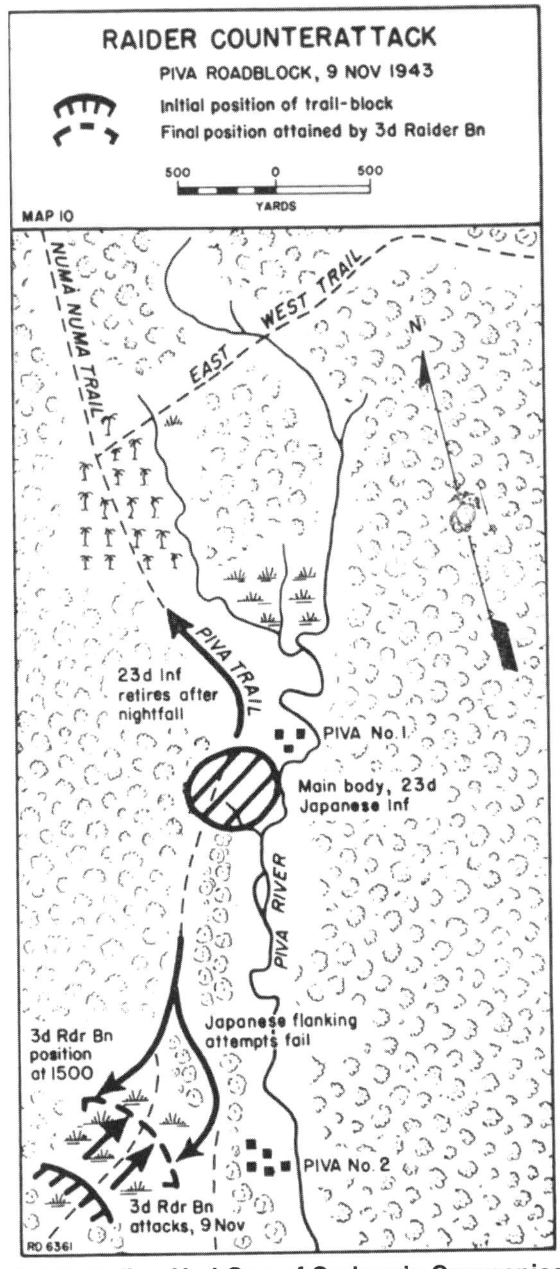

Map 9.3: 3rd Battalion Had One of Carlson's Companies Attached
(Source: "Isolation of Rabaul," by Shaw and Kane, vol. II, History of USMC Operations in World War II, HQMC, 1963, map 10)

> nies were forced to move along a narrow front between the swamps, and the enemy fire from a large number of machine guns and "knee mortars" stalled the Marine attack.
>
> Neither the tanks nor the half-tracks could negotiate the muddy corridor to reinforce the Marine attack. Unable to flank the enemy position, the Raiders could move forward only on the strength of a concentrated frontal attack. The fight along the corridor became a toe-to-toe slugging match, the Marines and Japanese screaming at each other in the midst of continual mortar bursts and gunfire. Slowly at first, then with increasing speed, the Marine firepower overcame that of the Japanese. The Raider attack, stalled at first, began to move.
>
> Suddenly, at 1230, the Japanese resistance crumbled and the Raider companies pressed forward against only scattered snipers and stragglers. By 1500, the junction of the Piva-Numa Numa Trail was reached.[7]
>
> – *History of USMC Operations in World War II*

When the Japanese tried to "double-envelop" 3rd Battalion's position, it had 2nd Battalion's Company F attached and to the right of the trail. (Refer back to Map 9.3.) With only one swampy flank available, Company F could only counterattack there. However, it and its sister companies were still in the double-envelopment mindset.

Succeeding Battles on Bougainville

On 13 November 1943, there was the Battle of Coconut Grove, and six days later the Battle of Piva Forks (or Numa Numa Trail). At the Battle of Coconut Grove, 2nd Raider Battalion was attached to 21st Marine Regiment and told to protect the supply line from the main line of resistance to 2/21. At the next Battle of Piva Forks, 2nd Raider Battalion was attached to the 3rd Marine Regiment and soon became one of its assault units.[8] On neither occasion do the war chronicles record any unusual tactics. However, at Piva Forks, 2nd Raider Battalion seemed to be more effective in the assault than its more conventional partner, for its opposition precipitously withdrew. If one were to try to guess the difference between the two units, decentralization of control would come immediately to mind. Carlson's former companies might have sent buddy teams crawling forward through the microterrain to outflank each bunker. Whereas, a regular line unit would have more carefully maintained its alignment to apply maximum firepower.

> . . . The 2nd Battalion of the Raider regiment, with two companies of the 3rd Raiders attached, was also ordered to move up behind the 3rd Marines for commitment to action.
>
> On the morning of the 25th [of November] . . . the 2nd Raiders and 1/9 [1st Battalion, 9th Marines] . . . moved east along the East-West trail to begin the day's attack. Randall's 1/9 was to move up Cibik Ridge and then attack almost directly east on a front of 400 yards to extend the left flank of 3/3 [3rd Battalion, 3rd Marines]. The 2nd Raiders were to attack on the left flank of 1/9 on a front of about 800 yards. The objective, an area of high ground north of the East-West trail, was about 800 yards distant.
>
> Randall's battalion [1/9] . . . [then] proceeded . . . to the crest. . . . [T]he attack was started straight down the opposite side of Cibik Ridge. At the foot of the ridge, both attacking companies were held up by extremely heavy machine gun fire from concealed positions on a small knoll just ahead. The fight for this knob . . . continued the rest of the day.
>
> The 2nd Raiders, meanwhile, had advanced against sporadic resistance. The attack was held up several times by enemy groups; but, as the Raiders prepared to assault the defenses, the enemy suddenly gave ground to retire to new positions. By afternoon, Major Washburn's battalion had occupied the hill mass dominating the East-West trail and established a strong perimeter defense on the objective to wait for the battalion from the 9th Marines to come up on line.
>
> Randall's battalion, however, had its hands full. Both attack companies had committed their reserve platoons to the assault of the small knoll facing them without making headway.[9]
>
> – *History of USMC Operations in World War II*

This would be the last major engagement for 2nd Raider Battalion. Largely due to Communist interest in the same common-sense approach to low-intensity combat, its contributions would not be fully appreciated for another 70 years.

Pictures of Marine Raiders fighting—while up to their waists in water—are some the most provocative reminders of those later battles, except—of course—for the casualty lists. To say that Bougainville was a muddy hell would be a gross understatement. In early January, 2nd Battalion was withdrawn from that hell. On 1 February, it was disbanded.[10]

Whatever Happened to 4th Raider Battalion?

The 4th Raider Battalion was composed of six companies. They were split between two task forces that separately forayed out of Guadalcanal. Back on 27 June 1943, the first task force had landed on New Georgia in the Central Solomons and begun an approach march to Viru Harbor.[11] (See Maps. 9.4 and 9.5.) *En route,* it managed a few nontraditional maneuvers.

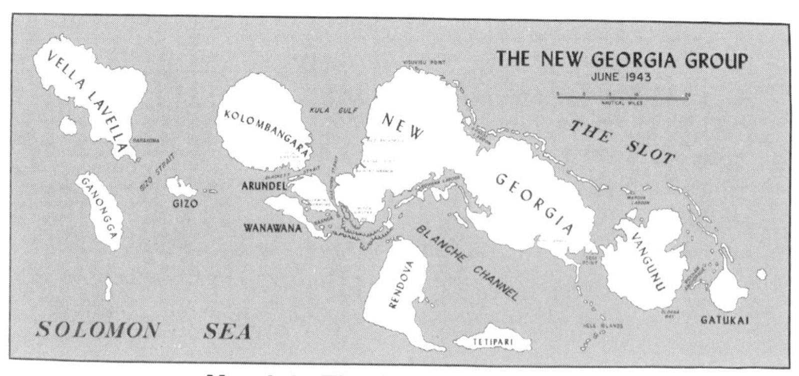

Map 9.4: The Central Solomons

(Source: "From Makin to Bouganville: Marine Raiders in the Pacific War," by Maj. Jon T. Hoffman, Marines in WWII Commemorative Series, HQMC, 1995, p. 30)

Hints of Maoist Encirclement at Viru Harbor

In true Carlson fashion, "native scouts served as [this overland maneuver force's] guides and . . . point." Along the way, one company did all the fighting at the Choi River while the other two moved on to comply with the battalion's attack schedule. In effect, an enemy concentration had been bypassed. Upon arrival at Viru Harbor, the two then split and moved to assault Tombe and Tetemara—towns on opposite shores. This in itself did not constitute a double-envelopment, but the "both-flank" advance upon encountering the former occupiers of Tetemara may have. During the overall pincers movement, there had been no attempt to coordinate the wings. Additionally, the Tombe force commander had been allowed to decide when and how to attack.

While using native bearers to carry the heavy ordnance, both elements still had a tough time with the terrain. To ford a six-foot-deep river, their members joined hands (or attached toggle ropes to each other). Just to stay in column after dark, they afixed luminescent vegetation to their backs. Having to ascend steep ridges during

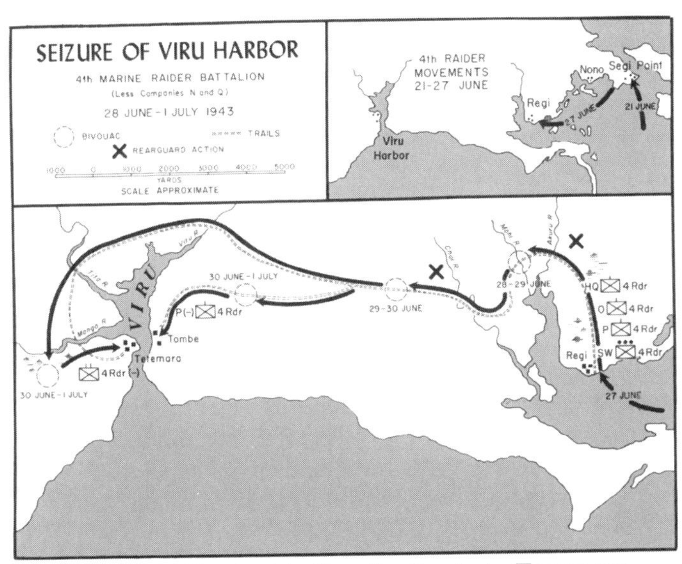

Map 9.5: Maoist Tactics *En Route* to Teremara

(Source: "From Makin to Bouganville: Marine Raiders in the Pacific War," by Maj. Jon T. Hoffman, Marines in WWII Commemorative Series, HQMC, 1995, p. 33)

the intermittent rain only added to their difficulties.[12] Only when Tetemara was finally in sight did the Mao-like maneuver occur. It was clearly both-flanks-oriented.

> Currin's force, moving along the high ground overlooking Tetemara, heard the explosions and firing during the airstrike, but the jungle screened the planes from view. Fifteen minutes later, Currin attacked the village. With First Lieutenant Raymond L. Luckel's Company O in the lead, the Raiders moved down the slope, then fanned out *[to the right]* in an attempt to confine the Japanese to an area bordered by the harbor and the sea. . . . A few outguard positions were overrun before the Marines were forced to halt under steady fire from the enemy's main line of defense.
>
> . . . Deciding that a buildup for an envelopment around his *left flank* was developing, Luckel committed his 3rd Platoon to that flank, and the advance continued. . . .
>
> The bottled-up enemy, realizing their predicament, began withdrawing toward the northeast with much frantic yelling. Anticipating a *banzai* charge in an attempt to break through the Marine's *left flank,* Currin dispatched his slim battalion reserve of the 3rd Platoon and two sections of machine guns from Company P to the aid of Company O. [Italics added.] [13]
>
> – *History of USMC Operations in World War II*

When all was said and done at Viru Harbor, this 4th Raider task force returned to Guadalcanal on 9 July.[14]

Another Double-Envelopment at Vangunu

Meanwhile, the other 4th Raider task force had been assisting 2nd Battalion, 103rd Infantry during the Battle of Kaeruka. This was being waged at Wickham Anchorage on Vangunu in the New Georgia group. (See Map 9.6.) The Raiders made a nearly catastrophic night landing on 30 June, and then—with native scouts in the lead—preceded all Army units in the approach march toward the Japanese garrison. (A Lieutenant from each contingent had been ashore since mid-June to recruit scouts and reconnoiter the objective.) During the subsequent assault, one of Army companies

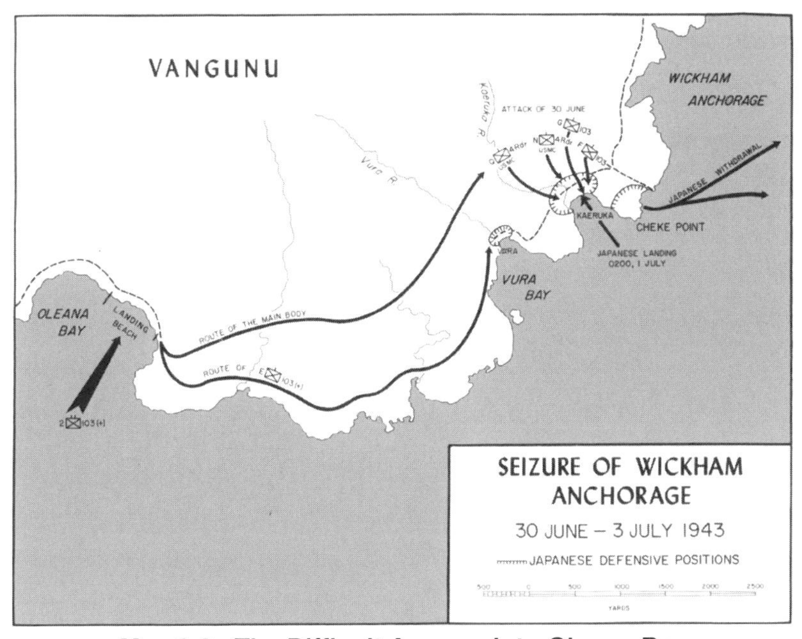

Map 9.6: The Difficult Approach to Oloana Bay
(Source: "From Makin to Bouganville: Marine Raiders in the Pacific War," by Maj. Jon T. Hoffman, Marines in WWII Commemorative Series, HQMC, 1995, p. 35)

moved left "to skirt around strong defenses" while a Raider company attacked to the right.[15] Again, such a maneuver is highly reminiscent of Chinese Mobile Warfare. An American line unit of the period would have driven straight into that enemy concentration. In tandem, the flanking moves constitute a double-envelopment. This has been confirmed by the official chronicle.

> The Marines, commanded by Major Clark, and the soldiers moved south from their line of departure at 1405. On the right, Company Q (Raiders) guided on the meandering Kaeruka River with orders to cross the river farther south to turn the left flank of the enemy. Company N (Raiders) in the center drove straight towards the Japanese; and on the

left, Company F of the 103rd Infantry moved to position for a partial envelopment of the Japanese right.[16]

— *History of USMC Operations in World War II*

On 9 July, two companies of this other 4th Raider task force moved to nearby Gatukai Island to conduct combat patrols. Shortly thereafter, they and their sister company returned to Guadalcanal.[17]

Another Maoist Maneuver at Bairoko

At 0100 hours on 18 July 1943, all 700 men of 4th Raider Battalion debarked their destroyer-transports at Enogai Harbor on the western end of New Georgia. As a part of 1st Raider Regiment, they

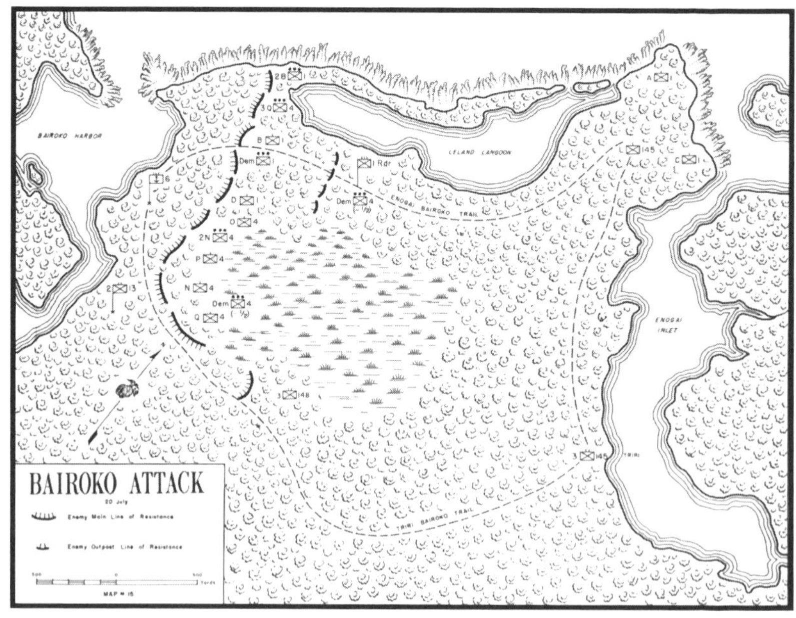

Map 9.7: Defenses Perfectly Meshed with Terrain at Bairoko
(Source: "Marines in the Central Solomons," by Maj. John N. Rentz, USMC Historical Monograph, HQMC, 1952, map 13)

were to try to seize Bairoko Harbor on the far side of Dragons Peninsula one day later. It was through Bairoko Harbor's barge base, that the Nipponese had been reinforcing their strategically vital airfield at Munda.[18] Unfortunately, Baikoro's garrison had foreseen an attack from the east. Its defenses were not only to stymie the Raiders, but also America's fledgling appreciation for light-infantry tactics. (See Maps 9.7 and 9.8.)

After a difficult approach march and skipped air attack, the Raiders finally made contact with the Bairoko defenders about 1000 hours on 19 July.[19] For a whole day, the battle raged—with 4th Raider Battalion on the left and 1st Raider Battalion on the right. In their path was a sophisticated matrix of defensive strongpoints.[20] After the Army battalion's flank attack from the south failed, the Raiders were forced to pull back without seizing the objective. The reason later proffered by the Joint Chiefs of Staff (JCS) was that "lightly armed troops cannot be expected to attack fixed positions defended by heavy automatic weapons, mortars, and heavy artillery."[21] Once again the myth had been perpetuated that light infantry can't hold its own in conventional battle. Actually, both the Raiders and JCS were right. Had Carlson and Roosevelt or Edson and Griffith developed the sophisticated assault techniques of true light infantrymen, this Raider attack could still have taken Bairoko Harbor. Either a Stormtroop-like penetration (with a mortar attack as the deception) or an Asian-style short-range infiltration would have worked. But, without any such advanced technique, the Raiders would have required more firepower to complete their mission.

Luckily, there are two fairly detailed accounts of the battle that should clear up any mystery as to what went wrong. The enemy's Bairoko defenses had not been properly reconnoitered,[22] nor had the Raiders adequately rehearsed assaults against mutually supporting bunkers. Thus, they had hastily attacked a prepared enemy position. This was no haphazard defense, but rather a prototype of what would create so much havoc on Peleliu, Iwo Jima, and Okinawa. It consisted of four separate bunker belts on parallel coral ridges. Each bunker had its own heavy machinegun, crisscrossing protective fire from neighbors, and "coconut-log-and-coral" construction.[23] With snipers in trees and "light Nambu machineguns in outpost foxholes,"[24] many possessed a perimeter defense of sorts. Because emplacements often existed on both sides of the same ridgeline,[25] one could expect tunnels between them (just like on Iwo Jima).[26] Such tunnels would have provided protection from preparatory fire

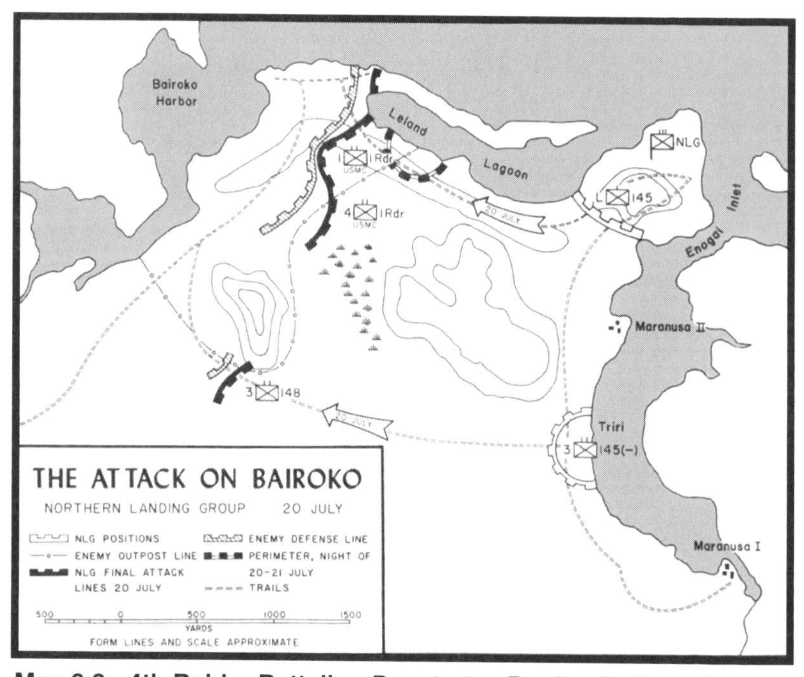

Map 9.8: 4th Raider Battalion Penetrates Bunker Belts at Bairoko
(Source: "From Makin to Bouganville: Marine Raiders in the Pacific War," by Maj. Jon T. Hoffman, Marines in WWII Commemorative Series, HQMC, 1995, p. 34)

anyway. Yet, through a communications mix-up, there would be no airstrike to confirm or deny this claim. True light infantry should be able to do well without any supporting arms, and that's what the Raiders ended up doing here. By all indications, they penetrated three of the four defensive belts through little more than fire team cooperation.[27] (See Figure 9.2.) If they had further possessed some advanced light-infantry assault techniques, they could have continued on to Bairoko Harbor after dark.

> Approach to Bairoko was to be made by two columns. Two full-strength companies (B and D) of the 1st Raider Battalion and the four companies of the 4th Raider Battalion were to make the main effort, advancing along the south shore of Leland Lagoon straight toward Bairoko and the north flank of the Japanese positions. Schultz' [Army]

Figure 9.2: Outflanking Each Gun Nest in the Matrix
(Source: U.S. Army Center of Military History, posters, illustration designator "1-38-49.jpg," Two Soldiers on Night Patrol, by Harold von Schmidt)

battalion was to move from Triri toward Bairoko to hit the south flank of the Japanese positions. . . . The departure time was set for 0730 [on 20 July], with an airstrike scheduled for 0900 to precede the actual attack on the harbor. . . .

Confronting the Raiders was a series of log and coral bunkers dug into the rising ground under banyan roots, and well camouflaged with palm fronds and branches. The ridge ahead blazed with [enemy] fire. . . . *[T]he emplacements supported each other with lanes of interlocking fire.* Further protection was furnished by Japanese soldiers in trees overhead who sniped at the Marines with Nambu (.25 caliber) light machine guns. . . .

By noon, the first line of enemy resistance crumbled, broken under the relentless pressure of the Raider units. Unable to use the 60mm mortars because of the jungle canopy, lacking the new flame-thrower weapons, and without air or artillery support, the Marines breached Okumura's defensive line by knocking out first one pillbox and then another by demolitions and overwhelming small-arms fire. But losses were heavy and progress was slow. . . .

Shortly after noon, . . . Liversedge committed Currin's [4th Raider] battalion to the fight. Company P (Captain Walker) was in close support behind Griffith's battalion, and thus able to move quickly into the line. Kemp's Company D . . . was receiving heavy fire on its *left flank and Walker now attacked toward this opposition. . . .*

Walker's fresh company, under orders to attack southwest to the shores of the inlet before turning north to hit the enemy's right flank, was barely able to move forward before crisscrossing fire from both right and left flanks held it back. While Walker scouted his front lines to determine the location of the machine guns facing him, Captain Snell moved his Company N into position behind Walker's unit to refuse the left flank and support Walker's attack. . . .

In the next two hours, the Raider attack slowly punched through *two different defensive lines*, uncovering a number of *bunkers on the reverse slopes*. Company D, riddled with casualties by the heavy and continuous enemy fire, scrambled to the top of a ridge line which overlooked the harbor at Bairoko, about 500 yards away. But between the Raiders and their objective lay *another series of formidable fortifications*. Hoping to cement Kemp's position on the commanding terrain, Liversedge directed First Lieutenant Raymond L. Luckel's Company O into the gap between Company D on the ridge and Company P. Both companies had been hit hard by several machine guns in this area, and Luckel's company was ordered to silence these weapons. As Company O lunged forward, the maneuver reduced fire on Company P and Company N. Walker and Snell then moved their companies forward to take a small ridgeline to the left front.

. . . Griffith's two companies and the demolitions platoon, on the right, had managed to move nearly to the end of the lagoon, but a slight gap still existed between the battalion and the lagoon's shoreline. Liversedge, in an attempt to plug this gap and . . . contact Christie [the unit on the sandspit], moved First Lieutenant Leonard W. Alford with a reinforced platoon from Company O [of the 4th Raider Battalion] to this flank. Alford's platoon made a spirited attack, but the volume of enemy fire prevented movement beyond that of Wheeler's company. . . .

At 1445, sporadic but accurate mortar fire from enemy positions on the inlet suddenly changed into an intense barrage that shook the attacking lines. The Marines, without weapons for counterbattery fire, could only press closer into their shallow positions behind scant cover on the ridge lines and try to weather the pounding. Estimated to be 90mm rounds, the shells inflicted further casualties, mainly from tree bursts overhead. The barrage was immediately followed by a screaming counterattack. . . .

Unfortunately, there were no ready reserve units. Nothing had been heard from the Army battalion which was supposed to hit the south flank of the enemy, but sounds of firing from that direction indicated that Schultz [its commander] was engaged. . . .

Following Company D's return to its former position, the 4th Battalion found movement easier, and Companies *N and P managed to move forward in the face of stiffening fire to extend the NLG lines more to the southwest.* But the move was costly; both companies received heavy casualties. Company Q (Captain Lincoln N. Holdzkom), the sole remaining company as yet uncommitted, moved up to the rear of the other three 4th Battalion units to be in position for an attack when directed.

By 1600, the Japanese had been pushed, still defiant and dangerous, into an area on the Bairoko Harbor headlands about 300 yards wide and 800 yards long. Their back to the sea, the enemy defenders kept up a sustained and murderous machine gun and mortar fire that showed few signs of slackening. In an effort to strike one last, conclusive blow, Liversedge ordered Company Q into the lines. *Holdzkom's company moved around the left flank of Company N in an attack* straight into the teeth of heavy enemy fire. . . .

The outcome of Liversedge's last attempt to take his objective was not long in doubt. Despite the vigor of Company Q's attack, the overwhelming fire of the enemy won. Badly depleted in a matter of moments, Company Q was forced to retire. Repulsed, the company reeled back, virtually noneffective through its losses. The tactical situation had been opportune for one last heavy punch to knock out the enemy defenders, but without artillery, air support, or other heavy weapons, the Raider battalions could not deliver it.

> For Liversedge, Schultz' failure to attack aggressively on the left flank was the final blow in a series of sharp disappointments. . . .
>
> By this time the Raiders (1st and 4th) had nearly 250 casualties, or about 30 percent of the force. We had another 150 men tied up getting them evacuated to aid stations and to Enogai. There was nothing to do but pull back. [Italics added.] [28]
>
> – *History of USMC Operations in World War II*

As had happened at Vangunu, some Raider units tried to skirt around the left end of the Japanese defenses, while others attacked at the right end. That's almost the same as a double-envelopment. Of course, most of the bunker rows could not be outflanked. For them, the Raiders would have had to launch separate fire teams against all composite emplacements at once. Most likely half of each team went left through the microterrain while the other half went right. That way, they could play off each other—advance only when the bunker occupants had been distracted. This maneuver should be remembered, for the 4th Battalion's direct descendent would do something similar against Half Moon on Okinawa's Shuri Line. That makes it a viable—if not more effective—alternative to the steam roller approach to state-of-the-art defenses.

A Precedent Had Been Set

After evacuating its casualties from Bairoko, the 4th Raider Battalion helped to "mop up" around Enogai Inlet for a month or so before heading back to Guadalcanal. There is another way of looking at what happened at Bairoko. Instead of proving that light infantry can't withstand the rigors of conventional combat, 4th Raider Battalion—despite its 156 casualties [29]—had shown something else. It had demonstrated that with a little guerrilla warfare training, U.S. infantrymen can practice MW at the squad level. Just to find out the extent of the Japanese defenses, 4th Battalion had needed recon pull. The official battle chronicle confirms it: "Walker [of Company P] scouted his front lines to determine the location of the machine guns facing him."[30] With no airstrikes, artillery, heavy mortars, flame throwers, or advanced assault technique, the Raiders had still gotten three-fourths of the way through what is still the state

Figure 9.3: There Was Japanese Artillery on New Georgia
(Source: U.S. Army Center of Military History, artphoto archives, illustration designator "112Cavalry.jpg," Cavalry Patrol at Umtingalu, New Britain, by Vidar Frede, 1943)

of the defensive art. Any who doubt the magnitude of such an accomplishment have only to review the battles of Iwo Jima or Okinawa. With the self-confidence that comes from guerrilla training and cooperation that comes from *Gung Ho* spirit, the Raiders had done the impossible. Not until an Asian force with no airplanes, tanks, or artillery, persevered in Vietnam has there been a better example of what light infantry can accomplish. While Americans are far too prideful to copy a former foe, they may be willing to emulate a Carlson or Roosevelt Raider.

What the Raiders Had Encountered at Bairoko

Bairoko's defensive scheme had been so fully developed as to include preregistered artillery concentrations. (See Figure 9.3.)

Elsewhere on New Georgia in July 1943, U.S. Army personnel were trying to capture Munda Airfield. Their accounts of its bunker systems may help to explain what the Raiders had faced at Bairoko.

> A line of pillboxes stretching from Laiana beach northwest for more than 400 yards had been breached. Typical of the defenses was a cluster of seven pillboxes which covered a frontage of only 150 yards, each position defending and supporting the next. Overhead and frontal protection consisted of two thicknesses of coconut logs and three feet of coral. Skillfully camouflaged, with narrow firing slits, the bunkers were virtually a part of the terrain and surrounding jungle. . . .
>
> . . . [E]nemy soldiers were dug in and covered by low, two-level camouflaged coral and log emplacements with deadly interlocking fields of fire. Trenches bulwarked by coconut logs connected the bunkers.[31]
>
> – *History of USMC Operations in World War II*

The Bairoko emplacements may not have been simple bunkers at all (Figure 9.4.), but more like the protected pillboxes of Iwo Jima.

Figure 9.4: Few Bunkers Were Out in the Open
(Source: TM-E 30-480 [1944], p. 159)

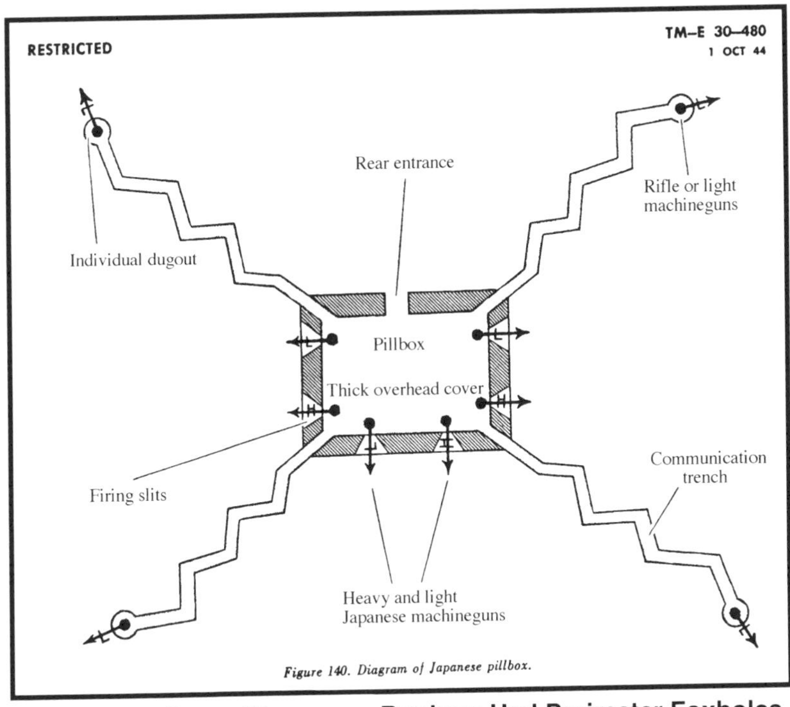

Figure 9.5: Some Nipponese Bunkers Had Perimeter Foxholes
(Source: TM-E 30-480 [1944], p. 160)

Each Iwo position had its own perimeter of fighting holes (Figure 9.5), and bomb-proof interior (Figure 9.6). A cross-section of those coral ridgelines may have looked something like Figure 9.7—a few years later excerpt from a Chinese manual.

What Finally Happened to the 4th Raider Battalion

After Munda Airfield had been taken around mid-August, two Army battalions cautiously entered Baikoro from the south. All defenders had left. Upon refitting at New Caledonia, 4th Raider Battalion was subsequently redesignated as the 2nd Battalion, 4th Marines (2/4) on 1 February 1944.[32] As such, its rather unusual military heritage would continue.

Figure 9.6: Japanese Pillbox Interior
(Source: TM-E 30-480 [1944], p. 161)

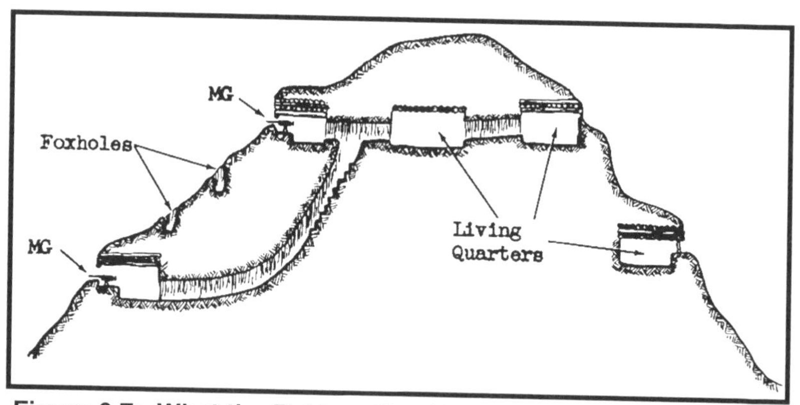

Figure 9.7: What the Raiders May Have Been Facing at Bairoko
(Source: Excerpt from Chinese Manual on Field Fortifications, in "A Historical Perspective on Light Infantry," U.S. Army Combat Studies Inst., Research Survey No. 6, p. 88)

Part Three

"Gung Ho's" Later Influence on the Corps

And when he gets to Heaven, Saint Peter he will tell:
"Another Marine reporting, sir—I've served my time in Hell!"

(Source: Attributed.)

10 The Raiders' Impact on the 4th Marines

- Where did Carlson's men end up in the 4th Marines?
- Did former Roosevelt Raiders later use any Maoist tactics?

The Japanese had greatly improved their defensive tactics.

(Source: Courtesy of Cassell PLC, from "World Army Uniforms since 1939," © 1975, 1980, 1981, 1983 by Blandford Press Ltd.; FM 21-76 [1957], pp. 77, 99)

Carlson's Influence on the 4th Marines

The Corps wasted no time in diluting whatever Maoist philosophies Carlson may have instilled into his Raiders. When 1st Raider Regiment became the new 4th Marines in February 1944, his 2nd Battalion was first "deactivated," and then its members "absorbed" into a new Weapons Company.[1] Luckily, Roosevelt's 4th Battalion was left intact as 2nd Battalion, 4th Marines. Thus, 2/4 was heir to Mao-like maneuvers. But, except for the fire team concept, most of the Carlson legacy would henceforth be limited to "working together" and "looking out for the man on one's right and left." No one really knows why the Carlson-developed expertise at one-on-one combat was so little valued by the Corps. Because of the type of fighting expected, it may have been trying to limit the amount of unsolicited initiative at the lowest echelons. But, those 2nd Raider Battalion self-defense experts also knew how to follow orders. In the close-quarters action that was to accompany the assaults against strongpoint matrices, that type of training made those Mao-emulating Raiders more survivable and productive. An assessment of the Roosevelt trainees in 2/4 bears this out. Luckily, a former 4th Battalion Raider and then 3/4 member—Dan Marsh—has carefully recorded all of his WWII experiences.[2] He and his 2/4 counterparts may now be able to transcend death to address America's current security shortfall. But, first comes the proof of their unique abilities.

After landing unopposed on Emirau Island (so U.S. planes could more easily bomb Rabaul), the 4th Marine Regiment went on to participate in the invasions of Guam and Okinawa. Of the two, Okinawa was the greater test. Due to the sophistication of the Shuri Defense Zone, it would equal anything on Peleliu or Iwo Jima. Of note, 2/4 was the first American unit to set foot on Japanese soil after the surrender. It went ashore at Tokyo Bay to help secure the huge Yokosuka Naval Base.[3] Such a risky assignment would have logically gone to former Raiders. Had the garrison resisted, only expert guerrillas would have stood any chance of survival. (See Figure 10.1.)

The Old 4th Marines Also Knew Something about the Chinese

By the time the 4th Marine Regiment's flag was captured on Corregidor in May 1942, all three of its battalions had seen considerable Chinese service. The 1st Battalion had served in Shanghai from February 1927 to September 1932. The 3rd Battalion had been sent to Shanghai in February 1927 and not deactivated until December 1934. Most notably, the 2nd Battalion had gone to Tientsin in April 1927, been reactivated at Shanghai in September 1932, and then not been withdrawn to Subic Bay until November 1941.[4] (Refer back to Table 1.1.) So, even before being rebuilt out of Roosevelt Raiders, 2/4 would have been the most likely battalion to emulate Maoist procedures.

Though 2/4 inherited most of the Chinese influence, Samuel Griffith did manage to bring some of Carlson's ideas over to 1st Raider Battalion (and thus its sequel).[5] As a result, the reconstituted 1/4 and 3/4 might also exhibit some very decidedly *Gung Ho* behavior. With any luck, it would be in how fire teams most effectively operate in combat.

Figure 10.1: Former Raiders Were to Be First Ashore at Tokyo Bay
(Source: U.S. Army Ctr. of Mil. Hist., artphoto archives, illustration designator "0806-4.jpg," Respect for New Emporers—Japan, by Robert McDonald Graham, Jr., 1946)

The Guam Campaign

As part of the 1st Provisional Marine Brigade, 1/4 and 2/4 were both in the first assault waves on the Agat-Bangi area of Guam. They were soon joined ashore by 3/4. Upon reaching the slopes of Mt. Alifan, the regiment was counterattacked. (See Map 10.1.) Then, 1/4 and 3/4 moved to its summit, and 2/4 went into reserve. Two days later, 2/4 moved north to help the 22nd Marines in its sweep across Orote Peninsula. Due to more resistance than expected, its sister battalions soon joined the fight. After stopping another Japanese *banzai* charge, 1st Brigade units resumed the assault.[6]

> Five days after D-Day and its seizure of the high ground behind the beach[head], the 4th Marines started moving to help take the brigade's next objective Orote Peninsula. With the 4th Marines attacking from the left and the 22nd Marines attacking on the right helped by armored reinforcements from the Army's 77th Infantry Division, the 1st Brigade captured the peninsula after four days of heavy fighting. This battle secured a valuable airfield and freed Apra Harbor for use by American ships.[7]
>
> — Official 1st Battalion, 4th Marines website

Details of the Orote Peninsula Operation

During the attack on Orote's airfield, there were only a few unusual tactics. (See Map 10.2.) The battle chronicles make no mention of the decentralized fire team activity with which 4th Raider Battalion had gotten three-fourths of the way through the Bairoko defense zone on New Georgia. However, they do say that 2/4 initially wanted no tank support after its more traditional sisters—1/4 and 3/4—had readily accepted it.

> The 4th Marines jumped off on time with the 3rd Battalion on the right, next to the road [on 27 July 1944]. A ridge 300 yards to the front, from which the Japanese laid down their withering fire, was the first objective. Beyond this a coconut grove extended 500 yards on gently sloping ground to meet a higher brush-covered ridge. Behind this, hidden from view, lay the important Orote airfield. . . .

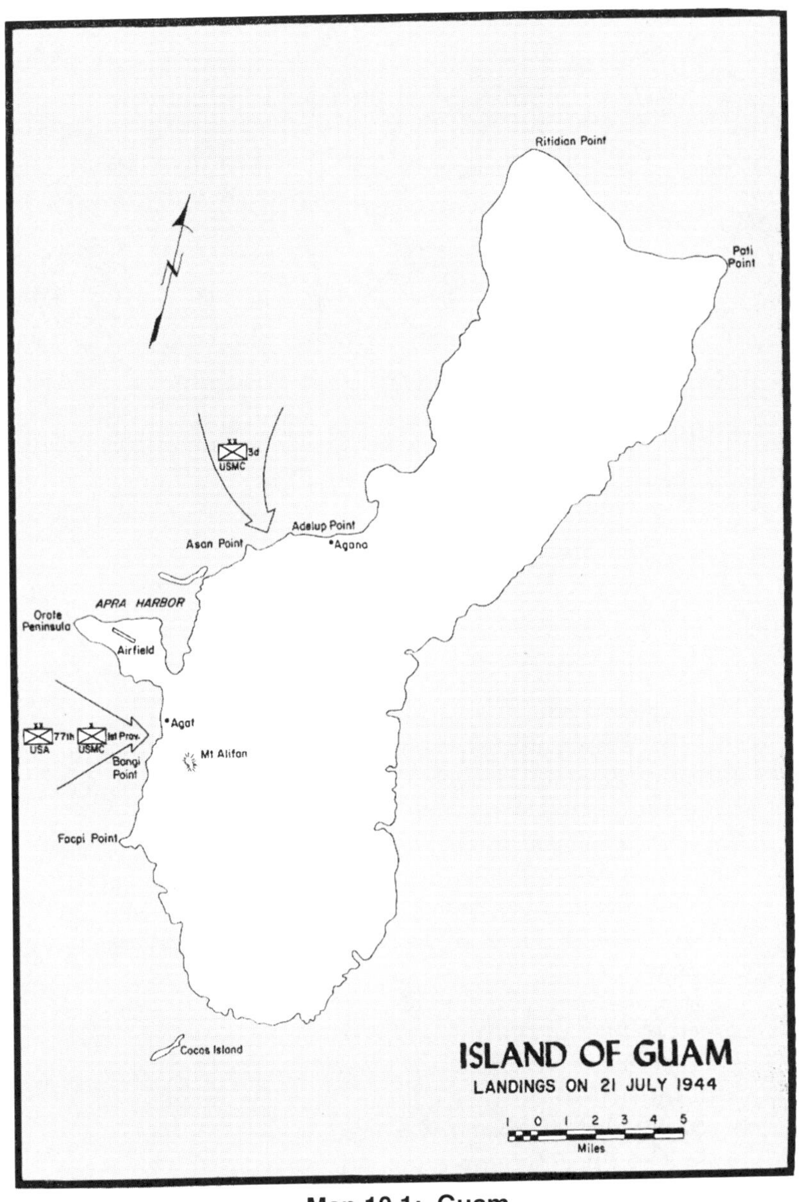

Map 10.1: Guam

(Source: "A Brief History of the 4th Marines," Marine Corps Historical Reference Pamphlet, by James S. Santelli, HQMC, 1970, p. 27)

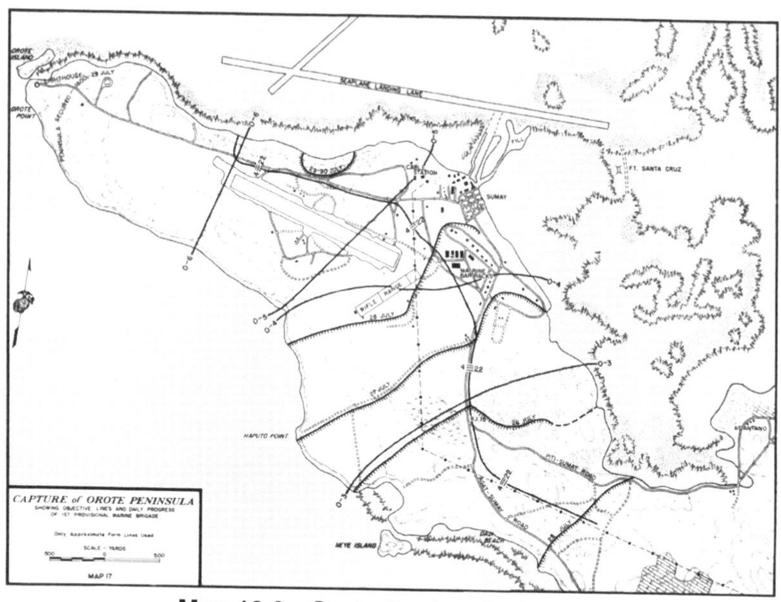

Map 10.2: Orote Peninsula Assault

(Source: "The Recapture of Guam," by Major O.R. Lodge, Historical Monograph, HQMC, 1954, p. 88)

Plagued by terrain covered with heavy vegetation, as well as a dug-in enemy who had cut fire lanes through the dense underbrush, the 4th Marines made slower progress [than the 22nd Marine Regiment]. Extremely bitter resistance developed in the center and on the right of the regiment's zone, with two strong points causing most of the trouble. Tanks were called in as quickly as possible, but the thick foliage made control and observation practically impossible.

Initially, two platoons of the tank company were assigned to the 3rd Battalion and the other to the 1st when *2/4 reported it could not use armor because of the terrain.* With the help of the tanks, 3/4 on the right broke through the coconut log pillboxes and reorganized prior to advancing to the O-4 line. Intense automatic-weapons fire kept the 2nd Battalion from making any headway, and when flanking fire from the left started to cut Company I to ribbons,

> Major Messer called for tank assistance. Regiment ordered a platoon of Shermans from the 3rd Battalion to report to Messer. The 2nd Tank Platoon withdrew and at 1430 was guided into position to help Company E. Unfortunately, it had been led into the midst of the strong point and could not fire because the 1st Battalion. . . .
>
> . . . General Shepherd went forward on a reconnaissance of his front lines. Quickly sizing up the gravity of the situation he sent a request to General Bruce for a platoon of Army tank destroyers to augment the fire from the brigade's tanks and a platoon of Army light tanks. . . .
>
> Shepherd then issued oral orders to Lieutenant Colonel Shapley to organize a tank-infantry attack, employing all available tanks in a mass effort to break through the strong line of Japanese-held bunkers. At 1530, Shapley launched the assault all along the regimental front. The massed armor cracked the rifle range defense line and infantry units followed closely behind to exploit the breakthrough. This had been one of the most formidable enemy positions encountered by the brigade. . . . Marines counted approximately 250 pillboxes and emplacements in this general area after the attack (TkCo, 4th Mar SAR, 15). [Italics added.] [8]
>
> – "USMC Historical Monograph," 1954

The III Corps Attack on Northern Guam

After seizing Orote Peninsula, 1st Brigade patrolled south of Mt. Alifan for a while before joining the Army's 77th Division in its drive toward the north end of the island. Though fighting was at times heavy, their joint goal was soon accomplished. Overall, the 4th Marines had suffered 900 killed and wounded. 1st Brigade was soon to be redesignated as 6th Marine Division.[9]

> Following the seizure of Orote Peninsula, the 4th and 22nd Marines were ordered to begin patrol operations to the south. In the later stages of the campaign, 7-10 August, the brigade was committed to the main III Corps' attack in northern Guam.[10]
>
> – Official 1st Battalion, 4th Marines website

Then Came the Meat Grinder

Thanks to the atomic bomb, Okinawa would be the final test of U.S. infantry resolve in the Pacific. (See Map 10.3 and Figure 10.2.) From April to June 1945, some 70,000 Americans would be killed or injured. Facing the 182,000-man U.S. invasion force had been roughly 100,000 enemy personnel (including both Japanese regulars and Okinawan "militia/laborers").[11] Their underground preparations had been so extensive that most were not harmed by the preparatory bombardment. Their main line of resistance—just north of Naha—was not discovered until after the landing. Its tenacity was soon to rival anything on Iwo Jima.

Figure 10.2: There Would Be Two Ways of Fighting on Okinawa

(Source: U.S. Army Center of Military History, posters, illustration designator "1-25-49.jpg," Beach Assault, by Amos Sewell)

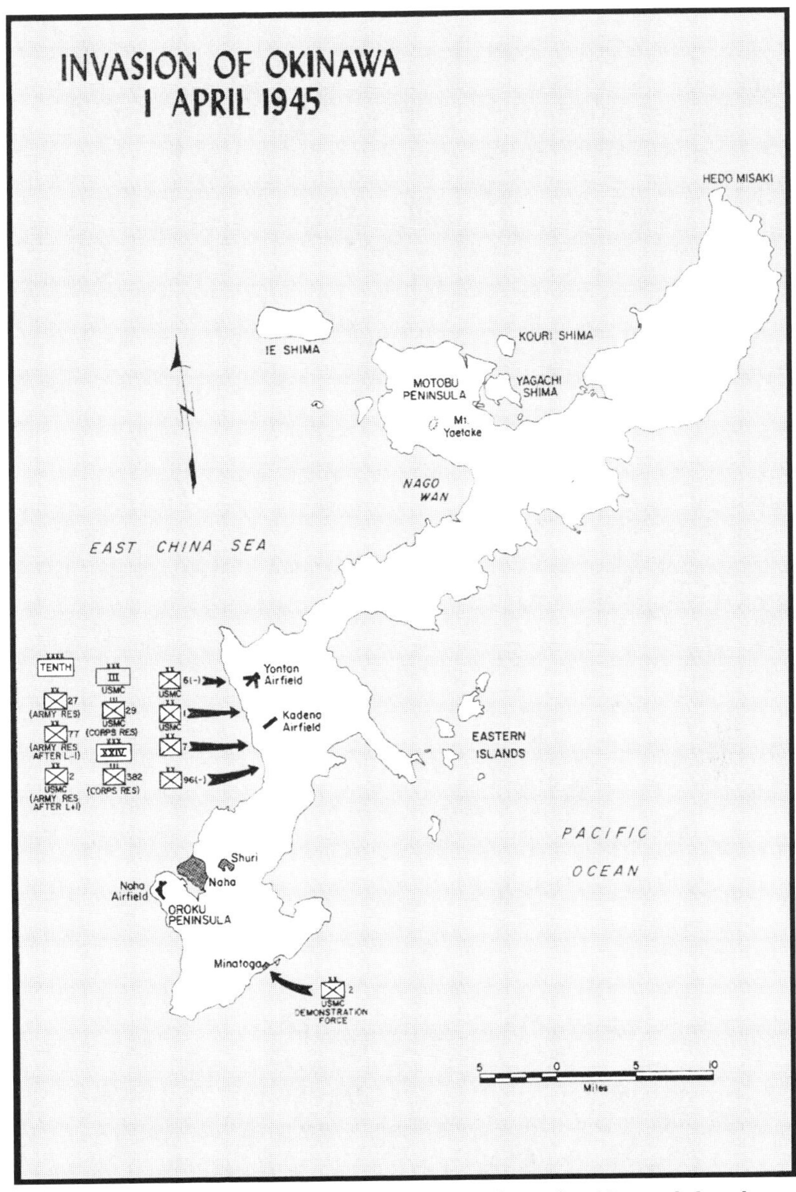

Map 10.3: Last Japanese Bastion before the Home Islands
(Source: "A Brief History of the 4th Marines," Marine Corps Historical Reference Pamphlet, by James S. Santelli, HQMC, 1970, p. 31)

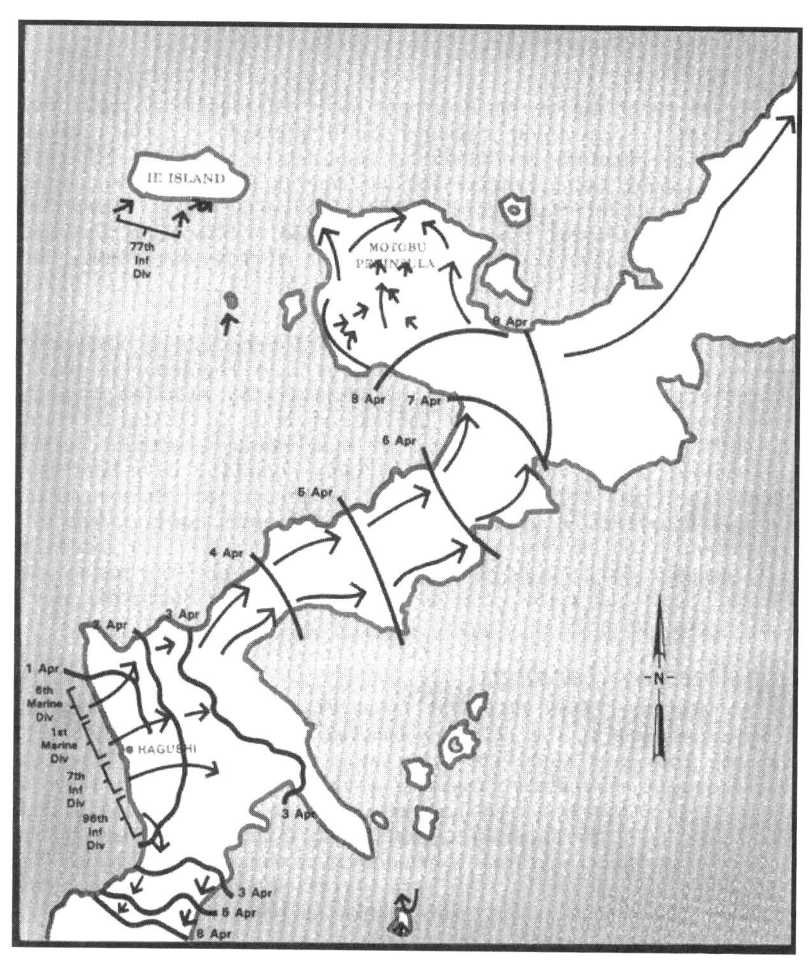

Map 10.4: Initial U.S. Advances on Okinawa
(Source: "Japan's Battle for Okinawa, April - June 1945," by Thomas M. Hubler, Leavenworth Papers No. 18, U.S. Army Cmd. & Gen. Staff College, 1990)

First There Was the Mobotu Peninsula

As part of 6th Marine Division, 2/4 got involved in the fighting at both ends of the island. Its first heavy contact occurred at the Mobotu Peninsula half way up its north side. (See Maps 10.4 and 10.5.) Its Raider skills were first manifested in some recon-pull-like patrolling.

29th Marines drove up the west coast in [a] column of battalions and reached its objective at Chuda by noon. The 4th Marines, similarly deployed, moved up the east coastal road in a contact imminent formation, with 2/4 reinforced by a platoon of tanks as the advance guard.

. . . Colonel Shapley's plan was . . . detaching patrols from the advance guard to investigate to their source all roads and trails leading into the mountainous and generally uninhabited interior. . . .

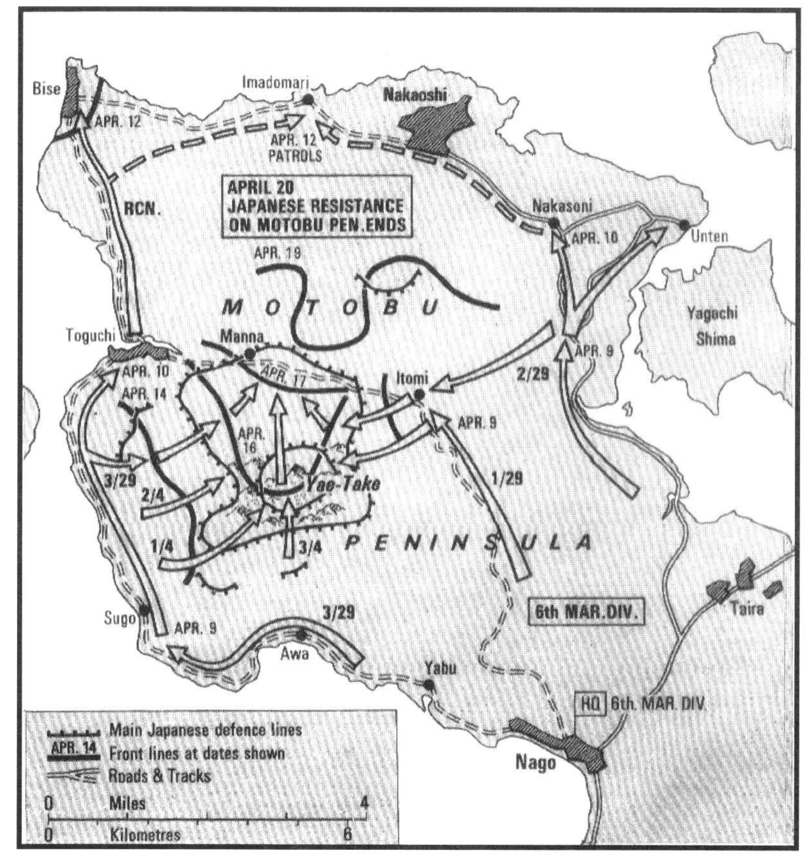

Map 10.5: 4th Marines' Initial Assault at North End of Okinawa

(Source: "The Final Campaign: Marines in the Victory on Okinawa," by Col. Joseph H. Alexander, Marines in WWII Commemorative Series, HQMC, 1996, p. 17)

> By 1300, 2/4 had been used up by the detachment of small patrols and was relieved by 3/4 passing through.[12]
>
> — "USMC Historical Monograph," 1955

Then came 2/4's attack on the low ridgelines guarding the 6th Division objective—Mount Yae Take. (Refer back to Map 10.5.) In it, 2/4 employed a very nontraditional maneuver—assaulting a prepared enemy position from two directions at once. (Normally, one Marine element assaults while the other provides a stationary base of fire.)

> Early on the morning of 14 April . . . the attack jumped off according to plan at 0800. From the vicinity of Toguchi, 3/29 attacked with two companies, G and H, in assault. On the right of 3/29, 2/4 moved out in a similar formation with Companies G and E in assault. . . .
>
> . . . 2/4 took the ridge to its front by a combined frontal attack and envelopment from the right (2/4 SAR, Ph I&II, 6-7).[13]
>
> — "USMC Historical Monograph," 1955

During the final approach to the mountain top, even Carlson's men got the chance to do more than handle crew-served weapons and protect the regimental command post (CP).

> [T]he Weapons Company of the 4th Marines, was ordered to patrol thoroughly the area to the right rear of 1/4 and 3/4.[14]
>
> — "USMC Historical Monograph," 1955

Big Problems at the Shuri Line

Meanwhile, the U.S. Tenth Army had been having trouble getting through the main enemy defenses at the south end of the island. The "Shuri-Yonburu Line" was anchored by a broken ridge that cut Okinawa in two just north of Naha. At its center was the ancient, and now heavily excavated, Shuri Castle. To its front were rows of tunnel-connected strongpoints. The Army's 27th Division had worn itself out getting through the outer rings of this formidable defense zone, so the 1st and 6th Marine Divisions were asked to take its place on the right end of the assault formation. (Look ahead at Map 10.6.) May 12-22 was to mark some of the most savage fighting in Marine Corps history.

Of course, the Shuri Line was not really a line at all, but rather a wide belt of mutually supporting underground strongpoints. They had been dug into the low rocky escarpments that fronted Shuri Heights. Not only could these strongpoints cover each other by fire, but they and most of the areas in between were visible to artillery spotters on Shuri Ridge. Thus, any attack on any one of the bastions could be met by fire from several inaccessible locations. To make matters worse, those strongpoints were mostly below ground and virtually impervious to direct and indirect fire. An estimated sixty miles of tunnels connected them to the Japanese subterranean headquarters inside Shuri Ridge and each other. Those tunnels made reinforcement, resupply, and spoiling attacks relatively easy for the Japanese. In addition, each had reverse-slope defenses and outlying spider holes (to thwart direct fire and discourage encirclement, respectively).[15] Even more than on Iwo Jima, the defenders of the Shuri Line were to counterattack through short-range infiltration and single-handed tank-killing forays. Thus, every Marine attack on one of those bastions involved a lot of short-range contact to its rear. Flush with the ground and covered with brush or dirt, the hidden holes in the ground may have caused the most consternation. That's because some of them were undoubtedly connected to the main tunnels. As a result, the Marines were constantly worried about who might suddenly appear behind them.[16]

> Japan's 32nd Army had spent the greater part of a year turning them [the escarpments] into formidable nests of interlocking pillboxes and firing positions. Connected by a network of caves and passageways inside the hills, their positioning enabled defenders to shift their strength constantly in response to attack.[17]
>
> — Col. Yahara, Japanese veteran of Okinawa

On Okinawa, there were even underground way-stations for the north-south shifting of Japanese units.[18] In these subterranean quarters, the island's defenders had little trouble weathering any amount of U.S. preparatory fire.

> The effectiveness of the . . . [U.S.] artillery was countered successfully to a great extent, by the elaborate system of underground fortifications. Heavy bombardments, such as came before attacks, caused relatively low casualties.[19]
>
> — Japanese Prisoner of War (POW) on Okinawa

At least some of the forward bastions on the several-hundred-yard-deep Shuri Line were linked by tunnel to those behind them. The Japanese had been using a daunting, triangular system of defenses,[20] in which the front of each position was crisscrossed by fire from the two behind it. Sugar Loaf, Horseshoe, and Crescent (also known as Half Moon) formed such an arrowhead-shaped complex at the western end of the Shuri Line. Even after Sugar Loaf had finally succumbed to assault, secret passageways from Half Moon and Horseshoe may have facilitated a few underground forays behind U.S. lines. Veterans of the campaign remember all too well the rearward activity.

On Okinawa, the Japanese periodically allowed themselves to be overrun so as to more easily attack. This was standard operating procedure for Japanese antitank troops.[21] They would wait in spider holes (or tunnel openings) for the forward echelon of a U.S. unit to pass. Then, they would pop smoke and run forward to afix satchel charges to American tanks. Japanese gun crews also hid in reverse slope bunkers to shoot passing infantrymen in the back. Whole units could have easily combined this form of below-ground maneuver with the dodging of U.S. supporting-arms fire.

> We received many reports of valorous fighting [for the Shuri Line], such as: "Our soldiers jumped out of their caves as soon as the enemy tanks passed, crawled forward, and engaged in hand-to-hand combat with enemy soldiers."[22]
>
> — Col. Yahara, Japanese veteran of Okinawa

6th Marine Division's Contribution at the Shuri Line

In the renewed attack against the Shuri Defense Zone, 6th Marine Division took the right end, and 1st Marine Division the part closer to the center. To its left in the assault formation were still the Army's 77th and then 96th Divisions.[23]

> The 6th Marine Division now planned an attack in force on the Sugar Loaf area. . . . Sugar Loaf and the other hills supporting it . . . offer[ed] exceptionally advantageous positions to the enemy. The crest, running generally east-west, curved back slightly at each end, affording the Japanese weapons on the reverse slope excellent protection from American flanking fire as well as from frontal attack. Supporting Sugar Loaf on its right rear was Crescent Hill, also known as Half Moon Hill; on its left rear was the Horseshoe, a long curved ridge harboring many mortar positions. These three hills supported one another, and any attack on Sugar Loaf would bring fire from the others. The Japanese here had excellent fields of fire to the northwest, obstructed only slightly by several tiny humps of ground which had their own reverse-slope defenses. Japanese on Shuri Heights commanded most of the ground (personal observations of Tenth Army and XXIV Corps historians).[24]
>
> — Official Army Chronicle, 2000

First into the breach for 6th Marine Division were the 22nd and 29th Marines. In a week of nearly constant combat, their troops were to assault the 75-foot-high, 300-yard-long Sugar Loaf Hill no fewer than eleven times.[25] Their problem was threefold. Sugar Loaf (and all of its approaches) had been thoroughly preregistered by Japanese artillery and mortars. Sugar Loaf had been completely blanketed by the small-arms fire from adjacent strongpoints. And Sugar Loaf had been continually resupplied/reinforced through its tunnels. Every time the gallant Marines seized a part of the hill, they were bombarded from above or infiltrated from below. Finally, the surface of Sugar Loaf Hill was occupied, and the 29th Marines even managed a few tiny footholds on the other hills in the complex—Horseshoe and Half Moon. Then, the 4th Marines tried their luck with the project. (See Maps 10.6 and 10.7.)

> On the next day, 19 May, the 4th Marines relieved the exhausted 29th Marines. . . . On 20 May, the 4th Marines gained more of the Horseshoe but were still unable to reach the crest of Crescent Hill [Half Moon]. An attack by an enemy force . . . of battalion strength was repulsed [at the Horseshoe]. . . . [T]he 4th Marines broke up the attack and inflicted on the enemy more than 200 casualties.

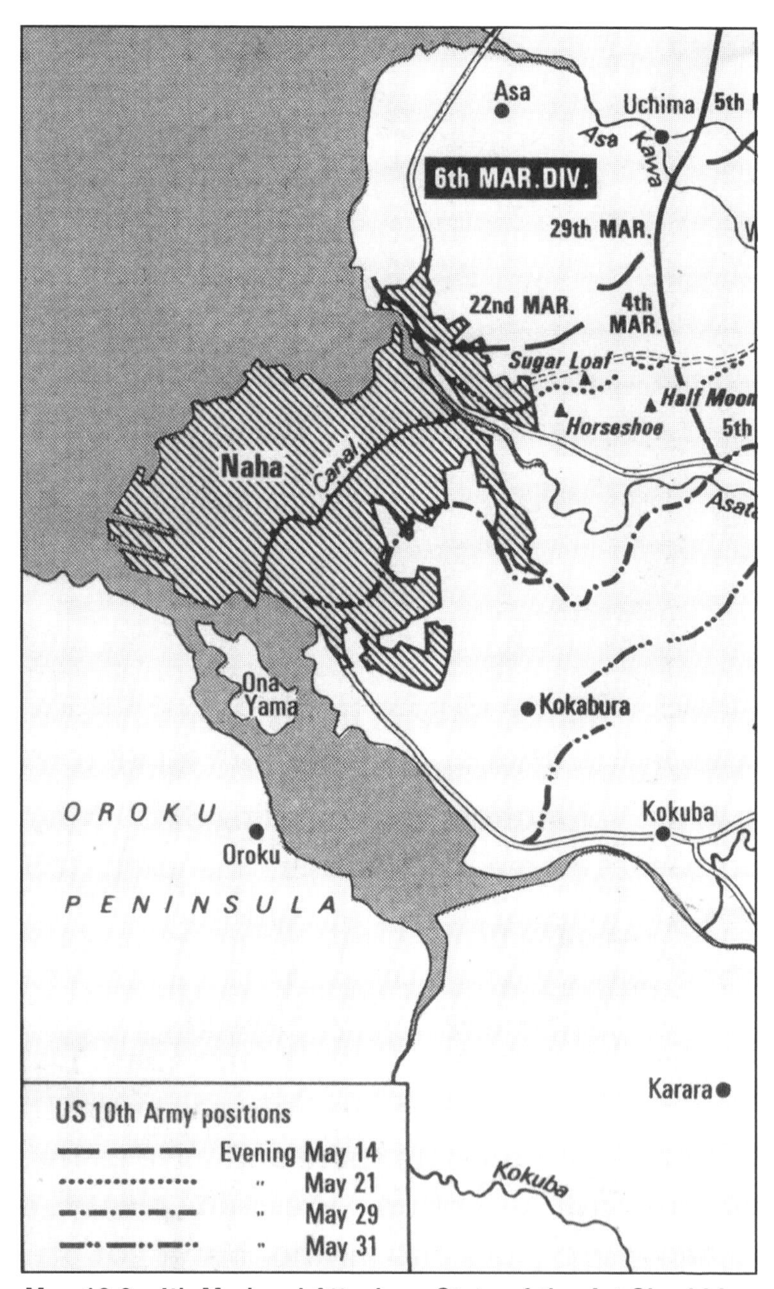

Map 10.6: 4th Marines' Attack on State-of-the-Art Shuri Line
(Source: "The Final Campaign: Marines in the Victory on Okinawa," by Col. Joseph H. Alexander, Marines in WWII Commemorative Series, HQMC, 1996, p. 38)

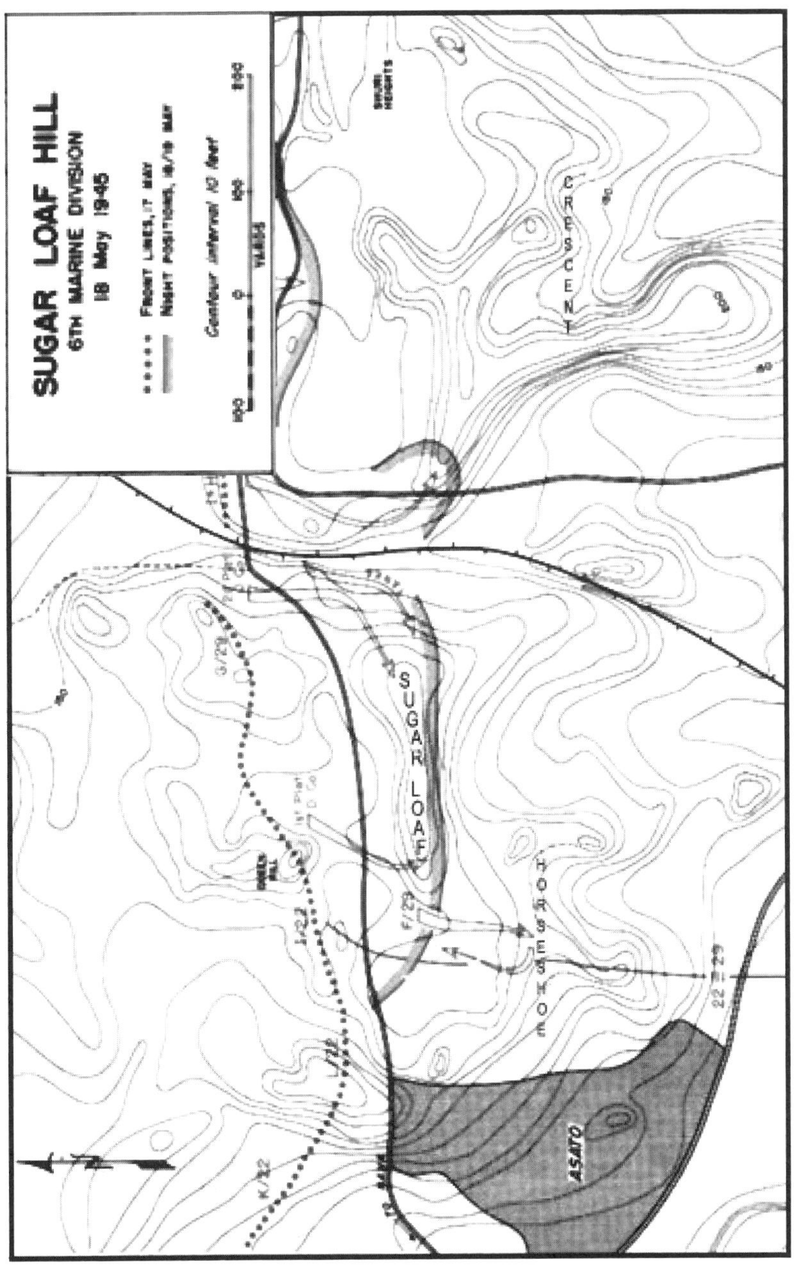

Map 10.7: Sugar Loaf Complex Progress As of 18 May 1945

(Source: "Okinawa: The Last Battle," by Roy Appleman, James Burns, Russell Gugeler, and John Stevens, U.S. Army Ctr. of Mil. History, 2000, map 38)

> On 21 May, the 4th Marines continued the attack toward the Asato River line. Troops advanced 250 yards into the Horseshoe but were unable to complete the seizure of Crescent Hill [Half Moon] because of intense enemy artillery and mortar fire. Much of this fire came from Shuri Heights. The next moves of the 6th Marine Division would depend on the outcome of the fierce struggle for those heights that was still being waged by the 1st Marine Division.[26]
>
> — Official Army Chronicle, 2000

Finally realizing that this part of the Shuri Line was just too strong to penetrate, the 6th Marine Division commander then wisely decided to concentrate on other sectors. The Marines had done nothing wrong *per se*. Their adversaries had simply come up with a nearly impregnable strongpoint. Only survivors of Iwo's triple defense belt may be able to properly empathize. By gradually improving their tactics, the Japanese had finally covered the perfect piece of terrain with enough fire. The result was an area through which no attacker could travel without excessive casualties.

> [A]n attempt to reduce either the Horseshoe or the Half Moon would be exposed to destructive, well-aimed fire from Sugar Loaf itself [and elsewhere]. In addition, the three localities are connected by a network of tunnels and galleries, facilitating the covered movement of reserves. As a final factor in the strength of the position, it will be seen that all sides of Sugar Loaf Hill are precipitous, and there are no evident avenues of approach into the hill mass. For strategic location and tactical strength it is hard to conceive of a more powerful position than the Sugar Loaf [Complex] terrain afforded. Added to all the foregoing was the bitter fact that troops assaulting this position presented a clear target to enemy machine guns, mortars, and artillery emplaced on the Shuri Heights to their left and left rear (6th MarDiv SAR, Ph III, Part III, 5).[27]
>
> — "USMC Historical Monograph," 1955

A Closer Look at 2/4's Assault on Half Moon

Double-envelopments currently violate U.S. doctrine. They

almost certainly did so during WWII as well. Yet, the former Roosevelt-led 4th Raider Battalion conducted one on Half Moon. (Refer back to Map 10.7.)

> The attack of 2/4 on Half Moon developed into a replica of the Sugar Loaf Hill battle during 20 May [in terms of the level of resistance]. Heavy and accurate flat trajectory fire coming from the direction of Shuri [H]eights raked the battalion's flank, and mortars firing from defiladed positions on the reverse slopes of Half Moon covered the entire zone of advance. . . .
>
> . . . With all three of his rifle companies in assault and the casualty toll mounting, Lieutenant Colonel Hayden decided to reorient his attack objectives from the front to the flanks of Half Moon. While Company F held its lines in the center and supported the advance by fire, Company E was to attack south down the division boundary and Company G was to drive past Sugar Loaf and then turn to attack the reverse slopes of Half Moon from the southwest. One company of tanks would furnish overhead fire support while a second company split to attempt a double-envelopment with Companies G and E.[28]
>
> — "USMC Historical Monograph," 1955

> 2/4 and 3/4 moved out in the assault on 20 May. Both battalions were supported by tanks and made rapid progress for about 200 yards, when they were brought to a halt by a torrent of enemy fire. The Japanese, who were deeply entrenched on Half Moon and Horseshoe, suddenly met the advance with a hail of small arms, machine gun, artillery and mortar fire. The enemy's artillery observers on Shuri Ridge were virtually looking down our throats, and could easily control and direct very accurate fire from hidden gun positions. . . .
>
> On the left Col. Hayden of 2/4 . . . decided to change his plan of attack. Instead of continuing the frontal assault, he would attempt to envelop both flanks of the enemy's positions on Half Moon. . . . [T]he attack was renewed with F Company laying down covering fire, [w]hile Company G assaulted the right flank and Company E the left. . . . Company G, moving closely behind the fire of the tanks, quickly reached and se-

> cured the western end of Half Moon. Traversing more open ground and subject to enemy fire from three directions, the advance of Company E was much slower. Despite heavy casualties, and the volume of mortar fire they encountered, E Company reached the forward slope of their objective and dug in for the night.[29]
>
> — *Dan Marsh's Marine Raider Page*

Thus, on 20 May, the front face of Half Moon was taken by 2/4, and part of Horseshoe by 3/4. That night 3/4 was heavily counterattacked from below ground. With the help of massed U.S. artillery fire, this assault was beaten off. The 4th Marines' advance continued on the 21st, but with little progress in 2/4's sector. To escape some of the direct fire from the south, 2/4 was ordered by the 6th Division commander to form a reverse-slope defense [on Half Moon's forward face].[30] 2/4 had not lost his confidence. As on the Orote Peninsula of Guam, Gen. Shepherd may have initially disagreed with 2/4's assessment of unsuitable terrain for tanks, but this time the contour intervals were definitely in 2/4's favor. It was clear to all who could read a map that Half Moon had very steep northern and western sides. (Refer back to Map 10.7.)

As suggested by the Horseshoe counterattack, the Japanese had merely concentrated all of their firepower on the only remaining part of the Sugar Loaf Complex. With a steady stream of bullets and shells coming in from Shuri Ridge, the area behind Horseshoe, and 1st Marine Division's sector, 2/4 had found itself in an unsurvivable killing zone. Using the same matrix-busting methods its 4th Raider Battalion personnel had so successfully applied at Bairoko on New Georgia, it had been doing well under the circumstances. According to HQMC, "the western slopes of Half Moon contained some of the most effective machinegun nests the Marines had yet encountered [in history]."[31] Gen. Shepherd had another reason for his decision. While 1/4 and 3/4 were free to advance, 2/4 was obligated to staying roughly on line with its 1st Marine Division neighbor.

> The First Battalion [of the 4th Marines] in the center encountered pockets of heavy resistance, and heavy rain made supply and evacuation of wounded a major problem. Nevertheless, the Battalion [1/4] advanced 200 yards and eliminated the resistance that had hindered their progress.

> Employing flamethrowers and demolition teams, 3/4 blasted and burned their way through elaborate enemy fortifications on the slopes of Horseshoe. By 1400, K and L Companies had destroyed the deadly, defiladed, enemy mortar emplacements in the Horseshoe depression, and were on a defensive line that reached half way between Horseshoe and the Asato River.
>
> Due to rough terrain, 2/4 at half Moon could not employ tanks effectively. Very accurate and heavy mortar and artillery fire from Shuri Heights made it impossible for the Battalion to make any significant gains on the 21st. On evaluating the situation at Half Moon Hill, General Shepherd changed his operational plans for the Division. Since 2/4 was being held up by fire originating out of the Division's zone of action, his plan called for that battalion to establish a strong defense on the rear slope. The focus of the Division's attack would then shift toward the south and southwest.
>
> Despite unfavorable conditions [to include incessant rain], 1/4 and 3/4 resumed their advance [in the] early morning of the 23rd, while 2/4 guarded the left flank and maintained contact with the 1st Division.[32]
>
> – *Dan Marsh's Marine Raider Page*

On May 24th, 2/4 was replaced by 3/22 on the slow moving left side of the line. It joined its sister battalions on the more fluid right—just south of the Asato River. Then, they all fully participated in the Battles of Naha and the Oroku Peninsula.

2/4 Had Again Employed the Bairoko Assault

There are no detailed descriptions of that piecemeal battle for the forward faces of Half Moon. While proponents of "strict historical research" might not miss that detail, this author thinks it important enough to extrapolate a little. The machinegun bunkers along those steep slopes had been mutually supporting. That means each was protected by this crisscrossing fire of two behind it. (See Figure 10.3.) Thus, 2/4 would have had fire teams moving forward (roughly on line) to try to double-envelop—through the microterrain—the bunkers in their lanes. While the most forward had the priority, they could not be seized without some rearward pressure. In other words, Marine buddy teams would have to provide impromptu assistance to those from different squads in other lanes. (See Figures 10.4 through 10.6.)

No frontline commander could have controlled such a convoluted evolution, nor would have more organization done any good. This was a fight to the death based on individual initiative and the surprise that only "micro-maneuver" can develop. The attack was simply happening. Only important was the constant cooperation between teams. While fire team techniques would have helped with the double-envelopments, the overall maneuver required no

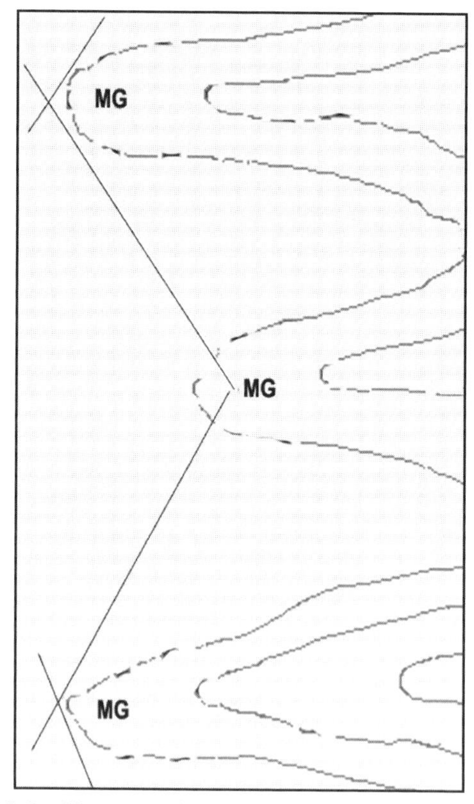

Figure 10.3: Mutually Supporting Machinegun Bunkers

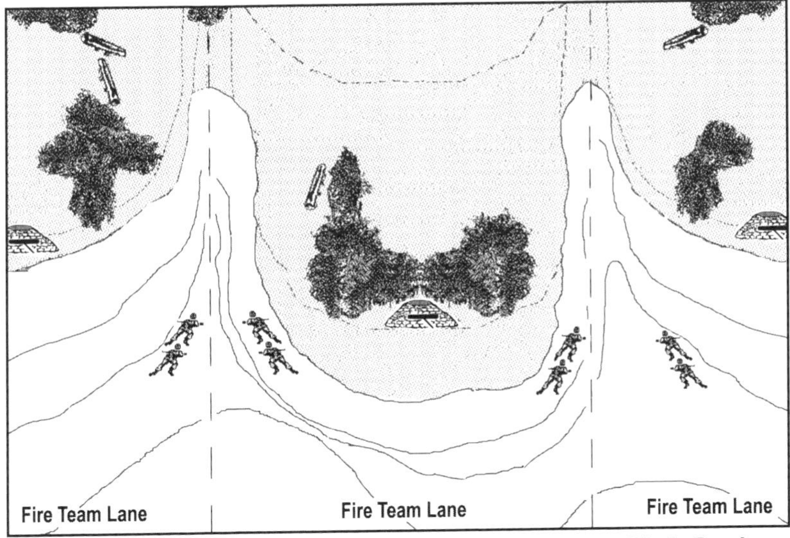

Figure 10.4: Fire Teams Subdivide to Double-Envelop Their Bunkers

Figure 10.5: Rearward Neighbors Fire across Front of U.S. Target

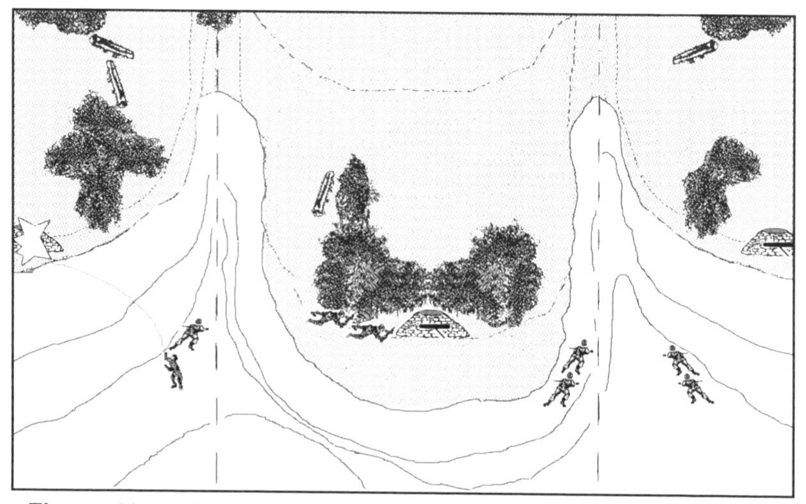

Figure 10.6: Adjacent-Lane Team Suppresses Crisscross Fire

structure other than lanes and alignment. The latter didn't need to be directed. Marines of this era knew instinctively not to get too far ahead of each other.

The closest Western parallel to a Bairoko Assault is "fire and movement with grenades added"—a decidedly "hasty" type of attack. However, that Assault also had recon pull, infiltration, and swarm characteristics. Because fire team technique would have made each bunker's double-envelopment a little easier, the entire evolution could be viewed as a "deliberate attack" of sorts. Yet, no procedural formula (or its rehearsal) could do justice to that many considerations. They must necessarily arise out of individual initiative and available microterrain. That's why this assault method replaced all leadership channels with lowest-echelon cooperation. There is something of major tactical significance here. 2/4 had once again proven that the Bairoko Assault needed no supporting arms to overwhelm a state-of-the-art defense.

The Bairoko Accompaniment

The Bairoko Assault had worked well at Half Moon because of enough troops occupying the ground behind it to prevent any subterranean envelopment. "Cushman's Pocket" would not have occurred at Iwo Jima if there had been more follow-on forces to the 9th Marines' "infiltration-style" night attack. Of note, 1/9 had worked with 2nd Raider Battalion on Bougainville.[33]

Clearly missing at Half Moon was a little Stormtrooper technique for the really stubborn emplacements. At night, it would not have drawn as much long-distance fire.

4th Marines May Have Had Slight Edge over Other Regiments

By comparing how the three regiments of 6th Marine Division did inside the Sugar Loaf Complex, one might be able to tell whether 4th Marines benefitted from having so many former Raiders. 22nd and 29th Marines first tackled the area, so to them fell the lion's share of the work. The 22nd had been formed in June 1942, with its cadre coming from the 6th Marines who had occupied Iceland. The 29th was formed during the summer of 1944, with its officers and NCOs being mostly returning veterans of the five active Divisions.[34] As such, 22nd and 29th Marine Regiments would have been using strictly traditional small-unit tactics.

By the time these two regiments had finally occupied Sugar Loaf Hill to stay on May 18, they had lost almost 4,000 personnel to either battle injury or fatigue.

> During the 10-day period up to and including the capture of Sugar Loaf the 6th Marine Division had lost 2,662 killed or wounded; there were also 1,289 cases of combat fatigue. In the 22nd and 29th Marines three battalion commanders and eleven company commanders had been killed or wounded.[35]
>
> — Official Army Chronicle, 2000

As the 4th Marines then went after other parts of the Sugar Loaf Complex (Horseshoe and Half Moon), it had a somewhat easier time of it. But the earlier carnage had bothered those in charge.

The left side of the 4th Marines' assault line was soon to be halted by the 6th Marine Division commander due to "too much fire from outside his zone of responsibility." Because of the way the enemy defenses were laid out, companies with the most pro-active fire teams and squads would have done better on the reverse slopes of all three bastions. One the famous *Leavenworth Papers* confirms that their defenses had been specifically designed to require a lot of decentralized activity on all rearward slopes.

> The [Imperial Japanese Army] IJA 32nd Army chose to build its main defensive positions across the Okinawa isthmus. . . . The rugged terrain in this area, which extended southward to the Naha-Yonabaru line, was superbly fitted to the methods the IJA had adopted of using hilltop pillbox caves and reverse-slope fields of fire that would force the Americans to engage as small infantry teams. The terrain here was rolling and hilly and "broken by terraces, steep natural escarpments, and ravines." It was characterized by "lack of pattern, steep slopes, and narrow valleys" and was "filled with twisting ridges and spotted with irregular knolls." Because the terrain was hilly and irregular, it provided innumerable short fields of fire but no long fields of fire. This was ideal for the Japanese whose defense relied on "large numbers of short-range weapons." The tangled, broken ground forced the Americans to fight a thousand small battles hand to hand instead of one large battle at a distance where their preponderant firepower would have given them the advantage *(Okinawa Area Infantry Strategy,* ed. Senshishiteu, 167-68; Inagaki, *Okinawa,* 134, 136).[36]
>
> — *Leavenworth Papers No. 18,* 1990

With all the close-encounter skill of a guerrilla, the former 4th Battalion Raiders excelled at this type of combat. The same *Leavenworth Paper* shows what the Japanese considered to be the most productive maneuver against the face of a Shuri strongpoint. They thought American tank-infantry teams would be of little use.

> At first, the Americans did not know the pillbox caves even existed and had no doctrine for dealing with them. . . . The Americans at the outset of the offensive advanced *en masse*

> and were mowed down in crowds by cave-hidden machine guns when they reached the reverse slopes (Inagaki, *Okinawa,* 139-140). American officers on the scene quickly developed a method for avoiding these unhappy effects, however. They would bombard the Japanese positions they faced, forcing the IJA off the surface. They would then infiltrate men in small numbers through narrow gaps in the Japanese fixed-cave fire line ("dead spaces").[37]
>
> – *Leavenworth Papers No. 18,* 1990

Second Look at Chronicle Confirms Many Tiny Skirmishes

During 4th Marines' attack toward the back side of the Sugar Loaf Complex, there were constant skirmishes with Japanese infiltrators. Former Raiders with the most guerrilla training would have fared best in these types of encounters. All Raiders had received some such instruction in school,[38] but only those from the 4th Battalion (those now in 2/4) had regularly been forced to apply it to combat.

> At daybreak [on 19 May] Companies K and L of 3/4 began relieving the units of 2/29 on Sugar Loaf, while Companies F and E of 2/4 took over the rest of the 29th Marines' front. The reliefs were effected smoothly despite the difficult terrain, steady bombardment, and *opposition from small enemy groups which had infiltrated the lines during the night.* Some advances were made along the regimental front as assault companies seized the most favorable positions from which to attack on 20 May. . . .
>
> Company E of 2/4, which had taken over 3/29's advanced positions on Half Moon Hill, sustained a strong counterattack in the late afternoon which began shortly after the relief was completed. . . .
>
> Promising gains were made by both assault battalions of the 4th Marines on 20 May. Jumping off at 0800 behind heavy artillery barrages and tanks, the attacking troops moved rapidly ahead for 200 yards before encountering fierce opposition from the Horseshoe and Half Moon. . . .
>
> Infantrymen [from 3/4] with demolitions and flame

throwers followed closely behind the tanks which blasted the cave positions honeycombing the forward slopes of the Horseshoe. . . .

The attack of 2/4 on Half Moon . . . [also occurred on] 20 May. Heavy and accurate flat trajectory fire coming from the direction of Shuri heights raked the battalion's flank, and mortars firing from defiladed positions on the reverse slopes of Half Moon covered the entire zone of advance [with exploding rounds]. . . .

The division attacked on 21 May with its objective the upper reaches of the Asato Gawa [a shallow river to the south]. The 4th Marines made the main effort with the 22nd conforming to its advance and delivering supporting fire. Under its new commander, Lieutenant Colonel George B. Bell, the 1st Battalion [4th Marines], less Company C in regimental reserve, attacked in the center of the line down the south slopes of Sugar Loaf toward the eastern extremity of the Horseshoe. Progress was slow and the fighting bitter as Companies A and B struggled to reach the river. A steady, soaking rain fell throughout the morning and most of the afternoon, making the loose, shell-torn ground muddy and treacherous. Adequate supply and evacuation through the thick, clinging cover of mud were almost impossible. *The day's advance of approximately 200 yards was won only by dint of prodigious efforts by men who had to fight* the weather as well as the *numerous enemy pockets that held out all along the river approaches (1 / 4 SAR, Ph III, 2).*

The 3rd Battalion drove down into the extensively tunneled interior of the Horseshoe, using demolitions and flame throwers to wipe out resistance in the nest of enemy mortar positions. Companies K and I halted their advance in mid-afternoon and set up a solid defense line approximately halfway between the Horseshoe and the river.

Advances in 2/4's zone of action were negligible because of the rugged terrain which prevented effective tank support and the intense mortar and artillery fire brought to bear on all ground exposed to the Shuri Heights. *After the fifth day of limited advances in the Half Moon area General Shepherd was convinced that the enemy power [long-range fire and below-ground resupply / reinforcements] that prevented the capture of Half Moon was [coming from] . . . outside of the*

> *division zone of action.* As a consequence . . . , he [became] determined to . . . "making no further attempt to drive to the southeast in the face of Shuri fire, and to concentrate the division's effort on a penetration to the south and southwest (6th MarDiv SAR, Ph III, Part III, 11)." [Italics added.] [39]
> — "USMC Historical Monograph," 1955

Proof of the Sophistication of the Shuri Defenses

On Okinawa, the Japanese had been planning to combine two assets: (1) the greatest number of large-caliber weapons the Marines had ever faced;[40] and (2) terrain that would largely negate U.S. firepower. That terrain spanned the narrowest part of the island. It stretched all along the northern side of Shuri Ridge.

> Everything about the terrain favored the defenders. The convoluted topography of ridges, draws, and escarpments served to compartment[alize] the battlefield into scores of small firefights, while the general absence of dense vegetation permitted the defenders full observation and interlocking supporting fires from intermediate strongpoints [and Shuri Heights].[41]
> — History and Museums Division, HQMC, 1996

Japan's new strategy was not to stop U.S. troops short of any stronghold, but rather to eject those who had gained a foothold. Then, all initially successful U.S. elements would take as many casualties withdrawing as they had during their initial assaults. There were three parts to this attrition-oriented formula.

> [T]he Japanese would contain and isolate an American penetration by grazing fire from supporting positions, then smother the exposed troops on top of the initial objective with a rain of preregistered heavy mortar [or artillery] shells until fresh Japanese troops could swarm out of their reverse-slope tunnels in a counterattack.[42]
> — History and Museums Division, HQMC, 1996

Of course, those counterattacks were greatly facilitated by the tunnels connecting the Sugar Loaf Complex with rearward staging areas. How else could a force of battalion size (700 or better) have counterattacked 3/4 on Horseshoe during the night of 20 May? [43] There had also been plenty of opportunity for tunneling between those three hills. Sugar Loaf's elevation was 230 feet, but it only rose 50 feet above its northern approaches. Horseshoe was 190 feet above sea level, and Half Moon 220.[44] All three bastions are known to have been honeycombed with caves and fighting holes. The bunkers on their precipitous northern faces might have more accurately been called "fire-port caves."[45] Every other surface was covered by preregistered direct and indirect fire from the sides and rear.

In essence, the Japanese had tried to create a string of killing zones of such lethality that no foe could cross them without unacceptable losses.[46] To anchor the left end of their Shuri Line, they had undoubtedly wanted such a trap at the Sugar Loaf Complex. "So sophisticated were the mutually supporting defenses of its three little hills that an attack on one of them would prove fruitless unless the others were similarly invested." All approaches to the Complex were within the beaten zone of heavy artillery from Shuri Ridge.[47] The Japanese also had any number of direct-fire 44mm guns. While normally for tank killing, they may have found a different purpose in this fight. As the Germans had with their infamous "88's," the Japanese may have aimed all such guns at Half Moon to prevent its consolidation.

Within this southeastern quadrant of the Sugar Loaf Complex, the Nipponese Army had made one last, desperate attempt to hold onto the western end of its defense belt. Half Moon had been the least accessible of the three hills. After losing so many people on Sugar Loaf, the American commander would not have wanted to match those losses on Half Moon. To help him make up his mind, the Japanese had simply concentrated much of their remaining firepower on that tiny piece of ground. Wherever possible, such kill zones should be bypassed.

What Those Strongpoints Looked Like from the Inside

There is no known diagram of what those tiny knolls in Southern Okinawa contained. That in Figure 10.7 was found at about the same time on Luzon in the Philippines. Yet, there are interior diagrams of the elongated escarpments on Okinawa. (See Figure

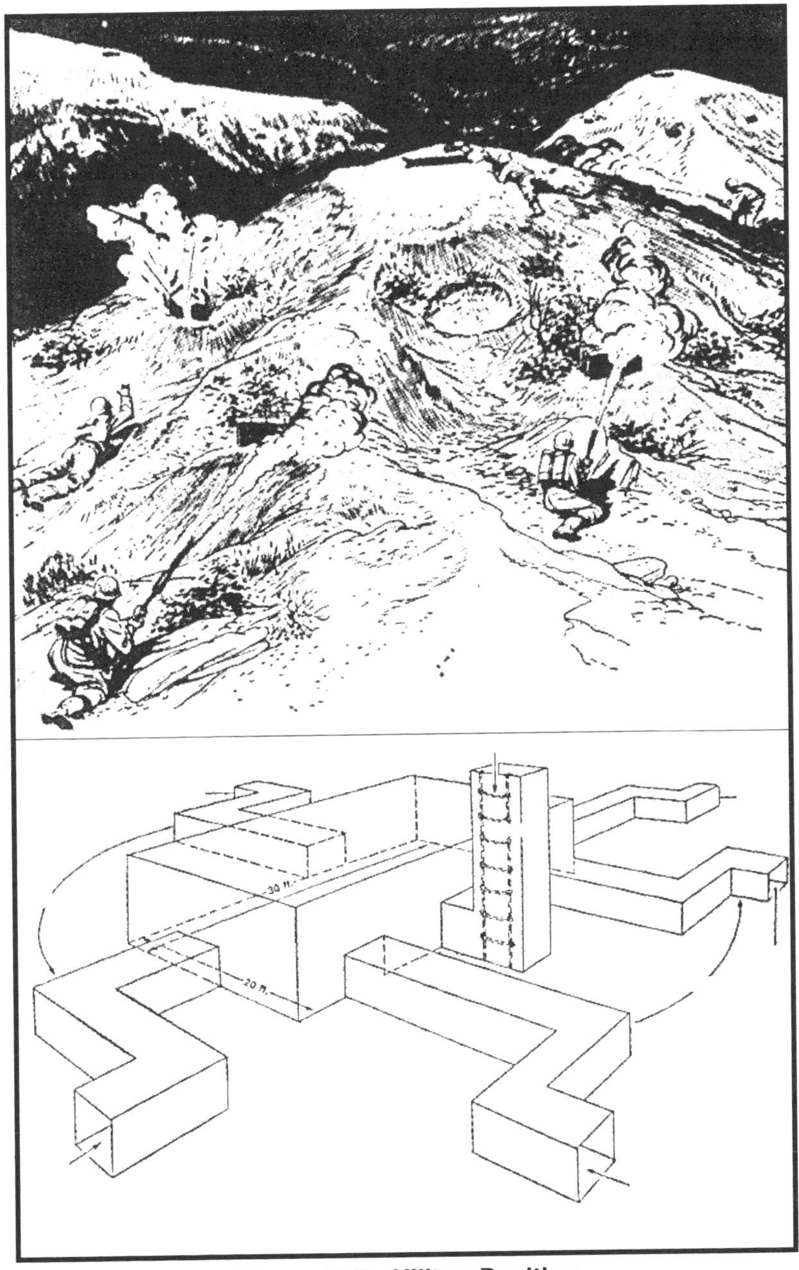

Figure 10.7: Hilltop Position

(Source: U.S. War Dept. sketch of hilltop position on Luzon in 1945, from "Japanese Army of WWII," by Philip Warner, © 1972 by Osprey Publishing Ltd., p. 25)

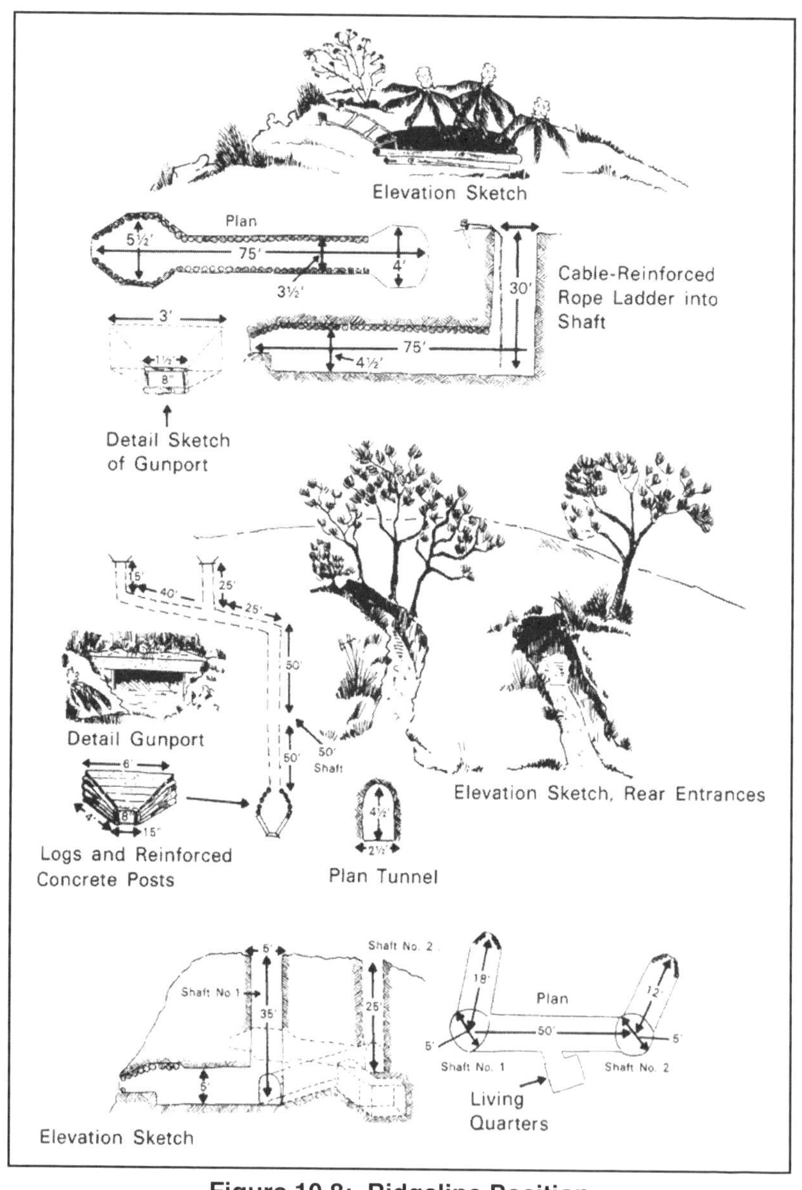

Figure 10.8: Ridgeline Position

(Source: "Japan's Battle for Okinawa, April - June 1945," by Thomas M. Hubler, Leavenworth Papers No. 18, U.S. Army Cmd. & Gen. Staff College, 1990, fig. 6)

10.8.) Clearly, each position was comprised of one or more fire-port caves that could be reached by vertical shaft from above. They also had living quarters and camouflaged rear entrances.

Of course, such positions would have been highly susceptible to smoke grenades and gasoline from anyone who had seized the ground above them. Because of the importance of the Sugar Loaf Complex, there would have been escape/reinforcement passageways leading below ground to the south. To protect these rearward leading tunnels from smoke and flame, one only needs a few fire doors and air shafts.

A Telling Maneuver at the Very End of Hostilities

After months of hard fighting, even the 4th Marine Regiment's commander—the same traditionalist who had initially replaced Carlson—was using Asian tactics. Though double-envelopments were still in violation of U.S. doctrine, Colonel Alan Shapley then tried one. (See Map 10.8.) His former 2nd and 4th Battalion Raiders

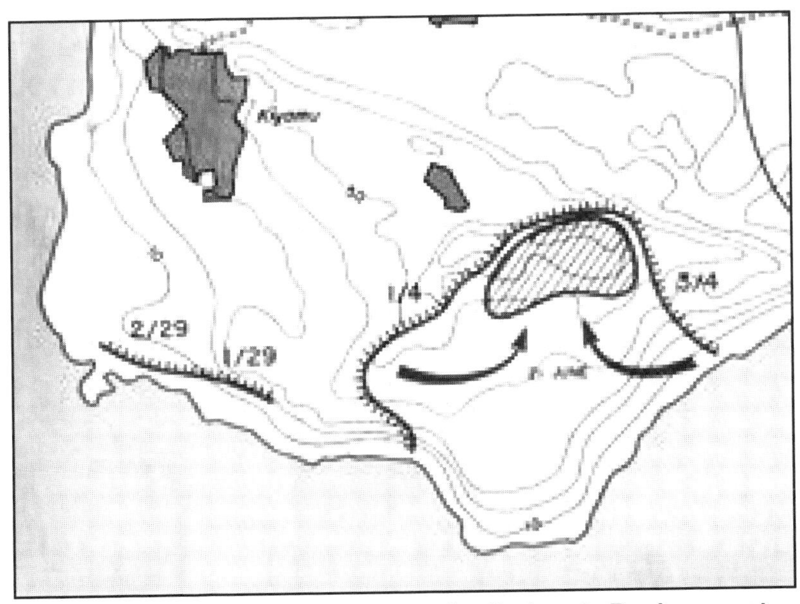

Map 10.8: An Unusual Maneuver by Carlson's Replacement
(Source: "Okinawa: The Last Battle," by Roy Appleman, James Burns, Russell Gugeler, and John Stevens, U.S. Army Ctr. of Mil. History, 2000, map 49)

had made a convert of sorts at the very end of the war. The enemy was less likely to escape an encirclement, and the distances and terrain between approaching forces had made fratricide unlikely.

> On 21 June . . . Colonel Shapley had directed 2/4 and 3/4 to make a double-envelopment of Hill 72 on Kiyamu-Gusuku ridge. Both battalions began their turning movements at 0800 and by 0930 had linked up and were driving north over the reverse slopes of the hill. In less than an hour the objective was secured and the troops, aided by tanks and armored flame throwers, were cleaning out the last enemy defenders.[48]
>
> — "USMC Historical Monograph," 1955

A Few of Okinawa's Lessons Have Yet to Be Realized

Like Iwo Jima, the Shuri Defense Zone had been a blood bath. With the pain of so many lost, it would be many years before any American would again speculate that more localized surprise would have allowed for less bombardment. With any heavy application of firepower comes friendly fire casualties and collateral damage. While the amount of supporting-arms-generated fratricide is not easy to ascertain for this battle, it most assuredly happened. Note the number of U.S. "nonbattle" casualties.

> Only 76,000 men in the Japanese force were uniformed and trained military; the other 24,000 persons were recently impressed indigenous militia and labor groups (Inagaki, *Okinawa*, 95). . . .
>
> To subdue these 76,000 IJA regulars cost U.S. Tenth Army exactly 6,319 KIA . . . , 32,943 [injured or missing in action, and died of wounds] . . . [and] an additional 33,096 casualties in the "nonbattle" categories ("Okinawa Area Infantry Strategy," *War History Series*, 2-3, chart 2).[49]
>
> — *Leavenworth Papers No. 18,* 1990

The amount of collateral damage is less difficult to ascertain. By this U.S. Army account, 24,000 Okinawan militiamen and laborers had been "impressed" into service. An American Vietnam veteran who—after marrying into a local family while working on

Okinawa—says that many of the older generation bore a tiny tattoo like that of a Nazi death camp inmate. In other words, many had been forced to help the Japanese.[50] This puts a new light on the number of noncombatant casualties. By some estimates, a full third of Okinawa's 450,000 civilian occupants perished in the melee, and another third were wounded.[51] Okinawa had not been voluntarily part of Japan at the time of the battle. It was instead the main island of an independent Ryukyu Kingdom that had been forcefully annexed by Japan in the 1870's.[52] Still, with some of the locals fighting alongside the Japanese and others thoroughly convinced of the anti-American propaganda, civilian identification was no easy matter for the invading GIs.

It would be not be fair to double-guess America's greatest generation as it fought for its life against a fanatical opponent in one of the most diabolical defenses ever devised. Yet, the Marines had been pushing for more maneuver than the Tenth Army from the time of the assault on Shuri Castle to the end of the conflict.[53] (See

Figure 10.9: U.S. Army Preferred the Sledge Hammer Approach
(Source: U.S. Army Center of Military History, artphoto archives, illustration designator "0806-3.jpg," Fire Mission—Okinawa—World War II, by Gerald W. Ferguson)

Figure 10.9.) So, it's only fitting that the modern-day Corps should now acknowledge the match that former Raiders had established between decentralized and undersupported maneuver and a constricted space. (By "undersupported" is meant relatively devoid of preparatory tank, artillery, and air bombardment.)

To the Maoist Raiders who had endured all the anguish of being rejected by their own organization, full credit for the Bairoko Assault must legitimately go. It worked well at Half Moon and to this day constitutes an evolutionary advance in infiltration-type assault tactics.

There Would Be No Direct Inheritance of Raider Methods

The 4th Marines' personnel (to which this chapter is dedicated) did not accompany 6th Marine Division to China in October 1945. Their battalions were all deactivated. The 3/4 that served in China from March 1946 to October 1947 was actually a redesignated 3/22.[54] Thus, no unit would directly inherit Raider procedure after WWII.

However, because the 4th Marine Regiment had such a long Oriental heritage, its future members would probably try harder to understand Asian culture than other Marines. That understanding would in turn translate into a few tactics emulated. 4th Marines was reactivated too late to see any action in Korea, but it did fight in Vietnam. All three battalions deployed to Southeast Asia in 1965 and would eventually find their way up to the Demilitarized Zone (DMZ). There, they participated in every major operation from "Hastings" on.[55]

11 Tackling Many Times Their Number

- Did Marines ever use any Maoist maneuvers in Vietnam?
- Which ones helped while they were fighting outnumbered?

The North Vietnamese are still the world's best light infantry.

(Source: Courtesy of Osprey Publishing Ltd. from "Armies of the Vietnam War 1962-75," Men-at-Arms Series, © 1980, plate C, no. 2)

Maoist Raiders Instantly Attacked during Chance Contact

While the point men from either a Carlson or Roosevelt patrol were quite stealthy, they would still jump whomever they met on the trail. Unlike the advance guards of regular infantry units, they never hung back to establish foe size or headquarters intentions. Nor did they bother with a hasty ambush. For them, it was all or nothing, right then and there. In the most successful skirmish on Carlson's Long Patrol, 70 bivouacking enemy soldiers were killed in a few minutes by the two or three members of a Raider element's point team.[1]

How Useful Is This Much Individual Aggressiveness?

Most U.S. infantry units prefer to do things as a group without much "hot dogging" from junior members. Thus, one wonders if this lopsided victory on Guadalcanal had been from luck, or something that could be regularly expected from low-ranking personnel with more initiative. To find out, the heir to the 4th Raider Battalion heritage will be closely studied in Vietnam.

The U.S. Unit with the Most Asian Background

Of note, 2nd Battalion was the first of the 4th Marines' units to reach Vietnam—possibly because of its guerrilla heritage. Its actions there may be the best indicator of Carlson's long-term effect on the Corps.

> In May of 1965 the battalion landed at Chu Lai. . . . The first major engagement for the battalion was Operation "Starlite" *[sic]* (the first regimental sized battle for American forces since the Korean War) in August 1965. It was a combined amphibious/helicopter-borne assault on enemy fortified positions of the Van Tuong Peninsula, 15 miles south of the Chu Lai airstrip. Six days after the operation had begun; the 1st Viet Cong Regiment was decisively defeated. . . .
>
> In 1966, combat operations measurably increased as several significant battles characterized by assaults upon well-fortified enemy positions occurred in March. The battalion had two major encounters with the enemy near Quang Ngai City that month during Operations "Utah" (4-7 Mar) and "Texas" (20-25 Mar). Because of the threat of infiltration across the Demilitarized Zone (DMZ) and enemy build-up in that area, the Marines launched Operation "Hastings," a coordinated Marine/South Vietnamese Army (ARVN) search and destroy mission, on 7 July near the DMZ. The battalion played a significant role in frustrating the North Vietnamese Army's (NVA) attempt to penetrate the area in force. Hastings was immediately followed by Operation "Prairie." . . .

> The next major confrontation between 2/4 and the enemy came during the siege of Con Thien [just south of DMZ] in 1967. The battalion, along with 3rd Battalion, 4th Marines, was involved in stopping the enemy's attempt to overrun the American outpost. . . . The 1968 "Tet Offensive" resulted in an increase in [the] tempo of combat activity for 2/4. Bitter clashes between the battalion and NVA broke out near Dong Ha [biggest U.S. base near DMZ]. In this area 2/4 moved forward to seize the fortified village of Dai Do. After three days of bloody fighting, 2/4, with the assistance of reinforcements, artillery and naval gunfire, was able to secure the enemy stronghold. Though the cost was high for both sides; the enemy lost nearly 600 killed, while 2/4 suffered 80 dead and 256 wounded [early estimate]. . . .
>
> Contact with the enemy tapered off during the fall of 1968, but picked up again in December. The battalion was involved in a series of violent clashes near the DMZ and, with the aid of artillery and airstrikes, they were able to overrun a massive bunker complex. Late in 1969, 2/4 was withdrawn to Okinawa as part of the United States policy of gradually turning the war over to the South Vietnamese.[2]
>
> — Official 2nd Battalion, 4th Marines website

More About the Dai Do Engagement

Three days before the battle's official start on 30 April 1968, several of 2/4's companies had been in contact with large numbers of NVA some 10 kilometers north of Dai Do. During a night march to a blocking position at Lai An for Echo Company's assault on An My, Golf Company had found itself in the middle of a southbound NVA column. (See the top portion of Map 11.1.) That company's subsequent withdrawal, along with all of its associated artillery and medevac support, had given 2/4 a good hint of what was to come. Everyone now knew their TAOR to be crowded. Though the occupiers of An My had fled, Echo had conducted a rare nighttime assault and then sidestepped a 32-round NVA artillery barrage on the way home. Though now fully primed for action, it was then unhappily "chopped" to 3rd Marine Division Headquarters for the defense of Highway #1's Dong Ha Bridge.[3] (See rest of Map 11.1.)

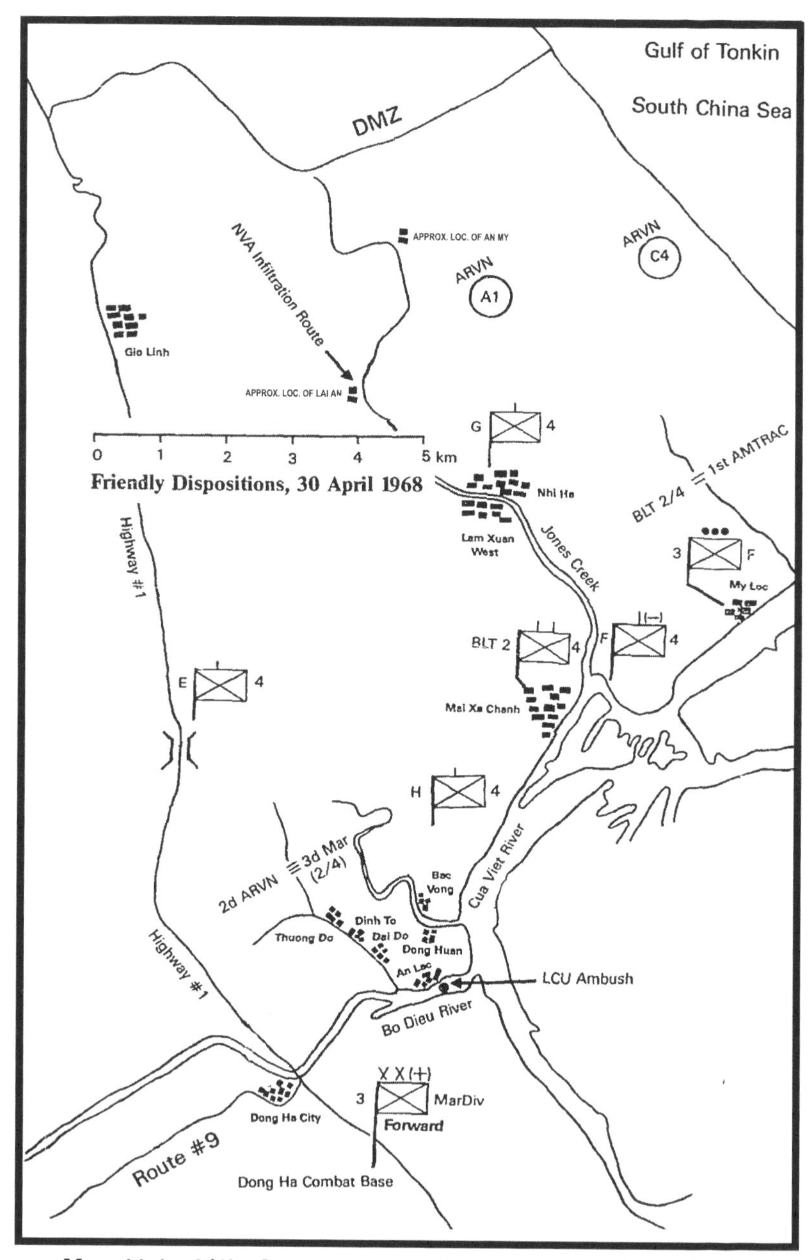

Map 11.1: 2/4's Company Locations at Start of the Battle

(Source: Map based on fig. 1, "Memories of Dai Do," by William Weise, © Sept. 1987 by Marine Corps Gazette)

By the time the sun rose over Vietnam's coastal plain on 30 April, 2/4 had all other companies strung out along the river that connected DHCB (Dong Ha Combat Base) to the South China Sea. (Refer back to Map 11.1.) It had just inherited responsibility for defending that vital supply conduit. To take the place of Echo, it was soon to be loaned B/1/3.[4]

After "Tet," things may have been winding down elsewhere in Vietnam. But, along the DMZ, they were just heating up. There was little doubt as to where that NVA column had been headed—either to the provincial capital of Quang Tri City or the northernmost U.S. airstrip at DHCB. A few miles northeast of the latter—where a tiny stream entered its Cua Viet outlet—was the village of Dai Do. Almost certainly an infiltration route way-station, it and the area to its immediate north were to become the site of one of the most instructional battles of the Vietnam War. What made this engagement different from most is the extent to which the enemy used large-caliber artillery from the DMZ, heavy machineguns, and mortars.

Just before dawn on that first fateful day, someone in An Lac started shooting at a Navy patrol craft with automatic weapons and rocket-propelled grenades (RPGs). In response, Lt.Col. William Weise decided to move all of 2/4's remaining companies toward An Lac.

First, Hotel went after a heavily contested Dong Huan. After shifting north to more safely ford the intervening stream, its members "literally crawled the last 700 meters of open rice paddy" while supporting arms prepared the objective.[5] That much crawling was quite out of character for a Western unit, but what happened next wasn't. "The grunts shouted and fired from the hip as they rushed forward through the cover of smoke rounds."[6] While the perimeter hedgerow was certainly entered on line, the rest of the *ville* must have been taken in more piecemeal fashion. All the battalion commander recalls is that "well-trained assault teams destroyed one fortified position after another."[7]

Then—all the while under heavy artillery and small-arms fire—Foxtrot crossed the same stream in Amtracs and headed southwest across the paddies for Dai Do. Only one platoon managed to gain a tiny toehold, while the others got pinned down in the open.[8] The successful platoon had first closed with Dai Do by fire team rush, then crawling (during the artillery barrage), and finally standup assault.[9] However, its beachhead was soon to be forfeited. After

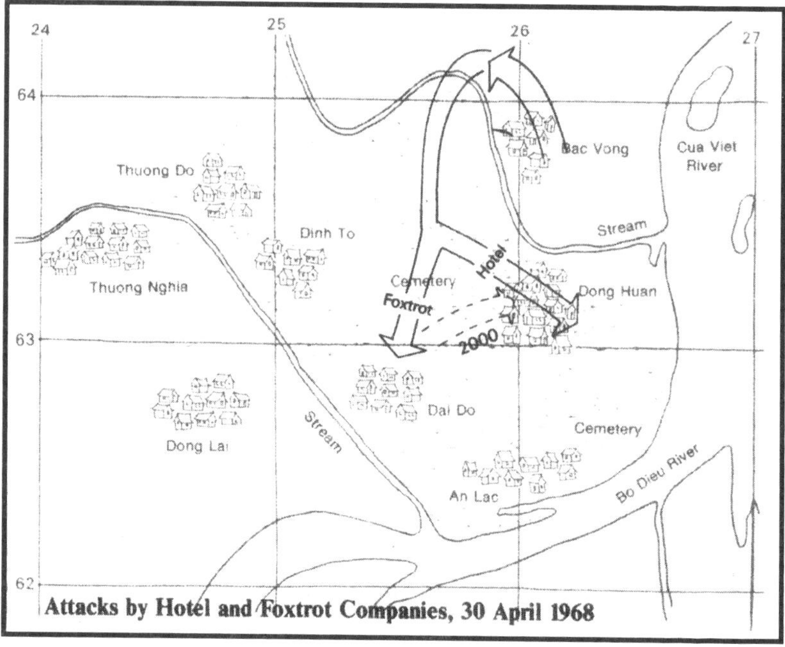

Map 11.2: Northern Initiative on the Morning of 30 April 1968
(Source: "Memories of Dai Do," by William Weise, © Sept. 1987 by Marine Corps Gazette, fig. 2)

being incorrectly informed that Foxtrot was down to 26 effectives,[10] Lt.Col. Weise had ordered every one of Foxtrot's platoons back to Dong Huan. With darkness approaching and lots of supporting arms—to include a few dry airstrikes [11]—that very dangerous withdrawal eventually took place. (See Map 11.2.) Meanwhile, B/1/3 (now attached to 2/4) and its Amtracs had hit the beach (riverbank) at An Lac under considerable enemy fire. Only with some difficulty did it capture the place. (See Map 11.3.)

After a night of intermittent contact, 2/4 resumed its offensive on 1 May. From the east end of An Lac, Golf and two tanks launched a morning assault on Dai Do's southern end. (See Map 11.4.) At first, the two assault platoons could get no closer than 150 meters. As was the Marine habit at that time, everyone had to be kept on line to prevent fratricide. Firepower was the name of the game, and most

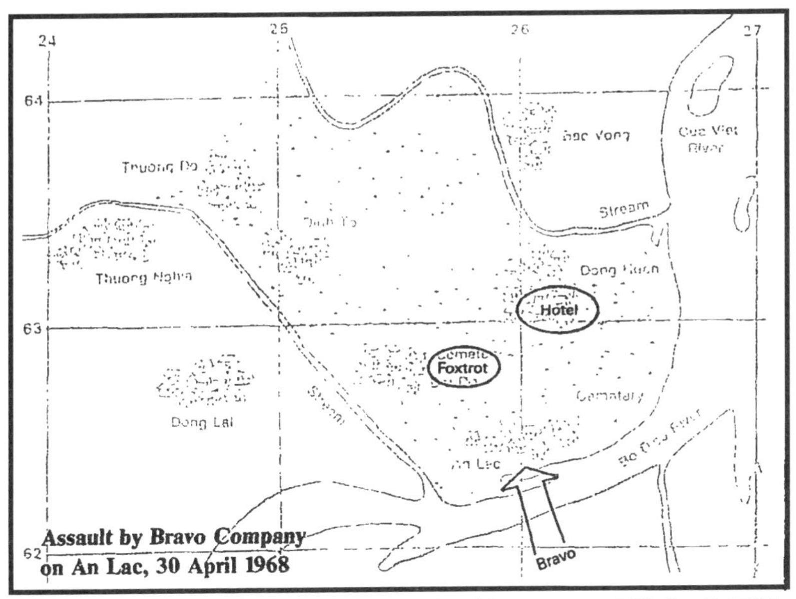

Map 11.3: Southern Follow-Up on the Afternoon of 30 April 1968
(Source: "Memories of Dai Do," by William Weise, © Sept. 1987 by Marine Corps Gazette, fig. 3)

movements were by whole platoons at once. This particular attack was supposed to have kicked off before dawn. However, it had gotten off to a late start, and the tanks run out of ammunition. When Dai Do's defensive fire had greatly increased with 300 yards to go,[12] the reserve platoon was brought forward (between the others) through a series of fire team rushes. Then, all three platoons spent two more hours in the open trying to establish fire superiority. Finally, the reserve platoon and supporting arms managed to suppress enough of the defenders' fire for the original assault platoons to "leapfrog in" to the objective.[13] Meanwhile, B/1/3 had tried to reinforce Golf by Amtrac across the paddies and taken so many casualties as to have to return to An Lac. (See Map 11.4.)

After moving through much of Dai Do, Golf's Leathernecks came upon bypassed positions. Before they could clean these out, they were heavily counterattacked (at least partially from Dinh To to the north). Then, G Company's survivors first withdrew to a drainage

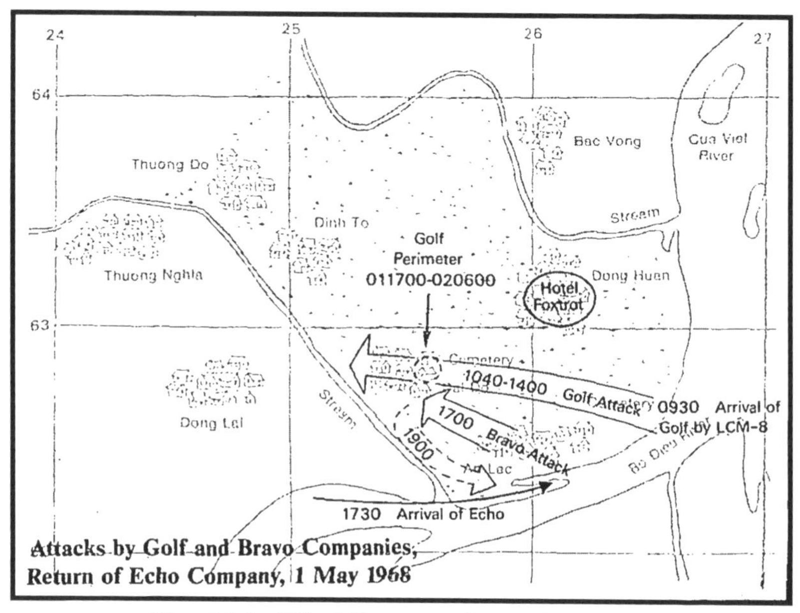

Map 11.4: What Happened on 1 May 1968
(Source: "Memories of Dai Do," by William Weise, © Sept. 1987 by Marine Corps Gazette, fig. 4)

ditch on the south side of Dai Do and finally to the burial mounds just outside its southeastern end. This gave them better fields of fire, and the overhead planes a more distinct target. (See Map 11.4.) Both would be required to fend off "two large enemy night attacks and several probes."[14]

After a long night of enemy interest, the Marines of 2/4 made their most historic advances on 2 May—the third day of the battle. Echo Company had been finally returned to the battalion from its bridge assignment and was to kick off the festivities. First, it attacked Dai Do from An Lac. As at An My, its troops launched their assault before dawn, with bayonets drawn and no smoke or rolling-artillery barrage.[15] Though not as surprise oriented as an enemy probe, the Marines were trying. "Enemy fire was again devastating and Marine casualties high, but the up-and-down assault line was able to breach the first hedgerow, a fire team here, a squad there."[16] Then, Echo's elements methodically reduced all of the tiny enemy emplacements [inside Dai Do]," while moving from west to east.[17] Such a thing is most easily accomplished by semi-autonomous fire teams that must stay roughly on line. However, only a crude facsimile of this probably occurred. Soon, Golf Company "broke out of its perimeter [at the east end of the village] to assist Echo Company [to] clear Dai Do."[18] At first, both companies were attacking towards each other.[19] (See Map 11.5.) Then, they joined up without incident.

Next—to exploit the NVA retreat from Dai Do—Lt.Col. Weise sent Hotel Company on an end run towards Dinh To. Having watched the back and forth flow since the 30 April assault on Dong Huan, Hotel did something that none of the other companies had so far attempted. Its two assault platoons advanced through well-decentralized "fire and movement" (separate elements alternately covering and moving). The individual rushes were probably from watching the NVA.[20] "Hotel [then] leapfrogged deeper into Dinh To,

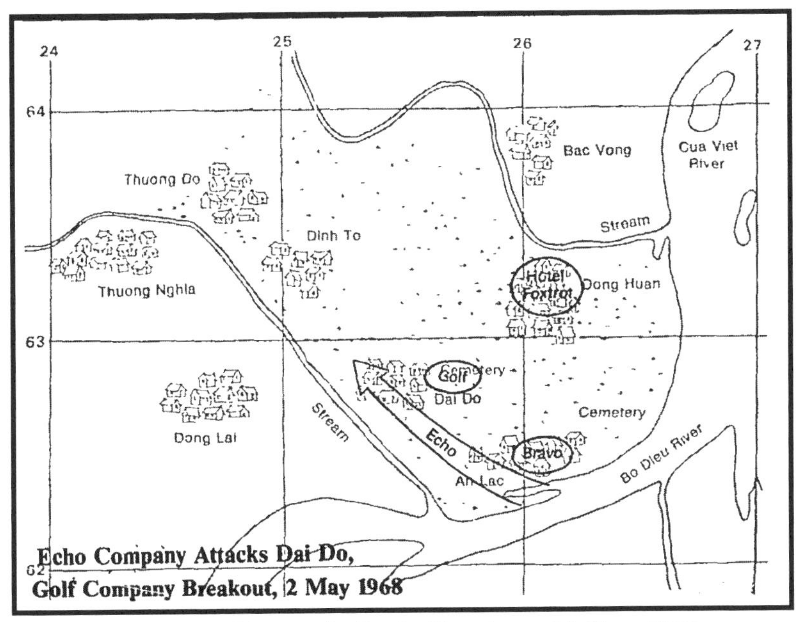

Map 11.5: Events in Early Morning of 2 May 1968
(Source: "Memories of Dai Do," by William Weise, © Sept. 1987 by Marine Corps Gazette, fig. 5)

returning the increasingly heavy fire but not suppressing it."[21] Thus, Hotel's formation involved not only composite movement, but also composite fire. If just buddy teams had been shooting in support of each other's advances (while roughly aligned), that would have been about as good as it gets anywhere in the world with regard to "fire and movement."

Sadly, Hotel's depleted number soon ran into a buzz saw, and the same Echo Company people who had come to Golf's assistance then did so for Hotel. (See Map 11.6.) By now, Hotel's Marines were also largely armed with AK47s.[22] Reinvigorated by the impromptu display of camaraderie, those in the combined force then continued onward into the heavily fortified village. Though the men of the two companies were now "jumbled together with bayonets fixed, they advanced in leaps and bounds between spots of cover."[23] Unfortu-

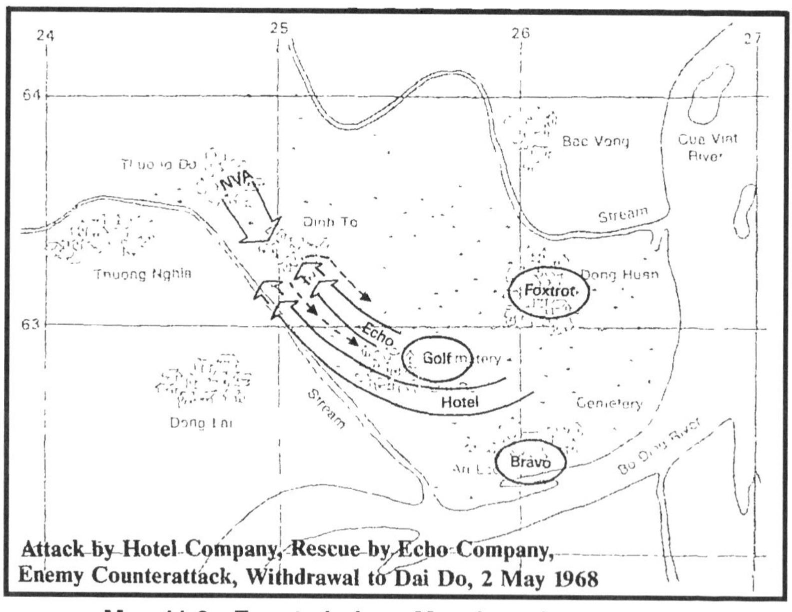

Map 11.6: Events in Late Morning of 2 May 1968
(Source: "Memories of Dai Do," by William Weise, © Sept. 1987 by Marine Corps Gazette, fig. 6)

nately, the odds were stacked too heavily against them. Realizing this, Lt.Col. Weise pulled both back to Dai Do. This gave him the chance to plaster Dinh To with supporting arms.

After already doing more fighting in two days than the average battalion did in six months, 2/4 was about to attack Dinh To again in the late afternoon of 2 May. This time, with Golf and Foxtrot to the right of the stream and an ARVN (Army of South Vietnam) mechanized battalion supposedly to the left of it. (See Map 11.7.) All in Golf—except for grenadiers, machinegunners, and commander—were now carrying AK47s.[24] Hundreds of enemy regulars still stood in their way. That mechanized ARVN battalion failed to keep up, and Foxtrot's orders got somehow confused (it ended up on Golf's flank instead of in trace).[25] After moving through Dinh To to Thuong Do, Golf ran into an even bigger meat grinder than Hotel and Echo had. The enemy strongly counterattacked its left flank from the ARVN's sector across the stream. Soon, it, Foxtrot, and

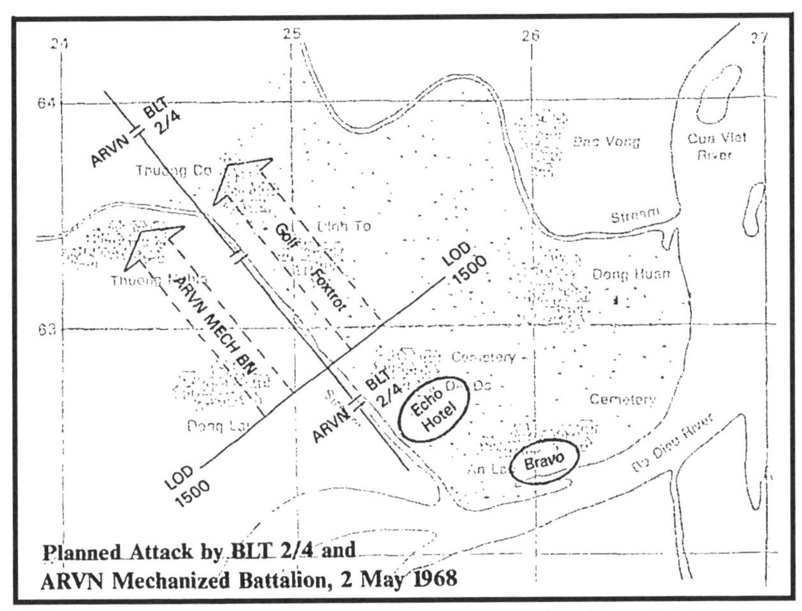

Map 11.7: Plan for Late Afternoon of 2 May 1968
(Source: "Memories of Dai Do," by William Weise, © Sept. 1987 by Marine Corps Gazette, fig. 7)

the Battalion CP were all moving rearward in a hurry. There had been no time to retrieve the dead or make a proper head count. The Forward Air Control (FAC) officer was directed by the now wounded battalion commander to organize a delaying action. Before long, he and half a dozen enlisted volunteers were "dinging" NVA who had become too engrossed with the chase. As, they progressively withdrew through the hedgerows, they picked up wounded. There had been both dry and wet airstrikes to cover the withdrawal,[26] as well as artillery barrages. When helicopter gunships tried to join in, at least one got confused as to the northernmost location of friendlies.[27] Then, as night fell, one Marine straggler had to be extracted by helicopter from his encirclement.[28]

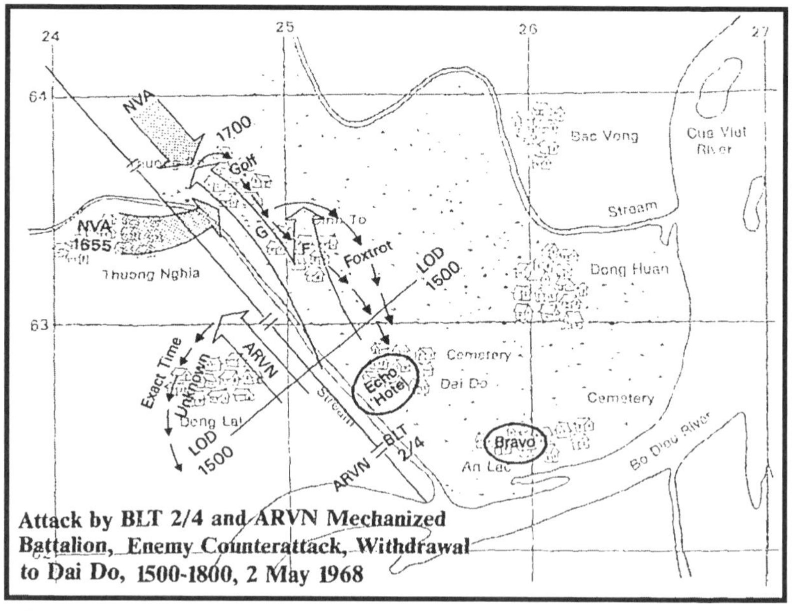

Map 11.8: Actual Events during Late Afternoon of 2 May 1968

(Source: "Memories of Dai Do," by William Weise, © Sept. 1987 by Marine Corps Gazette, fig. 8)

Finally, all of 2/4's companies were back together at Dai Do and preparing to defend it. (See Map 11.8.) Everything north of there was in enemy hands. Yet, those fine young Leathernecks had done remarkably well against a much larger and artillery-supported force of expert light infantrymen. Sadly, the enlisted rock of 2/4—"Big John" Malnar—had been killed that afternoon. During the night, "there was no final surge against this isolated pocket of Marines in Dai Do. The enemy [soldiers] had had enough, and were, in fact, using the cover of darkness to start marching back toward the DMZ."[29]

Soon 1/3 (from An Lac) and the U.S. Army's 3rd Battalion, 21st Infantry (from Nhi Ha) were following up on the battle. Within Dinh To, they found a few Marines who had been initially bandaged by the NVA and then executed.[30] However, the 320th NVA Division had also suffered from its encounter with the latest successor to Roosevelt's Raiders. Over 500 of its number were dead to ground action, and only 273 to supporting arms.[31]

How 2/4's Men Managed to Fend Off 10 Times Their Number

Possibly out of necessity, 2/4 had used some fairly Mao-like maneuvers while trying to compete with a whole NVA division at Dai Do. Either its leaders had made a thorough study of light-infantry tactics (not likely in 1968), or survivors of the first few encounters had started to mimic their opponent. All that is known for sure is that the men of 2/4 began to do things differently from other battalions. First, many traded easy-to-jam M16s for AK47s.[32] Then they inexorably moved toward more small-unit autonomy. All the while, their parent companies had been either struggling to push a much larger force from a fortified position or moving rearward to avoid counterattack.

This Willingness to Take Two Steps Backward

Having ample artillery and air support, U.S. infantry units almost never move rearward under pressure. They possess the doctrinal procedures for tactical withdrawal, but would rather measure their opponent with an all out defensive stand. There is only one exception. They will slightly back off of an adversary to more safely pound him with supporting arms. This tiny pullback is normally accomplished *en masse* and with no attempt at deception. Methodically retreating any farther in an attempt to chop a bigger adversary down to size is more Asian in origin. It was practiced by the Japanese late in WWII and the North Koreans during the Seoul battles.[33]

Then Moving Forward Again

U.S. infantry forces are no stranger to advancing under difficult conditions. They will mend any breach to their defensive lines and reattack any objective until taken. Some 101st Airborne troops were to assault Hamburger Hill in the A Shau Valley 11 times in succession in May 1969. Those who died in the effort will not be forgotten. But the Battle of Dai Do was different. Here, the foe not only had his own heavy artillery (with key parts of the battlefield preregistered),[34] but also a ten-to-one manpower advantage. Those 2/4 Marines continued forward after being repeatedly pushed rearward by overwhelming numbers. Their attacks more closely resembled an Asian "human-wave" effort. When properly practiced, such an assault is not nearly as dangerous as it looks. At the Chosin Reservoir, some of the Chinese attack formations were not subsequent rows of units on line, but rather a single row of Stormtrooper-type squads in column. As such, they were quite effective at evading enemy fire, breaching obstacles, and finally punching though U.S. lines.[35] By embracing some of those same skill sets, the Leathernecks in the Dai Do pushes also did better than might be expected.

The Emergence of a Dual-Hatted Formation

While moving backwards has sadly come to be viewed as un-American, it is sometimes necessary against a much larger opponent. Of course, any retrograde must at some point be replaced by advance. Quickly to reverse direction, one must use the same formation and movement method to both come and go. Some Asians have rearward-moving defenses that can be instantly turned into forward-moving assaults.

On Guadalcanal's Mount Austin, Carlson's Mao-oriented Raiders had also used a dual-hatted formation. Theirs was a cluster of company-sized perimeters that could either function as an offensive patrol base probe or defensive strongpoint matrix.

After the initial attack on Dai Do, Golf Company unconsciously developed a similar capability. First, it allowed its various components to cover each other by fire while randomly moving backwards. Then, it formed an essentially linear defense. (Such a thing would have been quite a help to realignment.) Finally, it (like Echo) allowed its various components randomly to advance.[36] The forward phase of this impromptu evolution was like a "hurry-up" or "no-huddle" offense in football. It may be common on America's gridirons, but extremely rare in its infantry exercises. American outfits much prefer to shift location as a group.

> Capt. Vargas led a fighting withdrawal to the eastern tip of Dai Do . . . and G/2/4 formed *a hasty, back-to-back [two-tiered and essentially linear] perimeter* behind the burial mounds of the village cemetery. . . .
>
> Except for this small last-stand position of grunts, the NVA had reoccupied Dai Do. To retake it, Capt. James E. Livingston and E/2/4 launched a fresh attack from An Lac on the morning of May 2. Enemy fire was again devastating and Marine casualties high, but the *up-and-down assault line* was able to breach the first hedgerow, *a fire team here, a squad there.* [Italics added.] [37]
>
> — *Leatherneck,* August 1994

Gradually More Sophisticated "Fire and Movement"?

Prior to the battle, 2/4's standard procedure for an objective in open terrain was almost certainly "two up and one back." If the first two platoons couldn't get in, then the reserve was summoned. This is what Golf did during the 1 May assault on Dai Do (using the reserve as a base of fire). Echo did it there again on the 2 May (assaulting with the reserve while the others covered.) [38] Echo, after all, had already assaulted An My *en masse,* and Hotel done likewise with Dong Huan.[39]

As the battle progressed, there were fewer examples of whole-units firing while moving forward on line, and more of squads, fire teams, and buddy teams taking turns covering and moving. Not only was the latter more effective under the circumstances, but the enemy was also doing it.

"Fire and movement" has been a familiar concept to the Marines for quite some time. Yet, it is so hard to accomplish with many elements at once that few platoons can do it with fire teams, much less buddy teams. Through lack of practice, they invariably make two mistakes: (1) not staying on line; and (2) not maintaining the same interval between teams (bunching up in the middle.) [40] So, as with Carlson's fire team concept, highly decentralized "fire and movement" is mostly an Asian capability.

In July 1968, NVA regulars were observed leapfrogging forward in fire-team-sized (three-man) rushes on Operation "Buffalo" just south of the DMZ.[41] They must have been doing likewise at Dai Do. When the Marines saw how effective it was, they almost certainly tried to emulate it. On the very first night of the battle, Golf had witnessed the following:

> The NVA . . . came at the grunts there as shadows that leapfrogged forward in the moments of darkness between illumination rounds—darting, dropping down, then popping up to fire AK47s.[42]

To assault Golf's perimeter, those NVA were almost certainly using randomly moving fire team columns that were roughly on line. During the first enemy counterattack on Hotel and Echo inside Dinh To, the opposition force was observed "rushing out of the brush in squad-sized groups."[43] Thus, assault element size may have been inversely proportional to the amount of resistance expected. As the Red Chinese volunteers had done—while simulating human waves—at the Chosin Reservoir,[44] the NVA were assaulting in tiny columns. Every Chinese squad of the period had its own machinegun,[45] so gradually advancing machineguns should come as no surprise at Dai Do.

> The NVA leapfrogged forward as the Marines withdrew, and at one point Livingston saw a 12.7mm. machinegun that had been brought forward and set up behind a berm.[46]
>
> — *Leatherneck,* August 1994

Within the "Overview of the Dai Do Engagement" paragraph lies the proof of how 2/4's fire-and-movement skills improved over the course of the battle. This part of Vietnam was so open that everyone could see what the others were doing. It is thus quite possible that the Marines got better at firing and moving from watching their foes do it well, and sister companies try to improve.

The first mention of this most difficult of platoon maneuvers is when Golf"s reserve had to use fire team rushes to come up even with the two other platoons outside Dai Do. Then, when those other platoons "leapfrogged" in, a certain amount of shooting and advancing within each was implied. Finally, Golf Company must have used some sort of stutter-step, fire-covered movement during its search, withdrawal, and reentry of Dai Do the next day. Echo seemed to go through a slightly more advanced growth process. During its initial attack on Dai Do, "the up-and-down assault line was able to breach the first hedgerow, a fire team here, a squad there." Then, its men "methodically reduced the enemy positions bunker by bunker, spider hole by spider hole."[47] Again inferred is some kind of incrementally moving on-line sweep.

After watching all of this for two full days, Hotel was to attempt more decentralized "fire and movement" during its attack on Dinh To. "[Its two] assault platoons were moving forward . . . methodically in team and *individual* rushes, using trenches, hedgerows, and tumble-down houches *[sic]* for cover."[48] One can assume that any element not rushing, was shooting. How else, during Hotel's assault on Dong Huan, could have its "assault teams destroyed one fortified position [bunker, trench, or spider hole] after another"? [49] Whether or not grenades were included in the Dinh To sequence is not known. Asian Communist troops would have thrown concussion grenades and not worried about who did it. U.S. troops would have had to limit all grenade throwing to the forward-most elements. While certainly implied by the Hotel account, there is no absolute proof that the Marine rushes were as random as they should have been. Still, one can legitimately conclude that the gradual improvement in 2/4's fire-and-movement ability was from actively competing with the world's best light infantry.

A Free-Floating Linear Defense?

Similarly, back-to-back (or severely elongated) perimeters—as

Figure 11.1: NVA "Double-Line" Defense
(Source: "Phantom Soldier: The Enemy's Answer to U.S. Firepower," © 2001 by H. John Poole, p. 120)

established by Golf at Dai Do—are almost never used by U.S. forces. Those that are more perfectly round seem better to comply with its preference for order in all things. What Golf did to defend itself against heavy pressure looks more like the front half to an NVA parallel-line formation.[50] (See Figure 11.1.) While facing one way, the rear portion provided defense in depth and a place for displaced front-line occupants to go. While facing the other, it offered rear security.

Other Non-Western Maneuvers by the Marines at Dai Do

In Vietnam, U.S. infantry units seldom did any of the following: (1) assault a prepared enemy position during the hours of darkness; (2) attempt much trickery during an attack; (3) regularly add snipers to their schemes of maneuver; or (4) assault an objective from two sides at once. Every one of these maneuvers is more characteristic of an East Asian Communist army. Yet, 2/4 still managed to do all four at Dai Do. That's because they work so well. They will continue to work as long as wars are fought.

An Unusual Propensity for Night Attacks

In Vietnam, only NVA and VC forces regularly ran attacks that involved both assault and consolidation at night. Still, there were exceptions. On 27 April 1968, E/2/4 had run an assault at An My on Jones Creek at 4:00 A.M.—well before dawn.[51] It was not of the flare-illuminated variety that most Vietnam veterans remember from Stateside schools,[52] but done completely in the dark. All exposed skin had been camouflaged, and much of the gear left behind (to include the sacrosanct flak jackets and helmets).[53] To be sure, this maneuver was due in large part to Lt.Col. Weise's new nighttime emphasis. Still, its sequels were to prove quite helpful over the next few days.

As 3/1 had done in this same general Area of Operations (AO) along the Cua Viet River,[54] 2/4 subsequently ran more predawn attacks during the Battle of Dai Do. They made the paddy expanse between wooded enclaves much easier to cross. (Refer back to Map 11.5.)

> I originally hoped to move Golf Company to An Lac by Navy LCM-8 landing craft during darkness, to land at night behind Bravo Company, and launch a predawn attack on Dai Do. The two LCM-8s did not become available until much later, and it was 0900 [on 1 May] before Golf Company and our two tanks were aboard and ready to move west. . . .
>
> My concern about Golf Company, isolated 500 meters from the rest of the BLT, increased greatly as it started to receive enemy probes. To take the pressure off Golf, I decided to launch Echo Company in a predawn attack on Dai Do [early on 2 May].[55]
>
> — Weise, in *Marine Corps Gazette,* September 1987

Battlefield Deception

This 4th Marines' battalion was also more interested in battlefield deception than the average U.S. unit. While all armies have attempted ruses, the Communist Chinese and their allies are more likely to do so at a small-unit level. The consummate reference on that subject is the *36 Stratagems*.[56] It soon became clear that 2/4 was also wanted a little trickery. For example, it regularly asked for a very powerful deception from supporting aircraft. By running a dry airstrike on enemy defenders, its people were much less likely to be seen (or shot) during the initial stages of an assault (or retreat). This trick was not used for the first time at Dai Do. A 1/4 Lieutenant had been told by one of his Basic School buddies at the Dong Ha exchange in 1967 that 2/4 had been using fake aerial bomb runs.[57]

> We had also intermittently run the Amtrac engines and moved them short distances to disguise the sound of our tanks when they landed with Golf Company at about 1040 [on 1 May]. Two A-4 Skyhawks delivered bombs and napalm on Dai Do prior to the assault, then made dummy attacks [no-bombs dropped] as Golf Company moved forward.[58]
>
> — Weise, in *Marine Corps Gazette,* September 1987

Full Sniper Utilization

Over the years, U.S. units have normally employed snipers only in an anti-sniper role. Eastern units use them for everything from an assault base of fire to a defensive ruse. There's still a mural in Tehran's military museum showing snipers keeping Iraqi defenders' heads down during an Iranian assault.[59] The North Vietnamese post-war literature also makes mention of "anti-U.S. sniper rings" around strategic hamlets. While positioned outside those villages, those snipers could either protect the entrances to underground assets or, in some cases, cause U.S. sweeps to veer away from the hamlet.[60] This Marine battalion had more appreciation for snipers than most. So much so, that one man in each squad of certain companies carried an M14 instead of an M16 precisely for that purpose.[61] This rather Eastern tendency was greatly to lessen the NVA machinegun threat during one of the Dinh To retrogrades.

> On his own initiative, our sniper, L.Cpl. Jim O'Neill, and his

assistant, PFC Bob Griese, crawled out into the open field to our right and found the murderous NVA machineguns. O'Neill killed 24 gunners and assistant gunners-one after the other.[62]

— *Marine Corps Gazette,* April 2004

Hints of a Raider-Like Double-Envelopment

There had been a partial encirclement of An My just prior to this battle, as with the blocking positions of any U.S. cordon operation. Then, Maps 11.2-11.4 and Lt.Col. Weise's first article show 2/4 trying to hit Dai Do from two different directions at once—Hotel with Foxtrot from the northeast and Golf with Echo from the south.[63] Whether this could be construed as a double-envelopment is a matter of opinion. But, there was one occasion in which two companies did end up assaulting the same limited space from opposite directions at the same time. It involved Echo and Golf inside of Dai Do. For a while on the morning of 2 May, one was assaulting through the village from the west, while the other was breaking out from its east end defenses.[64]

Still, the value of any offensive maneuver depends upon the enemy's readiness to defend. If the Battle of Dai Do had been a chance encounter between hordes of NVA moving south and a Marine battalion, that would be one thing. But it wasn't. This whole area had been thoroughly prepared ahead of time by the VC.

To What Extent Had Those Villages Been Fortified?

"These hedgerow-encased *villes* were patchy with brush and dotted with thatch-and-stucco hootches, and the NVA had expertly entrenched themselves amid this cover."[65] In all five deserted hamlets (Dong Huan, Xoi [An Lac], Dai Do, Dinh To and Thuong Do), "[t]he enemy [had] honeycombed the area with sleeping quarters, trench lines, fighting holes and spider traps, and camouflaged the whole lot."[66] Implicit is that even the sleeping quarters were below ground. To make matters worse, all five hamlets were also linked by strings of "bamboo and bush" (possibly concealing a communication trench).[67] Thus, a below-ground strongpoint matrix begins to

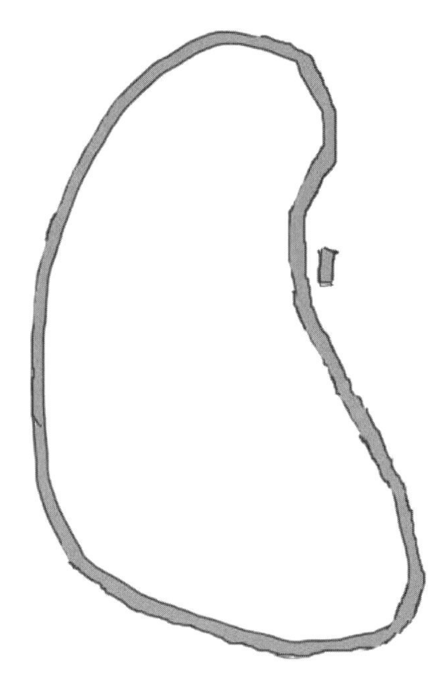

Figure 11.2: Village Trench with Nothing in the Middle

take shape, with each village sporting its own fairly sophisticated defense complex. Though not always developed to this extent, such things were common along major infiltration routes.[68]

The acting Hotel Company commander later marvelled at "[t]he immensity and complexity of their [the enemy's] fortifications." The complex at Dinh To alone was hundreds of meters "deep" with bunkers, fighting holes, gun pits, and connecting trenches.[69] This would suggest a big part in some important mission. While the Western mind imagines concentric trenchlines in a defense in depth, that may not have been the case. Such an arrangement would have invited airstrikes on an asset heavy center. At La Thap (2), a smaller infiltration route waystation south of Da Nang in August 1968,[70] only visible were a perimeter trench (with inclusive bunkers) and nearby bomb shelter. Located in the paddies just outside the one-family hamlet, that bunker would have looked like a burial mound. (See

Figure 11.2.) There was nothing of value at La Thap (2)'s center except for several rows of rice bags made to look like cultivated ground.[71] No amount of interior bombing would have done any good. Similarly, one can't assume anything around Dai Do.

Now to determine what manner of fortifications existed northeast of Dong Ha, one must look at every clue. Enemy trenches were recorded in Dong Huan,[72] Dai Do,[73] and Dinh To.[74] While most appear to have been hedgerow-covered communication trenches between bunkers, not all were at the village periphery.[75] Covered spider holes were also reported at Dong Huan,[76] Dai Do,[77] and Dinh To (in greater numbers).[78] Finally, enemy bunkers existed at Dong Huan,[79] Dai Do,[80] and Dinh To.[81] In only one village were enemy soldiers observed in treetops—Dinh To.[82] Of course, there were uncovered fighting holes throughout the villages as well. Most had probably been dug by the recently arrived NVA. The more sophisticated fortifications had been built over time by the local VC.

"Their [VC-built] A-frame, reinforced bunkers, well camouflaged from the air, could withstand the weight of a Marine M48 tank or all but a direct bomb hit."[83] Within one haystack had been a machinegun position.[84] Others had been predug into the rice paddy burial mounds. Each had its own covering mat.[85] Such things suggest a veritable network of interlocking machinegun fire that protected each village from the outside. There may also have been large underground "hide facilities" in Dai Do and Dinh To. This would help to explain Golf Company's sudden emergency in the former. Immediately after it had "discovered bypassed positions within the village . . . , the enemy furiously counterattacked."[86] During the subsequent assaults on Dinh To, the friendlies also espied enemy to their rear.[87] The likelihood that both were waystations along a well-traveled infiltration route would suggest a larger than average hide facility. This supposition is supported by Col. McQuown's comparison of Dai Do to Thon Tham Khe along Route #1, where a whole NVA battalion had once been able to evade a 3/1 sweep by simply moving below ground.[88]

Among the VC's responsibilities in Vietnam was to prepare future engagement sites for the NVA. McQuown's article infers that Dai Do and Thon Tham Khe had been similarly fortified.

> With respect to the battle at Dai Do, I, too, am convinced that the . . . (ARVN) forces knew that the NVA [soldiers] were creating defensive fortresses in the larger villages in

> the 3rd Marine Division TAOR. BLT 3/1 first encountered evidence of this complicity in the village of Thon Tham Khe on the "Street Without Joy" [Highway #1 between Hue Phu Bai and Dong Ha]. That village was prepared for defense as well as anything the Japanese [had] constructed in the Pacific.[89]
>
> — McQuown, *Marine Corps Gazette,* April 1988

Within Thon Tham Khe, a whole NVA battalion had not only evaded the Marines overhead, but also popped up piecemeal all over.[90] Possibly, extensive underground networks had been constructed at Dai Do and Dinh To as well, in which some of the so-called spider holes were really hide facility portals.

> This search [of Thon Tham Khe] revealed a village that was literally a defensive bastion. It was prepared for all-around defense in depth with a network of underground tunnels you could stand up in, running the full length of the village. Connecting tunnels ran east and west. This tunnel system supported ground level bunkers for machineguns, RPGs, and small arms around the entire perimeter of the village. Thus the NVA were able to defend, reinforce, or withdraw in any direction. All defensive preparation[s] had been artfully camouflaged with growing vegetation. Residents of Tham Ke *[sic],* questioned after the fight, disclosed that the NVA had been preparing the defense of this village for one year (McQuown, Comments on draft, 20 May 1981, MCHC, Washington, D.C.).[91]
>
> — Battalion Commander, 3rd Battalion, 1st Marines
> *Marines . . . Fighting the North Vietnamese, 1967*
> History and Museums Division, HQMC

Whether these villages were as well fortified as Thon Tham Khe will depend on the extent of the tunneling.

> [T]he NVA [and VC before them at Dai Do] had prepared heavily defended fighting positions, including *a few tunnels and alternate concealed routes*, using the terrain as a force multiplier. Hundreds were hiding and could not be seen until we were right on top of them. It was believed afterward

> that the . . . civilians . . . had assisted in preparing these positions. [Italics added.][92]
>
> — Echo Company Commander in his memoirs

There appear to have been mostly trenchlines (as opposed to tunnels) between positions in Dai Do and its neighbors. Though hard to see from the air, these overgrown ditches had yet to be covered.

> The elaborate fortifications that our Marines were forced to attack [at Dinh To]—the hundreds of meters of neck-deep bunkers, fighting holes, gun pits, and connecting trenches so cleverly woven into the hedgerows, buildings, and thickets—were constructed over the previous weeks by the full-time efforts of a local Viet Gong *[sic]* (VC) support battalion.[93]
>
> — *Marine Corps Gazette,* April 2004

Still, many of the fortifications were as well hidden from ground observation as they were resistant to bombardment.

> The great problem [in Dinh To] . . . was the well-constructed A-frame bunkers. These were strong enough to drive a tank over. In addition, many of the smaller positions were dug out under trees, where the enemy had boarded themselves up, roots and all. You really had to be within ten to fifteen feet before you could really see these bunkers, and, most of the time, the enemy would wait until we were that close to open fire.[94]
>
> — Echo Company Commander in his memoirs

The More Likely Starburst Design

While reports of the battle may suggest a series of parallel trenchlines inside Dinh To, there is no definitive proof of it. They were more likely built at different angles to coincide with the vegetation. Dinh To and Thuong Do were not far apart. The latter must have constituted its own separate strongpoint. That would put several segments of perimeter trenchline in the Marines' path.

> After fighting through a series of defended trench lines

[in Dinh To], they [H and E Company Marines] were halted by a large volume of heavy (12.7mm) machinegun fire and a counterattack. . . .

. . . [T[he 320th NVA [Division] troops could [not] have been so well dug in—mutually supporting bunkers, communications [trench] lines, and infrastructure [etc.]—without having [worked on the positions] over a period of days and probably weeks.[95]

— *Marine Corps Gazette,* September 1987

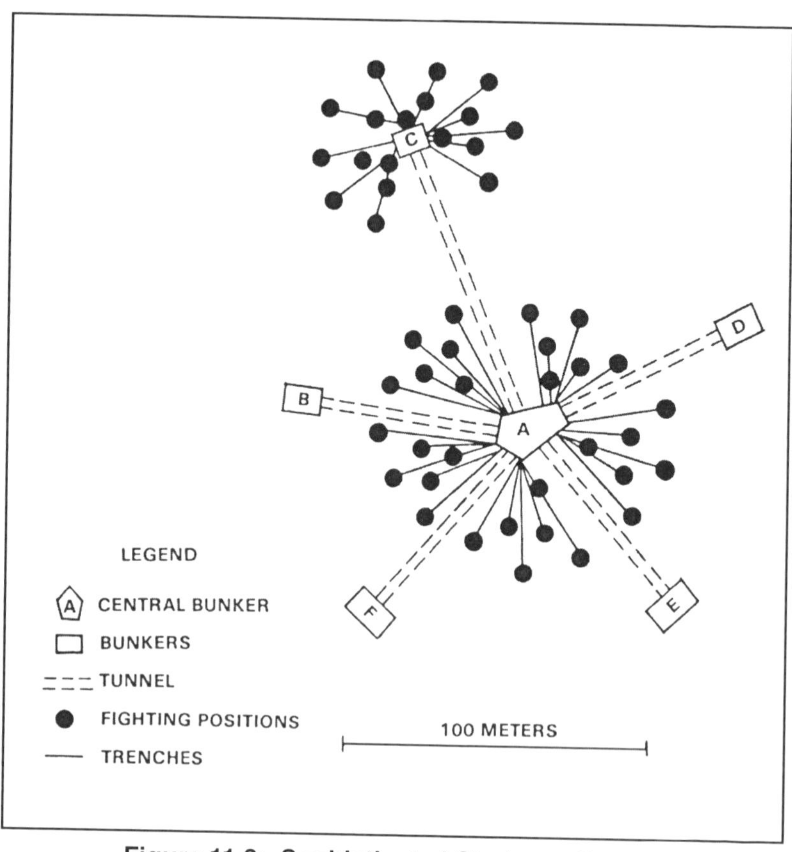

Figure 11.3: Sophisticated Starburst Design
(Source: "Counterguerrilla Operations," FM 90-8 [1986], p. A-6)

The defensive state of the art anywhere in the world is still the underground strongpoint matrix. It is with such an arrangement that local militiamen successfully repelled a massive Chinese invasion of North Vietnam in 1979.[96] The exact make-up of those defenses is a carefully guarded Vietnamese secret. Yet, seven years later, a U.S. Army manual on counterguerrilla operations contained a very interesting drawing. (See Figure 11.3.) It may be close to what those Vietnamese militiamen had used to repel the Chinese. A less "tunnel-heavy" version may be what 2/4 encountered at Dai Do and Dinh To.

All accounts of the battle have lone enemy soldiers appearing where they shouldn't have been—sometimes in front, and other times to the rear, of the Marines. After Dai Do had been captured, an enemy machinegunner suddenly emerged in a rice paddy (presumably from a burial mound) within 50 yards of the battalion CP at An Lac.[97] That's what a starburst formation would have produced, had spider holes been at the ends of covered trenches, and periphery bunkers connected to the center by rice paddy crawlways. This terrain was wet. (See Figure 11.4.) Where there had been too much water or insufficient time to build a tunnel, something else would have been needed. The Echo Company commander even talks of "alternate concealed routes" in his discussion of the tunnels.[98] When the Marines finally got to Dinh To, there were opposition individuals again emerging from the ground at a number of points.[99] A Figure 11.3 arrangement would explain them.

Of note, the best light infantry in the world seems to have had little trouble harnessing each individual's potential. Some might equate this much dispersion with too little regard for human life. However, bunching up around massed artillery and airstrikes (or streams of machinegun bullets) is not all that good for one's subordinates either.

Advisability of Firing and Moving against a Prepared Bastion

It is now generally accepted that a prepared enemy position (one with bunkers, interlocking machinegun fire, a barrier plan, etc.) should only be deliberately attacked. Minimally, it must be reconnoitered and an appropriate scheme of maneuver rehearsed. In other words, there has to be a concerted attempt at surprise. Approaching such an objective by "fire and movement" in the daytime is

Figure 11.4: A Few Streams to Cross
(Source: U.S. Army Center of Military History, posters, illustration designator "p_3_4_67.jpg," Perimeter Patrol, by SP4 Michael Crook)

generally equated with hastily attacking it. Thus, the most tactically correct attack of the battle may have been at Dong Huan, where the maneuver force at least crawled to within standup assault range. While Echo Company had attempted to use the cover of darkness to get that close to Dai Do, it had been prematurely detected. Then, it had little choice but to fire and move forward. In an armor-supported attack (like that of Golf on Dai Do), the surprise approach is less vital. But, the assaults of Foxtrot on Dai Do, B/1/3 on An Lac, and then Hotel/Echo and Golf/Foxtrot on Dinh To come close to violating this axiom. In their defense, it is only with 20/20 hindsight that one can now see how fully fortified these villages really were. For those who directed or took part in the latter attacks, there is also an exception to the above rule. Under certain circumstances, recon pull and rehearsed assault technique can be enough—just as it had been for German infantry in the Spring Offensives of 1918. Sadly, the Marines at Dai Do had never heard of Stormtrooper technique, whereas their adversary had.[100] Of course, once the periphery of a prepared enemy position has been breached, then the procedure of "fire and movement" is again the name of the game. Over the course of this battle (in true Maoist fashion), the Marines of 2/4 had learned some of its finer points.

How Much Had the Bunkers Been Outflanked by Tiny Teams

Those villages had contained hundreds of bunkers, and not all at their peripheries. Thus, one wonders how those 2/4 Marines could neutralize so many between enemy counterattacks. As Chapter 9 has shown, 4th Battalion Raiders found it most expedient to double-envelop each bunker at Bairoko with buddy teams. Might 2/4 have been doing the same thing here?

During Echo's attack through the interior of Dai Do, "several times . . . Marines gained the flank of trenchlines and placed killing enfilade fire on large numbers of NVA soldiers."[101] Some bunkers along those trenches had already come under the standard WWII assault method: (1) keep occupants' heads down with small arms; (2) blind them (with white phosphorus); (3) burn them (with white phosphorus or flamethrower); and (4) then blast them (with grenades, satchel charges, or LAAWs).[102] So at first, those 2/4 Marines did not appear to have used any Raider procedure. But then, in a description of Hotel's assault on Dinh To, a rather nontraditional (in its decentralization) method surfaced.

> To get at one bunker, you had to take the fire from another. By teams and pairs, the Marines would throw grenades, then flank the bunker, and fire up the trench.[103]
>
> – *Marine Corps Gazette,* April 2004

The Raider Correlation

The above excerpt implies grenades were directed against a supporting bunker to quell its fire long enough for the assigned bunker to be enveloped. That takes the cooperation of Marines in adjacent lanes—as at Okinawa's Half Moon. Wherever the roughly aligned buddy teams could assist a neighbor through suppressive fire or diversion, they did so. Because of terrain variations, such a thing cannot be preplanned or rehearsed. It must naturally flow from opportunistic and cooperative individuals. In effect, it was a combination of recon pull and piecemeal assault that randomly occurred across a wide frontage. This constitutes a highly unusual (at least in the West) and very powerful maneuver. It was almost the same as a Bairoko Assault.

The Composition of Those Tiny Teams

When the fight at Dai Do ended, the battalion commander was awarded the Navy Cross, and two company commanders the Medal of Honor. All three had remained actively engaged after being wounded. Yet, they would be the first to admit that those awards mostly reflect what their junior enlisted personnel did. It is true that supporting arms played a big role in the battle and that officers generally controlled them. Yet, it was the troops who assaulted the bunkers, and the troops who performed most of the hand-to-hand combat. Except for a few snipers, machinegunners, forward observers, and acting platoon leaders,[104] few of those troops received any reward for valor (except for the black-fringed Purple Heart). No words can now impart any more glory to their deeds. What was done where no one else could see has endeared them to God, their comrades, and all countrymen. If they could speak, they would simply ask that their tactical discoveries be passed along to future generations of enlisted men. There is no greater love than to lay down one's life for a brother. That's what every deceased PFC and Lance Corporal did at Dai Do. He would not want his hard-won lessons forgotten.

Many of 2/4's officers fired their personal weapons during the Battle of Dai Do, but most of the heavy fighting was by its junior enlisted. The difference was in the closeness of the encounter. The officers had radiomen and other Marines around them. The individual riflemen were more often on their own. Against a light-infantry expert, theirs was a much more risky endeavor. The following accounts made it into the battle chronicles, but most such stories never would. The first is what the young men of Golf endured inside Dai Do after being counterattacked from Dinh To (and possibly below ground) on 1 May.

> The result was a madhouse with some Marines shooting NVA at pointblank range, while others with jammed M16s wrestled individual enemy soldiers to the ground and bashed in their heads with entrenching tools.[105]
>
> — *Leatherneck,* August 1994

The second occurred after Hotel and Echo were counterattacked at Dinh To on 2 May.[106]

> Cpl. Richard R. Britton engaged in close combat, killing four NVA who attacked him in concert. He shot one with his Colt .45 and another with his M16; another he bayoneted in the throat, and the last man he killed with his issued K-Bar knife. Britton suffered a slashing wound to the inside left thigh for his effort; then a grenade landed near him, and it was over. He passed out from his wounds.[107]
>
> — Echo Company Commander in his memoirs

The third and last transpired on the afternoon of 2 May after Golf, Foxtrot, and the Battalion CP were forced by a massive counterattack to hastily pull back. Some readers may find it distasteful. War is not one of man's more noble inventions, and what happens from standoff range is not pretty up close either. An indeterminate number of NVA soldiers had outflanked the Marines through the ARVN sector, and things were not going well. This particular trio had a machinegun with which they were getting ready to shoot more Marines in the back. There was no time for surrenders and such. It was quite simply kill or watch more buddies be killed. This first-hand account reveals what the enlisted Centurian must routinely do while his officers kill people from a distance.

> [Private] Kachmar . . . was out of ammunition. . . . Spotting three NVA setting up a . . . light machinegun in a dugout, Kachmar . . . heaved a grenade at the position . . . . Kachmar charged in right after the blast. . . . "One tried to get at his SKS rifle . . . and I plunged my K-Bar into his chest." . . . He . . . turned toward the next enemy soldier. "I stabbed him, too, but . . . couldn't get it [the knife] out." The third NVA was sprawled against the back wall. . . . "I just choked him to death."[108]
>
> — Nolan, *The Magnificent Bastards*

Deep-seated courage wasn't all that low-ranking grunts brought to the table. Only they would experience—firsthand—how bottom-up adversaries fight. In Dai Do's killing fields, those fire team gladiators had ascertained two things: (1) that each bunker of a strongpoint matrix must be outflanked through the microterrain; and (2) that all infantrymen need more training in one-on-one encounters. It is no small coincidence that their Roosevelt Raider forefathers—who had been more thoroughly prepared for close combat—had gotten through three of the four defensive belts at Bairoko without a single tank, airstrike, or artillery round.[109] Nor is it a coincidence that the NVA would need only a few turncoat airstikes and only limited artillery and tank support to finally capture Vietnam.

Any American commander who now fails to connect these increasingly obvious dots does so at the risk of his beloved nation losing WWIII. Big wars are almost never won without first occupying enemy ground.

Those Generally Credited with This Much Unit Cohesion

It has often been said that the WWII Germans were so tenacious on the ground—despite their losing cause and insane leader—because of an extremely tight SNCO/NCO Corps. This Marine battalion did not only have fine officers; it also had a superb enlisted leadership cadre. At its head was legendary Sgt.Maj. "Big John" Malnar. He had seen action as a tanker and infantryman on Saipan, Tinian, and Okinawa in WWII; been awarded three heroism awards and badly wounded as a G/3/1 squad leader at Inchon in Korea; and already fought hard enough in Vietnam to be wounded twice. Never too "buddy-buddy" with the junior enlisted personnel or company grade officers, he soon became known as a "gruff sonofabitch."[110] In other words, he exuded the same aggressive spirit for which his battalion was soon to become famous. But, Malnar was not alone in this eagerness to close with the enemy. Foxtrot's Company Gunny—Staff Sergeant Balignasay—had fought the Japanese as a teenage *Huk* in the Philippines and was later to dispatch five VC sappers with his Bolo knife.[111] Many of Hotel's SNCOs were wounded in the Dong Huan assault.[112] Then, during the second Dinh To withdrawal, a Golf Company platoon sergeant—Richard F. Abshire—won a Navy Cross posthumously for staying behind to cover his troops' withdrawal. That was right before Malnar was killed.[113] At day's end on 2 May, the only NCO (senior or otherwise) left in Echo was Corporal Cardona.[114]

Thus, as a group, 2/4's enlisted leaders had displayed remarkable pugnacity. That would not have happened without a fully functioning (yet unofficial) NCO chain of command. Thus, it's far more likely that 2/4's "wartime" officers were living up to their career NCOs' expectations than the other way around.

Ultimate Credit for the Victory

All known chronicles of this battle are from officers and historians. For those who never got the honor of serving in a Vietnam-era rifle company, the following assessment is offered. It was not the officers, nor their supporting arms, that won the Battle of Dai Do. It was rather the flexibility and determination of their troops. No degree of charisma or bravery will get average 18-year-olds to reenter the Dinh To meat grinder four times in the same day. Nor will any size of preparatory barrage. To all those unsung heroes must legitimately go the credit. Theirs was to do or die, and they did it over and over where no one else could see.

Marine rifle companies of the period had a group *persona* that transcended whoever happened to be in charge. The overall discipline came from the tightness of their SNCO/NCO networks, but the dedication, aggressiveness, and moral compass was largely a group phenomenon. Thus, the officers were more accurately "extensions of the whole" than all-powerful bosses. Most valued was their skill with supporting arms. There was a good example of this "reverse relationship" at Dinh To. It was when the admittedly brave and already wounded Echo Company commander decided to stay behind to cover his troops' withdrawal. Two of his young Marines physically lifted and then "dragged" him to the rear under protest.[115] The good skipper had done his job; and it was time for the departing body to collect its parts. That those two junior enlisted personnel happened to be dark green and already wounded is a living testament to the lifelong bond between all Marines of whatever background.

For all enlisted veterans of that fight who may still harbor a little resentment against their commissioned leaders for the number of buddies lost, the following advice is offered. When one is up against a much larger foe who is also more proficient at small-unit tactics, there's only one way to limit the casualties—and that is to attack. To limit 2/4's losses, some Higher Power may have encouraged certain officers to keep moving forward. With what the U.S. military still has to learn from the battle, 2/4's Dai Do fatalities may end up making the decisive difference in WWIII. All things considered, they died as they would have wished—at the peak of their game on the field of honor. As such, they will be bathed in glory throughout eternity, and some future generation of U.S. infantrymen made more proficient (and survivable) through their sacrifices. Many a Vietnam casualty would have loved to have that many clearly visible targets before being hit. Strong young Americans do not join the U.S. Armed Forces to be underutilized.

What Training Had to Do with It

This particular edition of 2/4 trained more in the combat zone than most battalions. Just prior to the Battle of Dai Do, Hotel and Echo had both been drilling "their squads and platoons in live fire assaults" at Mai Xa Chan West.[116] (Refer back to Map 11.1.) According to the battalion commander, there was also bunker assault training.[117] Echo Company's troops had even been running in tight circles to increase their physical stamina.[118]

Most battalions did not train this much after being deployed. There may have been the occasional rehearsal for an impending attack, but not much small-unit instruction. Everyone had supposedly learned Stateside whatever they would need in Southeast Asia. Many would end up paying the ultimate price for that misconception.

This unique learning environment in 2/4 right before the battle may have helped its junior enlisted to more quickly assimilate the advanced light-infantry techniques they would need to survive. "Learning while fighting" is mostly an Asian concept, and more particularly Maoist.[119]

Dai Do's Yet-to-Be-Assimilated Contribution to U.S. Tactics

Strict traditionalists may still view what 2/4 did at Dai Do as the desperate actions of desperate men. That would be a tragic mistake. After too much pride comes the fall. Though not directly inherited, an Oriental heritage is still the edge 2/4 enjoyed over other battalions. This made its members more respectful of an Asian opponent. When that opponent showed up "to play" at Dai Do, the men of 2/4 became more than just tiny extensions of a stratified bureaucracy. They knew they had either to excel or die. Just as their 4th Raider forefathers had done against the unexpectedly tough Bairoko defenses on New Georgia, the Marines in each fire team rose to the occasion. To what they'd been taught, they added ongoing experiences. Out popped commonsense solutions to their predicament. The subsequent fire team maneuvers should thus be viewed as what U.S. tactics could usefully become.

The real lesson of Dai Do was not in its courageous acts, but in its decentralized operations. Against this big and skilled an opponent, 2/4 took amazingly few casualties. That would not have been possible without the highly aggressive yet still "retrograde-ready" mindset of all members. As the introductory chapters have proven, Carlson and his original Raiders were also like this. Too plodding an offensive is tantamount to fighting defensively. One cannot be sufficiently aggressive without occasionally withdrawing. As the Raider point men had done after killing whomever they could in the first few minutes of every encounter, 2/4's troops had pulled back to keep from being overrun by their immediate quarries' friends. They had not done so through any faintness of heart, but rather simple logic. Backing off a little had also helped them to apply the big stick—supporting arms—to enemy reinforcements. Another good reason for a little retrograde would be the reestablishment of enough surprise to resume the attack against a prepared enemy position.

Other infantry battalions would have simply defended against the enemy onslaught. A hasty defense had worked well against the Japanese *banzai* rushes of early WWII. But, against the more stealthy and deceptive assaults of the NVA, there was only one answer—attack them first. As always, it was the junior enlisted—and not their leaders—who carried the load.

> The young/old men in their teens and early twenties. They followed and led, fought and endured with loyalty and a soldierly steadfastness that inspired and sometimes humbled we who were privileged to lead them.

> In my mind's eye I can see their faces yet. As B.Gen. Weise points out—whatever success we achieved was due to them.[120]
>
> — first vocalized by Hotel Company's commander and then endorsed by the battalion commander

Figure 11.5: GI's Load Didn't Allow for Much Individual Maneuver
(Source: U.S. Army Center of Military History, posters, illustration designator "p_3_35_67.jpg," 9th Infantry Diviision GI, by Michael Crook)

Another Part of the Carlson Legacy Had Surfaced

While common sense may have produced every one of 2/4's innovative maneuvers, that commodity is harder to muster under extremely trying conditions. Not only had 2/4 just confronted a force ten times its size, but—like most U.S. battalions—it had been operating under a breakneck operational tempo since "Tet." In short, its 150-pound men had been regularly carrying 100-pound loads in near 100-degree heat with nothing more than power naps at night.[121] As a result, their tactical decisions had seldom deviated from either infantry manual or the most simplistic interpretation of orders. (See Figure 11.5.)

But, within 2/4, there had been not only collective learning but also another Carlson tradition: "Looking out for the guy to one's left and right." Its most obvious example was when one badly depleted company instantly responded—without orders—to another's plight. It did so not once, but twice. (Refer back to Maps 11.6 and 11.8.) The result was an instant renewal of that same aggressive spirit that every small critter knows to be his only chance against a much larger predator.

> Everybody [of Hotel] there knew we were in a bad spot, and things were about to get worse. The NVA had reinforced, regrouped, and they were reaching for our belt. . . .
>
> I heard somebody yell, "Echo!" I looked around and saw Capt. Livingston and 20 or 30 Marines coming toward us through the smoke. I could have kissed them. Scotty [1stLt. Prescott] was hit then and went down. He yelled to me, "You got it!"
>
> The Marines of Companies E and H mixed together, miserable and mad at everything. They literally jumped into another assault. We rolled over the NVA in front and shot, blasted, and stabbed for another 100 yards.[122]
>
> — Vic Taylor, in *Marine Corps Gazette,* April 2004

Without a doubt, it was this same zest for learning and joint responsibility that had produced such productive fire team and squad tactics. The fruits of decentralized control were once again apparent. Not only had the DHCB been saved, but the Pentagon had another outstanding example of how better to utilize its infantry. Sadly, few U.S. commanders have since been willing to delegate enough authority to match 2/4's performance. At Dai Do, all bottom-echelon members of a good-sized American unit had gotten a glimpse of their full warrior potential. Like their nickname, they had truly become "Magnificent Bastards." Through them, their leaders had partially displaced a ten-times larger force from a state-of-the-art defense complex. With Mao-like tactics, the standard "three-to-one" assault strength advantage had not been necessary.

12 Small-Unit Confidence

- How had Carlson changed the squad dynamic?
- Was this to pay any dividends in future wars?

NVA units *enroute* to an objective weren't easily distracted.

(Source: Courtesy of Cassell PLC, from "World Army Uniforms since 1939," © 1975, 1980, 1981, 1983 by Blandford Press Ltd.; FM 5-20 [1968], p. 14)

The Hill of Angels

Missionaries call this place "Hill of Angels," probably because of all the people who have died here. In which war and for what reason, no one really remembers. But, in May 1967, the men of 1st Battalion, 4th Marines were about to find out how strategically important it was to the NVA. Con Thien Combat Base was on a 158-meter-high rise some 10 miles northwest of the big U.S. installation (and airstrip) at Dong Ha. Each could be just barely seen from the other. Only two miles below the DMZ, Con Thien sat in a small indentation to that invisible boundary. (See Map 12.1.)

Con Thien was surrounded by elephant grass and three types of trees (Durian, Jambu, and Rafflesia) that grew in clumps and no higher than four meters. Its highest point was a squat pile of red mud. This was to be the key strongpoint along the McNamara Line—a bulldozed lane that had been intended to limit enemy infiltration. (See Map 12.2.) As of May 1967, that lane was 200 meters wide and 10,600 meters long. It ran eastward from Con Thien to Gio Linh on Route 1. A few of its westernmost towers had already been constructed.[1] Any further improvements were soon to be halted to more fully focus on Khe Sanh.

Actually, the Con Thien outpost was a "two-concentric-circle" affair that sat astride three interconnected mounds. (See Map 12.3.) On the night of 8 May 1967, its outer row of barbed wire was defended by an ARVN company, A/1/4, and D/1/4. Its inner cluster of bunkers (surrounded by mines and wire) was occupied by an Australian ARVN advisor and a few CIDG (Civilian Irregular Defense Group) personnel. Delta Company had just taken over the northeastern side of the ARVN sector.[2] Only four days earlier, engineers had begun to clear a 300-meter-wide strip around the camp.[3]

Unbeknownst to many Con Thien occupants, 8 May just happened to be the anniversary of the fall of Dien Bien Phu to the Viet Minh.[4] That might help to explain some of the NVA's precedents that night. Yet, through the actions of three understrength Marine squads with a 1st Raider Battalion heritage, there would be no repeat performance of that debacle. When confronted on ambush by hundreds of enemy soldiers, the first did what most from other regiments would not have. For lack of a better description, it displayed a remarkable degree of small-unit confidence. Something about this particular squad's "chemistry" had made that much confidence possible. First, a brief look at its most probable origins.

WWII Raider Squads Had Chemistry and Confidence Too

Carlson—with his Ethical Indoctrination, enhanced self-defense training, and other programs—had been trying to give his men more confidence. At least part of the 1st Raider Battalion heritage comes from him (and originally Mao). Maj. Samuel Griffith, Edson's XO "had studied British commando techniques" and observed Carlson's training for two weeks before taking over 1st Raider Battalion. While probably assessing fire team usage, he was also impressed by how

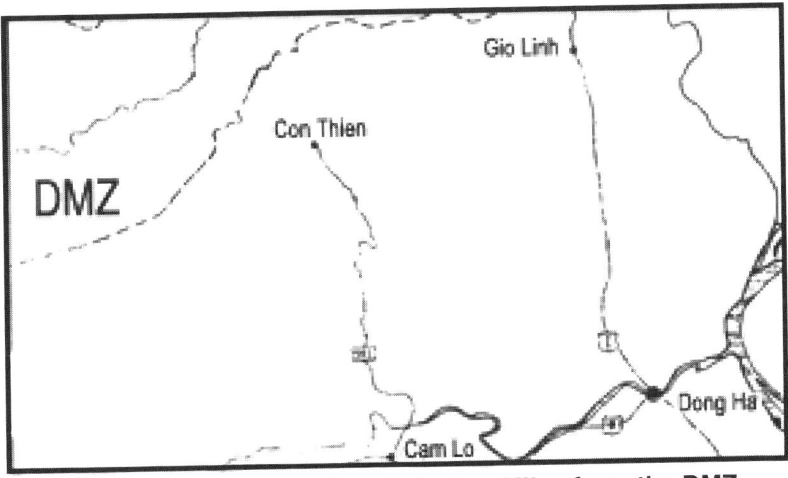

Map 12.1: Con Thien Was Only Two Miles from the DMZ
(Source: Map based on illustration designator "amtrac.org - bullal003.jpg," from official website for 1st Amtrac Battalion)

much the 2nd Raider Battalion members did together. They lived, worked, ate, slept, and trained together. Not only were the fire teams kept together day and night, but whole platoons were sometimes assigned to the same garrison task.[5] This gave them more unity of purpose in all things.

> Carlson assigned tasks by platoon, rather than to individuals—the platoon worked in the kitchen or policed the area.[6]
>
> — Wukovits, *American Commando*

As much familiarity with each other would have given this 1/4 squad more confidence in its own abilities. In effect, every unit member would have been more willing to back each other's play. That the *Gung Ho* spirit had already permeated 1/4 didn't hurt.

When Everyone Couldn't Wait to Get to Work

As late as 1967, 1/4's young Lieutenants looked forward to going to work.[7] They were now an integral part of something bigger than themselves, and their troops felt likewise. Those troops were

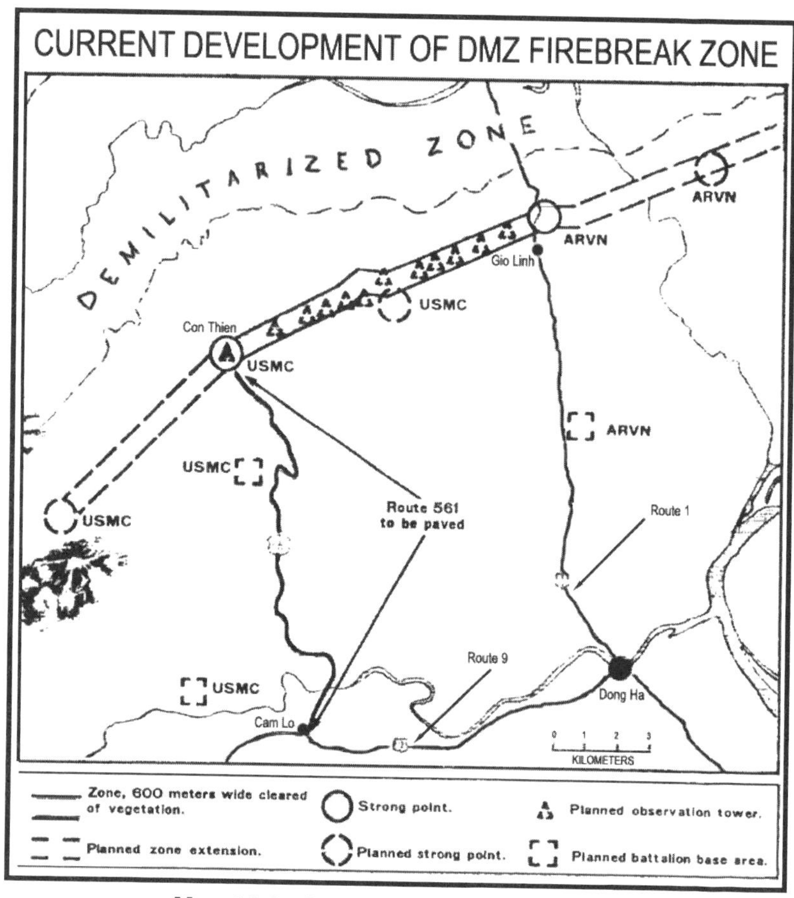

Map 12.2: Proposed McNamara Line
(Source: Map based on illustration designator "buffalo01.jpg," from the official website for 1st Amtrac Battalion)

largely the product of a Marine "squad bay," in which everyone had no choice but to live and work together. To varying degrees, each squad had its own internal chemistry. That chemistry fostered not only communication and cooperation, but also a tremendous bond. Whatever befell one would be endured by all. (See Figure 12.1.) How much of this chemistry survived the two-man room and rest of the 20th Century, one can only speculate. For as long as it lasts, great things are possible.

Figure 12.1: Buddy Teams Were the Backbone of the Squad
(Source: U.S. Army Center of Military History, posters, illustration designator "w_1_9_68.jpg," Ten Minute Break, by Sameul B. Alexander)

Subsequent Examples of Squad Chemistry

Vietnam era squad chemistry was more a matter of mutual dependency than tactical aptitude. People were assigned jobs they could handle. Those who were good at spotting boobytraps were put repeatedly on point. Then, over months of intermittent combat, enough OJT occurred to give each Marine squad a certain degree of confidence.[8] With better maneuvers, and more choice of missions, there is no telling what difference those squads might have made to the war's overall outcome.

During the final Marine Super Squad Competition for 1993 on Okinawa, an E-7 running the competition had the opportunity to observe the "best squads" in the Corps. The one from the 3rd Marine Regiment in Hawaii appeared to be head and shoulders above the rest, simply because of better unit chemistry. Its members were so tightly knit that 14 could operate almost as easily as one. They were not automatons all marching to exactly the same tune, but rather thinking individuals who saw no problem with collective decisions. Without taking advantage of any of the "shortcuts" that are often available at such competitions, they excelled at every subject (though too heavily based on the manuals).[9] Such a squad would have had unlimited combat potential—with some way for its parent company to develop advanced tactical techniques. But enough wishful thinking; Vietnam awaits.

What Separate Squads Did to Save Con Thien in May 1967

At about 0100 on 8 May, a lone squad from 1/4 (with no machinegun team attached) engaged part of what was undoubtedly a full NVA battalion moving westwards along the McNamara firebreak toward Con Thien. (See Figure 12.2.) Instead of annihilating the ambushers, the enemy force detoured around them so as not to upset its time schedule. Still, the damage had been done. What had previously been supremely confident soldiers with state-of-the-art assault technique and some very intimidating new equipment was now just fully detected cannon fodder. Quickly realizing the magnitude of the sighting, the Alpha Company squad leader alerted his headquarters to the impending attack. As the eastern side of the base was to bear the brunt of it, this early warning may have by itself saved the day.[10] It allowed for possible reinforcement and 100-percent alert in that sector.

At 0255, a green flare lit up the sky south of Con Thien. Then, the base was hit by 300 82mm mortar (and possibly a few 100mm artillery) rounds. Under cover of this barrage, tiny enemy elements with bangalores and satchel charges gained entry to the northeastern perimeter at two locations.[11] Killed in these penetrations had been many Delta Company defenders and an 81mm mortar crew.[12] Around 0400, part of two NVA battalions came flooding through those breaches in the wire. As hand-to-hand fighting developed,

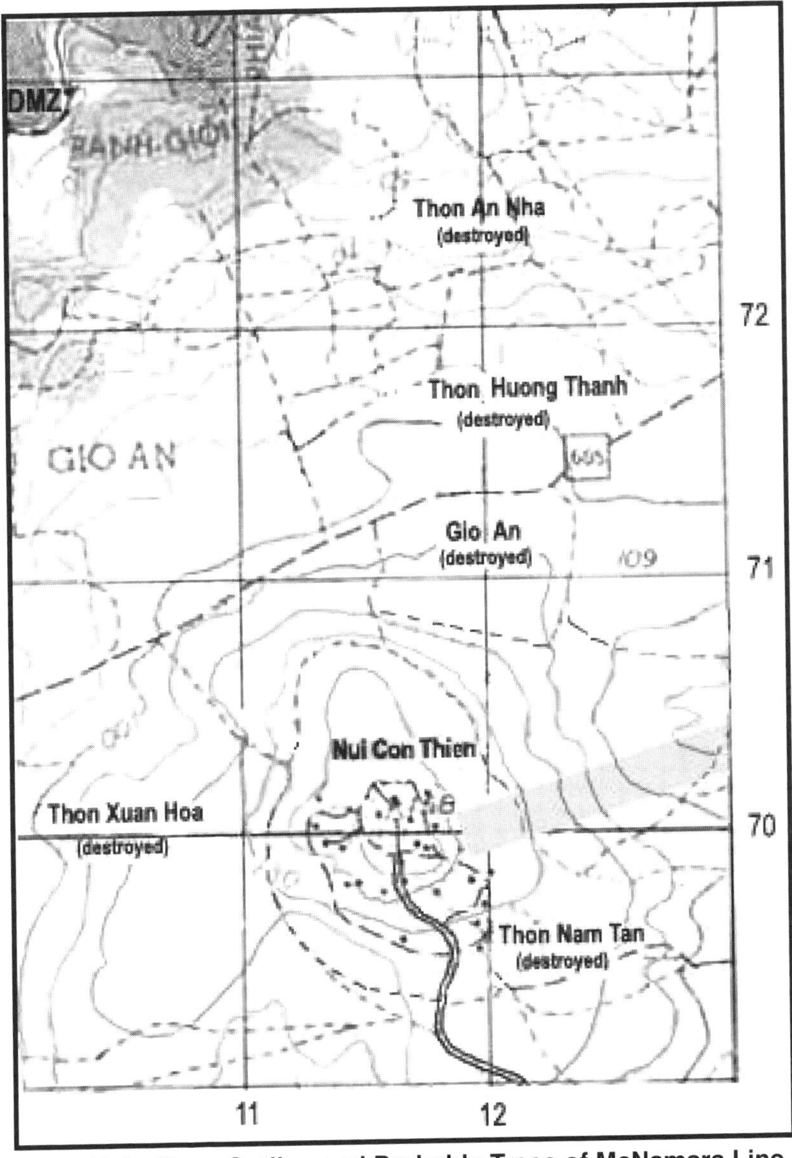

Map 12.3: Base Outline and Probable Trace of McNamara Line
(Source: Map based on "1:50,000 USGS, Vietnam Series L7014, Map Sheet 6342-1" and Lt. McDonnell's "Hill of Angels" article at official website for 1st Amtrac Battalion)

the battalion XO decided to send more ammunition and a few reinforcements to Delta by Amtrac. The tiny convoy came under attack. Aboard were separate squads from the other platoons of Alpha Company. They too were confident, but allowed to choose how best to cross the base.

At some point, the limited supply of 81mm illumination rounds ran out, and the only artillery with enough range to reach Con Thien (the 175mm guns at Gio Linh) lacked their own illumination round. So, until a C-47 "flare ship" showed up, the fight went on in the dark.[13] When the last enemy pockets were finally driven out of the perimeter after dawn, a damage assessment was made. Completely destroyed had been two Amtracs, an ONTOS 106mm recoilless rifle vehicle, and one or two 40mm Army "Dusters." There were 44 Marines dead (almost half from Delta [14]) and another 110 injured. The enemy had lost 197 killed and eight captured (probably also wounded). He had left behind 72 weapons, to include 19 RPGs, three flamethrowers, and three light machineguns.[15] It had been a fairly respectable showing for the NVA, but Con Thien was still in Marine hands. This is the story of what these three squads did to prevent disaster.

The Official Version of the Battle

There are some interesting details in "1/4's Afteraction Report for 8 May 1967." First is the unknowing reference to a very effective technique from WWI. The German Stormtroopers had possessed an assault method so deceptive that single squads could successfully spearhead all major attacks. It relied on artillery rounds to mask the barbed wire breaching, and concussion grenades (instead of shooting) to keep most defenders from ever realizing they were under ground attack. At Con Thien, small teams of NVA had also penetrated Marine lines to make way for a larger assault. Their bangalore detonations had been masked by mortar impacts, and their shrapnel-free satchel charges had taken the place of concussion grenades.

Elsewhere in the Report is a certain reticence about what had actually happened to the rapid reaction force. In charge of the two-squad contingent (one each from 1st and 3rd platoons of A Company), had been S.Sgt. Gustafson. With a love for the troops

Figure 12.2: The Hair Rose Up on the Back of Our Necks
(Source: FM 7-8 [1984], p. 5-22)

that was second only to John Basilone, he wanted to go wherever they went. As such, he was riding inside the lead Amtrac, while his right hand man—Sgt. Amos—was in the second.

> At 0245H on 8 May, Companies A and D with the Alpha [more probably Bravo] Command Group at Con Thien came under an intensive 82mm mortar attack, followed by a ground attack from the east in Company D sector. Sapper units breached the wire under cover of a mortar barrage with Bangalore Torpedoes and moved small units inside the wire. *These small elements were heavily armed with satchel charges* and TNT charges and used them to blow bunkers and trench lines. At approximately 0400H, two battalions of NVA attacked the perimeter through the breach made by the sapper units armed with flamethrowers, RPG rocket launcher and various assortments of small arms, explosives, etc. *The attached Engineer Platoon was moved to reinforce Company D's right flank where the attack seemed to be centered.* All 81mm illumination was utilized. Artillery illumination could not reach Con Thien from their positions at Gio Linh. A flare ship arrived after some delay

> and provided illumination until daylight. Company A was directed to send a platoon reaction force to assist Company D as well as escort two LVTs and two M-42's with ammo resupply. *En route* to Company D's right flank, the right rear sprocket of the leading LVT became enmeshed in barbed wire, freezing and stopping the vehicle. *The vehicle came under fire and the M-42's and one LVTH were struck by RPG rockets and set afire trapping personnel inside. The other LVTH was set afire with a satchel charge.* The penetration was limited and the breach in the perimeter was closed just prior to daylight, cutting off the escape route of this enemy element inside of the wire. By approximately 0900H all of these elements were either killed or captured. . . . The Battalion and supporting elements suffered 44 KIA's and 110 WIA's as a result of this attack. During the remainder of the day enemy bodies and equipment were collected. 226 enemy bodies were buried and covered by bulldozers. 8 NVA were captured and returned to Dong Ha. 43 AK47, 19 RPG rockets, *2 flamethrowers,* 1 radio, 400 lbs. of explosive, and over 100 Chicom grenades were collected in and around the perimeter. Company D was relieved in place by Company C late the afternoon of 8 May and returned to Dong Ha and relieved 1/9 as Sparrow Hawk responsibility.
> [Italics added.] [16]
>
> — "1/4's Afteraction Report for 8 May 1967"

The Intelligence Summary sent to 9th Marines (which had operational control over 1/4 at the time) was similarly vague as to what had actually happened. Still, it contained a few additional details.

> 080245H to 081100H–the Con Thien perimeter vic YD 117701 was attacked with a coordinated mortar attack and infantry assault by an estimated NVA Bn (rein). The Con Thien position received 250 to 300 rounds of 82mm/60mm mortar fire. The enemy assault troops breached defensive wire with bamboo Bangalore torpedoes and satchel charges, scattered pockets of resistance were driven out of the position as late as 080730H with some enemy stragglers still in contact as late as 081100H. Retreating NVA were taken under fire by Arty, air and friendly ambush (D/2/1/4). . . .

> Weapons [captured]: 42 AK47's, 5 SKS, 19 B-40 (RPG), *3 flamethrowers* (LPO), 3 RPD [light machineguns], 100 Chicom grenades, 5,000 rds. 7.62mm ammo, 470 lbs. TNT (taken from satchel charges and bamboo Bangalore torpedoes). . . .
>
> Conclusion: the NVA attack on Con Thien was well planned and rehearsed. . . . *The assault troops, to a man, carried satchel charges.* . . . Small pennant shaped paper-flags, stuck in 6-inch-long reeds and then stuck into the earth were used to mark the lanes through the barbed wire. [Italics added.] [17]
>
> — "1/4's Intelligence Summary for 7-8 May 1967"

Direct Recollections Will Be Needed

CWO4 Charles "Tag" Guthrie USMC (Ret.) was the squad leader of the infantrymen in the second Amtrac. At the time of the attack, he had been on a long postponed R&R (rest and recreation) leave to Hawaii. Since then, he has carefully researched all events of 8 May 1967 and personally talked with members of the ambush squad, surviving occupants of the second Amtrac, and the enlisted commander of the first Amtrac. Here are their descriptions of what happened.

An Eyewitness Account of the Saving Ambush

Steve Hohenstein participated in the ambush. He says it was a newly attached Corpsman who kicked it off when Cpl. Enrique Alvarez hadn't wanted to. Cpl. Alvarez was later awarded a Silver star, and that Corpsman nothing.[18] In all fairness to the squad leader, he may have been planning to attack the enemy some other way when the Corpsman opened up with his rifle. Hohenstein says all claymores for ambushing had been recalled to platoon headquarters (probably to bolster the front lines.) There is only one other way Cpl. Alvarez could have safely ambushed hundreds of NVA. That's with grenades alone. On a dark night, the enemy would have thought the noise to be a minefield or not known which way to assault. Such a deception had not been part of platoon procedure,[19] but it was still there for any commonsense-minded grunt to see. Or

Cpl. Alvarez may have been considering a mortar attack. Still, this is all speculation. The only thing that really matters is that this unsung Corpsman may have prevented a monumental defeat for 1/4, the Corps, and his nation. A pinpoint mortar barrage would not have as adequately alerted all attack force members to the loss of their surprise.

> When the Company [Alpha] arrived at Con Thien on 5 May, Second platoon was assigned on the southeast side of the perimeter, but on outside of Con Thien [inner] perimeter. We spent the past few days improving our fighting positions and the perimeter wire to our front. The old saying our back is to the wall was a true statement and the main perimeter to the U.S. Army Special Forces camp of Con Thien was at our back. They had a wall of wire then a perimeter of 30-meters wide in which land mines were placed and then another wall of wire. And then, the U. S. Army and ARVNs had cement and fortified bunkers that were dug deep into the ground. The firebreak was almost complete now and our positions face the east, and we can see Gio Linh and the Gulf of Tonkin.
>
> The night of 7 May 1967, Corporal Alvarez's squad was assigned the night ambush. The Squad prepares for this ambush with much trepidation, and we find out that the new Corpsman is assigned to the patrol. There were rumors again that the NVA was massing to attack Gio Linh and Con Thien. During the day we observed the new 25-foot towers on the firebreak that the SEABEES built and they had been receiving mortar rounds all day long. The squad moved out at dusk and moved on the south side of the firebreak. We moved to the ambush site without an incident.
>
> The squad set up in the ambush site on the south side of the firebreak. It was a place where the bulldozers had cut away from the bank, and we could overlook the firebreak. The bulk of the squad faced north toward the firebreak. I was facing away from the firebreak protecting the rear of the squad so no NVA could walk upon our position. We could hear Gio Linh getting pounded with heavy artillery. It was not a good night to be at any fire support base. The squad was 100 percent [awake] to 2400 and then we went 50 per-

cent after that. About 0100 hours, we noticed movement to our front. We counted about 20 heads go past us, and they were still coming. All of sudden Corporal Alvarez's [group] started firing to the front kicking off the ambush. We all joined in firing to the north.

The real surprise to us [was that] the bulk of the NVA did not return fire. We just had some isolated rounds shot in our direction. It was like we were an afterthought. They were not even interested in us. We contacted Con Thien about our contact and passed the word that [the] NVA was headed their way, and they said stay in place and hold what we have. It was at this time I wished we had a gun team attached to provide additional firepower. I was . . . [more] wishing we were back at the perimeter than here at that moment.

We heard movement all around us but the NVA stayed away from our position and it appeared that they had a different agenda. From my position I could observe the NVA moving in single file toward Con Thien. About 0245, it appeared like all of NVA in the world were attacking Con Thien. It seemed like Con Thien was in a hell of fight for its life. We could see and hear the mortar and artillery rounds impacting on Con Thien. Con Thien was bathed in light from the rounds impacting and exploding and then from the illumination rounds from the mortars from the Battalion 81mm gun crews. We could see red tracers coming out of the perimeter toward the NVA and green tracers going into the perimeter. All of sudden our situation did not seem so bad after all. We could see scores of NVA troops moving across the firebreak toward Con Thien.

Puff the Magic Dragon the U.S. Air Force Gun-ship came on station dropping illumination rounds, and they lit up the area like [a] stadium at night. Puff was the best friend a Marine could have when the NVA attacked. Then, all of [a] sudden Puff would spew fire out its side and the tongue of death reached out and touched the NVA. The weapon had a devastating effect for this night's interdiction. The gun ship was firing 6,000 rounds per minute with 450 tracer bullets coming out the gun barrel every second, and it was a stunning sight.

It was a long night and not a person slept. We had taken two casualties during the night but they were not serious wounds. The whole squad was alert and very attuned to all noise and movement during the night. This was one night we all practiced fire discipline. The squad moved into a tight 360-degree perimeter, and we each had utilized great cover and concealment. We knew the NVA would come back later in the morning and attack our position because they knew where we [were] at.

When daylight finally arrived, air support was circling above and they began their attack on the retreating NVA troops. The napalm was being dropped on the pockets of NVA. At this time, we were given permission to return to the perimeter. The first thing we did is sweep the area where the ambush was initiated. We were only able to come up with on[e] NVA body, and then we found a second NVA soldier wounded so the Corpsman bandaged the wounded soldier. Once he [was] bandaged up, we had ourselves a prisoner. While we were searching the area in the kill zone, we observed numerous blood trails leading to the north. The squad also recovered two submachine guns, and one radio.

We received the word that we could move back to Con Thien. Corporal Alvarez made constant radio contact [about] where we were; we did not want to be mistaken for the enemy troops moving in the direction of Con Thien. The entire time, the squad stayed very alert as the squad moved west, so friend or foe would not ambush our unit.

As we returned to Con Thien, we were seeing the carnage for the first time, and we can see how badly they were hit. There were two Dusters (twin 40mm guns mounted on a track vehicle . . . an anti-aircraft weapon) that were destroyed and burning in addition to the two amphibious tractors (Amtracs). There were dead NVA bodies everywhere and the smell of cordite, but the overwhelming smell came from the burned bodies of the NVA from the napalm strikes. This whole scene was so very surreal to each one of us as we walked into the perimeter. Amtracs were destroyed burning hulks. We had heard over the radio that portions of 1st and 3rd platoons had gone to the aid of their fellow Marines from Delta Company when the Amtracs were hit with a RPG and recoilless rifle rounds. As the Amtrac driv-

> ers lowered the doors of the vehicles to let the Marines out who were riding inside [is] when the NVA attacked with flamethrowers. The Marines were burned to death. Off to the side was a destroyed remains of an ONTOS which fired all six of it's 106mm recoilless rifle rounds at the oncoming NVA attack but was destroyed by a single NVA soldier with a satchel charge [who] threw himself against the ONTOS and blew it up. We arrived at 0700 hours, and we were in a very sullen mood, exhausted from being awake and alert all night. We were so drained and in shock [at] what we were seeing. We delivered our prisoner and the captured weapons and radio to Company Headquarters. Even as the terrible events were happening around us, Captain Corcoran still had time to speak to us and tell us what a great job [we had done] to the NVA this early morning. After the company commander spoke to us, he said get saddled up because he needed the squad to participate in the sweep of clearing out all pockets of resistance in and around the perimeter.[20]
>
> — Steve Hohenstein, ambush squad member

What May Have Been Averted That Night

During a CBS News Special Report in the fall of 1967, certain facts were divulged about nearby activity at the time of the Con Thien attack. Apparently, there had been as many as 35,000 NVA troops massed inside the DMZ, and Con Thien had been on a main infiltration route south.[21] The latter makes perfect sense as South Vietnam had only one interior southbound road. It ran from Con Thien to Cam Lo. One of the attacking NVA battalions had supposedly come up that road.[22] The Report also infers that the foe had not planned to fail on 8 May. That date would mark the start of an overall offensive that was to last well into the fall. Up to 100 large-caliber guns and rocket launchers then tried to pound Con Thien into submission from North Vietnam and the DMZ. To avoid counterbattery fire, those guns were being rolled in and out of deep caves. Finally, the U.S. was able to calm things down a bit with B-52 strikes and a ground operation into the DMZ.[23]

This same CBS Special indicates that Con Thien had been attacked by some 1200 enemy personnel that night in early May, with 200 left behind dead.[24] With little more than two understrength

Marine companies at the location, that might have given the enemy almost a 3 to 1 manpower advantage. During the first 25 days of September, the base was not only plastered by artillery, but also forced to fend off more ground attacks. Those infantry evolutions must have been squelched before they could fully develop. Yet, even Gen. Westmoreland agreed that the enemy had been after a tactical victory at Con Thien to weaken U.S. resolve.[25]

The official Army chronicle for the period alludes to additional ground attacks against Con Thien as well. "Beginning in May 1967, the enemy made repeated attempts to capture or destroy the Marine base at Con Thien." As the bombardment increased to over 3,000 rounds per week in September, most of that ground activity must have been sufficiently overshadowed. Then, massive U.S. bombardment and ground operations within the DMZ caused Hanoi to shift its focus elsewhere.[26]

In Retrospect

On 10 May, the ambush squad's parent platoon was to find the guidance section to a Russian built SA-2 (SAM missile) very close to Con Thien. Because Hanoi had used both flamethrowers and SAM missiles to support its attack on that base,[27] it almost certainly intended to take and hold it for a while. Word of flamethrowers inside a U.S. perimeter was initially suppressed. In fact, the official Vietnam War chronicle still talks of the lead Amtrac "running over a satchel charge." One of its photograph captions has the first Amtrac being "hit by mortars" and the second "entangled in barbed wire." Luckily, that same chronicle also admits to the capture of three flamethrowers.[28] Such is the nature of top-down government agencies. Their constant avoidance of embarrassment makes deficiencies harder to fix.

Still, great things had been done by those who seldom get any credit. There would be no new Dien Bien Phu. Many of the NVA attackers to be killed that night had just been bandaged,[29] so the ambushers may have hurt more people than they thought. Besides the God-sent Corpsman, their patrol had included Enrique Alvarez, Sam Briceno, Steve Hohenstein, and John Brown. Some of the following were also there: Kennedy, Wasick, Kent, Hogge, Carroll, Stanley, Pinette, Wade, and Constantine.[30] Both Edson and Carlson would have been proud of their gutsy effort.

Ill-Fated Relief Force May Have Discouraged the Attackers

Though fully warned, the eastern part of the complex had still been penetrated around 0300. Then, despite the problems with the rapid reaction force, the battle started shifting in the defenders' favor. Perhaps, their relief column had done its job after all. These were not ordinary LVTs, but rather LVTHs. The difference is a big gun barrel on top. On a dark night to overly sensitized assault troops, those Dusters and LVTHs must have looked like a whole platoon of heavy tanks coming down the hill at them. Even after all tracked vehicles were disabled, their surviving occupants keep fighting. As such, they may have forestalled an assault on the CIDG's inner perimeter. From such a commanding position, the NVA might have consolidated the base.

More Direct Recollections

There are two eyewitness accounts of the first Amtrac's fate. They come from Cpl. Aldo Betta, the vehicle commander and Lt. Patrick J. McDonnell, his Platoon Leader.

Betta remembers the Platoon Leader being aboard his vehicle when it was hit by an RPG. "The Amtrac driver was told to turn to the right, and the engine stopped." Then, Cpl. Betta crawled over to the driver's hatch. As the driver was wounded, he reached down and released the [compartment] door. After it dropped, the enemy flamethrower showed up. He pulled the driver out of the seat and down to the ground on the left side of the Amtrac. The machinegunner followed them. Small-arms fire was coming from the same place inside the perimeter that the RPG had. All three men soon moved to the other side of the Amtrac's rear. No one knew where the Lieutenant had gone. Meanwhile, the three soldiers aboard the trailing M-42 Duster had all been killed or wounded without firing a shot.[31]

To the best of Cpl. Betta's knowledge, all the Marines in the first Amtrac had either died inside or while coming out from gunfire and flame. The second Amtrac had been hit by a 57mm recoilless rifle. When its driver dropped the door, a second 57mm round entered the opening. That explosion killed some Marines. Then, others were engulfed by a second flamethrower. Among the wounded survivors were John McCoy, Bob Frederick, and Rick Gonyea.[32]

When later asked specific questions about the incident, Cpl. Betta said that his Amtrac platoon had been on the south side of the Con Thien complex near the helicopter pad when the call for support came in. Then, the Platoon Leader took over the commander's cupola on his Amtrac and established radio contact with the 1/4 Command Group. The order of march was to be one Amtrac, a M-42 Duster, another Amtrac, and then the other Duster. When the relief column ran into trouble, fire was coming from "the left (west) inside the perimeter, the front (north), and . . . outside of the perimeter (east)." Betta indicates the lead Amtrac then stopped because of an RPG hit to its left front, and not any tangle of barbed wire or command to do so. It had concurrently been the target of automatic weapons fire. "The flamethrower appeared from nowhere, and as soon as [the] ramp dropped we saw flames. I assisted the driver out of the top hatch of the Amtrac. The flames were everywhere." Then, enemy combatants came at the vehicles "from the left front [northwest direction]," and the three Amtrackers were forced to fight for their lives. Sadly, Betta's two men would never see another dawn. They were PFC Larry Milton Langan and Cpl. David Luhver Cleveland.[33]

> [T]here was lots of gunfire and explosions about 0300 hours. Everyone was alert, had our combat gear, and . . . [was providing] security for our tracks. When the NVA hit Con Thien, our Amtracs were parked near the Helo Pad, which was located on the southwest side of the perimeter. We were not part of the proper perimeter but inside; we were self-contained. No one knew what was happening until S.Sgt. Streck told me and Cpl. French to get saddled up and get the Amtracs ready. We were to take ammo and Marines to the other side of the perimeter. I was informed that my Amtrac was to take point and that Lt. McDonnell was riding with me and taking command of the relief convoy.
>
> Ammunition and grenades were staged inside my Amtrac. A grunt S.Sgt. [Gustafson] brought the Marines to our area, and they entered the Amtrac. I could tell they really did not like the idea of being inside the Amtrac and I do not blame them, and that is the main reason I rode on top of my track. I was scared of what we were going into,

and I could only imagine what they were going through down below. I do not remember how many Marines we carried that night but I do not believe it was . . . more than eleven. . . .

I could not believe the M-42 duster was going to follow us, when they should have taken the point with all the firepower mounted on each to clear the way. They could have made a wide open path for us to move especially with the Marines inside. Lt. McDonnell took my position inside the Amtrac where the copula was, and I had to sit on top with Cpl. Cleveland. PFC Langan was the Amtrac operator. Lt. McDonnell maintained radio contact with the Bravo Command Group [1/4 Headquarters].

As we were moving northeast toward Delta Company positions there was big flash of light and a[n] explosion and we were stopped. We did not realize that the weapons fire was coming from the west side (which is inside the perimeter) and we were on the east side. As soon as we were hit, I moved to the driver and instructed him to drop the ramp. The driver was having trouble, so I reached down and assisted him to drop the ramp. The flamethrower appeared from nowhere, and as soon as the ramp dropped we saw flames. I assisted the driver out of the top hatch of the Amtrac, and the flames were everywhere.

Once the flames engulfed the front of the Amtrac, I was able to get the driver and the gunner off the track. We were just trying to stay alive. There were hundreds of rounds pinging all over the place.

The NVA came from the left front (northwest direction—from inside and outside of the perimeter). . . . Lt. McDonnell disappeared when the RPG impacted the Amtrac. The Lt. was in the commander's position in the Amtrac. I was on top of the Amtrac with the Gunner. The gunner, the driver, and I slid off the Amtrac on the side of the perimeter but that was the side . . . where the NVA was firing from.

The NVA occupied the fighting positions . . . which the ARVN had vacated on the 7th of May. The NVA was to our front, to the left and the right. The three of us were

> fighting for our lives that night, . . . and we were hit by bullets, shrapnel and had burns. The Amtrac driver died of his wounds, and the gunner was seriously wounded. We had run out of ammo for our weapons. Cpl. Cleveland passed away, and I could not get help for either one of them.
>
> I was informed later that Lt. McDonnell and I were the only ones to survive from the first Amtrac. I heard all the Marines died inside. But later [I] found out three Marines did exit the Amtrac, but I do not know who survived.[34]
>
> — Cpl. Aldo Betta
> Enlisted commander of lead Amtrac

Lieutenant's Account Helps to Unravel Enemy Method

Years after the event, Lt. McDonnell—who had been riding the lead Amtrac—describes the experience. Of particular note is his reference to enemy concussion grenades. No Marine of this era had any inkling that such things were a distinct indicator of advanced assault technique. Those NVA soldiers were all carrying both satchel charges and Chicom grenades. They had undoubtedly been told to toss the former into a Marine position if possible, but minimally to keep enough of them exploding to keep up the impression of a mortar barrage. (Chicoms aren't as loud as 82mm mortar rounds.)

Some of those alleged 300 mortar impacts had undoubtedly been the random detonations of shrapnel-free satchel charges. As the Delta Company personnel hunkered down in their perimeter trench to escape the supposed shelling, those at the point of attack may have been bayoneted. Tag Guthrie remembers many being found dead in their holes.[35] The Lieutenant's statement further shows that the initial mortar barrage was almost immediately "extended" to the south side of the base. This could mean the initial concentration had been shifted (so as not to harm the assault troops), and the slackening in noise taken up by satchel charges.

In addition, Lt. McDonnell makes mention of another breach in the lines—where Delta Company's left flank tied in with the northern contingent of ARVNs.

Con Thien . . . was known as the Hill of Angels. . . . Most of the surrounding villages were abandoned. A road ran south [to] where it intersected Route 561, the road we had encountered on the Strip.

At the intersection of Route 561 and the Con Thien road were the remains of a village with several substantial concrete houses. Its most prominent feature was the shell of a large church with a bell tower. This area was called the "Churchyard," and it had changed hands several times over the past few months. Sometime later in the summer of 1967, a Marine tank took out the bell tower, which at the time was being used as an NVA observation post.

Farther south, 561 crossed a large ravine that was basically the headwaters of the Cua Viet. . . .

The defense of Con Thien consisted of Delta Company [and Alpha Company] 1/4 and a company of ARVN regulars with attached regional paramilitary irregulars known as Ruff Puffs. Advising the ARVNs was an Australian Warrant Officer and two NCOs. . . . [W]e set in on the south side of Con Thien. . . .

I often visited Delta's CP on the north perimeter to see an old Basic School friend. . . . Delta's lines tied into the ARVN on their left and with the Strip on the right. The [presumably other] ARVNs held the line from Delta back around to the Strip. The [Marine] engineer platoon spent most nights dug in behind the ARVNs on the north side of the perimeter. We were set up south of the hill, outside the lines, in a separate perimeter. A road ran parallel with, but outside, . . . [the] barbwire perimeter from our compound to the Delta CP. . . .

About 0300 on the 8th of May, an extremely intense and sustained mortar barrage hit Delta's lines. Soon after, as we monitored the net, we heard Captain . . . [Juul] advise the 1/4 XO that he had NVA in the wire. . . .

Over the next ten to fifteen minutes, as the mortars kept coming—*now on us as well,* it became evident that Delta was being penetrated. The NVA were through the wire and throwing satchel charges in Delta's bunkers and trenchlines. . . . *Captain . . . [John F. Juul] reported that they were holding their own, but he thought the NVA had breached the line where they tied in to the ARVNs.* He was also asking for reinforcements [of personnel] and ammo.

Knowing what that meant, I told [S.Sgt.] Streck to get a section [two Amtracs] ready and made my way through the barrage to the 1/4 command post and reported to the XO. The Major told me to get two tractors loaded with ammo and two squads of troops. He insisted that the troops be carried inside the vehicles instead of on top. I tried to talk him out of it, but he insisted that small arms fire was more likely than mines, and he wanted all the protection available. Accompanying me would be an Army "Duster," a vehicle with 40 mm guns mounted on a light tank chassis.

With this getting done, the Major and I raised the Aussie Warrant Officer who told us that his troops held the inner perimeter along the road and could hold it while we made our run into Delta's command post, which was at the end of the road. That had provided the answer to the question of route. The alternative to the road would have been to swing farther to the east toward the outer perimeter over what had once been an airstrip and now was the west end of the Strip. While creating some distance from the inner perimeter, the terrain was uneven, with depressions, rocks, some debris and piles of dirt. In the dark, that route would be slower and would include the risk of losing a track. Besides, the closer I would get to Delta, the closer I would come to the outer perimeter—now active with NVA. The XO directed that I use the [northern] road. I agreed.

With two tractors and the duster—me in the lead—we headed for Delta. We turned a tight corner to the left [possibly right] and through the flashes and smoke I could see Delta's command post several hundred yards down the road. I told the driver to step on it and stuck my head down in the tractor to tell the infantry to stand by.

Suddenly, we were under fire and I felt the tractor slowing down. I yelled at the driver, Langan, to step on it, but we slowly came to a halt. At the time, I could not understand why we had stopped, but we were under fire from the trench line. Langan was KIA, as was—eventually—the gunner on top of the tractor, Corporal Cleveland. By this time, my legs had been hit with shrapnel and phosphorous from the RPGs that were now impacting us. I dropped down in the tractor. It was a cauldron of smoke and fire. To this day, I do not know how the ramp dropped. Either Langan dropped it before expiring, or the infantry did it. At any rate, the survivors were scrambling to get out.

I came back up [into] the turret, told Cleveland to follow me, and dropped to the ground as more RPGs hit the tractor. My thought was to yell at the second tractor to go around me. But I was too late. I could see the section leader, Sergeant French, in the turret. The ramp was down and the infantry was strewn from the tractor to the wire. As Cleveland was found by Streck the next day in front of the tractor, it is unclear whether he did not hear me, or was hit before he could follow me over the side.

The last thing I remember was yelling at French and firing at the flashes and figures across the wire. The next thing I recall is lying on the ground between the tractors. I couldn't see, and I couldn't hear. French told me later that he had seen me fall among the small-arms fire and *concussion* grenades—and didn't move, he assumed I was KIA. Eventually, I do not recall how long I was out—my head began to clear, and I could begin to see light and confusion.

As I came around, it was obvious that crawling toward the trenchline was not an option. The incoming fire indicated it was full of NVA. Getting up and running was also out of the question. The only alternative was to slide downhill and take cover in a depression. Once out of the immediate area, I could then try to make my way toward Delta's lines. I recall crawling when I came across a wounded Marine. His leg was in bad shape. . . .

He seemed to come out of it as I spoke with him. He kept telling me that the trench was full of NVA and to not go there. He had been trying to get out of the trench . . . when he had been hit. . . .

We then started crawling as I pulled him. . . . We made it far enough that I felt we were out of the range of

1st Plt. (2nd Amtrac)	**3rd Plt.** (Lead Amtrac)	**Weapons Plt.** (Either Amtrac)
A/1/4 personnel wounded in action on 8 May 1967		
Anderson, Terry L.	Aukerman, John G.	Cassano, Anthony V.
Escalara, J.R. Jr.	Brown, Fred L. III	Curby, Denzel L.
*Frederick, Robert A.	Johnson, Nathaniel	Revels, Paul E.
*Gonyea, Richard L.	Keith, Clifford G.	Sanchez, Gilbert R.
*Guy, Charles R.	Mast, Albert S.	*Sanders, Richard D.
*Martin, Joseph A.	Wilkerson, Loren C.	Summerscales, S.T.
Martinez, Hector R.		
*McCoy, John L.		
Moro, Michael E.		
Nelson, Irwin D.		
Schlosser, Dean R.		
A/1/4 personnel killed in action on 8 May 1967		
Finley, Michael Paul	*Amos, Floyd Lehman	*Daut, Charles W.
*Jackson, Charles	*Gustafson, Donald L.	*Green, Robert J.
Jacobs, Del Ray	*(Jankowski, Larry)	*Harmon, James E.
*Kreh, Gary Harold	*Peters. Emmett Jack	*Huckleberry, J.R.
*Perry, William E.	*Valentine, James R.	*Leija, Mariano Jr.
	*Wicker, Henry Ray	*Montoya, V.H. Jr.

Table 12.1: People Possibly (*Definitely) in Those Amtracs
(Source: Names extracted from the Casualty Lists at 1/4 Assoc. website; asterisk determined from Tag Guthrie, on leave while squad leader of doomed squad)

the grenades. By now, the tractors were on fire and the ammo was cooking off. It was difficult to tell whether we were under fire from the NVA or the burning tractors.

We were in a depression so I thought we should just sit tight. . . .

From our vantage point, we could see the occasional figure get up and run—either back toward 1/4 or toward Delta. Each of them was hit. That confirmed that the NVA still held the trenchline. Several people also crawled under the tractors. That was suicide, because the fire would eventually ignite the gasoline. . . .

Eventually, the NVA began to break from the trenchline and head for the outer wire. It was approaching daylight, and the NVA knew it was time to go. . . . The ARVNs [probably CIDG personnel from inner perimeter] were now visible in the lines firing indiscriminately toward the outer wire—and over us. Every time I raised up to signal them, they shot at me. Fortunately, the depression was deep enough to protect us. . . .

It was now past dawn. At the sound of tractors, I looked up and saw three tractors with infantry now on top, led by Streck. One swung by, and we soon had the wounded Marine on board and we headed for Delta. Streck had reached Delta's lines, and he and the infantry were cleaning out NVA. By the time I got to Delta's CP, *Streck had moved west to where the Delta lines had met the ARVNs. His action was credited with sealing the breech* and trapping many NVA in the lines where they were now being slaughtered. He subsequently was awarded the Navy Commendation Medal with Combat V.

After off-loading the infantry and ammo, I picked up an M14, and together with the .30 and a box of grenades, the tractor crew and I joined the final stage of the battle—eliminating the NVA trying to leave our lines. Some were in holes returning fire, others were merely trying to escape. Very few at our end of the line escaped. Eventually, the firing tapered off for lack of targets. . . .

Next stop was Charlie Med at Dong Ha, then on to Phu Bai and the U.S.S. Repose. [Italics added.] [35]

— Lieutenant Patrick J. McDonnell
Commander of 4th Plt., Bravo Co.,1st Amtracs

What Happened to the Amtrac Survivors?

Not all of the grunts in the Amtracs died. Though severely wounded, about half of the men in the second were medevaced home—never to return to Vietnam.[36] According to Cpl. Aldo Betta, three of the lead Amtrac's occupants also made it out alive. What then happened to them is a mystery. The official casualty lists for 8 May tend to support infantry survivors from both vehicles. (See Table 12.1.) But, in trying to interpret those lists, one must remember that the battle around Con Thien was to go on for another day or two. Both NVA battalions got badly hurt while attempting to pull back across such open terrain. Unfortunately, so did a few more of the Marines—in sweeps around the base. They too would have been on the 8 May rosters.[37]

Specifically, the lists show eleven Marines wounded and five killed from 1st Platoon on 8 May. All those killed and about half the wounded had likely been on the second Amtrac with Sgt. Amos and a machinegun team (Weapons Platoon personnel). Those same lists show six wounded and five killed from 3rd platoon.[38] Most must have been with S.Sgt. Gustafson and a machinegun team in the lead Amtrac.

Of course, such lists are not always accurate under such trying conditions. For example, Finley is known to have died on a sweep the next day. Having just been transferred to Company Headquarters, Jacobs paid the ultimate sacrifice on 9 May while picking up weapons and wounded Marines on his MULE (a flat motorized carrier). Needless to say, he had been doing so within full view of enemy recoilless rifle gunners. On the 8th, there was also a Larry Jankowski killed in the lead Amtrac and Howard Swinehart wounded (presumably in the second). Neither appears on the Marine lists, because they were both Corpsmen. Sanders died from his wounds. Anderson, Escalara, Martinez, Moro, Nelson, and Schlosser may have been with the 1st Platoon squads that came to the rescue of the beleaguered Amtracs.[39]

The recollection that best illustrates the ongoing confidence of these two A/1/4 squads comes from a survivor of the second Amtrac. After the flame event, both vehicles came under concerted ground attack. The ensuing action tested the mostly wounded men. John McCoy had first been shot in the right inner thigh as the door dropped. Then, he took shrapnel in his back as the exploding 57mm round threw him out the door. When the NVA then sprayed the compartment with flame, his legs were burned. Then, as another occupant dragged him to safety, John was shot again in the left arm and his helper killed. His last wound occurred as enemy soldiers were throwing grenades at the Marines still able to fight. It consisted of more shrapnel to his left side.[40]

This had been a fight to the death, and the two squads from 1st and 3rd platoons of A/1/4 had given it their all. There had probably been many examples of extreme heroism around those burning Amtracs that night, but no way—from the hospital—to nominate more people for a medal. Kreh and Moro had both earned Silver Stars—one the hard way. (Neither of their award recommendations hold any specifics.) All other relief force members had been forced to settle for Purple Hearts (many with black edges). The next day, Finley won the Navy Cross posthumously during a sweep. There was no injustice in all of this. These had been true Marine grunts, so just having the opportunity to come to each other's assistance had been all the reward they wanted.

Most Probable Scenario

Con Thien's perimeter assignments for that night can now be fairly accurately ascertained. (See Map 12.4.) Lt. McDonnell says there had been ARVN defenders on either side of Delta. That would mean the ARVN company had not been totally replaced by Delta, but only relinquished the center of its lines to Delta. He

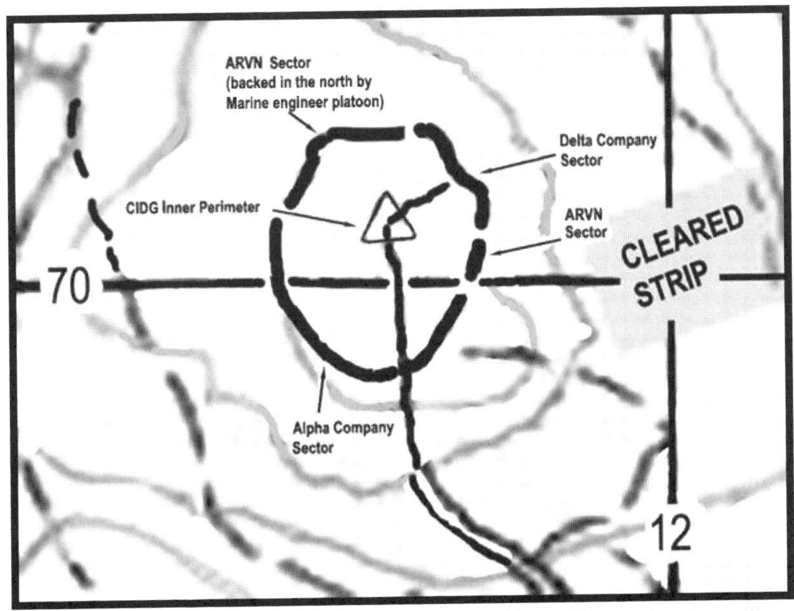

Map 12.4: How Security Sectors May Have Been Assigned
(Source: Map based on "1:50,000 USGS, Viet.Series L7014, Map Sheet 6342-1"; McDonnell's article; Guthrie's e-mails; foxco-2ndbn-9thmarines.com/ConThienFSB.gif)

further states that Marine engineers had been set in behind the northern ARVN contingent. According to the Afteraction Report for 1/4, those same engineers had—at the first sign of trouble—moved over behind Company D's right flank (to where the "attack had seemed to be centered.") In a radio conversation overheard by McDonnell, Capt. Juul thought "the NVA had breached the [Delta Company] line where they tied in to the ARVNs." The portion of trans-sector trenchline that the ARVNs bequeathed Delta would certainly have facilitated an envelopment from that direction. Still, the perimeter wire had been reportedly breached in at least two places, by parts of two battalions.[41] That would suggest a second breach somewhere else.

Whenever a Western perimeter gets this badly compromised, its defenders start shooting at whatever is still up and moving. According Lt. McDonnell, the CIDG personnel in the center enclosure were no exception. Their eagerness to shoot eastward into an ally-occupied area may indicate a recent encounter of their own with an enemy assault squad. After all, Lt. McDonnell did later mention another breach at the left end of Delta's line. Cpl. Betta had seen people coming at his disabled tractor from "both inside and outside the perimeter to the northwest." This would suggest an additional breach at the right end of the ARVN's northern sector.

After the fighting finally subsided, one could say that the enemy had done fairly well. He had captured enough of the perimeter to allow at least part of two battalions with flamethrowers to enter. Besides "rolling up" a good-sized segment of Delta Company trenchline with grenades and bayonets after the mortar fire had shifted, the initial assault squads had taken out an 81mm mortar crew. Their follow-on elements had then destroyed two Amtracs, two (or three) Dusters, a quarter-ton truck, and an ONTOS. At some point, three Marine tanks and a road grader were also damaged.[42] But, what is ultimately important is how the enemy got that close to all that equipment. It's far too easy to blame the ARVNs. Perhaps, the real problem had been one of enemy expertise.

Any blow-by-blow account of the foe's initial assault must necessarily be a guess based on an in-depth knowledge of his *modus operandi*. After bangaloring the outer wire during a mortar barrage, each of the NVA assault squads had probably gained entry to the perimeter trench by throwing enough satchel charges to simulate a mortar concentration. Then, the eastern squad had worked right along the trench, while the western squad went left. Still tossing enough satchel charges to keep up the mortar deception, those assault squads had done all trenchline killing with bayonets and Chicom grenades. Their assault technique had been deceptive enough that it didn't really matter that the defenders had been forewarned of an attack. Some of those Marines' grandfathers had been similarly tricked in the German Offensives of 1918.

Still, 1/4 had persevered—largely through the confidence of its small units. The ambush squad had provided the 1/4 CP with a two-hour warning and the attack's direction. The Amtrac relief squads had subsequently prevented too deep a penetration. Of course, others deserve credit as well. Though most likely outflanked on both sides, Delta Company had held its own. Five of its members (Stephen G. Herman, Peter L. Jette, John F. Juul, Jesus L. Limones, and Ralph H. Watington Jr.) had won Silver Stars—the last two posthumously. So had a tanker in their sector (Barnett G. Person). By wise relief force route selection, the 1/4 XO (Maj. E.H. Boyd) had blocked the foe's main avenue of approach to the base's highest point and strategic center. He had correctly surmised that even if his mechanized column got stopped, the foe's easiest route to the inner perimeter would soon be swarming with help. (Refer back to Map 12.4.) The NVA had be using state-of-the-art squad assault technique, but—on this particular night—the *Gung Ho* spirit of a unique Western force had trumped the *Gung Ho* tactics of an Eastern opponent.

Serving on the field of honor with A/1/4 and D/1/4 at Con Thien had been the following: (1) 4th Platoon, Bravo Company, 1st Amtracs; (2) 3rd Platoon, Company A, 3rd Tank Battalion; (3) Co D, 11th Engineer Battalion; (4) Detachment, Battery B, 1st Battalion, 44th Artillery, U.S. Army (the Dusters); (5) 3rd Company, 3rd Battalion, 2nd ARVN Regiment, 1st ARVN Division; and (6) Detachment, 104th ARVN Engineer Battalion.[43] There had also been SEABEES building nearby McNamara Line towers.[44]

One Mystery Solved

The research had shown Howard Swinehart to be a Corpsman wounded on 8 May, and assumed he was on the second Amtrac. Instead, a personal visit from Tag Guthrie in June 2012 discovered him to have been on ambush with Cpl. Alvarez's squad.[45] So, it was Howard "Butch" Swinehart who so luckily started shooting at all those crack NVA assault troops in the approach march. To him, and all the other tens of thousands of U.S. Navy Corpsmen who have so selflessly served over the years, goes the thanks of a nation.

If Only the Dead Could Speak

What had happened at Con Thien becomes much more obvious as one comes to better understand the worldwide advances in squad assault tactics. But, be warned—those advances have had less to do with applying one's own firepower than with dodging the enemy's. Any army that focuses too heavily on the former may find itself far behind its traditional foes with regard to maneuver. Wherever there is too little surprise, there is also too little casualty avoidance.

A lot of fine Marines had given the last full measure of their devotion during those early morning hours of 8 May 1967. Though far from pleasant, the mental images of the ones who died almost immediately *en route* to the Delta Company breakthrough should not be too quickly suppressed. Still looking down from heaven, those all-knowing souls would not want the present generation of U.S. service personnel to jump to any erroneous conclusions. No one person had been to blame for what happened to them. Organizational pride had simply taken precedence over keeping everyone informed of what other armies do better. Anywhere within East Asia today, the higher-tech version of a U.S. perimeter would be almost as easily penetrated.

13 Bottom-Up Learning

- Would squad expertise create more commander options?
- How did Raider background improve overall performance?

The NVA knew where to hide from "top-down" thinkers.

(Source: Courtesy of Osprey Publishing Ltd., from "Armies of the Vietnam War 1962-75," Men-at-Arms Series, © 1980, plate H, no. 1; FM 21-76 [1957], p. 88)

An Increasingly Distant Legacy

Carlson considered the PLA's approach to infantry leadership to be more productive than the U.S. version. Chinese leaders were expected to serve their unit and its fighters, not be served by them. As a result, responsibility (and not privilege) was the command guidance for all officers of 2nd Raider Battalion. Using an egalitarian and team-building approach, Carlson then promulgated a new way for his senior NCOs to mentor the junior officers. They would do so while working hand in hand with them for the betterment of the unit.[1]

Implicit in this upwards approach to mentoring was the rather nontraditional notion that the higher ranks actually had something to learn from their subordinates. In today's military, this whole syndrome has come to be known as "bottom-up learning." More than just NCO knowledge, it encompasses what each frontline fighter might have found out about the methods and objectives of a grassroots-oriented foe. Collectively, such observations would make an American victory much more likely against any Asian-emulating opponent.

Successors to the 3rd Raider Battalion

The 3rd Raider Battalion did not inherit all of Carlson's Maoist ideas, but thanks to Samuel Griffith, it did embrace a few. Most apparent were the fire team and its uses. One such "use" would have been tactical-intelligence gathering—learning (from those in closest contact) what a bottom-up adversary was initially doing. The Vietnam exploits of 3rd Battalion, 4th Marines—the descendent of 3rd Raider Battalion—will therefore be assessed for any direct evidence of bottom-up learning.

By having a Raider heritage, 3/4 may have been perceived by some to have special abilities with which to expand a conventional format. As such, it spent WWII attached to other regiments and fighting on Iwo Jima, instead of Okinawa, like its sister battalions. Then, the 3/4 that served in China from March 1946 to October 1947 was actually a redesignated 3/22.[2] Though re-activated for Korea, 3/4 arrived too late to see any combat. After being again decommissioned, it re-formed for Vietnam. Arriving there in April 1965, it soon participated in the biggest cordon operation to date—Operation Starlight south of Chu Lai. Then, it moved north towards the DMZ. On Operations "Hastings" and "Prairie" in 1966 and 1967, it helped to counter the NVA's crack 324B Division at the western end of Leatherneck Square. That division had been seeking control of the "Rockpile"—a rugged, 700 foot high outcropping that dominated the main valley approaches to South Vietnam.[3] In October 1966, 3/4 had to fight hard for Hills 400 and 484. Both were along the fortified Mutter's (Nui Cay Tri) Ridge that dominated the Rockpile's northern approaches. (See Map 13.1.)

Next, the battalion went into a rebuilding phase. After being fully reconstituted, many of its companies were detached for separate missions throughout Leatherneck Square. It was then that their Raider impulses became most apparent.

After reassembling those companies in May 1967, 3/4 moved to positions north and west of Con Thien during Operation Hickory—the first U.S. thrust into the DMZ.[4] From July through September of that year, it bore the brunt of some of the heaviest shelling at Con Thien. Then, it participated in Operations "Kingfisher" and "Kentucky" near Con Thien, "Robin South" and others along Route 9, and the fight for Hill 689 at Khe Sanh. As a part of the planned draw-down, the "Thundering Third" finally left Vietnam in November 1969.[5]

3/4's Most Famous Fight Was in Many Ways Unique

Just as the whole battalion had in WWII, 3/4's separate companies were to demonstrate certain qualities in Vietnam that enabled them to do well alone. One was a pronounced eagerness to close with their adversary. It became first apparent on Operation Prairie at Hill 400—along the northern route to the strategically vital Rockpile. There, Kilo was to do most of the fighting, but the battalion headquarters had followed so closely behind for protection that it also came under attack. The following account of the battle is from *Newsweek*.

Shortly after 10:00 A.M. on the morning of 27 September 1966, the lead elements of Kilo Company reach the top of Hill 400 after an exhausting climb. The point man stumbles over a bamboo pole that triggers a claymore mine and several grenades strung from branches. Then, the enemy machineguns open up. Within 15 minutes, mortar shells are impacting all around the company CP. Then, casualties start staggering back across the small clearing in which a 20-yard-wide perimeter has been set up spanning the trail. By this time, there are single rounds coming in from three sides of the tiny perimeter. Some Marines are digging frantically, while others provide covering fire. NVA troops can be seen crawling past no more than 50 feet below this location. Now, the lead squad falls back to the Kilo Company CP, and Capt. Carroll leads reinforcements forward toward a point no more than 100 yards away. All the while, two enemy machineguns keep up intense fire. The NVA now has the company almost surrounded.[6]

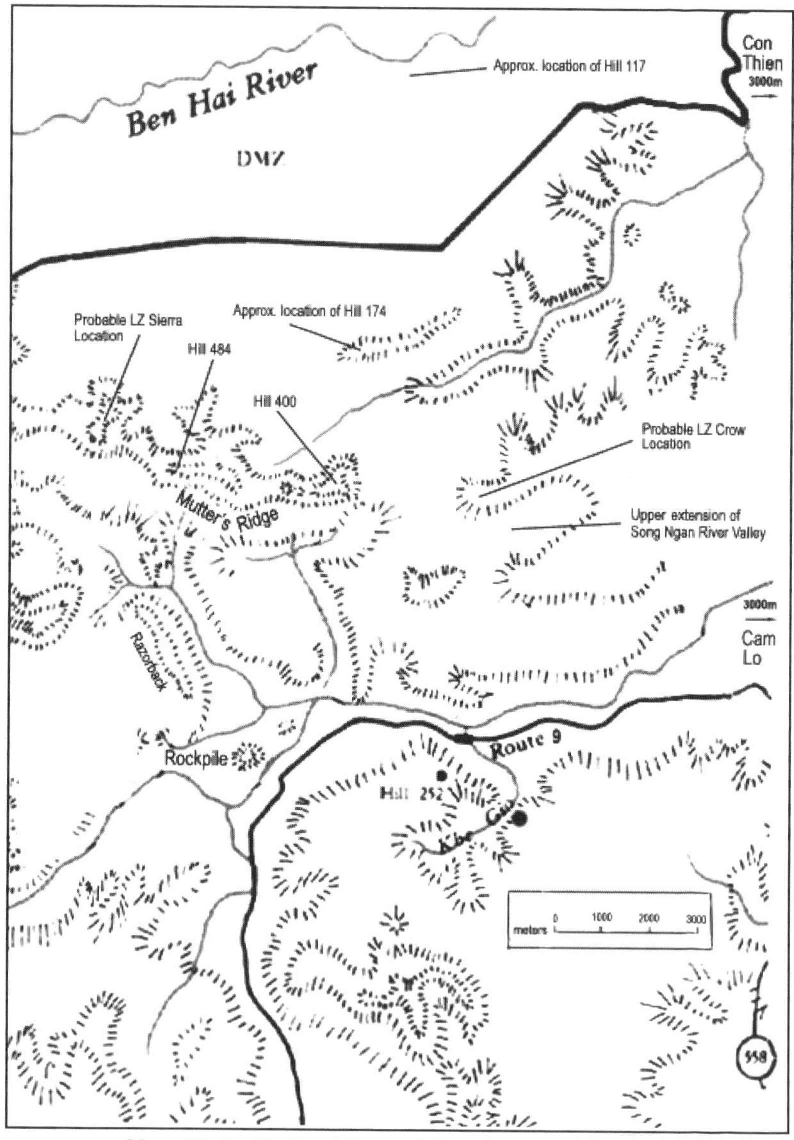

Map 13.1: To the West of Leatherneck Square

(Source: "Operation Prairie.jpg" plus http://marzone.com/7thMarines/MHist0202.htm, http://georgeharrisalphacompany.com/indexp7.html, and http://taskforceomegainc.org/da01k.htm)

At 10:43 comes in the first airstrike. "Not close enough," says Capt. Carroll to the FAC [Forward Air Controller]. He claims the ordnance fell 200 meters away, and he wants it 100 meters nearer. The next strike comes in at 75 meters away. Five minutes later, Captain Carroll leads his men forward again. Out of a whole company, only a few men can go forward at a time in single file. This is almost surely fatal for the point man. The tiny assault force is no sooner out of the perimeter than the NVA machineguns start firing again. Other NVA are still clinging to our positions. The closer they stick, the safer they feel from the napalm.[7]

At 11:00, there is a second devastating mortar attack, then more airstrikes just 100 meters away. Next, Captain Carroll hurls a smoke grenade and tells his FAC to drop ordnance 50 yards beyond where it lands. There are more airstrikes. Just after 13:00, a few casualties are hoisted out by helicopter.[8]

By 14:30, the trailing battalion command post (CP) is also experiencing enemy activity. There, engineers have been carving a landing zone (LZ) out of the jungle with 20-pound charges of high explosive. A couple of hundred yards ahead where Kilo is vying for the lip of Hill 400, all hell seems to be breaking loose. Sniper rounds begin zipping across the battalion CP. NVA soldiers appear to be working around its flanks. Headquarters Marines spray the bushes below the CP with bullets. Kilo's new wounded arrive but the LZ is not big enough. All agree mortar attack is imminent after all the LZ blasting. Sniper fire continues.[9]

For the next several hours, things are rumored to be still rough at Kilo. Its airstrikes have been almost continuous. The fighting has been supposedly seesawing across 100 yards of terrain. Then, at 02:30 A.M. on 28 September, 12 enemy mortar rounds land inside the battalion CP. By 08:20 A.M., there have been three more pinpoint mortar barrages. Next, a "friendly" 105mm shell falls short into the battalion perimeter. The artillery support is called off, and airstrikes ordered instead. Two hours later, there is another enemy mortar attack.[10]

By 10:45, there is good news from Kilo. Several NVA machinegun nests have been overrun. Intelligence also reports the displacement of 42nd NVA Regiment's CP from Hill 426—the protruding lip of Hill 400. At noon, there is another mortar attack on the battalion CP. Two hours later, firing breaks out on all sides of its perimeter. There is also an urgent call for more ammunition from Kilo. Its air-liaison team has just been wiped out. By 14:45, there are airstrikes coming in every 30 seconds. The ground trembles continuously. Almost miraculously, the firing dies down around 15:00. The NVA

Figure 13.1: Drinking Water Was at a Premium in the Mountains
(Source: U.S. Army Center of Military History, posters, illustration designator "w_1_14_68.jpg," Jungle Column, by Sameul B. Alexander)

on Hill 400 may be having second thoughts about continuing to defend it. Choppers are ordered in fast. No one has had enough to drink for 48 hours. (See Figure 13.1) The first "chopper" is driven away by ground fire. Rocket-launching "Hueys" silence it. Then the choppers start landing every two minutes—at first dropping off much needed ammunition and water and then taking out the casualties.[11]

More Respect for "Where the Rubber Meets the Road"

The above account implies some rather unique characteristics for this particular battalion. Besides having a decided interest in close contact, 3/4's officers seemed more willing to learn from their troops than was customary in other regiments. Such things require a certain proximity to the action. In the next account, the officer in charge moves forward with a few of his junior enlisted personnel. His skills at crawling and grenade-throwing undoubtedly improve along the way—from watching his riflemen do it. Evans Carlson would have approved.

> On 27 September as Company K moved through a thick jungle canopy toward Hill 400, the point platoon was hit hard by enemy automatic weapons fire, electrically detonated mines and booby traps, and the other platoons of the company came under intense mortar attack. Captain [James Joseph] Carroll quickly seized a piece of high ground, and utilizing it for a temporary landing zone was able to evacuate his wounded quickly and establish a company defensive position from which he could attack the determined and well-fortified enemy bunkers that defended Hill 400. On 28 September, he called in close-air support to within fifty meters of his front lines in an attempt to destroy the enemy positions that halted the Battalion for two days. Utilizing the shock action of bombs and napalm, Captain Carroll and seven of his Marines crawled to within hand-grenade range of the enemy. Aggressively and decisively launching the final assault and gaining a quick foothold on the hill, he employed the rest of his company to aid in securing the objective.[12]
>
> — Posthumous Navy Cross citation for J.J. Carroll

Proof of These Battalion Attributes

To now confirm a battalion-wide zeal for close contact and bottom-up learning, one must separately assess the actions of each company over the course of the war. Might these qualities be in some way related? If so, the commander who best listened to his junior enlisted personnel might have more chance at momentum. It may be no coincidence that Chapter 7 arrives at the same conclusion for Maoist Raiders.

Kilo Company's Other Adventures

Two months before Hill 400, Kilo's troops had seen some very heavy fighting a couple of miles to the southeast (in a small river valley). (Look back at Map 13.1 for LZ Crow.)

> On the morning of 15 July, . . . [Marine jets] began bombing . . . LZ Crow, 8 km northeast of the Rockpile, and LZ Dove at the mouth of . . . [a big] Valley, 5 km northeast of Crow. . . . [A]t 07:45, . . . [helicopters] began landing 3/4 Marines on LZ Crow [Shulimson, *U.S. Marines in Vietnam . . . 1966,* 165].
>
> Companies K and L . . . [were to establish] blocking positions around LZ Crow while Company I stayed in reserve. Company K took fire and soon located a 200 bed hospital and some 1,200 pounds of ammunition. Company K continued on to their objective . . . [at] 1.8 kilometers (1.1 mi.) south of LZ Crow, but they were repulsed by NVA fire as they tried to cross the Ngan River. Company K decided to set up night positions on a hill 180 meters (200 yds.) from the river. . . . At 20:15, a reinforced NVA Company attacked Company K's position and only withdrew after 3 hours of fighting [Ibid., 166]. . . .
>
> Company K was still unable to cross the Song Ngan [on 16 July], but the other two Companies were able to patrol unmolested to the north and northwest. . . . At 19:30, the NVA again attacked Company K's position, making three attacks over three and a half hours.[13]

Kilo Company had been assigned to a blocking position inside a "major enemy trail network." That position was presumably at the junction of resupply/reinforcement routes. After evicting the platoon of defenders from an enemy supply dump, Kilo was heavily counterattacked. For the next two and a half days, the NVA repeatedly tried to take back "this vital supply area."[14] On the second night (during an assault from an estimated NVA battalion), Kilo's Commanding Officer—Capt. Modrzejewski—won the Medal of Honor. How he did so is pertinent to the ongoing analysis.

> Although exposed to enemy fire, and despite his painful wounds, he [Capt. Robert J. Modrzejewski] crawled 200 meters to provide critically needed ammunition to an exposed element of his command.[15]
>
> — Medal of Honor citation for R.J. Modrzejewski

Kilo Company then somehow managed to make its way back to the battalion perimeter at LZ Crow. It was there that its most serious test would come.

> At 14:00 [on 18 July], 3/4 Marines began to move out leaving Company K as a rearguard. . . . At 14:30 the NVA began mortaring the position and then attacked with infantry [Shulimson, *U.S. Marines in Vietnam . . . 1966,* 169]. As the Marines had filled in their fighting holes, they quickly had to dig them out again as an estimated 1,000 NVA attacked. Company K's 1st Platoon bore the brunt of the assault and its squads were separated from each other as small groups of NVA moved between them. Airstrikes were called in as close as 45 m[eters] from the Marines.[16]

> [A]n estimated enemy force of 1,000 [had] hit two platoons of Company K, 3/4 on 18 July. Although the close-in fighting caused heavy casualties among enemy troops, the 3rd Battalion's forces were only able to withdraw after artillery and airstrikes were called in to support the beleaguered Leathernecks.[17]
>
> — "A Brief History of the 4th Marines"
> Historical Division, HQMC, 1970

It was during this second desperate K Company episode that S.Sgt. McGinty earned his Medal of Honor. While acting platoon leader, he had been instrumental in holding back a whole NVA regiment. Please note the similarities between his and Capt. Modrzejewski's actions. Both leaders were more troop service oriented than was the norm. Such menial assistance to the rank and file was most likely to emphasize that it was they who would have to win or lose the battle.

> [S.Sgt. John J.] McGinty's platoon, which was providing rear security to protect the withdrawal of the battalion from a position which had been under attack for 3 days, came under heavy small-arms, automatic-weapons and mortar fire from an estimated enemy regiment. With each successive human wave which assaulted his 32-man platoon during the 4-hour battle, . . . McGinty rallied his men to beat off the enemy. In one bitter assault, two of the squads became separated from the remainder of the platoon. . . . McGinty charged through intense automatic weapons and mortar fire to their position. Finding 20 men wounded and the medical corpsman killed, he quickly reloaded ammunition magazines and weapons for the wounded men and directed their fire upon the enemy. Although he was painfully wounded as he moved to care for the disabled men, he continued to shout encouragement to his troops and to direct their fire so effectively that the attacking hordes were beaten off. When the enemy tried to out-flank his position, he killed five of them at point-blank range with his pistol.[18]
>
> — Medal of Honor citation for J.J. McGinty III

From these citations, two things are clear: (1) Kilo's riflemen had seen plenty of close-combat prior to Hill 400; and (2) its leaders considered it essential to serve them. After all, how often in a firefight is ammunition personally delivered to frontline troops by a company or platoon commander? That much downward service is a rather pronounced admission that it is the troops who must ultimately carry the day, and not the supporting arms. Under such circumstances, a few rifleman discoveries cannot help but reach the commander.

Then came Hill 400 and numerous other struggles. Finally, on 25 May 1967 (toward the end of Operation Hickory), Kilo was to participate with H/2/26 in repeated attacks against a very difficult complex of mutually supporting bunkers on Hill 117. Hill 117 was located some three mile west of Con Thien and well inside the very dangerous DMZ. This was no small undertaking for Kilo Company. That bunker complex may have been occupied by a whole NVA battalion. After two unsuccessful Marine assaults, the foe decided overnight to go "to ground" or shift location. Though not widely acknowledged, the first option was always possible. Large underground hide facilities had already been detected deep within South Vietnam, so they could have easily existed at the DMZ. A whole NVA battalion had once eluded (by moving below ground) a Marine encirclement at Thon Tham Khe.[19] That had happened in southern Quang Tri Province.

India Company

India had been the first of 3/4's companies to reinforce Kilo on Hill 400. Then, in the early Spring of 1967, it demonstrated another rather unusual characteristic of the battalion. That's when the indomitable spirit of its junior enlisted personnel first became apparent. PFCs don't generally demonstrate this much initiative without being first weaned of their boot camp mentality. At this point in Marine Corps history, junior battlefield grunts still mostly followed orders. As in WWII and Korea, too slowly doing so could result in an uncomfortably irate senior.

> [O]n 6 March 1967, while conducting a company sweep near the village of Tan Lich in Quang Tri Province, Private First Class [Lamont D.] Hill was attached to the Third Platoon [India Company] when it was subjected to heavy automatic weapons fire from a well-entrenched enemy. In the initial burst of enemy fire, he was fatally wounded. However, realizing the gravity of the situation, Private First Class Hill, disregarding his own serious and painful wound, manned his machine gun and brought deadly, well-aimed fire to bear on the enemy. Refusing medical treatment except when he stopped to reload his weapon, he provided covering fire so that his wounded comrades could be moved to defiladed positions of relative safety. Then he immediately shifted his weapon and began to provide a base of fire on the entrenched enemy which enabled two squads of the platoon to make a

> successful assault, killing twenty of the enemy. Private First Class Hill, succumbing to his wound, fell unconscious upon his machine gun.[20]
>
> — Posthumous Navy Cross citation for L.D. Hill

Then, for two whole days in late May 1967, Company I participated in 3/4's follow-up attacks on Hill 174. Located four miles southwest of Con Thien (grid coordinates 063687), this hill helped to protect the northern end of the enemy's resupply/reinforcement routes to Mutter's Ridge and the Rockpile. As such, it was not only heavily fortified, but also fully preregistered for both mortars and rockets.[21] Slender in shape, it could only be assaulted by two companies at a time. (Refer back to Map 13.1.)

Next, during the summer of 1968, another of India's "lowly" PFCs made a rather bold statement about his self-sufficiency as a warrior.

> On the morning of 1 July 1968, Company I's defensive perimeter near the Khe Sanh Combat Base was assaulted by a numerically superior North Vietnamese Army force, and after the Marines successfully repulsed the hostile attack, Private First Class [William Walter] Hester's squad was assigned to search the area for any remaining enemy. Suddenly observing a small hostile group, one of the Marines immediately delivered a heavy volume of fire upon the enemy soldiers and exhausted his supply of ammunition. Reacting instantly, Private First Class Hester fearlessly assaulted the hostile unit, killing a North Vietnamese soldier with his M79 grenade launcher and preventing the remaining enemy from firing upon his defenseless comrade.[22]
>
> — Posthumous Navy Cross citation for W.W. Hester

That is more PFC Navy Crosses than most Marine regiments gave out over the course of the entire war. For someone that junior to win that high an award, he would have to earn the Medal of Honor several times over. Awards for enlisted Marines have always been lower than that recommended. These are very unusual, and speak well for India as a whole.

A little over a year later, while serving as Division "Sparrow Hawk" (a rapid-reaction force for Northern I Corps), India demonstrated the same degree of self-sufficiency as a unit. On 17 September 1969, it was told to help L/3/3 on Mutter's Ridge. The same enemy force that had been giving Lima a hard time must have seen the helicopters coming. Immediately upon landing, India took two dud mortar rounds. Then, as it "humped" around the ridge toward the beleaguered unit, "all hell broke loose."[23] Without a cohesive assemblage of well-seasoned riflemen, it could not have survived that hell.

Lima Company

Concurrently, there had been displays of Raider-like swagger from Lima. When a Marine reconnaissance team got surrounded five kilometers northwest of Cam Lo on 27 February 1967, it was L Company that was sent to the rescue. It had been patrolling with a platoon of tanks north of Cam Lo (presumably along the road to Con Thien). As might be expected, brush four to twelve feet high blocked their route to the beleaguered team. When the tiny armored force reached a point about 2,000 meters northwest of Cam Lo, one of its tanks threw a track. That's when part of 2/3 was dispatched from Camp Carroll to help with the mission. Before long, L Company was under concerted mortar and ground attack (from someone undoubtedly interested in capturing a U.S. tank or two). After defeating three separate assaults, Lima was reinforced by part of the 2/3 contingent.

That much success against so many skilled attackers in thick terrain would not have happened without an abundance of troop initiative. By then, the other part of 2/3 (a single company) and the recon team had linked up and moved to Hill 124—about 2,000 meters west of Company L. When that hill's occupants required forceful ejection, M/3/4 was called in. As 2/3 minus tried to join its company on Hill 124, it was ambushing coming out of L Company's perimeter. It subsequently helped Lima to resist more massed assaults. Then, two other Marine battalions were summoned, and the NVA soldiers disappeared back into the jungle.[24] Still, they would long remember the heroic stand of L/3/4.

While on a "search and clear mission" near Dong Ha some three weeks later, one of Lima's platoons came under the intense fire of a VC company in a village. The young platoon leader instinctively realized what to do. To keep from trying one of the standard (and totally predictable) squad maneuvers, he decided to go after the closest enemy machinegun himself.

> Second Lieutenant [George] Sullivan observed an enemy automatic weapon to his front and realizing the necessity of neutralizing the well-fortified position, he courageously moved across open fire swept terrain to within ten meters of the Viet Cong emplacement and silenced the enemy weapon with a grenade.[25]
>
> — Navy Cross citation for G.S. Sullivan

Someone from a different battalion might have ordered one of his squads forward. But, time was of the essence, and Lt. Sullivan didn't want his troops trying anything he wouldn't. With such a bond to his men, this young officer may have learned quite a bit about close combat.

Then, on 28 May 1967, Company L participated in 3/4's initial assault on Hill 174,[26] southwest of Con Thien. Its defense complex had been likened to that on Hill 117 inside the DMZ. As one of the first two companies to assault Hill 174, Lima paid a definite price. Besides small arms, it had been hammered with 57mm recoilless rifle, 82mm mortar, and 120mm rocket fire.

Mike Company

The theory that 3/4 enjoyed more bottom-up learning than the battalions of other regiments was definitely borne out by Mike. A few days after the Hill 400 fight, it seized a big ammunition cache from the defenders of Hill 484.[27] (Refer back to Map 13.1.) Then, it was sent to guard key outposts at Cam Lo and the mouth of the Cua Viet River. At this latter location, Mike's new company commander took full advantage of his troops' ingenuity.

The enemy in Vietnam liked to operate on a scale that was too small to be deemed important by U.S. leaders. This scale differential was not only in unit size, but also terrain dimension. To one and two man teams had been entrusted the most strategically important missions. Tiny teams moved most easily through microterrain—often crawling along its tiny depressions. To operate with impunity inside a U.S. base, they had only to make the mission look like an accident/coincidence and brush away their tracks. In this way, the Pentagon's wily opponent so depleted the American stock of war supplies and equipment that Congress finally called a halt to its replacement. He had made a decisive difference with his "extraordinary forces"—near-naked saboteurs—while his "ordinary forces" demonstrated.[28]

The only U.S. security personnel to regularly interact with the microterrain were junior "ground pounders." To avoid the trip wires, machinegun bullets, and mortar rounds, they had little choice. Then, while digging in every night, they began to think and talk about what might be happening below ground. How else could the bad guys keep popping up all over the place? While some of those young grunts may have had their initiative slightly suppressed at boot camp, they were still Americans. Having relied on a few of their own ruses to make life at the bottom of a Western bureaucracy bearable, they soon realized how their diminutive foes had been outsmarting American commanders. When Capt. Jackson got wind of these bottom-echelon rumblings, he took the only appropriate action under the circumstances. He adapted his company's strategy to whatever his fire teams had determined the grassroots-oriented foe to be doing.

Before long, the probing sticks of Mike Company's more inquisitive characters became routine company issue. They were called "Mike Spikes." Then, there appeared "J-Hooks."[29] Because the J-Hook was essentially a Mike Spike with a tiny, hook-like head and attached cord, it could be used to safely open a spider hole trap door. That door was often booby trapped or concealing a trigger-happy VC.

At the mouth of the Cua Viet River, there was a sandy and sparsely populated coastal plain. The rice paddies were only occasionally interrupted by narrow embankments, tree clumps, and hamlets. Mike's riflemen soon reasoned that the only possible hiding place for their foe was inside those embarkments. They would provide not only dry feet but also good fields of fire. Soon, the enthusiastic nonrates were sticking their Mike Spikes and J-Hooks into every rice paddy dike for miles in every direction. One day, the good Captain even found a trap door while fooling around with his K-Bar at a tree-lined rest stop.[30]

Capt. Jackson had been a graduate of the British Jungle Warfare School in Malaysia, so some of Mike's methods may have originated there.[31] But others carry a rather distinctive troop fingerprint.

Shifting position after digging one's holes smacks of the School, whereas patrolling in Amtracs is what someone tired of walking would do.[32]

Of course, a certain degree of speed is always necessary to catch an elusive foe. Once, after Mike had moved back to Cam Lo, the whole company broke out into a dead run to try to catch an NVA unit.[33] Running on patrol is a technique that is uniquely enlisted. It has been borne out of too seldom getting even.

Like 3/4's other companies, Mike was also quite self sufficient. On 28 February 1967, it went to the assistance of the previously mentioned elements on Hill 124. That was in the very dangerous area northwest of Cam Lo. Mike then escorted the beleaguered units southeastward through the enemy's line of retreat from the L Company fight.[34] Such a feat would not have been possible without self-assured troops.

Next, on Operation Hickory in the DMZ during mid-May 1967, M Company's microterrain assessment skills produced big dividends. This time it was a fully stocked underground hospital, 10 tons of buried ammunition, and 30 tons of rice.[35]

Right after Capt. Jackson's end of tour in late May 1967,[36] the men of Mike displayed their collective "metal" against a well-prepared enemy strongpoint. North of Mutter's Ridge and just below the DMZ, Hill 174 was its objective. Mike was to anchor every one of 3/4's multiple assaults. (Refer back to Map 13.1.)

> On 28 May, the 3rd Battalion, 4th Marines made heavy contact on Hill 174, approximately four miles southwest of Con Thien. The NVA were in bunkers, similar to the complex encountered on Hill 117. Two Companies, M and L, attacked late in the afternoon, only to be "blown off 174" by a heavy volume of fire from enemy small arms, automatic weapons, 57mm recoilless rifles, and 82mm mortars. . . .
>
> The 3rd Battalion, 4th Marines called in artillery throughout the night; the North Vietnamese responded with 82mm mortars. The following day, the 29th, Companies M and I, the latter led by Lieutenant Walter E. Deese's 1st Platoon, attacked up the hill. . . . [T]he Marines made contact with the NVA defenders around 1600. Enemy resistance remained firm. . . . This time, however, the Marines managed to hold positions on the western and northern slopes of Hill 174. The crest remained in enemy hands.

> On 30 May, I and M Companies attacked again. Despite heavy supporting arms fire and the Marines' use of flame throwers and 3.5-inch rocket launchers, the enemy retained control of the hill. . . . The North Vietnamese, however, decided to give up the contest. Company M reached the crest of Hill 174 on 31 May, meeting no resistance.[37]
>
> — *U.S. Marines in Vietnam . . . 1967*
> History and Museums Division, HQMC

In that 29 May confrontation, one of Mike's weapon operators combined an affinity for close contact with a rather unusual sense of his own strategic potential.

> Private First Class [Henry C.] Dillard, with complete disregard for his own safety, moved his rocket launcher, through the devastating enemy fire, to the main point of the ensuing battle and although completely exposed to the intense fire, he single-handedly assaulted the enemy stronghold. Stopping momentarily, only ten meters in front of the enemy stronghold, he fired his rockets with deadly accuracy at the position. As the exploding rockets threw him to the ground, he quickly rallied and regained his position. Expending all his rocket rounds, he continued his daring one-man assault with hand grenades and rifle fire, silencing the enemy position and killing six enemy soldiers.[38]
>
> — Navy Cross citation for H.C. Dillard

Then, a little later in the war, one of M Company's commanders was to behave more as if his unit had descended from the 4th Raider Battalion than the 3rd. With very little supporting arms, he and his men neutralized four separate bunker complexes in a row. Such an accomplishment would not have been possible without the total commitment of all troops. Young Marines tend better to cooperate when they have had a "say" in what's about to happen. There was no time for discussions here, but—as with Carlson—Mike's riflemen may have previously been allowed enough of an opinion to now assume good things from their officers. At LZ Sierra on Mutter's Ridge is where it all happened. (Refer back to Map 13.1.)

> On 13 March 1969, First Lieutenant [Edwin C.] Kelley

> [Mike's new company commander] was directed to retake Landing Zone Sierra . . . which had been previously abandoned by friendly forces and was subsequently occupied by a North Vietnamese Army force entrenched in well-fortified bunker complexes. After personally leading a reconnaissance patrol to within 100 meters of the hostile emplacements without detection, . . . [he] formulated his plan of attack and initiated an aggressive assault on the enemy positions. During the ensuing protracted engagement, . . . [he] directed his company in the destruction of a series of four bunker complexes without the aid of air support and with only limited artillery fire. When monsoon weather precluded helicopter resupply, he instructed his Marines in the employment of captured North Vietnamese Army weapons and grenades for a final assault against the remaining hostile fortification, thereby enabling his company to seize the objective and establish defensive positions. During the night, the Marines were subjected to a series of probing assaults, which increased in intensity until the early morning hours when the enemy penetrated a sector of the [Marines'] perimeter. . . . He fearlessly led a bold counterattack resulting in the defeat of the North Vietnamese Army force.[39]
>
> — Navy Cross citation for E.C. Kelley

During that same battle, one of M Company's squad leaders also felt it necessary to set the example as a service to his subordinates.

> When his platoon was pinned down by extremely intense hostile fire during an assault on a well-entrenched enemy position consisting of reinforced bunkers, Corporal [Clinton W.] Thompson maneuvered through the barrage of hostile fire, located the exact positions of the enemy emplacements, and launched a single-handed assault on the enemy bunkers, using fragmentation grenades to destroy the positions. . . .
>
> . . . It was during this period that an[other] enemy bunker began to deliver fire on Corporal Thompson and his men. Once again, he personally assaulted the position with grenades, destroying the bunker and three occupants.[40]
>
> — Navy Cross citation for C.W. Thompson

Two Very Distinct Trends within All Companies

Every 3/4 company had certainly sought out close contact. Only at issue is whether all had learned from their lowest echelons. India had produced two PFC Navy Cross winners and then handled big trouble on a Mutter's Ridge Sparrow Hawk. Kilo's leaders had hauled ammunition and joined their troops in the assault, prior to the Hill 117 fight. A Lima lieutenant had personally gone after a machinegun during the run-up to Hill 174. And by watching the troops probe, Mike had debunked the foe's subterranean strategy, before anchoring the Hill 174 assaults. In other words, all companies had honored their junior grunts before doing well in a prolonged battle. The latter takes cohesion. That much cohesion is not possible without very contented troops. They were contented because their leaders had been listening to them.

Most interesting from a tactical standpoint was the episode at LZ Sierra, in which Mike Company had—with very little help from supporting arms—neutralized four consecutive bunker complexes. As at Bairoko with 4th Raider Battalion and Half Moon with 2/4, that doesn't happen without tiny teams outflanking enemy machinegun nests through the microterrain. All contemporary U.S. military leaders should take note, for this—and not any technological advance—will remain the best way to occupy highly contested ground.

There should be no doubt as to why the "Thundering Third" had done so well in Vietnam. North of the Rockpile, it had participated in some of the hardest fought battles of the war. They had been unique in their degree of small-unit involvement.[41] Within 3/4, it had been all for one, and one for all. The "lessons learned" had flowed in both directions along its chain of command, but those from the bottom echelons had proven particularly useful in combatting that era's most proficient light infantry. The Raider heritage had once again made the difference.

14 Improvise, Adapt, and Overcome

- Does this phrase accurately portray life in the U.S. military?
- Is it from the Marine Raiders?

No technology is necessary to detect intruders.

(Source: Courtesy of Osprey Publishing Ltd., from "Armies of the Vietnam War 1962-75," Men-at-Arms Series, © 1980, plate C, no. 3; FM 21-76 [1957], p. 194)

3/4 Was Not Quite Done with Its Maoist Initiatives

Just as the Raiders had, 3rd Battalion, 4th Marines easily cooperated with an indigenous population. Thus, it may deserve partial credit for the West's most progressive counterguerrilla strategy to date. Called "Combined Action," it will continue to be the only way for a firepower-oriented army to defeat most insurgencies. There had been some mixing of Marines with paramilitary police during the Banana Wars in Haiti and Nicaragua, but this program was different in a number of ways. Nor were any of the U.S. Army's later "look-alikes" the same.

> Combined Action . . . seems to have started in August 1965 as a unit drawn from 3rd Battalion, 4th Marines . . . in the Phu Bai area. 3/4's TAOR included six villages. . . . [Its] executive officer suggested that they incorporate local militia units into 3/4's operations. . . . [Plan was forwarded] to III Marine Amphibious Force (III MAF). . . . Major General Lew Walt . . . agreed to the proposal. . . . [3/4] integrated four [Marine] squads with the local PF units in August 1965.[1]

An Actual Raider Had Made the Decision

A former member of 1st Raider Battalion was III MAF commander at the time (and later coordinator of all I Corps strategy). Thus, 3/4's proposal was being considered by someone with firsthand knowledge of the Carlson/Griffith insights. Having helped to protect Shanghai's International Settlement from August 1937 to February 1938, Lewis William Walt may have been one of the few Raider officers to fully understand those insights. Then, as a member of 1st Raider Battalion, he had applied them to some of the fiercest battles for Guadalcanal—Tulagi and Bloody Ridge.[2] From that rather unique background, he must have seen how most easily to get a civilian populace to contest an oppressor. It takes small-unit assistance at the local level, and that's precisely what Gen. Walt intended for Vietnam.

> "The struggle was in the rice paddies . . . in and among the people, not passing through, but living among them, night and day . . . and joining with them in steps toward a better life, long overdue."[3]
>
> — Maj.Gen. Lewis W. Walt USMC

Having won two Navy Crosses in WWII and a second Purple Heart during the Korean War, Gen. Walt was no stranger to close-quarters combat. Shortly after assuming command of 3rd Marine Division and III MAF in 1965, he initiated the forerunner to the highly progressive Combined Action Platoon (CAP). Ten months later, he fully implemented CAP. Gen. Victor H. "Brute" Krulak at Fleet Marine Forces Pacific was highly supportive of it. Having been with 4th Marines in China from 1937 to 1939, Gen. Krulak was already sold on the "Spreading Inkblot Theory," in which a government's control can be incrementally expanded throughout the villages.[4] As this was also Maoist guerrilla strategy, he may have only wanted to interrupt that strategy through similar activity. Thus, most credit for CAP procedure may still belong to 3/4, Gen. Walt, and their Maoist Raider backgrounds. Its design was so nontraditional as to have only one other source.

"Improvise, Adapt, and Overcome"

The old Marine Corps axiom—"Improvise, Adapt, and Overcome"—also suggests overcoming bureaucratic inertia through worker initiative. So, like the Combined Action concept, it may have Raider roots. Or, it may date all the way back to Leatherneck involvement in the Boxer Rebellion. (Refer back to Table 1.1.) In any case, this little organizational epithet has unmistakably Asian overtones. The British/French management model much prefers the lower echelons to simply follow orders.

This three-word formula carries with it a lot of hope and optimism. It conjures up visions of self-sufficient young Marines doing all kinds of smart things. Unfortunately, it also flies in the face of a long-standing Marine Corps' tradition—that of nonrates doing exactly what they have just been told.

The producers of the movie "Heartbreak Ridge" have done a credible job of explaining the inherent problem with strictly top-down instructions. Those instructions take a while to reach the bottom echelons of a tall organization. By the time they do, they almost never mesh with the quickly changing circumstances of active combat. As such, they would seldom work without a little bottom-echelon adjustment. That adjustment is often the result of individual initiative. Whether encouraged or not, that initiative must still occur. Otherwise, no Western military force would ever win a war.

As a result, "Improvise, Adapt, and Overcome" has—over the years—become the unofficial mantra of the USMC. That's what Gy.Sgt. Highway kept saying in the movie to justify his "interpretation of orders."[5] One encyclopedia goes so far as to attribute most of the Corps' magnificent heritage to the "creativity of its people and their success-based attitude."[6] Some of that creativity may have been unavoidable.

"Heartbreak Ridge" had been the name of an actual U.S. Army

objective during the "Punchbowl" battles of 1951,[7] so it carries with it a certain inference. Perhaps, less heartbreak would have been necessary through a different way of assaulting and holding that hill.

There has been no shortage of hard work and bravery over the years by U.S. military personnel. There is very little that some American hasn't—at one point or another—ascertained about warfare. Yet, poorly performing U.S. strategies seem impossible to discard. One can only conclude that many lessons failed to enter the institutional memory. How actually to do things—in the manuals—may have been too easily superseded by former habit or "untested visualization." The Chinese Communists don't have this problem. That's why they or their ancestors have been somehow behind this formula.

> [A]n attached observer has described Mao's soldiers as "constantly studying their mistakes, and *improvising* methods to . . . offset modernized equipment." [Italics added.] [8]
> — Wukovits, *American Commando*

A Former Raider Sees How to Win

As a fitting testament to Gen. Walt's pivotal role in the Vietnam struggle, *Life Magazine* featured him in a May 1967 cover story. That article documented the success of an "innovative program" he had initiated in August 1965. Then called the Combined Action Company (CAC), it sent squads of Marine volunteers into the villages to assist part-time militiamen known as Popular Forces (PFs). "His CACs all had the same orders: help protect the villages, get to know the people, find the local Communist infrastructure, and put it out of business." Gen. Walt was using the new program to win the confidence of the Vietnamese peasantry.[9] It was an integral part of his "Balanced Strategy": (1) search and destroy; (2) counterguerrilla; and (3) pacification.[10]

Because of the Vietnam War's ultimate outcome, the full brilliance of this initiative wouldn't be realized for many years. The flaw in the Pentagon's principal strategy—conventional battalions operating in free-fire zones to search out and destroy enemy formations—had not been immediately obvious. In a statement to reporters in 1965, General William Westmoreland is supposed to have given a rather profound clue to its essence. As a result of the U.S. strategy, the Vietnamese peasant would be confronted with three choices: (1) to stay close to his land [usually in a free-fire zone]; (2) to join the Viet Cong [the target in that free-fire zone]; or (3) to move to an area under South Vietnamese government control [and thereby become a refugee].[11] For all practical purposes, the Pentagon had declared war on that country's peasant society, just as the British had on Malaya's rural Chinese in the early 1950's.[12] But, unlike the Malay Peninsula, South Vietnam had an extensive mainland border across which the guerrillas could be reinforced and resupplied. What had marginally worked in Malaya had no chance in Vietnam.

Thus, the CAP program must now be viewed as one of the most productive parts of U.S. strategy. Unbeknownst to most veterans, it was not just a test, but instead a full-blown program that was eventually manned by over 2,200 U.S. personnel.[13] Though every bit as progressive and victory-enhancing as Carlson's Raiders, those courageous CAP members never received one tenth of the acclaim. What they did may have too greatly endangered the *status quo.* Might an extension of it have actually won the Vietnam War?

> Vietnamese people in some of the [CAP] hamlets still, twenty-five plus years after the fact, hold annual memorial services for the young men who died to keep them and their children free.[14]
>
> — Lt.Col. William R. Corson USMC (Ret.)
> former head of the CAP program

The Possibilities

The Vietnam CAP program was only tried at villages near big U.S. bases. This was undoubtedly done in the belief that its participants could be more easily rescued. However, when under attack from the best light infantry in the world, any overland relief effort would take far too long. Thus, one is tempted to blanket a whole region with mutually supporting CAPs, and then provide any required reinforcement by helicopter. Such a scheme would more closely approximate the strongpoint matrix of an advanced static defense.

The official casualty statistics seem to indicate that less than

15% of all the CAP compounds were ever overrun.[15] Of the 14-man U.S. contingent, no more than a third would have been inside their compound on any given night.[16] So wherever fewer than four Marines died, the defenses can be assumed to have held.

Those individuals had probably been encouraged to stand their ground. How else could they set the proper example for the PFs? But, the enemy often disappeared during a successful U.S. assault (to fight another day), so why shouldn't badly outnumbered friendlies be allowed to do likewise? One wonders how much more viable those CAPs would have been if members had practiced how to hide as a last resort—one of the UW skill sets. Is there something inherently dishonorable in bunkers with secret exits or a backup defense strategy? The survivors of such an attack could have then reemerged—as tiny killer teams—to take back their village. On at least one occasion, two Americans ended up doing just that. Their story must wait for a few of the preliminaries.

The Actual CAP Program in Vietnam

From 1965 to 1971, some 5,000 Marines and Navy Corpsmen operated virtually alone in isolated villages from Chu Lai to the DMZ as part of the CAP program. Though ostensibly pacified, most of those villages were thoroughly surrounded by difficult terrain, booby traps, and hostile elements. Each had a joint platoon comprised of a squad of Marines (with its Navy Corpsman) and 30 to 35 PFs. By 1969, the number of platoons had reached 102. They were organized into 19 companies under four Combined Action Groups—the 1st through the 4th.[17] (See Map 14.1.) Because of the difference in mission, most had been winnowed away from the infantry battalions.

The Four Combined Action Groups (CAGs)

To see how these joint platoons operated, one must look at the missions and chronologies published by their Group headquarters. All four were formed in late 1968 and remained operational until mid-1970. Only 2nd CAG lasted until May 1971. Of course, there had previously been CAPs since mid-1965. The earlier companies had letter, instead of numerical, designators. Then, from late 1968

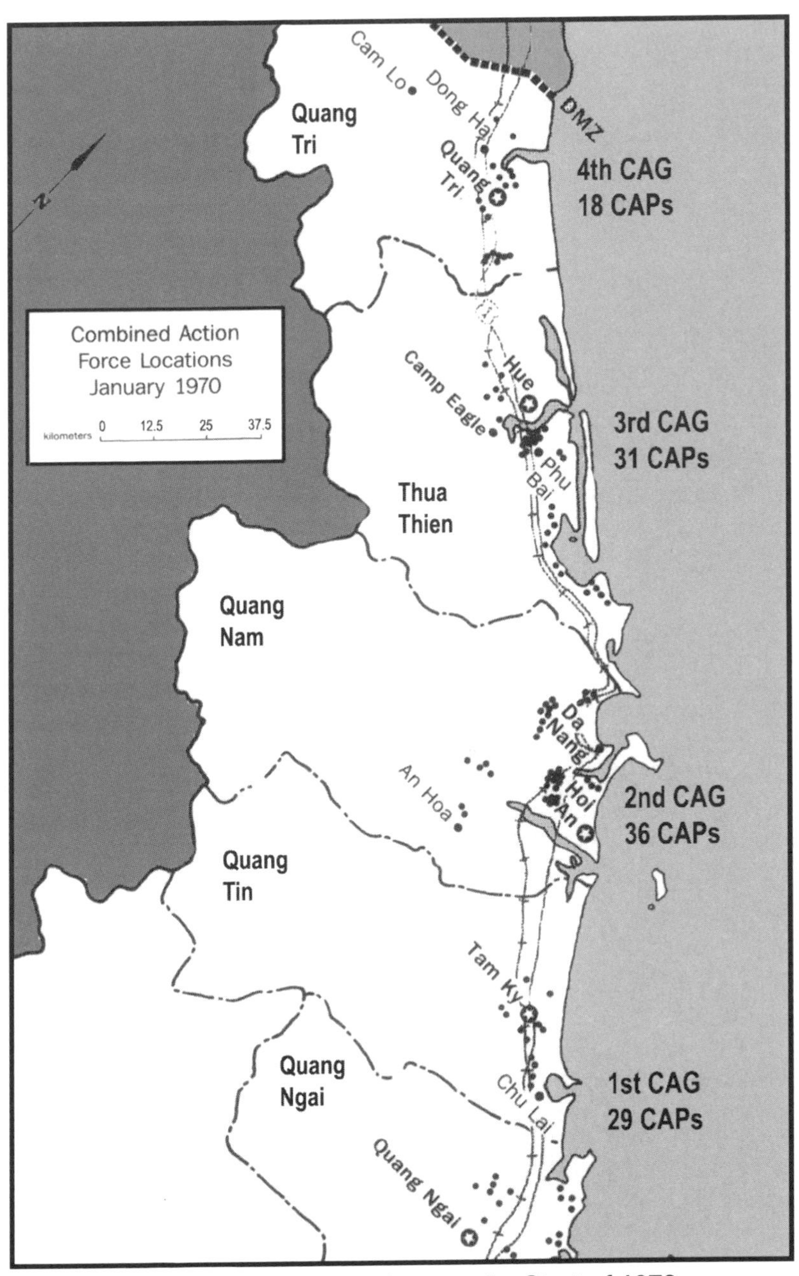

Map 14.1: CAP Locations at the Start of 1970

(Source: Map based on USMC Hist. Ctr. drawing by W. Stephen Hill, from "Our War Was Different," by Al Hemingway, © 1994 by Naval Inst. Press)

on, those from 1st CAG worked in Quang Tin and Quang Ngai Provinces (around Chu Lai Combat Base). Those from 2nd CAG were in Quang Nam Province (around Da Nang). Those from 3rd CAG operated in Thua Thien Province (around Phu Bai). And those from 4th CAG took up residence in Quang Tri Province (around Dong Ha).[18]

Each CAP had been given its own small TAOR. (See Figure 14.1.) As some TAORs comprised thousands of acres, its resident CAP had little choice but to focus on the immediate approaches to its village. Though Group headquarters ran various psychological programs (to include leaflets, aerial broadcasts, and awards for information/ordnance), those programs seldom infringed upon the CAP's principal mission—localized combat. Toward the end of the war, there was even talk of using CAPs to rain down artillery and airstrikes upon any enemy maneuver element that tried to cross their TAORs.

Early on, 1st CAG trained all CAP members in calls for fire and its subsequent adjustment. Most predominant of its civic-action projects was a new village water pump. Its platoons had an intelligence reporting requirement.[19]

2nd CAG was the closest to III MAF Headquarters, so its guidance was more complete. It considered CAP intelligence to be the most current and accurate source of enemy information. Besides medical assistance, its platoons ran mostly construction projects. Throughout 2nd CAG, there was one Marine fire team assigned to each of the three PF squads. That fire team's mission was so well to train its indigenous counterparts as to no longer be needed. Two-thirds of each Marine contingent was to stay outside its compound at night. Yet, they were still part of a "fixed CAP." There were also "mobile or roving CAPs." At the start, 2nd CAG had only six of the mobile variety but plans for 75% of all platoons to become that way.[20]

To all incoming CAP Marines, 3rd CAG taught intelligence gathering, call for fire, and claymore use. Its members were to become particularly adept at locating and then investigating spider holes.[21]

For civic action, 4th CAG also preferred construction projects within the villages. Like 2nd CAG, it thought roving CAPs to be a good idea.[22]

There were also a few outlying CAPs that may not have been

Group-affiliated. Near the DMZ, one existed right next to Con Thien,[23] and others named Oscar near Khe Sanh.[24] There were also two CAPs right next to the An Hoa Combat Base. (Refer back to Map 14.1.)

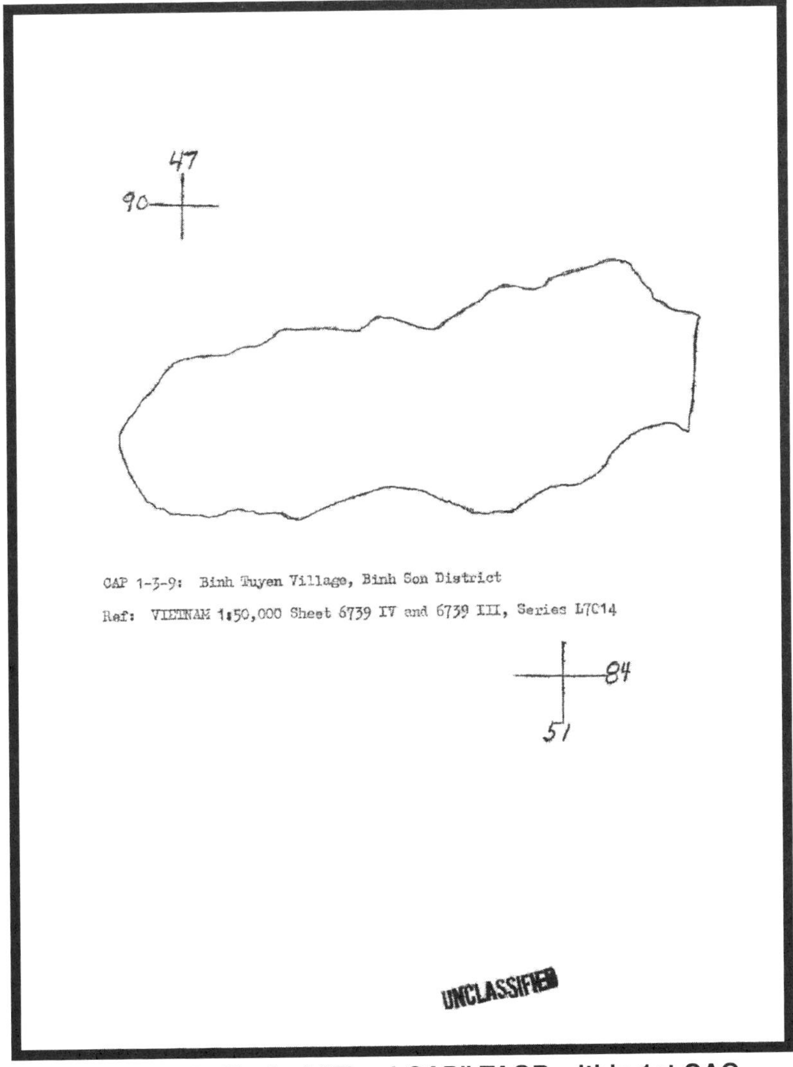

Figure 14.1: Typical "Fixed-CAP" TAOR within 1st CAG
(Source: 1st CAG Command Chronology, 1-31 December 1968, p. 19, from Assoc. of the CAP website, http://www.cap-assoc.org/)

The Full Extent of the CAP Mission

To assess the CAPs' overall effort, all available mission statements were considered. According to the official website, their primary job was to provide local defense. The PFs contributed knowledge of the local area, people, customs, government and VC activities. The Marines provided them with military training and artillery, airstrikes, and reinforcement as necessary. Of note, only a few of the CAP members were given much local language training. Their hand-and-arm signals and a few of the more common pleasantries seemed to suffice. Additionally, some of the PFs spoke a little English or French. While the CAGs were theoretically part of III MAF, operational control of each platoon remained with the Vietnamese district (subsector) commander. CACs were collocated with District headquarters, and CAGs with Province headquarters. That helped to coordinate the supporting arms.[25]

In 1967, a 2/4 inspector describes the early CAP role this way. "Their mission was to protect the village against Viet Cong infiltrators and to assist in the general pacification programs." The latter included everything from medical and construction aid to protection against enemy confiscation of food and conscripts. The CAPs around Phu Bai had too little preplanned artillery to keep from being overrun.[26]

Then, when the CAGs took over, 1st CAG headquarters published the following CAP objectives: (1) to find and destroy local VC and VC infrastructure; (2) to protect assigned villages and friendly infrastructure; and (3) to attack the conditions supporting the insurgency by civil action, psychological operations, and population and resources control. These only partially mirrored Gen. Walt's guidance. His additional objectives were: (1) protect Vietnamese authorities; (2) provide military training to the PFs; and (3) collect intelligence. By 1970, III MAF even called CAPs an "aid to local law enforcement."[27]

The mutual threads with regard to war making were village defense (from continually circumnavigating it) and information gathering. The Marines were not only to be a force multiplier for the PFs, but also to collect and relay VC intelligence. During the initial month of control, 1st CAG ran not only an equal number of day patrols, night patrols, and listening posts (LPs), but twice that number of ambushes. During the same period, 4th CAG ran the same number of day patrols, night patrols, and ambushes, but only half as many LPs.[28] Both efforts involved nearly constant crisscrossing of the village outskirts. (See Figure 14.2.)

The Roving CAP

Roving CAPs had no established home. They moved back and forth between two or more villages after spending all nights in the field. Their mobility kept the enemy guessing as to their next location. Though the roving CAPs had sacrificed some of their control over the villages, III MAF supposedly continued with their creation. By 1970, many of the previously static platoons may have been converted. According to a III MAF staff letter, the justification for this conversion was fivefold. First, all links with the PFs were left intact. Second, the "mole" mentality of a static position was removed. Third, the enemy had trouble ascertaining its exact location. Fourth, by being outside the populated areas, the Marines could make better

Figure 14.2: CAP Patrols Were Seldom Larger Than a Fire Team
(Source: U.S. Army Center of Military History, posters, illustration designator "1006-1.jpg," Friend Today—Foe Tonight, Vietnam, by Augustine Acuna, 1966)

use of their supporting arms. And fifth, by not being tied down to one base, the Marines could better concentrate their forces. These mobile CAPs set up temporary command posts (CPs) at various locations throughout their TAORs. There they would rest during the day (just as the NVA used paddy islets for pre-assault assembly areas). Each CAP's nighttime CP would then be manned by only one fire team. Everyone else would be out patrolling and ambushing.[29]

While this makes perfect sense tactically, one wonders how much enemy intelligence might have been lost in the changeover from fixed to mobile. That part of the mission had heavily depended on occupying a space so small as to have real trouble missing any occurrence—animate or inanimate. Had the original vision been too Westernized? That is always the risk where perspectives grow larger. Not only had the CAPs' TAORs been expanded, but also their mission. The latter now looked more like maneuver force interdiction by forward observer teams or (Special Forces) SF-led strike units. No longer was there as close a relationship with the villagers. An ally who occasionally passes through is much harder to tip off than one who lives there. After all, VC sympathizers were almost certainly watching.

Degree to Which the CAP Concept Has Now Been Accepted

That Bing West's book—*The Village*—is still on the "Commandant's Required Reading List" is the best testament to the viability of the original concept. Peterson's work hints at something better than the established way of doing things. "These CAP units were unique to the war. Their function was to 'capture and hold' rather than to 'search and destroy.' While the main forces of the Army and Marines all too often waged war on the Vietnamese hamlets, the CAP Marines waged war from the hamlets. Their intent was to keep the hamlet intact."[30]

With regard to Hemingway's study, *Publishers Weekly* admits to the CAP program's success amidst general failure. "Between 1965 and 1971, the Marines in Vietnam allocated 4% of their resources to an experimental effort that turned into one of the rare American successes of the war. The . . . (CAP) program was based on the belief that winning the support of the Vietnamese people was of primary importance. The CAP concept . . . was a simple one: a squad of Marines . . . joined forces with the local militia to protect villagers from the Viet Cong—denying the latter recruits, food, and intelligence."[31]

The CAPs represented an effective, long-term commitment to combatting Vietnamese Communists at the grassroots level. As most rural insurgencies are based on Mao's teachings, wouldn't Maoist procedure most easily defeat one? Yet, the CAP program was never fully implemented throughout the coastal plain, as Gen. Walt had wanted. Either it had made all the other strategies look bad by linking too little economy-boosting wherewithal to a better kill ratio. Or, it had relied on a scale that most senior officers thought to be insignificant.

The Hidden Brilliance behind the CAP Program

When it comes to guerrilla warfare, U.S. troops quite often complain about being forced to fight in someone else's backyard. The implication is that their foe has so fully memorized every fold in the ground as to easily "attrit" them. But, this is the opinion of frontline troops. Even those who subsequently rise to the rank of general seldom retain this perception of the battlefield. At best, their viewpoint changes to what everything looks like from 500 feet overhead in a helicopter; at worst, how it looks like from a satellite. With that new perspective comes different strategies. What Gen. Walt had managed with his CAP program was to bring the proper scale back to the American counterguerrilla effort. By assigning a small TAOR to each Marine squad, he had made sure that anyone wanting to attack one of his bases would have to go through some hard-charging rifleman's backyard. While the good general appears to have made no attempt to train those Marines in microterrain appreciation, he didn't really have to. By simply requiring them to spend the vast majority of their time circumnavigating a village, he had insured that they would learn every surface wrinkle. Still, most officers can only vaguely describe why such a small thing is important.

> The enhanced knowledge of the terrain allowed the CAP Marines to move more easily through the countryside, thus

> avoiding possible ambush sites, discovering infiltration routes, covering more area in less time, etc.[32]
>
> — U.S. Army Cmd. and Gen. Staff College thesis

Most probably Gen. Walt had remembered—from his Raider days—how the world looks to an indigenous mantracker. Other than a profound interest in extremely tiny clues, that tracker is no different from anyone else. Having learned to follow such clues from a distance, he sees a wide swath for what it more precisely is. This enhanced "attention to detail" allows him to more than just spot three-pronged detonators, trip wires, and bunker apertures. He can also tell which trees have been recently climbed, bushes have recently passed, and ground recently entered. Where a trail holds too many footprints for the occasional farmer, he suspects an infiltration route. Where a few footprints suddenly end, he is looking for a spider trap or tunnel entrance. And where the puddles are still muddy or the grass bent, he gets ready for company. Thus, almost everything that has lately happened in the vicinity is available to him. If he has been additionally required to circle a village, he cannot help but "cut the trail" (encounter the tracks) of any intruder. Thus, over the course of the average day, he gets a fairly accurate picture of enemy intentions. This is what the CAP Marines had going for them that sweep battalion personnel did not. It made them much more effective in combatting guerrillas. The key had been a tiny area around which to move, and the leeway to take advantage of any discovery.

To enhance the already inquisitive nature of a young American, one has only to put him into a very dangerous situation with enough time to think about how to survive it. All this Gen. Walt must have recalled from his Raider days. As such, the big lovable football player may be remembered as one of the Corps' most progressive tactical thinkers.

And That Wasn't All

The absolute brilliance of the CAP concept went far beyond the use of terrain. Guerrillas depend for much of their support on the local population. That's why winning over that population has always been a good way to defeat them. Maoist guerrillas like to apply the "Inkblot" method—gradually expanding the rural areas they control until all areas run together. The CAP Marines had been dropped right in the middle of this bottom-up strategy. They were to contest its initial objectives—the rural villages. Their constant interaction with village occupants gave them considerable insight into the enemy's grassroots approach. Too few Western leaders see the value of so mundane a relationship. Again, their problem is one of scale. What a peasant farmer might share with a junior Marine wouldn't seem all that important to a top-down or big-picture thinker. Yet, as a group, such tidbits of information might clearly define any nuances or amendments to a bottom-up strategy. Besides Generals Walt with Krulak and 3/4's XO, there were some U.S. Army officers who realized what had been gained from CAP members living inside the villages. Such an arrangement was like a "witness protection" program. It protected the villagers from subversion.

> The appreciation the Marines gained as to the people brought with it an insight into their routine. This familiarization of village routine, allowed his Marines to notice auspicious deviations of that routine that indicated something was awry.[33]
>
> — U.S. Army Cmd. and Gen. Staff College thesis

To make a junior Marine more aware of his animate surroundings, one has only to give him too little to do. Whether intentional or not, the CAP Marines had more time on their hands than their sweep battalion counterparts. From Tet onward, the average rifle company grunt got no more than nightly "power naps" between constant forays into every corner of God's green acre. So with enough "down time" to monitor each village's gossip, comings or goings, and body language, the CAP Marines could accomplish two things. One was to determine who their friends were. The other was to insure a viable community model—one based on trust and respect as opposed to suspicion and intimidation. For those who are now so intent on protecting junior GIs, all that danger helped with the people equation. It did not take long for those PFCs and Lance Corporals to realize that their best chance at survival lay in being nice to the villagers. The literature contains no power abuse examples. Screening alone would not have produced as happy a result.

The All-Important Village Cadre

As tiny North Vietnamese Army contingents would later do to evict the Khmer Rouge from Cambodia, the CAPs also promoted a reliable leadership cadre for each village. Their mission included "protect local Vietnamese authorities,"[34] but not all villages were totally friendly. Whether this cadre building was intentional or not, it still happened. That's the beauty of thinking like an Asian while trying to quell an Asian insurgency. All initiatives have side benefits. The young Marines were performing civic-action projects to win the trust of the villagers, but what actually resulted was more credibility for the South Vietnamese government. Training local militiamen similarly resulted in a more robust leadership cadre. As did the North Vietnamese contingents in Cambodia, the CAP Marines had no intention of staying on indefinitely in every village. They wanted only to shore up its "town council" and then move on to a different location.

The Extent of Headquarters Genius

III MAF had assigned the term "tactical mobility" to the fixed CAP concept. With this phrase, it had only intended to move each village's defensive formation beyond its outskirts. That formation was still to be static—as in a screen of stationary ambushes.

> A CAP does not defend . . . from behind bunkers and barricades. The idea is not to put up a wall around the hamlet, but rather to put out a screen of ambushes. . . . When coupled with stealth, [such] mobility provides . . . the protection afforded by elusiveness. . . . [T]he CAP seems to be everywhere, but never predictably anywhere. . . . [This] is the basis for CAP security against surprise attack by overwhelming enemy forces.[35]
>
> — CAP "Fact Sheet," III MAF, 1970

As with any bottom-up scheme from a top-down headquarters, the troops were soon forced to modify this one a little. It was they who were supposed to rely on a few ambushes to keep an enemy assault force from crossing the imaginary line that stretched hundreds of meters around most villages. Their foe wasn't stupid. He wasn't going to come in along existing trails. So, the Marine squad leader had little choice. To have any chance of preventing an enemy onslaught, he had to divide his two dozen or so ambush personnel into six roving fire teams. Standard patrolling technique would not have worked against this clever a foe. It would have created too much of a motion signature to permit much surprise. At a minimum, that squad leader would have thus needed roving ambushes—those that sit at one place for a while and then move on to another. Or, as the Japanese and other Asian armies had done, he would need roving LPs and defensive scouts.[36] He couldn't call them that, because such things violate U.S. doctrine. All that moving around at night created another problem. With everyone's location continually shifting, he could no longer rely on protective artillery fires.

Some extrapolation has obviously gone into the above assessment. There is no way of proving any of this statistically. All that is known for sure is that most CAPs patrolled very heavily at night. Every young Marine instinctively knows that the real struggle for any defensive perimeter happens outside it. If that perimeter additionally lies inside a village, then shifting all the fighting to its outskirts also saves villager lives. So, those CAP Marines had no intention of protecting their village with the standard routine of preregistered artillery, minefields, and interlocking machinegun fire. At best, they had a few strands of barbed wire and some fighting holes around the periphery of their compound. Its triangular shape would have also permitted an automatic weapon on each corner, so that two could target any assault.

Such an inverted defensive scheme was quite progressive for the American military. As opposed to an impenetrable strongpoint, the villages had become traps for overconfident VC, according to *Life*. Though each village's CAP continually patrolled and ambushed, its occupants still had the freedom to move around and earn a living. However, if any VC dared to enter that village to collect taxes, proselytize, or terrorize, they might have to fight their way out.[37] This is a great way of only inconveniencing the guilty.

Fully Utilizing One's Assets

The beauty of a bottom-up plan is that it can be more easily adapted to the frontline situation. Though partially flawed (as are all plans), this one had appropriately evolved. Gen. Walt had done what only Asians usually can. He had turned a defensive problem into an offensive opportunity.

Because those triangular CAP compounds stood almost no chance of holding out the old fashioned way against good light infantry, Gen. Walt had also uncovered the Holy Grail of short-range combat. He had created a manageable way for each fledgling combatant to reach his full warrior potential. As a fully vetted CAP member, that combatant was more useful to the war effort and less likely to be killed. Sgt. Anthony Price was a squad leader in a CAC unit north of Phu Bai. His subsequent exploits as a platoon sergeant with A/1/4 are almost legendary. One was to team up with Gy.Sgt. Winebar on a dark night in August 1966 to single-handedly rid an overrun perimeter (at Cam Lo) of unwanted visitors.[38]

War is an inherently dangerous business, so why not take advantage of that danger. Just to survive in many locations, those young CAP Marines would have to "contact patrol," and their senior commanders knew it.

Structural Anomaly Helps with the Operational Details

Also apparent from the CAP method was a Chinese and then Carlson Raider perception of leadership. Unlike the *Guardia Nationale* contingents of the Banana Wars, the CAPs contained no Marine officers, or even E-6's in most cases. All emphasis was on a Sergeant or Corporal "facilitating," as opposed to directing, the actions of a dozen men. As a result, those men developed the field skills, ingenuity, and tactical-decision-making ability to operate virtually alone in Indian country. Only then could they go on to collectively accomplish the most productive campaign of the Vietnam War.

The CAP program leader's reasons for such a deep delegation of authority in an increasingly "officer-centric" Marine Corps are quite interesting. According to the *Life* article, Lt.Col. William R. Corson became the III MAF deputy director for Combined Action, when Gen. Walt formalized the program in February 1967. Corson wanted the CAPs to have a separate chain of command, because "the average battalion commander in Vietnam . . . was trained and oriented toward offensive large-unit warfare." He saw the CAP as both mobile and offensive in nature, a concept that was later to translate into more roving CAPs.[39] What Corson may not have realized is how a bigger backyard gives roving CAPs less of an offensive edge. Through nearly constant patrolling, the fixed CAPs were already hard for the enemy to pin down. Plus, roving CAP members no longer enjoyed the same rapport with the villagers. This had intelligence gathering ramifications.

Most interesting are Corson's rationale for using so little rank in the CAPs. He was afraid a Gunnery Sergeant would look like "a tough old pro," and he didn't want an officer as platoon leader because "people associate them with corruption." That left only an NCO in charge (NCOIC) of the Marine portion of the platoon, as the PFs could more easily relate to him. Though most NCOICs had the benefit of combat experience, they were also chosen for their lack of resentment against the Vietnamese people (ambassador potential).[40]

This rank anomaly was not the only exception to the Marines' stratified system. Their resupply channels were occasionally circumvented. Any shortages of wherewithal that bartering could not remedy, were acquired through scrounging.[41]

PF Trainer to Become a Different Kind of Infantryman

No 3/4 officer or general may have realized it, but—with the CAP program—they had created the perfect OJT school for truly light infantrymen. NVA regulars were also required to instruct local militia—as the final stage of their training regimen—before heading south. This was not only to prepare them to teach VC, but also to hone their light-infantry skills to commando quality.

> The typical North Vietnamese regular fighting in the South was twenty-three years old—four years older than his U.S. counterpart. . . . [H]e had already logged three years of compulsory service, undergoing military training and also instructing local militia.[42]
>
> — Maitland and McInerney, *Vietnam Experience*

Any longtime infantry instructor ends up learning more from his students than they do from him. That's because he invariably dissects his topics to improve his presentation. The grunts who joined the CAP program had a good working knowledge of U.S. infantry basics: (1) shoot; (2) move; and (3) communicate. When they tried to teach those basics to people who were already "woods-wise," they realized that each had subcategories. Instead of just moving "stealthily," one could silently glide through dry leaves, swampy ground, or thick brush. Instead of just keeping a low profile on patrol or approach march, he and his buddies could all but disappear. That took the following: (1) staying off the skyline; (2) blending in with all backgrounds; (3) avoiding any watery reflections; (4) moving among the shadows; and (5) varying one's stance and speed with lighting conditions. Most of these abilities were significantly enhanced by having prior knowledge of all microterrain along the way. Because of the tiny strip around each village that the CAP members continually traversed, these things more easily occurred to them. That their foe was working for the best light infantry in the world also helped with their education. The confines of the defensive battle space had forced the young grunts to do two things: (1) appreciate microterrain; and (2) forsake firepower. The continuous danger had further forced them to sneak around. As a result, they became more able to surprise someone than their sweep-battalion counterparts. For all practical purposes, that's the definition of a truly light infantryman.

To accelerate this process, their enemy had provided the role model. He was an expert at both stealth and deception. Without more attention to tiny clues, the Marines couldn't "hang" with him. They had either to learn—through OJT—how to interpret all types of enemy sign, or die. As one III MAF "Fact Sheet" very succinctly stated, the CAPs' "classroom was the 'bush' where the VC provide the necessary training aids."[43]

The idea of learning on the job from one's foe is distinctly Maoist in origin. U.S. forces seldom have that much respect for any enemy and much prefer an actual classroom where "doctrinal correctness" can be assured. Whether intentional or not, putting non-infantry Marines into these CAPs may have helped to expand the infantry skills. It provided a partial break from traditional procedures so that more situationally appropriate ones could take hold.

CAPs Were Also the Best Hope in Non-Martial Arenas

As a later *Life Magazine* article covers, many CAP members even worked against local graft (with its inevitable links to the

South Vietnamese government). A few CAG headquarters people had apparently threatened corrupt officials with assassination,[44] so there is no telling how far certain CAP NCOICs may have gone with their graft rebuttal. That's one of the risks of actually winning a guerrilla war. Sorting things out at the local level will always stand a better chance than top-echelon negotiations.

All villages probably had turncoats, and the Marine's job was to so strengthen the local cadre as to make those turncoats unwelcome. In the vast majority of cases, they did so in a completely professional manner. Those who had the honor of commanding the idealistic 18-year-olds of this period found their collective opinions to be their most reliable moral compass.

Some of the CAPs' More Interesting Tactics

There must have been hundreds, if not thousands, of very interesting small-unit contacts between these Marines and the VC or NVA. In many, they may have used more ingenuity than in their manuals. Yet, sadly, most of these technique variations have been lost to history. All that is known is that these Marines found and destroyed many caches and bunkers. That takes particular attention to microterrain, just as M/3/4 displayed in the last chapter. Once the battle moves into the microterrain, more maneuver options are available. At night, a village drainage ditch becomes an invisible envelopment route and a break in the neighbor's fence works as handy escape route. There are no more standup contests of will, but only the surprise elimination of intruders. As a result, fewer friendlies get hurt. Two partially accessible CAP encounters help to make the point.

In December 1968, CAP 3-1-8 spotted a small VC column somewhere near Phu Bai and then "moved to ambush them." This act alone is almost never managed by a regular grunt unit. It takes intimate understanding of the local terrain—where all paths lead and how to get there first. Then, when the bullets started to fly, this particular CAP patrol was reinforced by a PF ambush team from the same platoon. Again, only through complete familiarity with the terrain could such a link-up be made. The combined force then tried to "fire and move" against the foe, but had instead to repel an assault from 40 NVA. Gunships were called in, and the CAP extracted due to a shortage of ammunition.[45] This is how short-range combat is supposed to be conducted—in an aggressive and innovative manner, but still capable of backing up a little.

During the same month in 1968, a patrol from CAP 4-1-4 established an "area ambush" somewhere around Dong Ha. Implied, of course, is the dispersal of several teams throughout a small locale, like at every entrance to a trail junction. Due to the increased possibility of fratricide, this type of maneuver is generally disallowed by U.S. doctrine. But, it is completely consistent with Maoist encirclement tactics and, when properly executed, poses very little friendly risk. Thus, one can legitimately call it progressive. Unfortunately, it also landed this particular group of Marines a healthy dose of combat—so much so, that they had to initially leave a wounded buddy behind and return to their village. Luckily, a reaction force was immediately launched and the Marine successfully recovered.[46] Again, this had been a very aggressive patrol. When things go too smoothly against this talented an enemy, it generally means that someone would rather demonstrate than fight.

Rare Firsthand Account of a CAP Being Overrun

After serving as a machinegunner with G/2/5, one particularly dedicated young Marine became a CAP contingent leader. From an intelligence background, he may have had more interest in graft elimination than most. Though fully Marine, his contingent worked under the protection of the 502nd Infantry of the 101st Airborne west of Hue City in late 1969. It is one of the few CAPs to have been completely overrun. Of the 13 Marines on its roles at the time, six were killed, five wounded, and two survived to take back the village.[47] That squad leader just happens to be one of the avengers. From him come the following insights.

This squad leader claims to have hidden beneath a pile of "pig crap" to keep from being shot or bayoneted during the final assault on his compound. With the other survivor, he then reemerged to systematically eliminate all enemy occupants. As his original weapon had been fouled, he was forced to contest his first opponent with a helmet to the base of the nose. (See Figure 14.3.)

That rather self sufficient Marine now describes the CAP mission as one of an intelligence screen around the big bases. In other words, the CAPs were not just there to help the villagers protect themselves, but also to keep the bases from coming under assault. He describes this defense effort as mostly a patrolling evolution that happened outside the villages so as not to endanger their occupants. On any given night, there were several "three-man-ambush" patrols out. During the average day, "strategic" patrols looked for enemy "weapons sites" (like makeshift rocket launchers or buried ammunition). Before being admitted to the CAP program, this Marine remembers being interviewed by Lt.Col. Corson. "He was making sure that no joinee held any animosity toward the populace." The Marine also recalls many CAP members with military occupational specialties other than infantry. He says this was good for civic action but a problem on defense, because most knew too little about tactics. He further volunteers that the original CAP acronym of "CAC" had meant oversexed young man in Vietnamese. For the program to succeed, all Vietnamese women had to be off-limits to Americans.[48]

Of note, this same Marine went on—after the war—to take an Okinawan bride and revisit Vietnam many times. He is thus quite knowledgeable of not only the Oriental mindset, but of its tactical heritage. He confirms that one of the reasons the CAP worked so well was its lack of an officer. He says all members were forced to take an oath to protect their village occupants. All further realized the increased risk from not treating their villagers well. They knew some of the local militiamen were unreliable, but could not figure out which until an attack.[49] Ahead of time, there was no attempt to harm them. The mutual respect that then developed between Marines and villagers is what made the concept work. It was an advanced way of supporting a beleaguered population.

Sadly, as had Carlson's more autonomous small units, the whole CAP concept contradicted established U.S. military procedure. In short, giving any squad leader that much authority detracted from the absolute control deemed necessary to run a stratified unit. As such, both concepts—though extremely beneficial to their respective war efforts—went away. Without spreading the CAP program throughout Vietnam's most heavily populated area—its coastal plain—as Gen. Walt had originally wanted, the U.S. phalanx had little chance. Nor will it in Afghanistan. An SF veteran of several tours to that country confirms that only by living with mutual respect and skepticism among the people were his tiny teams able to disenfranchise the local Taliban. When a firepower-oriented French unit took over his TAOR, it almost immediately got into a big fire-

Figure 14.3: He and a Buddy Had Just Retaken the Compound
(Source: U.S. Army Center of Military History, artphoto archives, illustration designator "0207-4.jpg," The Pause That Refreshes—Vietnam, by Dennis O. McGee, 1967)

fight that negated most of his progress. He says there was a game of sorts going on, and the rules of that game could not be learned through too prominent a display of Western *machismo*.[50]

Success Rate

The CAP program had been born in August 1965. By August 1967, there were 75 CAPs and another 39 authorized. Between

January and August 1967, 15 all-out attacks were made on those platoons, with four suffering "heavy casualties," according to *Life Magazine*.[51] However, the official casualty statistics for that period show only one or two being overrun (having more than 4 killed in action (KIA): (1) 5/67, 2-3-4, 2 KIA; (2) 6/67, Bravo-4, 5 KIA; (3) 6/67, Oscar-3, 4 KIA; and (4) 7/67, Hotel-7, 2 KIA.[52] This *Life* article goes on to claim that Echo-2 in the village of Hoa Hiep some 12 miles north of Da Nang had already been "overrun" in November 1966.[53] There may be a problem with semantics here. Of the six Marines in that village at the time of the attack, one had been killed and four wounded. This sounds more like the VC had penetrated the CAP compound and then exited without bothering to consolidate. If this is to be the definition of overrunning something, then every American base and permanent outpost in Vietnam was about to be overrun repeatedly.[54]

Only one or two fully compromised units out of 75 is a fairly respectable record. Those casualty statistics show only 11 more collapses of compound defenses over the next four years.[55] This is when the heaviest fighting occurred. Relatively cheap to operate, CAPs seldom resorted to supporting arms and enjoyed a very high kill ratio for that size of unit.[56] To be sure, those dozen or so Marines in each location lived in constant fear of being overrun. After winning the villagers' trust, they must have regularly had to contemplate such threats. But, they also experienced great satisfaction. By end of 1967, 25 fully pacified villages were ready to be turned over to their PFs. When the platoon totals peaked in 1970, 93 Marine contingents had been shifted away from villages deemed capable of defending themselves. "Of the 209 villages protected by CAP units [some undoubtedly mobile], not one ever reverted to VC control." To this day, that remains the best indicator of almost unparalleled success.[57]

Even Gen. Westmoreland later admitted in his memoirs that the Combined Action Program had been one of the more "ingenious innovations developed in South Vietnam."[58] However, it was a former Raider who best envisioned its future potential.

> Of all our innovations in Vietnam, none was as successful, as lasting in effect, or as useful for the future as the Combined Action Program.[59]
>
> — Maj.Gen. Lewis William Walt USMC

And That Was That

Tracing the effects of a Raider (or Maoist) heritage on any U.S. unit beyond Vietnam would be an exercise in futility. Too many years would have passed, and too many other variables intervened. Still, truth has a way of resurfacing. This one would emerge from its Headquarters-induced slumber some 20 years later.

Part Four

21st-Century Follow-Up

"We are also firm believers in 'bottom-up' training."
— Special Operations Training Group (SOTG) Commander

(Source: West Coast SOTG commander while Gen. Mattis was the head of I MEF.)

15 The Belated End to Carlson's Research

- What had Carlson been working on before being relieved?
- Did a 1980's Platoon Sergeant School finish his research?

Best techniques through collective opinions and trial runs.

(Source: FM 100-5 [1994], p. 37)

Gung Ho Spirit Finally Resolves Age-Old Problem

Right before being relieved of command in a rest camp on New Caledonia in 1943, Evans Carlson had been running *Gung Ho* experiments.[1] Among them may have been how—through *Gung Ho* Sessions and follow-up field trials—to develop a full portfolio of advanced small-unit techniques. But this was never to be. As he departed, so did the *Gung Ho* Session from acceptable Marine Corps procedure.

Corps leaders had been afraid that the individual initiative generated by those Sessions would later prove counterproductive in bunker busting. Their concerns were partially justified. When a Marine squad is within 50 feet of an enemy bunker with no chance for maneuver, and its presence known to the occupants, then all forward movement must be by the numbers. In other words, all squad members must do exactly what they have been just told or previously practiced. If the barbed-wire-breaching bangalore goes off before the bazooka man finishes his shot, then he will lose part of his head. Because proper assault step sequencing is so important under these circumstances, there is little room for individual initiative. Yet, Carlson's close-combat skills would still help if enemy soldiers suddenly surfaced behind the assault squad. Sadly, along with the *Gung Ho* Session also disappeared as much emphasis on individual protective measures.

In essence, the Session had been scrapped because it might impinge on the commander's degree of control, and the advanced self-defense training because of less emphasis on each rifleman's contribution. When it came to enemy machinegun fire, that rifleman was now a member of a team, and what mattered most was whether that team as a whole could get its mission accomplished. Unfortunately, both parts of the original rationale had been flawed. That much control is not necessary where the bunker occupants are farther away or unaware of the squad's presence. Neither is maneuver in a constricted lane always impossible. If there exists any microterrain at all, tiny elements can sometimes crawl through it. Finally, with enough planning and rehearsal, 14 men can accomplish almost any task without any leader at all. Then, much of their overall effectiveness depends on each member's individual skills.

Infantry Training Can Be Quite Boring for Most Involved

In a top-down military organization, unit training generally takes precedence over individual training. While large-unit exercises may help principal leaders and supporting staff to interact, they hold very little instructional value for most unit members—all the NCOs and riflemen.

Almost all of Carlson's unit training had been of the "free-play" variety in which all unit members got to "aggress" and then "be aggressed." Even his self-defense training gave each rifleman the opportunity to out-think his attacker. Then, the *Gung Ho* Sessions gave everyone—however low in rank—a way to influence their leaders.

When a new Platoon Sergeants Course was created at the U.S. Marine Corps' East Coast School of Infantry (SOI) in 1986, a combination of factors led to the following: (1) a symbiotic relationship between instructor and student; plus (2) a way to develop state-of-the-art tactical technique. The new school had unknowingly completed Carlson's 45-year-old research. Below is that story, and its future significance.

The Camp Geiger Miracle

What developed at the south end of Camp Lejeune from 1986 to 1992 was a course of instruction for infantry platoon sergeants that contained more information than in the manuals. That's right—the very running of the course had generated additional knowledge. Everything taught was still doctrinally correct, but it now included vital steps that the directives had either skipped or never considered. For example, the manual for the M203 grenade launcher made no mention of an often defective barrel latch. And the manual for small-unit attacks failed to discuss how partially compromised surprise can often be reestablished through standby ruses.

Nothing particularly mysterious had happened. The Camp Geiger instructors had done little more than fill in the holes in the official body of knowledge, as had been the SNCOs' tradition. Their sources of information had been the students themselves (mostly career infantrymen from line units) and some of the more obscure government pamphlets. Wherever they detected a step missing from a procedure, they sought out an official reference to it. If such a reference could not be found, they added the step to their lecture but not to its subsequent test. This had been their guidance at the School for Instructors at Camp Johnson. It had given them the authority to add elements of information to their classes without backup, as long as they weren't considered to be formal ELOs (Essential Learning Objectives). This had been sage advice. It had allowed for a learning dynamic where there might otherwise have been rote memorization. The Geiger instructors had another reason to avoid humdrum presentations. Whether or not they could remain on the "platform" was almost totally dependent on student critiques.

Just as Carlson had with his nonrates for the 2nd Raider Battalion, Camp Lejeune had allowed its students to arrive at training specifics. Among those specifics were the most life-preserving maneuvers.

What Ever Happened to That School

This Platoon Sergeants School had been new and, as such, initially exempted from CCRBs (Course Curriculum Review Boards). About 1992, that exemption was rescinded. CCRBs were then regularly conducted in all of their initiative-absolving glory. Any element of information that was not specifically referenced in the most mainstream of manuals was summarily removed from all courses of instruction. Today, the school's successor looks more like an abbreviated version of Quantico's Infantry Officer Course. Much of the detail on how successfully to get "the rubber to meet the road" has vanished. In its place are "How to Land the Landing Force" and other broad topics that mostly help Staff Sergeants to understand their senior officers' perspective. Unfortunately, close-quarters combat involves much more than that. It requires considerable technical skill—much of which (due to its seemingly mundane nature) has never been put into print. For lack of a better description, it is all the subgroups of what officers call "basics." That's what Sgt. Stryker had been trying to tell his squad members in the movie "Sands of Iwo Jima." This immense body of unwritten knowledge has traditionally been brought to the table by career NCOs. While there is no way for each to understand everything, it still resides in their collective memory.

To claim that the school has been ruined is too harsh an indictment. Suffice it to say, it no longer enjoys the same reputation it had in the late 1980's and early 1990's. Just prior to the first Gulf War, it had been really humming. The students were happy, and instructors couldn't wait to get to work. Regimental Sergeant Majors regularly stopped by to see how their people were doing and share latest deployment "scoop" with the class. Trips to the field were punctuated by long bonfire chats (complete with ghost stories), an instructor for every 10 students, and an abundance of realism (to include machinegun and artillery simulators). After the local newspaper reported a large deformed critter attacking somebody in South Carolina, rumors began to circulate that a "Lizard Man" inhabited the Verona Loop area. That instructor invention had to be retracted, when the length of student flashlights on the night land navigation course began to exceed 12 inches.

In other words, this school was not only professional, but also fun. Because it was fun, people learned more. No student was ever dropped from the program because of poor grades. Those who found certain subjects difficult were given extra tutoring and further testing. All eight instructors had agreed that the minds of quick thinkers sometimes race in combat, so why discriminate against the ones that wouldn't. When a combat order was to be written, the "duty solution" was sometimes modified. If a number of students arrived at a scheme of maneuver that was better than that intended, they too were given credit. In this way, the instructors grew smarter, the courses of instruction improved, and the school became a much sought after destination for East Coast Marines.

Day to Day Functioning of the School

For whatever reason, this fledgling "course of instruction" was only loosely controlled by its Officer in Charge (OIC). There was a 1st Sergeant, but he spent most of his time on administrative matters and seldom bothered the instructors. There was also an enlisted Chief Instructor. He did little more than combine instructor input on class duration into a finished schedule, and then provide logistical assistance as required. In other words, each separate instructor was in charge of almost every aspect of his classes. Among other things, he had the authority to use any or all of the other instructors as assistants. On one occasion, an E-5 Sergeant—on short notice—requested and received a continuous 72 hours of field assistance from an E-7 Gunnery Sergeant.[2] As with the Raiders, rank held few privileges.

Whenever possible, related topics were taught in Round-Robin fashion—just like in WWII. (See Appendix A). All coordination glitches were worked out by the instructors themselves (i.e., no intervening leader). The best example was the marriage of "Close-Air Support" and "Call for Fire" with the "81mm Mortar" package. One overcast afternoon in 1991 at OP-2 on Lyman Road (where

Range Control Forward used to be), there was a rather unusual sight. Fighter jets were screaming in over the observation tower to drop dummy bombs into the G-10 Impact Area. What made this evolution different from most was the degree of enlisted involvement. Platoon Sergeants School students had just marked the target from a collocated 81mm mortar and were now controlling the aircraft. As the two explosive projectiles were entering the same space, any error in timing could have been unpleasant.

Those E-6's had not spent all morning rehearsing their part in this rather delicate dance. They were instead rotating between four very busy training stations. Those stations were as follows: (1) call for fire; (2) operating an 81mm mortar; (3) running a Fire Direction Center (FDC) to arrive at the proper gun settings; and (4) requesting and controlling a close airstrike. Because of the noise and risk involved, such training was quite inspiring to the junior SNCOs. It is doubtful that anything like it has been tried with new Lieutenants at Quantico. Only later would the rewards of so challenging a package be realized. During the Light Armored Reconnaissance (LAR) battle that highlighted the initial stages of the Kuwait invasion, it was an E-6 graduate of this school who was to run all the airstrikes for three days.[3] Of course, this OP-2 practice session had only been the final stage of a somewhat longer learning progression. The students had already been to classes on all four subjects and through a miniature Round Robin on three. With a compass, plotting board, and tiny compressed-air mortar, they had all practiced hitting a target in a cardboard town. That town had been constructed—complete with grid line strings—on half a soccer field.

The Situation Station

Among the school's many discoveries was what to do when a combat scenario has no official solution. An outdoor "Situation Station" is created within a Round Robin of more traditional training. While pretending to know the scenario's answer, the instructor first walks the area and describes all circumstances to a stick of 15 to 20 students. Then, he asks for their opinion (as is often done to reestablish interest). But this time, his reason is different. He is instead searching their "combined knowledge" for a legitimate solution. When he hears something that seems—through his own experience—to be close to an answer, he quietly assesses the other students' degree of concurrence. If the majority seem to agree with the suggestion, then that's the duty solution for this particular group. After following the same procedure with the next three groups, the instructor becomes fairly confident of the answer. At no time do his students suspect he has just given a class on something he knew very little about. In effect, he has been a facilitator of knowledge, instead of its trumpet. Appendix A shows Lieutenants doing something similar at Geiger during WWII. Though counter-intuitive in an authoritarian setting, this type of training is actually quite helpful to student and instructor alike.

The "Fire and Movement" Drill

Often within tactical training, physical toughness becomes an additional unsolicited objective. For career Marines, this constitutes harassment. They're tough enough now. What they really need is more ways to outmaneuver their foe. Assuming that happy students tend to learn more, one can make a good case for removing all unnecessary labor from their training. A good example would be the use of rubber rifles for small-unit maneuver rehearsal. Mock weapons are not as hard to check out, clean, or return; and the whole base doesn't get shut down every time one is mislaid.

There are other ways to limit the amount of administrative time associated with training. Small-unit maneuvers can be first demonstrated in a sand box with miniatures, and then practiced in the woods behind the barracks. Unless live fire is required, there is no need for a lengthy trip to a formal training area. Individual movement courses can even be designed so that participants don't have to return to the starting point to try it again. The following "fire and movement" exercise is like that. It's every bit as strenuous as running around the block.

With kite string, parallel lanes are laid out across a soccer field. Those to be trained are split up into three equal sections. All are issued rubber rifles and told to pair up. The assistant instructor takes Section One to the other end of the lanes, while the primary keeps Sections Two and Three at the near end. The buddy teams in Section One each drop to the ground and prepare to count three-second sight pictures of people in their lanes. Then, Section Two buddy teams fire and move toward them. Next, Section Three assumes the role of defender, while Section Two fires and moves back the other way. There is no "hurry up and wait" or "returning to the starting point." By keeping each student informed of how many times he is killed, the instructor further captures the Holy Grail of instruction. He puts the responsibility for improvement squarely on the shoulders of the student himself. What a person can self-monitor and correct will almost always exceed what he is told to do. To increase that motivation, the section taking the least number of hits will escape clean up.

During the above evolution, random fire and movement with everyone guiding toward the center proves to be far less costly than that directed by a squad leader. The prospective rushers could play off more diversions that way. In effect, advanced technique had been born out of training format expediency.

Urban Assault Collaboration

Just as random fire and movement had been, an unexpected insight occurred during the urban assault training. There, it was learned that two squads can move up a street quicker through mutual cooperation than under a platoon leader's direction. In battle, and particularly urban battle, momentum is everything. To have much chance at a difficult cross street, the two squads must traverse each block faster than the enemy thinks possible. This is best accomplished by squad leaders deciding who should attack next. If a vacant lot lies between houses on one side of the street, the far-side squad may have to assault twice in a row. Simply alternating responsibility would be far too predictable anyway. As soon as a house is cleared, the occupying squad signals with a green teeshirt that it's ready to cover. If the other squad doesn't want to attack next, it signals back with a white teeshirt. The Lieutenant only gets involved on request or to insert the reserve squad.

Such management by exception is not only more expedient, but it gives the leader time to do other things. Take, for example, what he might accomplish during a chance contact. His people have been "stalking and moving" until fired upon. Then, they automatically advance until any of the following: (1) fresh dirt (indicating a prepared enemy position); (2) complete loss of cover on one side of the line; or (3) well-directed enemy machinegun fire. As soon as they stop, control reverts back to the squad leader. In the meantime, he has more easily come up with a six-digit coordinate for the initial call for fire. When dealing with an opponent of indeterminate size, the first mortar round must land no nearer than 400 yards from friendlies. All too often, the leader makes an error in this computation.

Similarities in Carlson's Approach to That at Geiger

For the 2nd Raider Battalion, small-unit techniques were sometimes proposed in *Gung Ho* Sessions and then haphazardly attempted in combat. But the two were never part of a systematic process. That may have been what the Raiders' commander finally realized. If he had regularly arrived at new techniques through group discussions and then tested all in combat, he would have eventually arrived at world class methods. That's what was happening at Geiger, just in a slightly different format. Group opinions controlled the maneuvers taught there as well. For each, the instructor could add steps (like a little deception) to the official sequence. If the students did not like the result, they could fire the instructor. These modified maneuvers additionally underwent field trials. Instead of active combat, the Geiger procedures were assessed against simulated casualties. Through the number of beeping MILES sets or three-second sight pictures, the effectiveness of each assault or defense technique could be fairly accurately ascertained—at least in comparison to its last variation.

There are any number of other similarities between Carlson's program and the Platoon Sergeants Course—all coincidental. None of the Geiger instructors knew much about him. The common denominator had simply been respect for actual fighters. He had allowed his people training suggestions. He had also been preparing the instructors of indigenous guerrillas. So, the inflated role of the student at Geiger was totally in keeping with Raider tradition. He also took the mainstream manuals with a grain of salt. He saw them more as general guidelines than doctrinal edicts. Similarly, the Geiger instructors were not content to base all instruction on paragraph headings. That's what created the wonderful learning dynamic. Anything to do with close-quarters combat, Carlson depended more on the collective opinions of his junior Raiders than on the advice of his officers. In a similar vein, group perceptions of well-seasoned enlisted students had been the source of the instructional detail at Geiger's new school.

Carlson had been trying to instill self-discipline and confidence into people who already had unit discipline and morale. Similarly, the Geiger school made it almost impossible for any student to use another as a crutch. Even night land navigation was conducted alone. Then, if anyone was having problems, he was allowed to try over and over until finally finding a legitimate way to overcome his deficiency. Not every grunt can be a superman. His productivity and survival are more fully dependent on understanding (and then compensating for) his limitations. By allowing each Raider to experiment with ways to trick an oncoming aggressor, Carlson had instilled this same aspect of self-confidence.

It's clear from the records of 2nd Raider Battalion that all members helped to design both fire team techniques and battalion scheme of maneuver. On the Long Patrol, that scheme of maneuver was mostly for tiny teams to hit hard and then quickly withdraw before any counterpunch. Similarly at Geiger, most courses of instruction had been fine-tuned by the students themselves. They had eliminated through student critiques anyone who wouldn't listen, and then guided the surviving instructors into advanced methods. That's why they had been so contented. It was in knowing that their best interests were finally being served.

From how training was conducted at Geiger during WWII (Appendix A) and the late 1980's, a way for each rifle company to develop its own portfolio of advanced techniques emerges (Appendix B.) While exciting in theory, this inexpensive option poses big problems in practice. What then is to become of the massive bureaucratic apparatus that has yet to provide state-of-the-art tactical methods?

Carlson's Experiments Have Now Come Full Circle

The above-mentioned "Platoon Sergeants Course" was offered by SOI's Advanced Infantry Training Company. Its current successor is the "Infantry Unit Leaders Course" of the same command's Advanced Infantry Training Battalion. That the course's name has been changed speaks volumes as to how closely its operating procedures may have corresponded with those of the summarily discontinued Raiders.

Figure 15.1: Fire Teams Played a Significant Role in Iraq
(Source: U.S. Army Center of Military History, artphoto archives, illustration designator "Another Day at the Office.jpg," by MSG Christopher Thiel, in Iraq, 2006)

Somebody somewhere needs to reassess the principal tradeoffs between a tightly controlled military and one that can win a guerrilla war or take minimal casualties at short range in all-out war. With regard to small-unit maneuvers, too much standardization equates to a lack of surprise. Organizational hype is good for instilling pride and securing the next budget, but it has much less utility on the battlefield. This was a very productive course of instruction that has since fallen by the wayside. Any senior U.S. infantry officer who sees no problem in this should really be looking for another line of work.

A single organizational procedure had been the initial culprit at Geiger, but subsequent events suggest a deeper problem. Small units had been instrumental late in the Iraq War, but then never allowed to rise to their potential in Afghanistan. (See Figure 15.1.)

The school had gone away for many of the same reasons that Carlson's Raiders had—the precedence of complete control over bottom-echelon competence.

Future War's Most Promising Model

- How are Carlson's methods best applied to modern era?
- What may be the consequences of not doing so?

The next big threat is from China.

(Source: "Handbook on the Chinese Communist Army," DA Pamphlet 30-51 [1960], fig. 110; FM 21-76 [1957], p. 89)

Mixed Reviews on Past Wars

WWI and WWII were victories, but not without cost. Though both foes had been far better than the Allies at squad maneuver, they were beaten through an overwhelming display of firepower. One can only guess at how many young Marines might have been saved if the Belleau Wood wheat field and Peleliu airfield had been crossed piecemeal at night.[1]

Rumors of tactical deficiency did not end with WWII. When North Korea's defenses stiffened along the 38th Parallel in 1953, all that firepower could not breach them.[2] Nor would it work in

Vietnam. The Asian Communists had come up with some tactical nuances that the Japanese and Germans hadn't. From that point forward, 2GW-oriented U.S. heavy infantry could no longer be expected to defeat 4GW-adept light infantry.

> I'm afraid we haven't recognized the most important lesson from Korea. The Communists have developed a totally new kind of warfare. . . . This is a total warfare, yet small in scope, and it's designed to neutralize our big . . . weapons. Look at Vietnam. The French outnumbered the Communists two to one, yet they [the French] were massacred.[3]
>
> — B.Gen. Lewis B. "Chesty" Puller USMC (Ret.)

By the end of the Iraq War, a few of the overdue tactical adjustments had been made in theater (allowing for smaller units), only to be ignored by the Stateside bureaucracy. Then came Afghanistan. What the individual U.S. fighter knew to be possible against a rather primitive foe was never tried. American leaders feared the political backlash—from more casualties and the occasional embarrassment—of fully dispersing their personnel. They preferred the impression of victory through targeting (with drone missiles) the relatively inconsequential leaders of a bottom-up movement.

Something was wrong with U.S. infantry capabilities, and everyone knew it. While catering to public opinion, government officials had been overcontrolling what had—by necessity—to be opportunistic at the lowest echelons. Instead of creating the truly light infantrymen who could win a 4GW-oriented war, they had been making all ground pounders dependent on vehicles and supporting arms. Within these last few pages lies a better way to defend America.

Raider Contribution Applauded

First and foremost of Evans Carlson's contributions was the three-fire-team squad. Now available were enough tiny elements to outflank each mutually supporting bunker in a defense matrix. This was most important where there were too few supporting arms or impervious emplacements.

As part of a three-component squad, the fire team also allowed for more maneuver during less demanding scenarios. Instead of the highly predictable "bounding overwatch" routine (wherein one element fires while the other moves), a third element was available to trick the enemy. While Carlson and the Maoists often turned this capability into a double-envelopment, U.S. doctrine forbade any encirclement for fear of fratricide. Still, with more potential for surprise, the three-fire-team squad helped to win many engagements.

A Maverick's Partially Welcomed Additions

With this decentralization of control inside the squad had also come enough initiative to better handle a constantly changing situation. Its ultimate byproduct was more emphasis on the individual rifleman and his capabilities. 2nd Battalion Raiders did not just rehearse the canned motions of bayonet fighting. They separately experimented with ways to deceive an onrushing opponent. This much thinking at the lowest echelons was soon to run into considerable resistance.

With the guerrilla warfare training, Carlson had created America's first UW experts. His Raiders were thus the forerunners of all modern-day special operators. (Upstaging the Army's Rangers by four months, the Raiders were also the first deployed.[4]) For infantrymen, UW consists of how to fight like a guerrilla and then escape and evade (E&E) the foe. He had been preparing his Raiders "for infiltration [behind enemy lines] and the attainment of objectives by unorthodox and unexpected methods."[5] They were then able to handle many times their number through hit-and-run and swarm-type tactics. Both maneuvers worked well because of the greater aggressiveness of loosely controlled lead elements. The significance of such UW capabilities to conducting MW at the squad level cannot be denied. This so-called maverick may be the only American to have ever done the latter. That would suggest that HQMC can't fully embrace its new doctrine without first training all riflemen in UW. With the above-mentioned self-defense experiments, the Raider Colonel has provided the key to the new instructional model.

Raider Methods Scorned

Carlson's other big contributions—those that eventually led to the demise of his beloved Raiders—were a new leadership paradigm for working together and the decidedly counter-cultural *Gung Ho* Session.

From the Chinese Communists, the Colonel had discovered that infantrymen do not need as much management as commonly believed in the West. With an ethical orientation, proper reconnaissance of objectives, and detailed rehearsal of methods, small infantry elements can work quite well together without any leader at all. Of course, this rather shocking conclusion flew right in the face of a system that had always prided itself on strict compliance of bottom-echelon orders.

The alternative *Gung Ho* Session was too progressive for the 1940's. While a little collective thinking didn't violate American ideals, arriving at better tactics that way discredited not only the manuals, but also their producing headquarters. In a hierarchical organization, Carlson's "democratic seances" were not thought to be good for unit discipline. They may have helped the Raiders to improve their techniques, but they also limited the amount of officer and SNCO control.

For the belts of bunkers that would soon dominate WWII's battlefields, the Raiders' confidence and initiative were not considered particularly helpful. Each emplacement appeared to require a by-the-numbers (attrition warfare) assault. But, that formula had assumed no opportunity for maneuver. If there were ground undulations to the front and sides of the emplacement, couldn't a few crawling riflemen envelop it? (See Figure 16.1.)

"Keeper" Maneuvers from Converted Raiders

The 4th Marine Regiment had been exposed to the Oriental thought process long before its 1943 Raider infusion. (Refer back to Table 1.1) From whatever source, many of its WWII and Vietnam tactics then mirrored Mao.

On three separate occasions during the battle for Okinawa, battalions from the 4th Marines conducted doctrine-violating double-envelopments: (1) 2/4 at Mount Yae Take on the Mobotu Peninsula; (2) 2/4 at Half Moon in the Shuri Line; and (3) the whole regiment at Hill 72 on Kiyamu-Gusuku Ridge. Having also occurred was something like a Maoist infiltration attack. Forgoing tank and artillery support to instead rely on buddy teams to envelop the

Figure 16.1: Stalking Adjacent Bunkers through the Microterrain
(Source: MCRP 3-02H [1999], fig. 1-2)

separate bunkers of a defense matrix had happened several times: (1) 2/4 at the Guam's Orote Peninsula; and (2) 2/4 at Okinawa's Half Moon. First developed by the Carlson-emulating 4th Raider Battalion at Bairoko (where no tanks or artillery were available), this grassroots maneuver had now proven preferable where both were abundant. Half Moon's frontal faces were too steep for tanks, and its passageways too well protected from bombardment. Thus, only the Bairoko method would work.

Modern-day defenses are nearly impregnable to armor and supporting arms as well. Where devoid of barbed wire, they may be most easily taken by Bairoko Assault. (Refer back to Chapter 10.) Each assault line must be backed by enough troops to prevent its subterranean envelopment.

From the Sugar Loaf Complex struggle, one can also see that former Raiders better survived intense combat. Complex occupiers were constantly skirmishing with infiltrators who had just surfaced a few feet away. The Marines who did the best had formerly experimented with ways to trick an onrushing assailant.

An Evolutionary Advance in Tactics?

The Bairoko Assault may at first look fire team "fire and movement," but it really isn't. It involves enough cooperation between lanes to facilitate the double-envelopment of each bunker in a row. Advanced defenses are no longer linear, so narrow penetrations of their frontal zones accomplish very little. The initially successful attackers will still have active bunkers to their front and sides. Instead, the first two rows of mutually supporting emplacements must all be invested at once. That's the only way to suppress the fire that will crisscross the face of each one.

Such a complicated maneuver cannot be planned or even directed from above. It must simply happen after fire team lanes have been assigned. For reasons not completely clear to the author, it no longer constitutes as a hasty attack. There is certainly enough recon pull to meet the deliberate-attack requirements. Perhaps, two-man assault elements don't require as much rehearsal.

Where there is no barbed wire, this maneuver would be every bit as effective as a more carefully planned attack (and without the delay). As shown in Chapter 11, it worked well for the 4th Raider Battalion successors in Vietnam. But, beware; during WWII, both the Germans and Russians liked to combine strongpoint matrices with barbed wire—some around each strongpoint and then more to make the defenses look linear.[6]

4th Marines Use Maoist Tactics in Vietnam

An in-depth study of the 4th Marine Regiment in Vietnam

reveals Mao-like tactical tendencies for all three battalions. Their precise source is less important than the obvious exception to established procedure.

At Con Thien, 1/4 displayed an unusual degree of small-unit confidence. Separate squads so disrupted the timing of the Dien Bien Phu anniversary attack force as to cause it to fail at its mission.

At Dai Do, while engaging a much larger force, 2/4 took these rather unusual steps: (1) withdrew to more easily attack; (2) continued to attack despite being repeatedly thrown back; (3) formed a single-line defense; (4) used the same formation for both offense and defense; and (5) conducted random fire and movement with increasingly smaller elements. By the following, it further broke with tradition: (1) attacking more at night; (2) attempting more deception in the assault; (3) using snipers to counter enemy machineguns; and (4) investing many objectives from two sides at once (double-envelopment). Last but not least, Hotel and Echo Companies had both used tiny teams to separately outflank the bunkers in a strongpoint matrix (namely, the Bairoko Assault).

While fighting at the periphery of Leatherneck Square, 3/4 liked to close with the foe and learn from its own troops. Both had helped it to confront a bottom-up thinker who most heavily relied on frontline elements. Like 2/4 in WWII and Vietnam, 3/4 had also demonstrated enough excellence at fire team maneuver to take four consecutive bunker complexes with no supporting arms. In fact, all of 3/4's composite elements, however small, were quite self-sufficient. Though not a direct descendent of a Mao-emulating Raider Battalion, 3/4 had apparently seen why Mao and Carlson put so much emphasis on the individual fighter. Kilo's leaders served their riflemen. India's leaders honored their riflemen. Lima's leaders depended on their riflemen (not supporting arms) to win the difficult fights. And Mike's leaders learned from their riflemen how to combat the foe's most obscure strategy.

Mao Tse-tung's tactical influence on this American infantry regiment seems to have been greater in Vietnam than during WWII. How could this be? There had been an interim war against the Communists in 1950, but the 4th Marine Regiment had not participated. Had Japan's small-unit maneuvers been less worrisome than the North Vietnamese variety? While confronting the latter, had these U.S. battalions learned a better way of operating themselves?

Then Came the Maoist CAPs

The proposal to put Marines and militiamen into the same platoons had come from 3/4 and been approved by a former 1st Battalion Raider. The resulting CAP was a "friendly blotch" with which to interrupt the Communist Inkblot strategy. So, the CAP concept was more Maoist than anything else. Its underlying intent was, after all, to fortify the leadership cadre within each village. As the number of friendly villages grew, the insurgents' base of support dwindled. This vision still has great utility—with regard to 4GW. Instead of a physical barrier that cannot forestall subversion, the Marines had followed the Asian example to create an imaginary barrier that could. Such an arrangement might be likened to a political strongpoint matrix.

From the standpoint of tactical evolution, the CAPs had also provided a much more significant service. Just as the Chinese leader had been forced during his Long March to rely on the individual fighter, so too had CAP headquarters. In a loosely controlled and constantly dispersed platoon, the young Marines had largely to rely on self-discipline. They soon realized another need—to match the woods skills of a more numerous foe. With the CAP program, III MAF had created the perfect environment in which Western troops might acquire light-infantry expertise. That environment had been the product of three factors: (1) the diminutive size of the unit and constant threat of its annihilation; (2) the tactical expertise of the enemy; and (3) continually traveling the microterrain around each village. Instead of relying on protective artillery fires, the CAP members had been forced to develop enough observation, movement, and contact skills to keep their tiny compound from ever being attacked. Herein was something that Mao had also determined. For light-infantry skills, actual battle experience is the best teacher. That's because initiative and self-confidence only result from continual exposure to highly challenging situations. Should the Pentagon ever decide to create some truly light infantrymen, it won't be able to do so in any classroom. Minimally required will be simulated-casualty assessment with which to emphasize (and eventually correct) any ill-advised action.

Besides the extreme danger, every CAP member had been motivated by an oath to "serve" his villagers. He would soon realize that his best chances for survival lay in treating them well. Such an oath may be required for enough discipline to conduct 4GW.

Had Vietnam Magnified the Carlson Tradition?

The above-mentioned 2/4 was only a redesignated 3/22, and its sister battalions had no direct Carlson input. Yet, 2/4 and 3/4 were both exhibiting Maoist tendencies. Just to survive at Dai Do, 2/4 had copied a bigger adversary's bottom-echelon tactics. By following the advice of the troops, 3/4 had embraced the same techniques. Their mutual foe—the NVA—had based their procedures on Mao. So, like the Raiders of Carlson and Roosevelt, these two battalions had opted for Communist small-unit maneuvers over their own. A somewhat isolated WWII trend had been greatly expanded.

Raiders and 2/4 Had Both Been Doing Squad Level MW

While exactly copying all of Carlson's methods may no longer be possible, none should totally rejected. His was the only example of how the Chinese model—for producing tiny self-sufficient elements—might work for a Western military. He had accomplished some things that the modern-day Marine Corps has yet to match. On Guadalcanal, he had performed a small-unit version of Chinese Mobile Warfare. That, except for a few more parameters (for reassembly after dispersion, short-range infiltration, deception, and non-martial alternatives), is the same as MW at the squad level. Without some Carlson-like guerrilla training, contemporary squads may never have this capability.

Replacing the meat grinder approach to a bunker complex with concurrent buddy team envelopments of all accessible bunkers is also a good example of squad-level MW. Roosevelt's Raiders had developed it out of necessity at Bairoko, and 2/4 (its redesignation) had used it on Okinawa's nearly impossible Half Moon. Had either combined it with Stormtrooper technique (for the really stubborn emplacements), they might have fully taken their objectives.

What Had the Communists Invented?

With the massive infusion of "volunteers" from the north, the Red Chinese proficiency at maneuver became quite apparent in Korea. Next came Vietnam. There, the whistles and bugles of the Chosin Reservoir were replaced by silent signalling.

Because Asian Communist armies alternately practice Mobile, Positional, and Guerrilla Warfare, they sometimes pick the wrong style for the situation. Then, they look bad (like when a fully supported PLA army failed to penetrate Vietnam in 1979).[7] Still, their well-documented ability to learn from past mistakes makes them extremely dangerous. Asian Communist troops don't need to study the WWI Stormtroop, WWII Carlson, Vietnam CAP, or any subsequent wartime experience. Their "corporate knowledge" has already embraced all evolutionary changes to small-unit maneuver. It did so while the American system was focusing on technology, and in large part to counter that technology. Having a guerrilla background, tiny groups of Asian soliders can more easily move around a battlefield in a semi-autonomous role. That's the same as practicing MW at the squad level. It's why Carlson had been working so hard on self-discipline and self-sufficiency. If the Asian Communists long ago assimilated German MW parameters, then their current guidelines for Mobile Warfare may be more refined than those for U.S. Marine MW.

In all likelihood, the Chinese, North Koreans, and Vietnamese already enjoy state-of-the-art squad tactics. To what Mao had contributed for fire teams, they have added what the WWII Germans and Japanese ascertained for squads. Included would be the short-range infiltration of the Japanese and rearward moving strongpoints of the Germans. Any Communist mistakes in Korea have since been rectified. While the Japanese were good at camouflage and the Germans at unexpected assault, the Asian Communists have become masters of every kind of deception. Among them would be non-martial efforts. This much diversity is now known as 4GW. Its power has been painfully evident in Vietnam, Southern Africa, Central America, Iraq, and Afghanistan. The most advanced version may already be at work inside the borders of China's sole remaining competitor. For its specifics, one has only to review the leftists' political and economic progress throughout the rest of the Western Hemisphere.

The way to handle this more subtle threat is not through additional firepower. It is with squads of commensurate UW, MW, and 4GW skill to deal with the subversion. While it is unlikely that the Pentagon will ever follow an Eastern model to train special-operations-qualified infantry squads, that's what's now needed to slow the Communist, Islamist, and criminal expansion. There are not enough SF, SEAL, and Marine Special Operations Command (MARSOC) teams to get the job done. Even they have too few techniques for UW (hiding and fighting like a guerrilla) and noisy surprise assault (bangalore and concussion grenades during feigned mortar attack). All Vietnamese and North Korean special operators know such things well enough to routinely instruct line infantrymen. That's why they make such good force multipliers.

The Infantry Squad's Ongoing Role

In the "Sands of Iwo Jima," Sgt. Stryker shared with his squad "stuff that would never be printed."[8] Much of that stuff had been passed down over the campfire. This documentary movie suggests that credit for getting to the top of Suribachi and then through Iwo Jima's defense belts rightly belongs to the rifle squad.

When Marine squad bays (group living arrangements) went away around 1970, the troops could less easily inform their NCOs and SNCOs (who also lived there). In turn, the officers became less aware of squad, fire team, and rifleman potential. Quickly to take its place was the economy-driven fascination with everything technological. Only now, the sellers of overhead surveillance and precision bombardment were promising victory. Most wars can't be won without first occupying the ground. In many places, that can only be done on foot. If the Pentagon continues to phase out its "straight-leg infantry," this nation may never again win a war. To upgrade that infantry, the military services have only to allow a little bottom-up training.

The Arms Manufacturers' Opposition

U.S. arms manufacturers and their Pentagon contacts are in no hurry for the American public to find out that light infantry can hold its own with acceptable casualties in conventional battle. Israel's so-called Second Lebanon War with *Hezbollah* provides a perfect example. In the West, light-infantry skills have historically been associated with low-intensity combat, and all that expensive firepower with high-intensity combat. The *Hezbollah* clinic at the Lebanese border in 2006 should be enough to dispel that myth forever.[6] Among other things, limited numbers of *Shiite* militiamen had destroyed over 50 tanks (by the Israelis' own count).[9]

Israeli troops are only slightly better at light-infantry subjects than their U.S. counterparts. Neither are fully trained in man-tracking or microterrain appreciation. As a result, the Israelis had trouble locating the camera/computer triggered anti-tank rockets that were to eliminate so many *Merkava* tanks. (See Figure 16.2.) More troops might have helped to occupy that contested ground, but what was really needed was more light-infantry skills from the ones already there. Journalists have since speculated that more air support could have suppressed the anti-tank rockets. There had been plenty of planes overhead, but nothing to shoot at. The tanks had been spotted by camera, rockets raised and targeted by computer, and shots triggered remotely. With all of the Moslem fighters well dispersed in hidden bunkers, there had been no heat signature to attack.

War's Most Likely Face Has Changed

If the last few deployments are any indicator, U.S. squads will

Figure 16.2: Light Infantry and Gadgets Stop Tanks at Bint Jbeil
(Source: U.S. Air Force Clipart Library (www.usafns.com/art.shtml), image designator "scott_et_al_long%20war%20presen copy07 copy.jpg")

need more proficiency in non-martial subjects as well. Again the Chinese model may help. In addition to an Ethical Indoctrination and self-discipline practice, U.S. troops will need some police training. In so heavy a drug and extremist infested world, the most productive way of quelling unrest is different. The drone missile enthusiasts have yet to realize that.

> When the only tool you have is a hammer, the whole world looks like a nail.
> — Mark Twain

Within the Squad Is Still the Key to Victory

Through enough maneuver comes the minimal-force option. Safely to assault a defense matrix, one has only to sneak up on—and then stick a pistol in the ear of—every enemy machinegunner. As with Carlson's fire team probes on Guadalcanal, this much maneuver is only possible through serious decentralization of control. Small elements are harder to detect; and really small elements can virtually disappear. From high overhead, the latter are indistinguishable from locals. Yet, when facing the most sophisticated surveillance equipment, they need only a foot-deep ditch to sneak up on someone. Herein lies the future of warfare, not with chair-bound technocrats trying remotely to dominate a battlefield. One is terrain anchored, and the other isn't. Whoever actually occupies the ground after an engagement is—and always has been—that engagement's winner.

Squad Maneuvers Are Best Designed by Squad Members

Collective NCO opinion and field experimentation will always produce better maneuvers than a headquarters think-thank. (See Figure 16.3.) Tactical technique is only as useful as it is unexpected. Thus, there is little harm in letting every rifle company arrive at its own. Three things are accomplished that way: (1) less predictability; (2) more situationally appropriate maneuvers; and (3) a better learning dynamic. Following the manuals too closely—when people are tired, rushed, or uninspired—can create real problems. It may have its place in a parade or canned competition, but seldom works in combat.

Past Attempts to Correct the Deficiency

Some years ago, Commandant C.C. Krulak (one of "Brute's" sons) announced the "Strategic Corporal" initiative. Before long, mantracking and movement skills had been added to the enlisted infantryman's training. Though well intended, both programs made little difference. Squad self-sufficiency is less a matter of NCO status and force-fed training, as it is of continual practice. It takes letting squad members run their own show to a certain extent—during both training and operations. By the end of 1917, the Germans had NCOs in charge of all ground attack spearheads,[10] and all elastic-defense forts.[11] They had made the change to try to salvage an all-out war. Within training or any limited deployment, U.S. commanders are not likely to delegate this much authority. That's because one squad's mistake could end their careers. Yet, every foolish action in training is one avoided in combat.

If the 95-year duration of this squad deficiency is any indication, neither U.S. infantry branch has any intention of decentralizing control over training and operations enough to fix the problem. Their preference is completely standardized top-down training. That requires too little maneuver selection, technique input, and initiative from each NCO. To improve, those service branches need a bottom-up training supplement. That in Appendix B has been shown to 40 battalions, and adopted by three.[12]

At fault is the hierarchical nature of the organizations themselves. Bureaucracies tend to focus more on self-perpetuation than doing every part of their job well. What suffers most in a top-down military is bottom-echelon proficiency. This is no one's fault *per se,* simply what happens in a Western country when a government agency tries to copy civilian procedure. That's what Carlson had been attempting to change. However, his vision had been too ambitious for the period. Even today, the best that can be realistically expected is for the bureaucratic damper on NCO initiative to be counteracted by in-unit-technique experimentation.

East Asian Communists don't have this problem. The armies of Mainland China, North Korea, and Vietnam all rely on bottom-up training and operations while drawing their methods from bottom-up societies. This allows them more easily to produce self-sufficient squads. From Hanoi still come the best light infantrymen in the world.

Figure 16.3: The Most Logical Designer of Squad Tactics
(Source: U.S. Army Center of Military History, artphoto archives, illustration designator "avop08-01.2.jpg," An Army of One, by Henrietta Snowden)

The Corps' Next (and Possibly Last) Opportunity

Of America's two infantry branches, the Marine Corps has always been the one pushing for more maneuver. It did so while attacking the Shuri Line on Okinawa, and it did so again with CAP program in Vietnam. Now it must exploit its Maoist heritage to give this country the best chance of winning WWIII.

With the CAPs, some of the Corps' highest generals had displayed a depth of understanding for the lowly Maoist method that still amazes most Asia-philes. Yet, this had been an aberration in an otherwise Western strategy. America's battlefield "Intelligence" was of no help to its rifle company commanders.[13] Those coming up with it must have known very little of the evolution of small-unit tactics or Asia's bottom-up thought process.

Without first reading of the WWI Germans' tactical advances, a Vietnam participant would have had no clue as to the depth of his relative deficiency. Unbeknownst to most U.S. grunts, the NVA had been regularly using a variation to the Stormtrooper assault. So had the Chinese, North Koreans, and Japanese before them. In fact, many Korea and WWII participants may have died from simply not knowing enough about history.

As might be expected, such a realization doesn't make modern-day war veterans very happy. Their respective systems had clearly opted for strict compliance of orders over rifle squad welfare. Of course, there had been some system members attempting to compensate for the oversight. During WWII, Marine SNCOs all but took over the everyday workings of the infantry companies—only sharing what was absolutely necessary with their officers. Then, during Korea, they came to work two hours early to accomplish some training without interference. With an exceptional platoon sergeant, the Vietnam era lieutenant could have also done well. But, not every Staff Sergeant is exceptional.

For the average company, consistently excelling at close-quarters combat takes a different approach. Some 20 or so of its NCOs must be continually polled on the tactical options. That's after all NCOs have arrived at a universally practiced technique portfolio. As in football, each tiny element needs at least three ways to handle every contact. To keep the foe guessing, those ways must occasionally change. To be the world's best at short-range combat, the Corps must now embrace this reasoning.

The Most Logical Fix Costs Nothing

Surprise maneuvers cost nothing. That may be why there's so much manufacturer emphasis on firepower. Continually learning to operate a new piece of equipment leaves little time for stealth and deception practice. This ordnance-oriented way of fighting is not without risk. By some estimates, a full fifth of all casualties in Vietnam came from friendly fire.[14] Encircling every objective, however small, would have produced less fratricide.

There is little doubt a squad of Marines who had been together long enough and allowed to do their own training could "hang" with the best in the world. Unfortunately, that much time and leeway are seldom possible. That's why every squad's techniques are more usefully acquired through historical lessons, group proposals, and field trials. For the best squad maneuvers, each company's NCOs must be allowed to develop the component moves. This requires only an occasional show of hands and simulated-casualty assessment. Once practiced, those techniques need not be exactly followed in combat. Their very existence makes momentum possible.

What is most trustworthy in combat comes from the observations and logic of junior enlisted personnel. That's because they're the next to die. Unfortunately, Western bureaucracies like to treat all nonrates like new guys. That leaves too little opportunity for their input. To compensate, each company needs a way to harness and incorporate junior-enlisted wisdom.

The NVA and Chinese way of instructing infantrymen works well for Asians. Carlson's controversial *Gung Ho* Session was the mirror image of the NVA's Kim Thao Session. For Americans, something a little less democratic might stand a better chance. For starters, it should deal only with tactics.

An Original MW Prerequisite Had Been Ignored

In recent years, the U.S. Marine Corps has moved forward a little. Its doctrine has been MW since Gen. Gray was Commandant, and its battlefield contingents smaller late in the Iraq War. Yet, below platoon level, it has yet to attempt MW.

A key step in the Germans' conversion to MW has been skipped. It was to let every rifle company commander train as he saw fit.[15] However, by the end of 1917, this freedom was far from open-ended. To help each company commander focus, Hun Headquarters provided Stormtrooper assault and strongpoint techniques, as well as how to teach them.[16]

Marine company commanders haven't enjoyed enough control over their small-unit training for years. By the early 1990's, even what was taught by the very proficient Division schools had been usurped by HQMC. The first step in any rejuvenation process must therefore be delegating more authority to the company commander. Then, his former training assistant must be returned to that role.[17] Each company's most experienced infantryman is its Gunnery Sergeant. While no expert on squad tactics, he has a better chance than the officers of collecting troop wisdom on the subject.

A More Conservative Route to Carlson's Vision

MW is the same, no matter who does it. What Carlson had learned from Mao was also MW. Thus, his training regimen may be of help to modern-day commanders. Of all its parts, the *Gung*

Figure 16.4: Too Many Lives Will Be Lost or More Wars
(Source: U.S. Army Center of Military History, artphoto archives, illustration designator "20KFlags.jpg," Planting 20,000 Flags on Memorial Day, by Ellen White, 1976)

Ho Session was most controversial. Within the world's most individualistic society, giving average troops that much power could be risky. It had worked in the Orient because of its more group-oriented societies. There is no evidence of the Germans ever trying it. Still, the whole idea of harnessing troop wisdom is attractive. Only needed is a more discreet way to collect it.

Appendix A compares how most Marine riflemen and squads were trained during WWII with Carlson's way. Appendix B shows how indirectly to acquire troop input on tactics alone. Each company commander would enjoy more tactical options in combat if his nine squads were to have already practiced a full portfolio of advanced techniques. While the Stormtrooper methods would qualify, their original format may no longer surprise an Eastern opponent. So, there is plenty of room for alternative versions or something new. Unlike the WWI German, today's American commander has a way to develop such things from scratch (Appendix B).

Exploiting Past Progress

When the Corps discontinued its squad bays, the bottom up learning suffered. As the SNCOs heard about fewer of the troops' training needs, so did the officers. Then, when promotions became mandatory, many leaders had to focus on their boss's mission or just keeping the system running. A few small-unit improvements were still proposed, but the underlying bureaucracy made existing procedures almost impossible to supersede. Thus occurred a further delay to the much needed advances in squad tactics.

The SNCO Corps is no longer as helpful as it once was for a reason. Within the infantry, it first ran into trouble in mid 70's. That's when the rifle company's Gunnery Sergeant became its "bean counter," and its First Sergeant was relieved of most disciplinary and administrative responsibilities. By 1992, the infantry SNCO had still acquired considerable warfighting skill. Then, the East Coast Platoon Sergeants School got reined in, and almost every Sergeant Major with an infantry background transferred to the Air Wing.[18] After Gen. Gray's doctrinal switch to MW (a close facsimile to Chinese Mobile Warfare), these two occurrences seemed like the disbanding of 2nd Raider Battalion all over again.

Of late, the Marine Corps has had more peacetime pressure, to include a number of misplaced civilian rules. One of the most ludicrous is for every recruit to now have a "stress card" with which to tone down his Drill Instructor. A nation's military culture must often differ from its civilian culture. Any Western society that thinks otherwise should not plan to win many more wars. (See Figure 16.4.)

Many Vietnam regiments had not relied as much on squads as the 4th Marines. That was because of the enemy's rather obvious edge in that department. At the time, the Corps didn't know how to create better squads. The CAP experience came too late to influence the overall training pattern. Now, there's enough water under the bridge for a solution. It involves letting each company's NCOs collectively develop their own portfolio of tactical techniques. That should only bother those who have come to value a career over America's future. It is unlikely that wars will ever again be fought in battalion or even company formation. Yet, with HQMC so firmly in control of every aspect of individual and small-group training, world class squads will never be possible.

The U.S. Army May Get There First

What makes sense to Marines also motivates soldiers. In the last year or so, the U.S. Army has greatly increased its focus on squad-level proficiency. The name of its new initiative is "The Squad As the Cornerstone of the Force."

Like America's Marine Corps, its Army also needs some truly light infantry. What it has previously called that really isn't. It travels mostly by truck and fights mostly with supporting arms. Truly light infantrymen depend more on surprise than firepower. Contrary to the arms' manufacturers claims, they can hold their own in high-intensity conventional combat with an acceptable level of casualties. To enhance what commandos do, one has only to make them light-infantry instructors. That's the lesson of North Korea's Light Infantry Training Guidance Bureau.[19] At one point, its members may have had to infiltrate alone across the DMZ and up to 40 kilometers into South Korea as part of their commando certification.[20]

Again for the Army, overcontrol by the command hierarchy is what makes it all but impossible to create self-sufficient squads. To counteract this organizational foible, the NCOs from each line company have only to expand their portfolio of techniques. In the process, they will get all necessary practice in initiative and tactical-decision making. Such bottom-up training would not replace the existing curriculum, just augment it. It would cost nothing, and be accomplished by every NCO teaching a 12-man stick during some delay in the normal training schedule. See Appendix B for the most refined version of this method. It has been tested throughout the Fleet Marine Force, but only adopted for a short while by its most progressive battalion commanders.

How Late the Hour

WWIII won't be like WWII. It may well be lost unless both U.S. infantry branches allow units in closest contact with an Asian foe to learn and operate from the bottom up. Only by "systematically" working together (as in Appendix B) will they achieve Carlson's dream—MW at the squad level.

Appendix A: Extent of Rifleman Training

WWII Boot Camp Training

After Pearl Harbor, Marine Commandant Thomas Holcomb realized he could not achieve his assigned end strength without reverting to a five-week course of recruit training. The new curriculum called for three weeks in garrison and two weeks at the rifle range. A total of 188 hours were scheduled: (1) 96 hours of weapons training; (2) 56 hours of drill, interior guard, and other garrison subjects; (3) 32 hours of field subjects; and (4) four hours of physical conditioning.[1] By March 1942, the duration of recruit training was back up to seven weeks. At MCRD San Diego, it included 138 hours of weapons instruction, 62 hours of garrison subjects, 57 hours of field training, and 14 hours of physical conditioning. Throughout 1943, the training day was lengthened—with much of the extra time dedicated to physical training. The new regimen included swimming and various contact exercises—boxing, wrestling, judo, and hand-to-hand fighting.[2] Then, in early 1944, Lt.Gen. Holcomb's successor—Lt.Gen. Alexander A. Vandegrift—went to an eight-week recruit training schedule "in response to complaints from the Fleet and Marine Corps schools about the quality of knowledge of boot camp graduates."[3]

> [I]nadequacies in recruit training were so great that from 25 to 50 percent of the time in the Replacement Training Centers had to be devoted to very basic instruction.[4]
>
> — Marine General in charge of all West Coast Training

That expanded schedule (which remained in effect until the end of the war) contained 421 hours of instruction: (1) 195 hours for weapons; (2) 39 for physical training; (3) 89 for garrison subjects; and (4) 98 for field training.[5] Among San Diego's field subjects were the following: (1) 19 hours of bayonet training; (2) four hours of chemical warfare; (3) four hours of "protective measures" (possibly first aid); (4) three hours of map and compass; (5) four hours of squad combat principles; (6) one hour of rifle fire technique; and (7) three hours of individual emplacements.[6] Regardless of each Marine's eventual occupational specialty, he was being initially prepared as a rifleman.

During those years, boot camp emphasized three things: (1) attention to detail; (2) teamwork; and (3) shooting. There may have been a few short classes on advanced subjects, but not many. While knife-fighting demonstrations occurred at San Diego,[7] there is no evidence of the "scouting and patrolling" or even "grenade throwing" packages that had been available before the war.[8] That's because those subjects were to be covered at follow-on training. Unlike the Marine Corps of today, most of this era's boot camp graduates were headed to the infantry.

> They [the graduates] might be assigned to any one of a variety of specialist courses. . . . The majority would attend advanced training in the infantry camps, where the skills needed to survive on the modern battlefield were learned.[9]

Extent of Recruit Training at New River and Elliott

During December 1941, 5,272 recruits descended on MCRD Parris Island. With 9,206 arriving the following month, it became necessary to add the 5th, 6th, 7th and 8th Recruit Training Battalions. As the war influx continued, there is some evidence of five more battalions at New River, North Carolina.[10] However, the official chronicle only shows recruits being transferred to New River and Camp Elliott for three weeks of "range instruction" after an initial four weeks at Parris Island and San Diego. This splitting of recruit training location only occurred between August and December 1942.[11] The California Military Museum account tends to confirm the official version.[12]

Individual Training While Existing Units Got Ready to Deploy

As the regiments of 1st Marine Division were rapidly fleshing out at New River, they did some training of Parris Island accessions. Much was monotonous (e.g., countless hours of gun drill and nomenclature) and physically demanding. However, the rest helped to get those recent recruits into a different mindset.

Much of the latter occurred after a seven or eight mile hike into the Verona Training Area from their temporary quarters near New River Barracks (now Camp Geiger). (See Map A.1.) It first covered individual skills under realistic conditions. Then, there were open-ended field problems (scenarios in which all hands had to participate in a solution). While Marines scaled walls, negotiated mud pits, dodged shell holes, and crossed logs (all with dynamite exploding nearby),[13] officers covered subjects they knew little about.[14] One trainee recalled being sent out on a "compass march," in which the platoon and lieutenant were dropped off at midnight in the middle

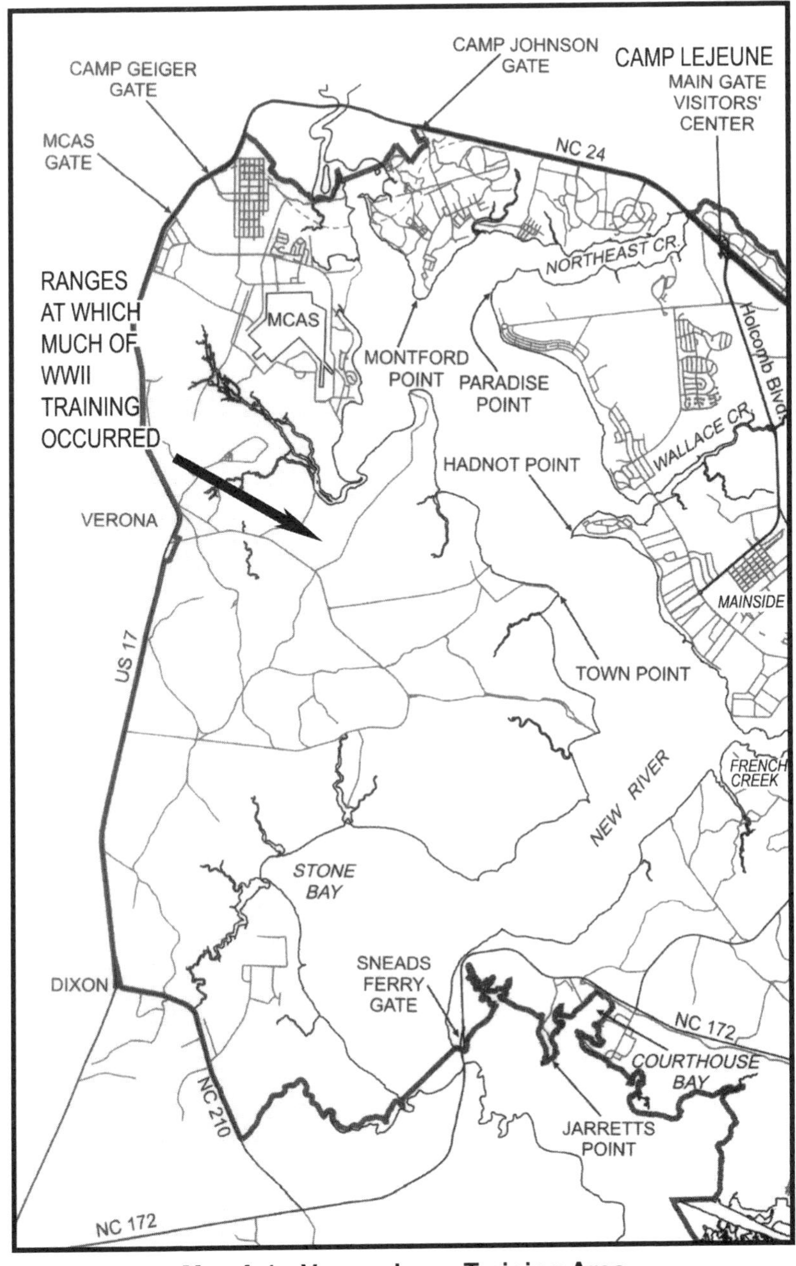

Map A.1: Verona Loop Training Area

(Source: "Semper Fidelis: A Brief History of . . . Camp Lejeune," with Lt.Col. Lynn L. Kimball as consulting historian, Environmental Mgt. Div., 2006)

of the woods with only a compass, map, and teamwork to get them back to base.[15] While instruction this loose might seem less than professional, it was actually farseeing. It not only got everyone thinking, but also created a way (through group Situation Station input) to address issues without answers. Some very useful techniques may have resurfaced this way after never making it into the manuals. Such a regimen was also quite good for the officers. It showed them how to facilitate group knowledge.

Formal Post-Boot-Camp Schooling

When, 1st Marine Division left for the West Coast in April 1942, New River became a place for forming new units and creating their technical and leadership cadre. Included in the latter were enough infantry NCOs to man 21 new grunt battalions. For the first few months of WWII, most units had conducted their own training. Then, in May 1942, the Corps initiated "individual replacement training" at New River (just south of present-day Camp Lejeune) and Camp Elliott (south of what is now Camp Pendleton).[16]

New River and Elliott had slightly preceded their more famous neighbors. While the higher-ups called the East Coast training center Marine Barracks New River, its occupants soon dubbed it "Tent City." It was located where Camp Geiger is today. Camp Elliott had previously been Camp Holcomb on Kearny Mesa, just north of San Diego and east of Miramar. Both were soon to become the epicenter for the reactivation and mobilization of the wartime Marine Corps. Most forming units were temporarily in residence.[17]

The New River Training Center

For New River, the additional grunt training was called the "Graduate School of Invasion." At one outdoor exercise in mid-October 1942, students had their "shallow foxholes" overrun by a 12-ton tank and then mock-strafed by actual airplanes. In the latter, it was a lieutenant who designated the direction in which everyone was to fire. His underlying message was that it was folly to try to outrun such an attack. Nearby was how to make—and then use from a foxhole against mock armor—a Molotov Cocktail. Elsewhere, troops in full gear were running an obstacle course. But, this was no ordinary course. Besides the standard wall to scale, fence to vault, and rope to swing, it had the following: (1) culverts to penetrate; (2) barbed wire to "submarine"; and (3) gullies to leap. Nearby, another group roughly practiced how to kill with one's bare hands, knife, and bayonet. A little further away, other Marines learned how to lay and detonate land mines.

Most noteworthy of this very realistic training (all had been done on a range with live training aids), was the sapper-style patrolling package. "In open fields, men are slithering though the grass learning scouting and patrolling."[18] This may have been as a result of reports from Guadalcanal on how the Japanese liked to patrol near U.S. lines.[19] Or it may have just been the safest way for a whole group to cross a danger area. From whatever source, it was highly intuitive (and would almost never be seen today). Other activities in adjacent areas were obviously part of some other package. There was road building and flag signaling.[20]

Over the years, this method of instruction has come to be known as Round Robin training.[21] It involves rotating small groups among the same number of outdoor stations. For some reason, this particular Round Robin included non-combat subjects. At one station, an officer was showing everyone how to erect shelter halves. At another, troops in full combat gear were climbing down rope nets. This Round Robin was to go on all day, with a short break for lunch. At the end of the full curriculum was to be awarded an M.A.—for Master of Assault. As such, the full course of instruction may have been only for NCOs (and the occasional SNCO who had spent too long on independent duty). Its modern equivalent would then be the Squad Leaders and Platoon Sergeants Schools at the East Coast School of Infantry. Instead of more infantry training for boot camp graduates, its job may have been to create an enlisted leadership cadre. Many battalions were forming at the time. This course was only part of a rather extensive FMF Training Center offering.[22]

The Camp Elliott Training Center

One successful recruit—John Barry—arrived at Camp Elliott from MCRD San Diego in September 1943. For whatever reason, he was then given additional infantry training. A contemporary was quite impressed with it. "Gerry Nelson said nothing was as hard as boot camp, but he didn't go through a 'stone crusher's' (infantryman) training. It's boot camp all over again except we have 2nd Lieutenants over us."[23]

The training of which he speaks focused on infantry weapons, tactics, and deployment. His weapons instructors were often NCOs with wartime experience. Barry also took lengthy conditioning marches. "Mornings, afternoons, and once at night, we went out on battle problems, just like maneuvers," he wrote. Barry learned to throw live hand grenades on one expedition to the boondocks. "They are bright yellow, and just fit in your hand nice. Two at a time, we pulled the pins and threw them at some mark on the ground. They really explode and fling the pieces around. As far as 200 yards away, we found little squares of yellow steel." He also describes a "combat reaction course."[24]

Out there, they put on a [phonograph] record of all sorts of loud

Figure A.1: Bayonet Practice Was Standard
(Source: OPNAV P34-03 [1960], p. 406)

> noises—men screaming, bombs bursting. They actually set off land mines near you; and when you see about five heavy lumbering tanks coming at you, you drop in a foxhole—already dug out—and the tank drivers . . . drive right over each and every foxhole twice. While it's going on it isn't bad, but afterwards, I wondered how I went through with it.[25]
>
> — Boot camp graduate after follow-on training

That sounds a lot like what went on at New River. NCOs and boot camp graduates must have been attending the same course of instruction on both Coasts. That means all fledgling infantrymen earned an M.A. The Elliott students also took courses in judo, advanced bayonet training, and how to fight the Japanese hand to hand. Eugene Sledge's instructor told pupils to "kick him in the balls before he kicks you in yours." They were further taught how to use their K-Bar knife. "I guarantee that you or the man in the next foxhole will use a K-Bar on a Jap infiltrator before the war is over," said Sledge's instructor.[26]

After weeks of training, the new Masters of Assault got their final assignments. Some were sent as replacements to divisions already in the war zone. Others went to forming units. Some of the 1943 graduates ended up at Pendleton as part of the brand-new Fourth Marine Division.[27] A few were even lucky enough to work for Gy.Sgt. John Basilone.

Unit Training in the Pacific

As portrayed in the movie "Sands of Iwo Jima," all rest periods for deployed units involved training. It consisted of long foot marches, bayonet fighting, and obstacle course running. (See Figure A.1) Later in the war, it almost certainly included practice in the "Blind 'em, Burn 'em, and Blast 'em" technique for assaulting enemy bunkers.[28]

There must have been subtle variations to this theme for different units (each envisioning a slightly different scenario). Assault groups were formed with flamethrower men, demolition men, and BAR men. At the time, the technique may have been called "Corkscrew" or "Blowtorch." The BARs were to suppress each emplacement with a heavy volume of automatic-weapons fire, while the flamethrowers dispatched its occupants. Only after the position had been neutralized were the demolitions to destroy it. Often, it took that third step to get all resistance to cease. That's because the flamethrower operators—with what amounted a napalm bomb strapped to their back—had to get fairly close to the bunker to be effective.[29]

Raider Training Was Different

Whereas boot camp had taught everyone unit discipline, Carlson was trying to enhance their self-discipline, individual skill, and personal initiative. This took a slightly different approach to training. No longer was it strictly group oriented. He gave each Marine the chance to experiment with his own self-defense methods.

Carlson's initial training emphasis was on how to win every one-on-one encounter between individuals. He wanted only those Marines who were prepared to kill or be killed at close range with a knife. Then, he gave them advanced training in close combat and endurance. His troops learned to watch for an attack against their person from any direction and then—through various ruses when necessary—to instantly gain the upper hand against an onrushing assailant. Their command guidance at this point was "always to expect the unexpected."[30]

At some point, Edson also realized that his junior enlisted personnel needed more self-confidence to do well at short-range combat. As had Carlson, he found free-play to be the most realistic way of training both them and their tiny groups.

> If I had to train my regiment over again, I would stress small group training and the training of the individual....
>
> Our basic training is all right....In your training put your time and emphasis on the squad and platoon rather than on the company, battalion and regiment.
>
> In your scouting and patrolling,...have the men work against each other. Same thing for squads and platoons in their problems....
>
> ...With proper training, our Americans are better [than the Japanese], as our people can think better as individuals. Encourage your individuals and bring them out.[31]
>
> — Col. Merritt A. Edson USMC

While the first Raider preparation had been at Jacques Farm, a satellite facility of Camp Elliott, the "Raider Training Center" was eventually at Camp Pendleton. There occurred eight weeks of instruction. Its subjects ranged from guerrilla warfare to individual cookery. The culmination was a week-long field problem in which students alternately made up a main body of friendlies and two opposing guerrilla groups. There was also rubber boat training. The rest of the curriculum dealt mostly with traditional methods: (1) marksmanship; (2) scouting; (3) patrolling; (4) personal conditioning; and (5) individual combat. Among the group skills were vaulting barbed wire, crossing rivers on two-rope bridges, crawling through low obstacles, and parallel-column road hiking. Among the individual skills were knife fighting,[32] wall scaling, barbed-wire crushing, and invisible-obstacle vaulting (like one would do over a stream of machinegun bullets).[33]

Particularly productive of initiative was each Raider's chance to trick an onrushing assailant during self-defense training. This had come through Roosevelt from Carlson. (See Figure A.2.)

ITR Only Emerged Many Years Later

All of the above happened well before the Infantry Training Regiment (ITR) of the Vietnam era and Infantry Training School (ITS) of modern times. There is evidence that the two WWII Training Centers were run by the Marine divisions responsible for Coastal defenses. It was not until 1953 that Individual Combat Training (ICT) was created as a Base function at both Lejeune and Pendleton.[34] It was only for boot camp graduates destined for infantry units. Advanced Combat Training (ACT) was added in 1956. Among its more specialized subjects were helicopter operations (probably how most safely to embark and debark), plus E&E and survival techniques. As an important aspect of UW, this E&E may have been quite progressive for its time.

All three active duty divisions conducted their own infantry skill courses until the early 1990's. As had the 2nd Marine Division's Guerrilla Warfare Center during Vietnam,[35] such schools heavily focused on battlefield conditions. They had E-5's for instructors and "rankless" students.

Shortly after the Schools of Infantry from both coasts consolidated their curricula in 1987,[36] their separate capacities for improvement started to wane. The amazing progress of the Camp Lejeune "Platoon Sergeants School" (as outlined in Chapter 15) had been largely because of its fledgling status. When forced to institute a CCRB around 1991, its curriculum quickly lost much of its hands-on detail.[37] That detail had never made it into the manuals, just as Sgt. Stryker had predicted.[38]

Figure A.2: Thanks to the Raiders
(Source: Courtesy of Edward Molina © 2012)

Appendix B: Harnessing Frontline Wisdom

1. In modern 4GW, U.S. grunts will always be outnumbered.

2. For enough skill to operate alone and in small units, they will need to work together on some bottom-up training. (See Figure B.1.)

   a. There can be no full Maneuver Warfare (MW) capability without decentralizing control and lowest-echelon initiative.

   b. Each company must learn to operate as nine semi-independent maneuver squads.

      (1) Squads can fight like football teams.

         (a) If they've practiced and numbered several "plays" for each category of enemy contact.
         (b) If the squad leader asks his fire team leaders (by hand-and-arm signal) which play to run before picking.
         (c) If that play need not be run exactly as rehearsed (so individuals can react to unforeseen circumstances).

      (2) Each squad leader will have adequate control if all plays are practiced in varied terrain before attempted in war.

      (3) Training for squad combat is like football too.

         (a) Individual, buddy team, fire team, and squad drills are followed by force-on-force scrimmage.
         (b) Instead of daily physical training (PT), squads do battledrills on cross-country runs with boots and rifles.

   c. Training must give every squad member initiative, tactical-decision-making practice, and nonpredictability.

      (1) The best way is to let the junior NCOs of each company collectively identify and fix their own tactical deficiencies.

(2) Companies no longer need identical squad maneuvers.

(3) Only through local experimentation can the lowest echelons of a top-down organization gain "world class" tactical proficiency.

d. Officers must control bottom-up training indirectly.

(1) By providing options from history.

(2) By choosing situations to be solved.

(3) By monitoring improvement in surprise generated and simulated-casualties suffered.

3. Planning Phase.

a. CO and Platoon Leaders publish "mission-type" training order to Gy.Sgt.—short list of squad combat situations to be solved.

(1) E.g., security patrol, counterambush, ambush, chance contact, day attack, night attack, short-range infiltration, urban attack, urban defense, sapper-oriented defense.

(2) Best are those involving large numbers of enemy soldiers, because they will require total surprise.

b. Gy.Sgt. will function as facilitator of group knowledge (as opposed to enforcer of organizational procedure).

c. Gy.Sgt. convenes NCO Conference to record on the blackboard what will be needed to comply with officers' goals.

(1) Group arrives at prerequisite skills for each situation—what squads, fire teams, buddy teams, and individuals must do.

(2) Elementary "basics" will no longer be enough.

(a) All must be able to covertly shoot, move, and communicate.
(b) All must also have microterrain appreciation, harnessing of senses, night fighting, deception, and decision practice.

d. Gy.Sgt. then schedules supplementary instruction for each level of embedded element (individuals first).

(1) Any weapons training will have one of two formats.

(a) Explain, demonstrate, imitate, practice, test.
(b) Create situation for students to solve (more retention and applicable to enemy weapons).

(2) Established tactical maneuvers taught through battledrills.

(a) Attention gainer and lecture.
(b) Demonstration and practical application.
1 Outdoors.
2 Blackboard or overhead projector.
3 Sand table with miniatures.
(c) Practical application testing (e.g., count U.S. losses).

(3) New tactical maneuvers taught through Situation Stations (with participants allowed to arrive at own solutions).

(4) NCO assigned to each period of instruction.

(a) Leaders of next-higher echelon will do the teaching.
(b) Situation station "experiments" given to NCOs with "by-the-book" mentalities.

(5) Instructors told to refer to *The Last Hundred Yards* and *The Tiger's Way* for guidance on what to teach.

(a) Fully tested maneuver warfare methods.
(b) No squad-level maneuver in conflict with U.S. doctrine.

(6) All instruction will takes place near unit's headquarters or barracks with rubber rifles and makeshift training aids.

4. Execution Phase.

a. Training is conducted for whole company at once.

(1) Either sequentially or in Round-Robin format.

(2) Normally in 20-minute sessions for 12-man sticks.

(3) Assigned instructor can ask any number of peers to help.

(4) Most training consists of movement technique rehearsal.

(a) Success measured through surprise generated (speed, stealth, deception) or simulated-casualties suffered.
(b) Individuals and subunits are asked to compete with each other or improve themselves on successive tries.
(c) "Super squad" determined for each training period.

(5) Instructors statistically track how well the techniques they are teaching work, and keep notes on how to improve them.

b. Next comes the "Tactical Demonstration."

(1) Officers arrange training support and recreate situations.

(2) Squads run through situations under simulated fire.

(a) Machinegun and artillery simulators add realism.
(b) Surprise indicators and friendly casualties measured.

(3) Only recourse for dissatisfied officers is to change situations or pick another group facilitator (SNCO).

c. Then comes "Free-Play"—a force-on-force exercise in which the side with the fewest simulated casualties wins.

(1) Sides required to solve—twice—certain situations for which technique was taught (e.g., two assaults on foe's camp).

(a) One side reverses its shirts.
(b) Sides assigned command posts (CPs) not too far apart.
(c) One third of each force defends own CP with no outposts.
(d) Two thirds of each force must assault enemy CP.
(e) Each man records any three-second sight picture of upright foe or flour grenade hit within 10 feet of himself.
(f) Casualties reenter problem via own CP after short delay.
(g) Secretly seizing the enemy's flag nets bonus points (flag must be unattached and at ground level in CP).
(h) Umpires assess demerits for any bodily contact or not doing required events.

(2) At end of the event, sides are moved beyond earshot of each other while all counts are made and winner determined.

d. Finally, a "Lessons-Learned Field Day" is held.

(1) All junior enlisted personnel are assembled in bleachers.

(2) Lowest ranks given chance to demonstrate better ways.
(3) Gy.Sgt. gauges worth of each way through show of hands.
(4) No promises made as to training changes.
(5) Troops reminded of existing NCO Conference techniques.
(6) New PT method demonstrated.

5. All squads are expected to practice existing NCO Conference movement techniques during daily PT.

   a. First some combat warm-ups.

      (1) Crawling races (with squad leader participating).
      (2) Duck walking as if as under a wall aperture.
      (3) Practice in window entry over any horizontal obstruction.

   b. Then each squad takes its own combat run with boots and rifles.

      (1) Move in "Indian" file (column) through all types of terrain.
      (2) Periodically slow to practice one of the squad techniques.
      (3) Make mental note of terrain limitations to each maneuver.

Figure B.1: Squad Level MW by Systematically Working Together
(Source: Redrawn from Chinese lettering at the start of movie, "Gung Ho," copyright © by Universal Studios, 1943)

6. Gy.Sgt. convenes all NCOs quarterly to modify the company's portfolio of squad, fire team, buddy team and individual techniques, and to plan the next training evolution.

    a. Shortfalls in last training session identified.

        (1) If fewer mock casualties possible than with existing techniques.
        (2) Whether all instructor modifications considered.
        (3) Whether officers' and lowest ranks' expectations met.
        (4) Whether overall organizational doctrine still followed.

    b. All techniques modified as necessary.

7. Gy.Sgt. arrives at next training schedule.

8. This bottom-up cycle becomes a recurring and supplementary part of each company's training program (whether in garrison or deployed).

9. Only now is each battalion fully capable of employing its new tactical doctrine—Maneuver Warfare.

10. Only now can theater commander employ the state of the tactical art—by starting an attack with a squad-sized penetration or building a defensive matrix from squad-sized strongpoints. (Look back at Figure B.1.)

Notes

SOURCE NOTES

Illustrations:

Picture on page vi was created by a U.S. government agency and is thus considered to be in the public domain. This is an OFFICIAL RECRUITING POSTER with image designator "post_usmc_168th-birthday_ww2.jpg." It was retrieved from U.S. National Archives and Records Administration through www.bluejacket.com.

Pictures on pages 7, 18, 30, 36, 56, 72, 85, 88, 115, 123, 155, 268, 283, 299, and 302 reprinted from ARTPHOTO ARCHIVES of the U.S. Army's Center of Military History. As they all appear to have been painted by active-duty personnel, they are considered to be in the public domain. They have the following illustration designators: "avop03-98_1.jpg"; "0806-1.jpg"; "avop05-98_2.jpg"; "0107-4.jpg"; "avop05-98_1.jpg"; "jungle.jpg"; "avop05-99_1.jpg"; "avop07-98_3.jpg"; "112Cavalry.jpg"; "0806-4.jpg"; *0806-3.jpg"; "0207-4.jpg"; "Another Day at the Office.jpg"; "avop08-01.2.jpg"; and "20KFlags.jpg," respectively.

Pictures on pages 8, 20, 32, 111, 128, 184, 192, 199, 230, and 255 reprinted from POSTERS of the U.S. Army's Center of Military History. As they all appear to have been painted by active-duty personnel, they are considered to be in the public domain. They have the following illustration designators: "couldnt_fight.jpg"; "1-36-49.jpg"; "1-18-49.jpg"; "1-38-49.jpg"; "1-25-49.jpg"; "p_3_4_67.jpg"; "p_3_35_67.jpg"; "w_1_9_68.jpg"; "w_1_14_68.jpg"; and "1006-1.jpg," respectively.

Illustrations on pages 11, 22, 33, 42, and 81 reprinted from "FIRST OFFENSIVE: THE MARINE CAMPAIGN FOR GUADALCANAL," by Henry I. Shaw, *Marines in WWII Commemorative Series,* Headquarters Marine Corps, 1992.

Illustrations on pages 12 and 44 reprinted from "CLOSING IN: MARINES IN THE SEIZURE OF IWO JIMA," by Colonel Joseph H. Alexander, *Marines in WWII Commemorative Series,* Headquarters Marine Corps, 1994.

Picture on pages 15 reprinted under provisions of GNU Free Documentation License, from *WIKIPEDIA ENCYCLOPEDIA,* s.v. "Carlson's Raiders." As an educational nonprofit, Posterity Press considers the reproduction of this image to be fair usage, but others must be more mindful of its possible copyright.

Illustrations on pages 19, 73, 104, 105, 107, and 110 reprinted from "FROM MAKIN TO BOUGAINVILLE: MARINE RAIDERS IN THE PACIFIC WAR," by Major Jon T. Hoffman, *Marines in WWII Commemorative Series,* Headquarters Marine Corps, 1995.

Illustration on pages 21 reprinted from "UP THE SLOT: MARINES IN THE CENTRAL SOLOMONS," by Major Charles D. Melson, *Marines in WWII Commemorative Series,* Headquarters Marine Corps, 1993.

Map on page 23 reprinted from one of the *GREEN BOOKS* of U.S. Army's Center of Military History. It has illustration designator "Imap-vi.jpg."

Pictures on pages 157, 225, and 245 reproduced after asking permission of Osprey Publishing Ltd., London, from "ARMIES OF THE VIETNAM WAR 1962-75," *Men-at-Arms Series,* issue 104, text by Philip Katcher and Lee E. Russell, with color plates by Michael Chappell. The illustrations are from plate C (number 2, "Viet Cong," 1960's-70's), plate H (number 1, Enlisted Man, North Vietnamese Army, 1975), and plate C (number 3, "Khmer Rouge," 1960's-70's), respectively.

Pictures on pages 27, 83, 93, 121, and 195 reproduced after written assurance from Cassell PLC, London, that the copyright holder for *WORLD ARMY UNIFORMS SINCE 1939,* text by Andrew Mollo and Digby Smith, with color plates by Malcolm McGregor and Michael Chappell, could no longer be contacted. The illustrations are from part II (plate 80), part I (plate 155), part II (plate 88), part I (plate 156), and part I (plate 136), respectively.

Pictures on pages 55 and 57 reproduced with permission of Stefan H. Verstappen, from *THE THIRTY-SIX STRATEGIES OF ANCIENT CHINA.* Copyright © 1999 by Stefan H. Verstappen. All rights reserved.

Illustrations on pages 76, 96, and 97 reprinted from "TOP OF THE LADDER: MARINE OPERATIONS IN THE NORTHERN SOLOMONS," by J.C. Chapin, *Marines in WWII Commemorative Series*, Headquarters Marine Corps, 1997.

Picture on page 81 reprinted from *A CONCISE HISTORY OF THE UNITED STATES MARINE CORPS 1775-1969,* by Captain William D. Parker, with sketch by Captain Donald L. Dickson, Historical Division, Headquarters Marine Corps, 1970.

Maps on pages 94 and 108 reprinted from *MARINES IN THE CENTRAL SOLOMONS,* by Major John N. Rentz, "USMC Historical Monograph," Headquarters Marine Corps, 1952, from an un-numbered chapter 1 map and map 13, respectively.

Map on page 101 reprinted from "ISOLATION OF RABAUL," by Henry I. Shaw and Major Douglas T. Kane, volume II, *History of USMC Operations in World War II Series,* Historical Branch, Headquarters Marine Corps, 1963, from map 10.

Picture on page 151 reproduced after written assurance from Osprey Publishing Ltd., London, that this is a U.S. War Department (public domain) sketch from "JAPANESE ARMY OF WORLD WAR II," *Men-at-Arms Series,* text by Philip Warner, with color plates by Michael Youens, page 26. Copyright © 1972 by Osprey Publishing Ltd. All rights reserved.

Maps on page 125 and 129 reprinted from *A BRIEF HISTORY OF THE FOURTH MARINES,* by James S. Santelli, "Marine Corps Historical Reference Pamphlet," Historical Division, Headquarters Marine Corps, 1970, pages 27 and 31.

Map on page 126 reprinted from *THE RECAPTURE OF GUAM,* by Major O.R. Lodge, "Historical Monograph," Headquarters Marine Corps, 1954, page 88.

Maps on pages 130 and 137 reprinted from "JAPAN'S BATTLE FOR OKINAWA, APRIL - JUNE 1945," by Thomas M. Hubler, *Leavenworth Papers Number 18,* U.S. Army Command and Staff College, 1990.

Maps on pages 131 and 136 reprinted from "THE FINAL CAMPAIGN: MARINES IN THE VICTORY ON OKINAWA," by Colonel Joseph H. Alexander, *Marines in WWII Commemorative Series,* Headquarters Marine Corps, 1996, pages 17 and 38.

Maps on pages 135 and 153 reprinted from *OKINAWA: THE LAST BATTLE,* by Roy Appleman, James Burns, Russell Gugeler, and John Stevens, U.S. Army's Center of Military History, 2000, from maps 38 and 49.

Maps on pages 160, 162, 163, 164, 165, 166, 167, and 168 reprinted with permission of the Marine Corps Association. They come from "Memories of Dai Do," by William Weise, in the September 1987 issue of the *MARINE CORPS GAZETTE.*

Maps on pages 201 and 221 reprinted with permission of Ray Smith. They are based on enlargements of part of the 1:50,000 Vietnam Series L7014 found at RAY'S MAP ROOM (http://rjsmith.com/topo_map.html). His map designator is "Central DMZ: Con Thien, SPOS, Map Sheet 6342-1 (401kb)."

Map on page 251 is based on a U.S. Marine Corps Historical Center drawing by W. Stephen Hill, from *OUR WAR WAS DIFFERENT,* by Al Hemingway, Naval Institute Press, 1994. As an educational nonprofit, Posterity Press considers its reproduction and then modification to be fair usage, but others must be more mindful of its copyright.

Illustration on page 296 reprinted from U.S. AIR FORCE CLIPART LIBRARY (www.usafns.com/art.shtml). The image designator is "scott_et_al_long%20war%20presen copy07 copy.jpg."

Illustration on page 313 reprinted with permission of EDWARD MOLINA.

Picture on page 319 redrawn from Chinese lettering at the start of Universal Studios' movie, "*GUNG HO!*" Factual story by Lt. W.S. LeFrancois USMC, with Lt.Col. Evans Carlson USMCR as technical advisor. As an educational nonprofit, Posterity Press considers this facsimile reproduction to be fair usage, but others must be more mindful of the original image's copyright.

Text:

Excerpt on page 40 reprinted with permission of Random House (New York) from *VIETNAM AT WAR – THE HISTORY: 1946-1975,* by Phillip P. Davidson.

Excerpt on page 41 reprinted after being unable to contact Dodd Mead (New York) or Foreign Languages Press (Beijing, China), from *TWIN STARS OF CHINA,* by Evans Fordyce Carlson.

Excerpts on pages 139-141 reprinted with permission of Louie Marsh from *ONCE A RAIDER . . . U.S. MARINE RAIDERS IN WW2 AND ONE RAIDER'S EXPERIENCE* and Dan Marsh's Marine Raider Page (http://www.usmcraiders.com).

Excerpts on pages 180, 181, and 187 reprinted with permission of Zenith Press (Minneapolis), from *NOBLE WARRIOR,* by James E. Livingston, Colin D. Heaton, and Anne-Marie Lewis.

Excerpt on page 187 reprinted after asking permission of Random House (New York) from *THE MAGNIFICENT BASTARDS: THE JOINT ARMY-MARINE DEFENSE OF DONG HA, 1968,* by Keith William Nolan.

ENDNOTES

Preface

1. Memorandum for the record by H.J. Poole.

Chapter 1: *Historical Backdrop*

1. Bruce I. Gudmundsson, *Stormtroop Tactics—Innovation in the German Army 1914-1918* (New York: Praeger, 1989), pp. 43-50, 94, 146, 147.
2. "From Makin to Bougainville: Marine Raiders in the Pacific War," by Maj. Jon T. Hoffman, *Marines in WWII Commemorative Series* (Washington, D.C.: Marine Corps Hist. Ctr., 1995), pp. 1-5.
3. Ibid.
4. Ibid.
5. Ibid.
6. "What Was the Long March," by Kallie Szczepanski, *Asian History About.com.*
7. *Mao Tse-tung: An Anthology of His Writings,* ed. Anne Fremantle (New York: Mentor, 1962), p. 69.
8. Ed Gilbert, *U.S. Marine Corps Raider 1942-43* (London: Osprey Publishing, 2006), p. 4.
9. "From Makin to Bougainville," by Hoffman, photo annotation, p. 25.
10. Gilbert, *U.S. Marine Corps Raider 1942-43,* p. 4.
11. Former member of 3rd Raider Battalion and then 3/4, in conversation with author during August 2011.
12. Truong Chinh, *Primer for Revolt,* intro. Bernard B. Fall (New York: Praeger, 1963), pp. 114-117.
13. *The Strategic Advantage: Sun Zi & Western Approaches to War,* ed. Cao Shan (Beijing: New World Press, 1997), pp. 7, 11, 49, 50.

Chapter 2: *The Marine Raiders' Initial Contribution*

1. *Semper Fidelis: A Brief History of Onslow County, North Carolina, and of Camp Lejeune,* document prepared by the Louis Berger Group Inc. under contract with the U.S. Army's Corps of Engineers and with Lt.Col. Lynn L. Kimball USMC (Ret.) as consulting historian (Camp Lejeune, NC: Environmental Mgt. Div., 2006), p. 37.
2. LaVarre Daley, *United States Marine Corps Raiders: A Personal Account* (N.p.: Pal-Mit Industries, 2002), pp. 1-4; "From Makin to Bougainville," by Hoffman, pp. 1-5.

3. Joseph H. Alexander. *Edson's Raiders: 1st Marine Raider Battalion in World War II* (Annapolis, MD: Naval Inst. Press, 2001), p. 242; "From Makin to Bougainville," by Hoffman, p. 5.
4. *Handbook on the Chinese People's Liberation Army,* DDB-2680-32-84 (Washington, D.C.: DIA, November 1984), pp. 16, A-5.
5. "From Makin to Bougainville," by Hoffman, pp. 5, 24.
6. Gilbert, *U.S. Marine Corps Raider 1942-43,* pp. 1-25.
7. "From Makin to Bougainville," by Hoffman, p. 5.
8. John Wukovits, *American Commando* (New York: New American Library, 2009). p. 213.
9. Geoffrey Perret, "Warrior Mao," *MHQ: The Quarterly Journal of Military History,* issue 19, no. 3, Spring 2007, p. 6, in *American Commando,* by Wukovits, pp. 10, 11.
10. Wukovits, *American Commando,* p. 7.
11. "From Makin to Bougainville," by Hoffman, pp. 5, 19-22.
12. "Article Details Everyday Life in Army," *Chungang Ilbo,* 15 April 1993, p. 1, as cited in FBIS-EAS-93-092, 14 May 1993, pp. 32, 33; "North Korean Army Training Is Steadily Progressing," *Defense Intelligence Digest,* June 1968, pp. 29-31; and "North Korean People's Army Operations," *FC 100-2-99* (Washington, D.C.: Hdqts. Dept. of the Army, 5 December 1986), chapt. 16; all from *North Korean Special Forces,* by Joseph S. Bermudez, Jr. (Annapolis, MD: Naval Inst. Press, 1998), p. 219.
13. "From Makin to Bougainville," by Hoffman, p. 5.
14. Ibid., p. 10.
15. Ibid., p. 5.
16. Ibid.

Chapter 3: *The Counter-Cultural "Gung Ho Session"*

1. *China Page,* s.v. "gung ho."
2. *Wikipedia Encyclopedia,* s.v. "gung ho."
3. *Merriam-Webster Dictionary,* s.v. "gung ho," as retrieved from the following url on 1 August 2011: www.merriam-webster.com/dictionary/gung%20ho.
4. Evans Carlson, as quoted in "Gung Ho," by Alfred F. Moe, *American Speech,* vol. 42, no. 1, Feb., 1967, p. 58, and originally from interview associated with "Carlson of the Raiders," by Don Burke, *Life,* 20 September 1943.
5. "From Makin to Bougainville," by Hoffman, p. 5.
6. *The Strategic Advantage: Sun Zi & Western Approaches to War,* by Cao Shan (Beijing: New World Press, 1997), pp. 21, 22.
7. *Gunny G.'s Globe and Anchor,* s.v. "gung ho."

8. "Some Interesting Facts about Korea: The Forgotten War," *DAV Magazine,* May/June 2000, p. 28.

9. H. John Poole, *Phantom Soldier: The Enemy's Answer to Firepower* (Emerald Isle, NC: Posterity Press, 2001), chapt. 15.

10. Gen. Vo Nguyen Giap, "Once Again We Will Win," as quoted in *The Military Art of People's War,* ed. Russel Stetler (New York: Monthly Review Press, 1970), pp. 264, 265.

11. "Gung Ho!: The Story of Carlson's Makin Island Raiders," movie, 87 minutes, Universal Studios, 1943.

12. *Handbook on the Chinese Armed Forces,* DDI-2680-32-76 (Washington, D.C.: DIA, July 1976), pp. 5-21, 5-30; *Global Security,* s.v. "PLA Uniforms and Insignia."

13. *Handbook on the Chinese People's Liberation Army,* DDB-2680-32-84 (Washington, D.C.: DIA, November 1984), p. 16.

14. Ibid., appendix E, p. A-5.

15. H. John Poole, *The Tiger's Way: A U.S. Private's Best Chance for Survival* (Emerald Isle, NC: Posterity Press, 2003), chapt. 12; *The German Squad in Combat,* trans. and ed. U.S. Mil. Intell. Service from a German manual (N.p., 1943), and republished as *German Squad Tactics in WWII,* by Matthew Gajkowski (West Chester, OH: Nafziger, 1995), p. 15; *Soviet Combat Regulations of November 1942* (Moscow: [Stalin], 1942), republished as *Soviet Infantry Tactics in World War II: Red Army Infantry Tactics from Squad to Rifle Company from the Combat Regulations,* with trans., intro., and notes by Charles C. Sharp (West Chester, OH: George Nafziger, 1998), p. 26.

16. "Gung Ho!," Universal Studios.

17. Ibid.

18. Wukovits, *American Commando,* pp. 46, 53, 212.

19. "Gung Ho!," Universal Studios.

20. Former member of 3rd Raider Battalion and then 3/4, in conversation with author during October 2010.

21. Gudmundsson, *Stormtroop Tactics,* pp. 43-51.

22. Ashida Kim, *The Invisible Ninja: Ancient Secrets of Surprise* (New York: Citadel Press, 1983), pp. 13-16.

23. PFC Kent, as told to CWO4 Tag Guthrie USMC (Ret.) in 1966, and further related to the author in August 2011.

24. *Mao Tse-tung,* ed. Fremantle, p. 71.

25. Poole, *Phantom Soldier,* parts One and Two; Poole, *The Tiger's Way,* parts Two and Three.

26. Poole, *Phantom Soldier,* p. 37.

27. *Phrases.org,* s.v. "gung ho."

28. Lt.Col. Gregory H. Kitchens USMCR, "Building the Team for Unit Excellence," *Marine Corps Gazette,* December 2003.

Chapter 4: *What Carlson May Have Finally Realized*

1. Wukovits, *American Commando,* pp. 4, 5.
2. "From Makin to Bougainville," by Hoffman, p. 3.
3. Phillip B. Davidson, *Vietnam at War—The History: 1946-1975* (New York: Oxford Univ. Press, 1988), p. 64.
4. "Twin Stars of China: China's Valiant Struggle for Existence by a U. S. Marine who Lived and . . . ," by Evans Fordyce Carlson (N.p.: Dodd Mead, 1940), excerpts as quoted in *Gunny G.'s Globe and Anchor,* s.v. "gung ho."
5. *Handbook on the Chinese People's Liberation Army,* DDB-2680-32-84, p. 16.
6. Wukovits, *American Commando,* p. 12.
7. Gilbert, *U.S. Marine Corps Raider 1942-43,* p. 14.
8. Ibid., p. 12.
9. Wukovits, *American Commando,* p. 4.
10. Poole, *Phantom Soldier,* chapt. 6; Poole, *The Tiger's Way,* figs. 12.7 and 12.9.
11. Wukovits, *American Commando,* p. 53.
12. Ibid., p. 56.
13. Ibid., p. 54.
14. Wukovits, *American Commando,* p. 4.
15. "From Makin to Bougainville," by Hoffman, p. 22.
16. George W. Smith, *Carlson's Raid: The Daring Marine Assault on Makin* (Novato, CA: Presidio Press, 2001), p. 59; former member of 3rd Raider Battalion and then 3/4, in conversation with author during August 2011.
17. Poole, *Phantom Soldier,* chapt. 7.
18. *Mao Tse-tung,* ed. Fremantle, p. 82.
19. Wukovits, *American Commando,* p. 46.
20. Bill Onstad and Jayson Lowry, *"Trust. Truth. Evil."* (Victoria, B.C.: Trafford Publishing, 2005), p. 65, in *American Commando,* by Wukovits, p. 212.
21. Wukovits, *American Commando,* pp. 6, 9.
22. Joseph S. Bermudez, Jr., *North Korean Special Forces* (Annapolis, MD: Naval Inst. Press, 1998).
23. Terrence Maitland and Peter McInerney, *Vietnam Experience: A Contagion of War* (Newton, MA: Boston Publishing, 1968), p. 94.
24. Gudmundsson, *Stormtroop Tactics,* p. xiii.
25. Ibid., p. 49.
26. Maitland and McInerney, *Vietnam Experience,* p. 97.

27. *Vietnam Interviews,* Interview "K-5" (Santa Monica, CA: Rand Corporation, K Series, n.d.), pp. 32, 33, from *Cohesion: The Human Element in Combat,* by Wm. Darryl Henderson (Washington, D.C.: Nat. Defense Univ. Press, 1985), p. 28.

28. Bermudez, *North Korean Special Forces,* p. 222.

29. James F. Dunnigan and Albert A. Nofi, *Dirty Little Secrets of the Vietnam War* (New York: Thomas Dunne Books, 1999), pp. 276-279.

30. Ibid.

31. Memorandum for the record by H.J. Poole.

32. Dunnigan and Nofi, *Dirty Little Secrets of the Vietnam War,* p. 279.

33. Arthur Zich and the editors of Time-Life Books, *The Rising Sun: World War II* (Alexandria, VA: Time-Life Books, 1977), p. 35.

34. Sun Tzu, *The Art of War,* trans. Samuel B. Griffith, foreword by B.H. Liddell Hart (New York: Oxford Univ. Press, 1963), p. 82.

35. "From Makin to Bougainville," by Hoffman, p. 22.

36. *Mao's Generals Remember Korea,* trans. and ed. Xiaobing Li, Allan R. Millett, and Bin Yu (Lawrence, KS: Univ. Press of Kansas, 2001), pp. 70, 71.

Chapter 5: *Modern War Precepts from Ancient China?*

1. William S. Lind, "Fourth Generation Warfare's First Blow: A Quick Look," *Marine Corps Gazette,* November 2001.

2. William S. Lind, *The Maneuver Warfare Handbook* (Boulder, CO: Westview Press, 1985); *Warfighting,* FMFM 1 (Washington, D.C.: HQMC, 1989); *Tactics,* FMFM 1-3 (Washington, D.C.: HQMC, 1991).

3. Sun Tzu, *The Art of War,* trans. Thomas Cleary (Boston, MA: Shambhala Publications, 1988), p. 54.

4. Sun Tzu, *The Art of War,* trans. Griffith, p. vii.

5. *Sun Tzu's Art of War: The Modern Chinese Interpretation,* by Gen. Tao Hanzhang, trans. Yuan Shibing (New York: Sterling Publishing, 1990), p. 28.

6. *Sun Tzu: The New Translation,* by J.H. Huang (New York: William Morrow, 1993), p. 46.

7. Sun Tzu, *The Art of War,* trans. Griffith, p. 85, in *Warfighting,* FMFM 1 (Washington, D.C.: HQMC, 1989), p. 55.

8. Sun Tzu, *The Art of War,* in *Sun Tzu's Art of War: The Modern Chinese Interpretation,* by Gen. Tao Hanzhang, trans. Yuan Shibing (New York: Sterling Publishing, 1990), p. 95.

9. H.J. Poole, *The Last Hundred Yards: The NCO's Contribution to Warfare* (Emerald Isle, NC: Posterity Press, 1997), p. 31.

10. *Warfighting,* FMFM 1 (Washington, D.C.: HQMC, 1989), p. 29.

11. Sun Tzu, *The Art of War,* trans. Samuel B. Griffith, p. vii.

12. *The Strategic Advantage,* ed. Cao Shan, p. 21.

13. Samuel B. Griffith, in intro. to *The Art of War,* by Sun Tzu, trans. Griffith (New York: Oxford Univ. Press, 1963), p. xi.

14. Mao Tse-tung, "Mao's Primer on Guerrilla War," trans. B.Gen. Samuel B. Griffith, in FMFRP 19-9, *The Guerrilla and How to Fight Him* (Quantico, VA: Marine Corps Combat Develop. Cmd., 1990), p. 7, and in *Marine Corps Gazette,* January 1962 (plus a 1941 issue).

15. Truong Chinh, *Primer for Revolt,* pp. 114-117.

16. Lind, *The Maneuver Warfare Handbook,* p. 6.

17. *Morning Sun* (morningsun.org, China), s.v. "the long march."

18. H. John Poole, *One More Bridge to Cross: Lowering the Cost of War* (Emerald Isle, NC: Posterity Press, 1999), table 10.1.

19. Mao Tse-tung, "Mao's Primer on Guerrilla War," trans. Samuel B. Griffith.

20. *Warfighting,* FMFM 1 (Washington, D.C.: HQMC, 1989), pp. 23, 24.

21. Poole, *The Tiger's Way,* chapt. 10.

22. Gudmundsson, *Stormtroop Tactics.*

23. Chesty Puller, as quoted in *Marine,* by Burke Davis (New York: Bantam Books, 1964), p. 390.

24. Maitland and McInerney, *Vietnam Experience,* pp. 100, 101.

25. *Wikipedia Encyclopedia,* s.v. "Marine Raiders."

26. *Warfighting,* FMFM 1, p. 71.

27. Poole, *The Tiger's Way,* pp. 169, 170.

28. Wukovits, *American Commando,* p. 12.

29. H. John Poole, *Terrorist Trail: Backtracking the Foreign Fighter* (Emerald Isle, NC: Posterity Press, 2006), pp. 35, 36; ABC's Nightly News, 28 July 2006.

30. Abraham Rabinovich, "Militants Seen As Able to Hit Tel Aviv," *Washington Times,* 18 July 2006.

31. H. John Poole, *Tequila Junction: 4th-Generation Counterinsurgency* (Emerald Isle, NC: Posterity Press, 2008), chapts. 1-9.

Chapter 6: *Mao's Influence on Raider Tactics*

1. Mao Tse-tung, as quoted in *Handbook on the Chinese Communist Army,* DA Pamphlet 30-51 (Washington, D.C.: Hdqts. Dept. of the Army, 7 December 1960), p. 19.
2. Lind, *The Maneuver Warfare Handbook,* pp. 6, 7; *Warfighting,* FMFM 1, p. 31.
3. Lind, *The Maneuver Warfare Handbook,* pp. 9, 10.
4. Ibid.
5. *Handbook on the Chinese Communist Army,* DA Pamphlet 30-51 (Washington, D.C.: Hdqts. Dept. of the Army, 7 December 1960), p. 29.
6. Poole, *Phantom Soldier,* p. 37.
7. *Handbook on the Chinese Communist Army,* DA Pamphlet 30-51, pp. 23, 24.
8. Lind, *The Maneuver Warfare Handbook,* p. 5.
9. Sun Tzu, *The Art of War,* trans. Cleary, p. 91.
10. "From Makin to Bougainville," by Hoffman, p. 1.
11. Alexander, *Edson's Raiders,* p. 27.
12. Ibid., p. 28.
13. David H. Hackworth and Julie Sherman, *About Face* (New York: Simon & Schuster, 1989), pp. 680, 681.
14. Wukovits, *American Commando,* pp. 7, 8.
15. Sun Tzu, *The Art of War,* trans. Samuel B. Griffith, pp. 41, 42.
16. Ibid.
17. *Wikipedia Encyclopedia,* s.v. "Merrill's Marauders, "Chindits," "X-Force," and "Chinese Troops in India."
18. Gilbert, *U.S. Marine Corps Raider 1942-43,* p. 48.
19. Ibid.
20. Wukovits, *American Commando,* p. 183.
21. "From Makin to Bougainville," by Hoffman, p. 22.
22. Ibid., p. 21.
23. Wukovits, *American Commando,* p. 191.
24. "From Makin to Bougainville," by Hoffman, p. 22.
25. Ibid., p. 20.
26. Wukovits, *American Commando,* p. 188.
27. "From Makin to Bougainville," by Hoffman, p. 22.
28. *Handbook on the Chinese Communist Army,* DA Pamphlet 30-51, p. 5.
29. *Handbook on Japanese Military Forces,* TM-E 30-480 (Washington, D.C.: U.S. War Dept., 1944), reprint (Baton Rouge, LA: LSU Press, 1991), p. 86.
30. Maj. John L. Zimmerman, *The Guadalcanal Campaign* (Washington, D.C.: Hist. Div., HQMC, 1949), p. 145.

31. "From Makin to Bougainville," by Hoffman, p. 22.
32. *Handbook on the Chinese Communist Army,* DA Pamphlet 30-51, p. 26.
33. Maj. Scott R. McMichael, "The Chinese Communist Forces in Korea," *A Historical Perspective on Light Infantry,* chapt. 2, *Leavenworth Research Survey No. 6* (Ft. Leavenworth, KS: Combat Studies Inst., U.S. Army's Cmd. & Gen. Staff College, 1987), p. 70.
34. "From Makin to Bougainville," by Hoffman, p. 22.
35. Wukovits, *American Commando,* p. 235.
36. "From Makin to Bougainville," by Hoffman, pp. 19-22.
37. Geoffrey Perret, "Warrior Mao," *MHQ: The Quarterly Journal of Military History,* issue 19, no. 3, Spring 2007), p. 6, in *American Commando,* by Wukovits, pp. 10, 11.
38. *Handbook on the Chinese Communist Army,* DA Pamphlet 30-51, p. 54.
39. Ibid. p. 29.
40. Gudmundsson, *Stormtroop Tactics,* pp. 147-149, in *The Last Hundred Yards,* by Poole, p. 31.

Chapter 7: *"Gung Ho's" Gift to Combat Momentum*

1. "From Makin to Bougainville," by Hoffman, p. 23.
2. Ibid., p. 25.
3. Wukovits, *American Commando,* p. 212.
4. Toggle drawing, in *U.S. Marine Corps Raider 1942-43,* by Gilbert.
5. Alexander, *Edson's Raiders,* p. 58.
6. Ibid., pp. 242, 243.

Chapter 8: *Collective Wisdom or Headquarters Control*

1. "From Makin to Bougainville," by Hoffman, p. 5.
2. *Webster's New Twentieth Century Dictionary Unabridged (Second Ed.),* s.v. "consensus."
3. Memorandum for the record by H.J. Poole.
4. Maj. Norman L. Cooling, "Russia's 1994-96 Campaign for Chechnya: A Failure in Shaping the Battlespace," *Marine Corps Gazette,* October 2001, pp. 62-66.
5. Lt.Col. Timothy L. Thomas and Lester W. Grau, "Russian Lessons Learned from the Battles for Grozny," *Marine Corps Gazette,* April 2000, p. 48.
6. Ibid.
7. BBC's News, Public Radio East, 2 October 2011.
8. Memorandum for the record by H.J. Poole.

Chapter 9: *Further Maoist Raider Participation in WWII*

1. Assoc. of U.S. Marine Raiders website, s.v. "Chronology" and "Commanding Officers."
2. Ibid.
3. Ibid.
4. Ibid.
5. *Isolation of Rabaul,* by Henry I. Shaw and Maj. Douglas T. Kane USMC, part III, chapt. 3, "Assault on Cape Torokina," vol. II, *History of U.S. Marine Corps Operations in World War II* Series (Washington, D.C.: Hist. Br., HQMC, 1963), pp. 211-213.
6. Ibid.
7. Ibid.
8. *Isolation of Rabaul,* by Shaw and Kane, part III, chapt. 5, "Advance to Piva Forks," pp. 247-270; *Bougainville and the Northern Solomons,* by Maj. John N. Rentz, *USMC Historical Monograph,* chapt. 2, "Establishing Bougainville Beachhead" (Washington, D.C.: Hist. Br., HQMC, 1946), pp. 55-72; Assoc. of U.S. Marine Raiders website, s.v. "Chronology."
9. *Isolation of Rabaul,* by Shaw and Kane, part III, chapt. 5, "Advance to Piva Forks," p. 260.
10. Ibid., p. 65.
11. Assoc. of U.S. Marine Raiders website, s.v. "Chronology."
12. Ibid.
13. Ibid.
14. Ibid.
15. Ibid.
16. *Isolation of Rabaul,* by Shaw and Kane, chapt. 2, "Elkton Underway," p. 76.
17. Assoc. of U.S. Marine Raiders website, s.v. "Chronology."
18. *Marines in the Central Solomons,* by Maj. John N. Rentz, "USMC Historical Monograph," chapt. 4, "From Rice to Bairoko (Washington, D.C.: Hist. Br., HQMC, 1952).
19. Ibid.
20. Assoc. of U.S. Marine Raiders website, s.v. "Chronology."
21. "From Makin to Bougainville," by Hoffman, p. 34.
22. *Isolation of Rabaul,* by Shaw and Kane, chapt. 4, "The Dragon's Peninsula Campaign," pp. 130-145.
23. "From Makin to Bougainville," by Hoffman, p. 33.
24. *Marines in the Central Solomons,* by Rentz, "USMC Historical Monograph," chapt. 4.
25. *Isolation of Rabaul,* by Shaw and Kane, pp. 137, 138.
26. *Iwo Jima: Amphibious Epic,* by Lt.Col. Whitman S. Bartley (Washington, D.C.: Hist. Br., HQMC, 1954), p. 140.

27. *Marines in the Central Solomons,* by Rentz, "USMC Historical Monograph," chapt. 4, pp. 113, 114.
28. *Isolation of Rabaul,* by Shaw and Kane, part II, chapt. 4, "The Dragon's Peninsula Campaign," pp. 130-145.
29. *Marines in the Central Solomons,* by Rentz, "USMC Historical Monograph," chapt. 4.
30. *Isolation of Rabaul,* by Shaw and Kane, chapt. 4, "The Dragon's Peninsula Campaign," p. 138.
31. "From Makin to Bougainville," by Hoffman, pp. 35, 40.
32. *Isolation of Rabaul,* by Shaw and Kane, part II, chapt. 3, "Munda Victory," pp. 104-107.

Chapter 10: *The Raiders' Impact on the 4th Marines*

1. "A Brief History of the 4th Marines," by James S. Santelli, *Marine Corps History Reference Pamphlet* (Washington, D.C.: Hist. Div., HQMC, 1970), p. 26.
2. *Dan Marsh's Marine Raider Page,* created by former member of 4th Raider Battalion, main page.
3. All official 4th Marines' websites.
4. Ibid.
5. Wukovits, *American Commando,* p. 61.
6. "A Brief History of the 4th Marines," by Santelli, *Marine Corps History Reference Pamphlet.*
7. Official 1/4 website.
8. *The Recapture of Guam,* by Maj. O.R. Lodge, "USMC Historical Monograph" (Washington, D.C.: Hist. Br., HQMC, 1954), pp. 89-92.
9. "A Brief History of the 4th Marines," by Santelli, *Marine Corps History Reference Pamphlet.*
10. Official 1/4 website.
11. *Okinawa: The Last Battle,* by Roy E. Appleman, James M. Burns, Russell A. Gugeler, and John Stevens, *United States Army in World War II Series* (Washington, D.C.: U.S. Army's Ctr. of Mil. Hist., 2000), appendix; "The Final Campaign: Marines in the Victory on Okinawa," by Joseph H. Alexander, *Marines in WWII Commemorative Series* (Washington, D.C.: Hist. and Museums Div., HQMC, 1996), pp. 5, 9.
12. *Okinawa: Victory in the Pacific,* by Maj. Chas. S. Nichols, Jr., and Henry I. Shaw, Jr., "USMC Historical Monograph" (Washington, D.C.: Hist. Br., HQMC, 1955), p. 91.
13. Ibid., p. 98.
14. Ibid., p. 101.

15. "Victory in the Pacific," PBS's *American Experience,* NC Public TV, 1 April 2012; *Military History Online,* s.v. "Battle of Okinawa"; *Okinawa: The Last Battle,* by Appleman et al, p. 217.

16. Hiromichi Yahara, *The Battle for Okinawa,* trans. Roger Pineau and Masatoshi Uehara (New York: John Wiley & Sons, 1995), p. 35.

17. Ibid.

18. Ibid., pp. 25, 26.

19. Unidentified Japanese POW, as quoted in Yahara, *The Battle for Okinawa,* p. 219.

20. Yahara, *The Battle for Okinawa,* pp. 56, 215; "History of the Sixth Marine Division" (N.p., n.d.), from Yahara, *The Battle for Okinawa,* p. 61.

21. *Handbook on Japanese Military Forces,* TM-E 30-480, p. 117.

22. Yahara, *The Battle for Okinawa,* p. 60.

23. *Okinawa: The Last Battle,* by Appleman et al, p. 311.

24. Ibid., pp. 317, 318.

25. Synopsis of *Killing Ground on Okinawa: The Battle of Sugar Loaf Hill,* by James J. Hallas (Annapolis, MD: Naval Inst. Press, n.d.), from Tom's Recommended Reading Roster.

26. *Okinawa: The Last Battle,* by Appleman et al, pp. 322, 323.

27. *Okinawa: Victory in the Pacific,* by Nichols and Shaw, "USMC Historical Monograph," p. 176.

28. Ibid., p. 183.

29. *Dan Marsh's Marine Raider Page,* created by former member of 4th Raider Battalion, s.v. "Okinawa: The Last Battle."

30. "The Final Campaign: Marines in the Victory on Okinawa," by Joseph H. Alexander, *Marines in WWII Commemorative Series* (Washington, D.C.: Hist. and Museums Div., HQMC, 1996), p. 39.

31. Ibid., p. 35.

32. *Dan Marsh's Marine Raider Page,* created by former member of 4th Raider Battalion, s.v. "Okinawa: The Last Battle."

33. Bill D. Ross, *Iwo Jima—Legacy of Valor* (New York: Vintage Books, 1986), pp. 297-300; *Isolation of Rabaul,* by Shaw and Kane, part III, chapt. 5, "Advance to Piva Forks," p. 260.

34. Association of the 6th Marine Division website, s.v. "Introduction."

35. *Okinawa: The Last Battle,* by Appleman et al, pp. 322, 323.

36. Thomas M. Huber, "Japan's Battle for Okinawa, April - June 1945," *Leavenworth Papers No. 18* (Ft. Leavenworth, KS: Combat Studies Inst., U.S. Army's Cmd. & Gen. Staff College, 1990), chapt. 3.

37. Ibid.

38. Former member of 3rd Raider Battalion and then 3/4, in conversation with author during November 2011.

39. *Okinawa: Victory in the Pacific,* by Nichols and Shaw, "USMC Historical Monograph," pp. 182-184.

40. "The Final Campaign: Marines in the Victory on Okinawa," by Alexander, p. 19
41. Ibid., p. 28.
42. Ibid., p. 19.
43. "The Final Campaign: Marines in the Victory on Okinawa," by Alexander; *Okinawa: Victory in the Pacific,* by Nichols and Shaw, "USMC Historical Monograph," p. 184; "Victory in the Pacific," PBS.
44. "The Final Campaign: Marines in the Victory on Okinawa," by Alexander, p. 36.
45. Ibid., p. 9.
46. Ibid., p. 19.
47. Ibid., pp. 35, 36.
48. *Okinawa: Victory in the Pacific,* by Nichols and Shaw, "USMC Historical Monograph," p. 255.
49. Huber, "Japan's Battle for Okinawa, April - June 1945," *Leavenworth Papers No. 18.*
50. Vietnam era Marine intelligence, infantry, and CAP veteran, in telephone conversations with author during May of 2012.
51. *Tennozan: The Battle of Okinawa and the Atomic Bomb,* by George Feifer (Boston: Houghton Miflin, 1992), p. 578, and *Okinawa: The Last Battle,* by Appleman et al, p. 468, in *Military History Online,* s.v. "Battle of Okinawa."
52. *Wikipedia Encyclopedia,* s.v. "Ryukyu Kingdom" and "The Ryukyu Islands."
53. "The Final Campaign: Marines in the Victory on Okinawa," by Alexander, pp. 41-52.
54. Assoc. of 3rd Battalion, 4th Marines website.
55. Official 4th Marines' website.

Chapter 11: *Tackling Many Times Their Number*

1. "From Makin to Bougainville," by Hoffman, p. 22.
2. Official 2nd Battalion, 4th Marines website.
3. Keith Nolan, *The Magnificent Bastards: The Joint Army-Marine Defense of Dong Ha, 1968* (New York: Ballantine, 2007), pp. 6-24.
4. Max McQuown, "Learning from Dai Do," *Marine Corps Gazette,* April 1988.
5. William Weise, "Memories of Dai Do," *Marine Corps Gazette,* September 1987.
6, Keith William Nolan, "The Battle of Dai Do," *Leatherneck,* August 1994.
7. Weise, "Memories of Dai Do."
8. Nolan, *The Magnificent Bastards,* p. 74.

9. Ibid., p. 73.
10. Ibid., p. 84.
11. Ibid., p. 86.
12. Ibid., pp. 148, 149.
13. Ibid., pp. 105, 112.
14. William Weise, "Memories of Dai Do [a Sequel]," *Marine Corps Gazette,* April 2004.
15. Nolan, *The Magnificent Bastards,* pp. 148, 149.
16. Nolan, "The Battle of Dai Do."
17. Ibid.
18. Weise, "Memories of Dai Do [a Sequel]."
19. Ibid.; Nolan, *The Magnificent Bastards,* p. 153.
20. Nolan, *The Magnificent Bastards,* p. 169.
21. Ibid., p. 170.
22. Vic Taylor, "Hotel Company-Day Three," *Marine Corps Gazette,* April 2004.
23. Nolan, *The Magnificent Bastards,* p. 177.
24. Ibid., p. 256.
25. Ibid., p. 257.
26. Ibid., p. 282.
27. Ibid., p. 292.
28. Ibid., pp. 287-294.
29. Nolan, "The Battle of Dai Do."
30. Nolan, *The Magnificent Bastards,* pp. 295, 302.
31. Ibid., p. 301.
32. Nolan, "The Battle of Dai Do."
33. Poole, *The Tiger's Way,* p. 153.
34. James E. Livingston, Colin D. Heaton, and Anne-Marie Lewis, *Noble Warrior* (Minneapolis: Zenith Press, 2010), p. 51.
35. "The Chosin Reservoir Campaign," by Lynn Montross and Capt. Nicholas A. Canzona, *U.S. Marine Operations in Korea 1950-1953 Series,* vol. III (Washington, D.C.: Hist. Br., HQMC, 1957); Poole, *Phantom Soldier,* chapt. 7.
36. Nolan, "The Battle of Dai Do."
37. Ibid.
38. Weise, "Memories of Dai Do."
39. Ibid.; Nolan, *The Magnificent Bastards,* p. 20.
40. Memorandum for the record by H.J. Poole.
41. Keith William Nolan, *Operation Buffalo: USMC Fight for the DMZ* (New York: Dell Publishing, 1991), pp. 72, 73.
42. Nolan, *The Magnificent Bastards,* p. 137.
43. Nolan, "The Battle of Dai Do"; Weise, "Memories of Dai Do."
44. Poole, *Phantom Soldier,* chapt. 7.

45. Wukovits, *American Commando,* p. 4.
46. Nolan, "The Battle of Dai Do."
47. Ibid.
48. Nolan, *The Magnificent Bastards,* p. 169.
49. Weise, "Memories of Dai Do."
50. Michael Lee Lanning and Dan Cragg, *Inside the VC and the NVA: The Real Story of North Vietnam's Armed Forces* (New York: Ivy Books, 1992), pp. 206-208.
51. Nolan, *The Magnificent Bastards,* pp. 7-20.
52. Memorandum for the record by H.J. Poole.
53. Nolan, *The Magnificent Bastards,* p. 7.
54. McQuown, "Learning from Dai Do."
55. Weise, "Memories of Dai Do."
56. *36 Stratagems: Secret Art of War,* trans. Koh Kok Kiang and Liu Yi (Singapore: Asiapac Books, 1992).
57. Memorandum for the record by H.J. Poole.
58. Weise, "Memories of Dai Do."
59. Memorandum for the record by H.J. Poole.
60. Poole, *The Tiger's Way,* p. 116.
61. Livingston, Heaton, and Lewis, *Noble Warrior,* p. 82.
62. Taylor, "Hotel Company-Day Three."
63. Weise, "Memories of Dai Do."
64. Nolan, "The Battle of Dai Do"; Livingston, Heaton, and Lewis, *Noble Warrior,* p. 79.
65. Nolan, "The Battle of Dai Do."
66. Otto Lehrack, "Dai Do: The Strategic Battle for Dong Ha." *Leatherneck,* March 2009, pp. 38-43.
67. Ibid.
68. Memorandum for the record by H.J. Poole.
69. Taylor, "Hotel Company-Day Three."
70. H. John Poole, *Dragon Days: Time for "Unconventional" Tactics* (Emerald Isle, NC: Posterity Press, 2007), p. 309; Poole, *The Tiger's Way,* map 10.1.
71. Memorandum for the record by H.J. Poole.
72. Nolan, "The Battle of Dai Do"; Weise, "Memories of Dai Do."
73. Weise, "Memories of Dai Do."
74. Ibid.
75. Nolan, *The Magnificent Bastards,* p. 162.
76. Nolan, "The Battle of Dai Do"; Weise, "Memories of Dai Do."
77. Nolan, "The Battle of Dai Do."
78. Weise, "Memories of Dai Do"; Nolan, *The Magnificent Bastards,* p. 176.
79. Weise, "Memories of Dai Do."
80. Nolan, "The Battle of Dai Do."
81. Weise, "Memories of Dai Do."

82. Nolan, *The Magnificent Bastards,* p. 171; Livingston, Heaton, and Lewis, *Noble Warrior,* p. 84.
83. Lehrack, "Dai Do."
84. Nolan, *The Magnificent Bastards,* p. 303.
85. Ibid., p. 187.
86. Lehrack, "Dai Do."
87. Weise, "Memories of Dai Do."
88. McQuown, "Learning from Dai Do."
89. Ibid.
90. Paul R. Young, *First Recon—Second to None: A Marine Reconnaissance Battalion in Vietnam, 1967-68* (New York: Ivy Books, 1992), pp. 219, 220.
91. *U.S. Marines in Vietnam: Fighting the North Vietnamese 1967,* Maj. Gary Tefler, Lt.Col. Lane Rogers, and V. Keith Fleming, Jr. (Washington, D.C.: Hist. and Museums Div., HQMC, 1984), p. 179.
92. Livingston, Heaton, and Lewis, *Noble Warrior,* p. 68.
93. Taylor, "Hotel Company-Day Three."
94. Livingston, Heaton, and Lewis, *Noble Warrior,* p. 82.
95. Weise, "Memories of Dai Do."
96. Poole, *The Tiger's Way,* pp. 168-173.
97. Weise, "Memories of Dai Do."
98. Livingston, Heaton, and Lewis, *Noble Warrior,* p. 68.
99. Ibid.; Taylor, "Hotel Company-Day Three."
100. H. John Poole, *Global Warrior: Averting WWIII* (Emerald Isle, NC: Posterity Press, 2011), chapt. 20.
101. Weise, "Memories of Dai Do."
102. Ibid.
103. Taylor, "Hotel Company-Day Three."
104. Nolan, *The Magnificent Bastards,* pp. 158, 159, 179, 184, 273, 295; Nolan, "The Battle of Dai Do"; Livingston, Heaton, and Lewis, *Noble Warrior,* p. 93.
105. Nolan, "The Battle of Dai Do"; Nolan, *The Magnificent Bastards,* p. 116.
106. Nolan, *The Magnificent Bastards,* p. 179.
107. Livingston, Heaton, and Lewis, *Noble Warrior,* p. 93.
108. Nolan, *The Magnificent Bastards,* p. 286.
109. "Isolation of Rabaul," by Shaw and Kane, part II, chapt. 4, "The Dragon's Peninsula Campaign," pp. 130-145.
110. Nolan, *The Magnificent Bastards,* pp. 37, 38.
111. Ibid., p. 110.
112. Taylor, "Hotel Company-Day Three."
113. Nolan, "The Battle of Dai Do."
114. Nolan, *The Magnificent Bastards,* p. 195.
115. Ibid., p. 189; Nolan, "The Battle of Dai Do."
116. Nolan, *The Magnificent Bastards,* p. 53.

117. Weise, "Memories of Dai Do."
118. Livingston, Heaton, and Lewis, *Noble Warrior.*
119. *Mao Tse-tung,* ed. Fremantle, p. 82.
120. Weise, "Memories of Dai Do."
121. Memorandum for the record by H.J. Poole.
122. Taylor, "Hotel Company-Day Three."

Chapter 12: *Small-Unit Confidence*

1. *U.S. Marines in Vietnam: Fighting the North Vietnamese 1967,* by Tefler, Rogers, and Fleming, pp. 19-21.
2. Ibid., pp. 33-35
3. "1/4 Afteraction Report for May 1967," as retrieved through the 1/4 Assoc. website, from the following url: http://jones-thompson.com/onefour/AFTACTREP/1967/MAY67/aftactrep2-may67.htm.
4. *Wikipedia Encyclopedia,* s.v. "Dien Bien Phu."
5. *Gunny G.'s Globe and Anchor,* s.v. "gung ho"; "From Makin to Bougainville," by Hoffman, p. 5.
6. Wukovits, *American Commando,* p. 59; Griffith interview with HQMC of November 1968, pp. 53, 54, in op.cit., p. 59.
7. Wukovits, *American Commando,* p. 59.
8. Memorandum for the record from H.J. Poole.
9. Ibid.
10. Steve Hohenstein, an ambush squad member, in written recollections for Tag Guthrie, as relayed by e-mail to the author in the Fall of 2011.
11. *U.S. Marines in Vietnam: Fighting the North Vietnamese 1967,* by Tefler, Rogers, and Fleming, pp. 33-35.
12. CWO4 Charles "Tag" Guthrie, A/1/4 member at Con Thien, in e-mail to the author during December 2011.
13. *U.S. Marines in Vietnam: Fighting the North Vietnamese 1967,* by Tefler, Rogers, and Fleming, pp. 33-35.
14. CWO4 Charles "Tag" Guthrie, A/1/4 member at Con Thien, in e-mail to the author during December 2011.
15. *U.S. Marines in Vietnam: Fighting the North Vietnamese 1967,* by Tefler, Rogers, and Fleming, pp. 33-35.
16. "1/4 Afteraction Report for May 1967," as retrieved through the 1/4 Assoc. website.
17. "1/4 Intelligence Summary for 7-8 May 1967," as retrieved from the 1/4 Assoc. website, at the following url: http://jones-thompson.com/onefour/AFTACTREP/1967/MAY67/intelsum2-may67.htm.
18. CWO4 Charles "Tag" Guthrie, A/1/4 member at Con Thien, in e-mail to the author during December 2011.
19. Memorandum for the record from H.J. Poole.

20. Steve Hohenstein, an ambush squad member, in written recollections for Tag Guthrie, as relayed by e-mail to the author in the Fall of 2011.

21. CBS News Special Report, "The Ordeal of Con Thien," 30 min., as aired as a Vietnam Special in 1967.

22. "1/4 Afteraction Report for May 1967," as retrieved through the 1/4 Assoc. website.

23. CBS News Special Report, "The Ordeal of Con Thien," 30 min., as aired as a Vietnam Special in 1967.

24. Ibid.

25. Ibid.

26. "The War in the Northern Provinces: 1966-68," by Lt.Gen. Willard Pearson, *Vietnam Studies* (Washington, D.C.: Hdqts. Dept. of the Army, 1975), p. 19.

27. "1/4 Afteraction Report for May 1967," as retrieved through the 1/4 Assoc. website; *U.S. Marines in Vietnam: Fighting the North Vietnamese 1967,* by Tefler, Rogers, and Fleming, pp. 33-35.

28. *U.S. Marines in Vietnam: Fighting the North Vietnamese 1967,* by Tefler, Rogers, and Fleming, pp. 33-35.

29. "1/4 Afteraction Report for May 1967," as retrieved through the 1/4 Assoc. website.

30. CWO4 Charles "Tag" Guthrie, A/1/4 member at Con Thien, in e-mail to the author on 26 March 2012.

31. Cpl. Aldo Betta, the lead Amtrac commander, in interview with Tag Guthrie, as relayed by e-mail to author in December 2011.

32. Ibid.

33. Ibid.

34. Cpl. Aldo Betta, the lead Amtrac commander, in written recollections for Tag Guthrie, as relayed by e-mail to the author in December 2011.

35. Capt. Patrick J. McDonnell, 4th Platoon Amtrac leader, in written recollection "Hill of Angels—My 1967," at official 1st Amtrac Battalion website (Amtrac.org), s.v. "1st Amtrac Battalion History" and "Bravo Company Arrives First."

36. CWO4 Charles "Tag" Guthrie, A/1/4 member at Con Thien, in e-mail to the author on 26 March 2012.

37. Ibid.

38. Casualty Rosters, as extracted from 1st Battalion, 4th Marines website.

39. CWO4 Charles "Tag" Guthrie, A/1/4 member at Con Thien, in e-mail to the author on 26 March 2012.

40. John McCoy, wounded occupant of 2nd Amtrac, in conversations with Tag Guthrie, as relayed by e-mail to the author in May 2012.

41. CWO4 Charles "Tag" Guthrie, A/1/4 member at Con Thien, in e-mail to the author on 26 March 2012.

42. Ibid.

43. "1/4 Afteraction Report for May 1967," as retrieved through the 1/4 Assoc. website.

44. Steve Hohenstein, an ambush squad member, in written recollections for Tag Guthrie, as relayed by e-mail to the author in the Fall of 2011.

45. CWO4 Charles "Tag" Guthrie, A/1/4 member at Con Thien, in e-mail to the author on 9 June 2012.

Chapter 13: *Bottom-Up Learning*

1. *Wikipedia Encyclopedia,* s.v. "Carlson's Raiders."

2. Assoc. of 3rd Battalion, 4th Marines website.

3. Official, 3rd Battalion, 4th Marines' website, s.v. "History Section."

4. Ibid.

5. *U.S. Marines in Vietnam: The Defining Year 1968,* by Jack Shulimson, Lt.Col. Leonard A. Blaisol, Charles R. Smith, and Capt. David A. Dawson (Washington, D.C.: Hist. and Museums Div., HQMC, 1997); *U.S. Marines in Vietnam: High Mobility and Standdown 1969,* by Charles R. Smith (Washington, D.C.: Hist. and Museums Div., HQMC, n.d.); *Wikipedia Encyclopedia,* s.v. "3rd Battalion, 4th Marines."

6. "The Battle for Hill 400," by Arnaud de Borchgrave, *Newsweek,* 10 October 1966, at Assoc. of 3rd Battalion, 4th Marines website.

7. Ibid.

8. Ibid.

9. Ibid.

10. Ibid.

11. Ibid.

12. Carroll Posthumous Navy Cross citation, at Assoc. of 3rd Battalion, 4th Marines website.

13. *Wikipedia Encyclopedia,* s.v. "Operation Hastings."

14. Modrzejewski Medal of Honor citation, at Assoc. of 3rd Battalion, 4th Marines website.

15. Ibid.

16. *Wikipedia Encyclopedia,* s.v. "Operation Hastings."

17. "A Brief History of the 4th Marines," by Santelli, *Marine Corps History Reference Pamphlet.*

18. McGinty Medal of Honor citation, at Assoc. of 3rd Battalion, 4th Marines website.

19. *U.S. Marines in Vietnam: Fighting the North Vietnamese 1967,* by Telfer, Rogers, and Fleming, p. 179; Young, *First Recon – Second to None,* pp. 219, 220.

20. Hill Posthumous Navy Cross citation, at Assoc. of 3rd Battalion, 4th Marines website.

21. Command Chronology for 3/4 for May 1967, #1201045092, USMC Hist. Div., Vietnam War Documents Collection, the Vietnam Ctr; and Archive, Texas Tech University; *U.S. Marines in Vietnam: Fighting the North Vietnamese 1967,* by Telfer, Rogers, and Fleming.

22. Hester Posthumous Navy Cross citation, at Assoc. of 3rd Battalion, 4th Marines website.

23. Commemorative website at the following url: http://bellsouthpwp.net/p/d/pdavison/memorial.html.

24. *U.S. Marines in Vietnam: Fighting the North Vietnamese 1967,* by Telfer, Rogers, and Fleming, pp. 10-13.

25. Command Chronology for 3/4 for March 1967, #1201045090, USMC Hist. Div.; Sullivan Navy Cross citation, at Assoc. of 3rd Battalion, 4th Marines website.

26. *U.S. Marines in Vietnam: Fighting the North Vietnamese 1967,* by Telfer, Rogers and Fleming.

27. Command Chronology for 3/4 for October 1966, #1201045084, USMC Hist. Div.

28. *Sun Bin's Art of War: World's Greatest Military Treatise,* trans. Sui Yun (Singapore: Chung Printing, 1999), p. 9.

29. Richard D. Jackson, *Yesterdays Are Forever: A Rite of Passage through the Marine Corps and Vietnam* (Galt, CA: Working Title Publishing, 2007), pp. 160, 179.

30. Ibid., pp. 168, 172.

31. Ibid., pp. 133, 142.

32. Ibid., p. 157.

33. Ibid., p. 211.

34. *U.S. Marines in Vietnam: Fighting the North Vietnamese 1967,* by Telfer, Rogers and Fleming, pp. 10-13.

35. Ibid., p. 223.

36. Ibid., p. 226.

37. *U.S. Marines in Vietnam: Fighting the North Vietnamese 1967,* by Telfer, Rogers and Fleming.

38. Dillard Navy Cross citation, at Assoc. of 3rd Battalion, 4th Marines website.

39. Kelley Navy Cross citation, at Assoc. of 3rd Battalion, 4th Marines website.

40. Thompson Navy Cross citation, at Assoc. of 3rd Battalion, 4th Marines website.

41. "A Brief History of the 4th Marines," by Santelli, *Marine Corps History Reference Pamphlet.*

Chapter 14: *Improvise, Adapt, and Overcome*

1. *Wikipedia Encyclopedia,* s.v. "Combined Action Platoon"; Al Hemingway, *Our War Was Different* (Annapolis, MD: Naval Inst. Press, 1994), pp. 3, 4,

2. Michael S. Smith, *Bloody Ridge: The Battle That Saved Guadalcanl* (Novato, CA: Presidio Press, 2000), p. 202.

3. Unofficial website of the CAP Program, as retrieved from this url: http://capmarine.com/index.htm.

4. Ibid.; *Wikipedia Encyclopedia,* s.v. "Lewis William Walt" and "Victor H. Krulak."

5. "Heartbreak Ridge," movie, 130 minutes, directed and produced by Clint Eastwood, Warner Home Video, 1986.

6. Answers.com, s.v. "Improvise, Adapt, and Overcome."

7. *Wikipedia Encyclopedia,* s.v. "Battle of Heartbreak Ridge."

8. Wukovits, *American Commando,* p. 12.

9. Colin Leinster, "The Two Wars of General Walt," *Life,* 26 May 1967, pp. 83–84.

10. "The Marine War: III MAF in Vietnam, 1965-1971," by Jack Shulimson (Washington, D.C.: Marine Corps Hist. Ctr., 1996).

11. Gen. William Westmoreland, as quoted at the unofficial website of the CAP Program.

12. "Malaysia: A Country Study," DA Pamphlet 550-45, *Area Handbook Series* (Washington, D.C.: Hdqts. Dept. of the Army, 1984), pp. 50-59.

13. Al Hemingway, *Our War Was Different* (Annapolis, MD: Naval Inst. Press, 1994), p. 5; *Wikipedia Encyclopedia,* s.v. "Combined Action Platoon."

14. Lt. William R. Corson, as quoted at unofficial website for the CAP program.

15. "List of Killed in Action: Combined Action Program, 1965-1971," as compiled and published by HQMC, and retrieved from Assoc. of the Combined Action Program website.

16. 2nd CAG Command Chronology, 1 October-30 November 1968, as retrieved from Assoc. of the Combined Action Program website.

17. Unofficial website for the CAP program; *Wikipedia Encyclopedia,* s.v. "Combined Action Platoon."

18. Assoc. of the Combined Action Program website; Jackson, *Yesterdays Are Forever,* p. 113; Leinster, "The Two Wars of General Walt," pp. 83, 84; "The Future Role of the Combined Action Program," by Major Michael Duane Weltsch USMC, thesis for U.S. Army's Cmd. and Gen. Staff College, 1991.

19. 1st CAG Command Chronology, 1-31 December 1968, as retrieved from Assoc. of the Combined Action Program website.

20. 2nd CAG Command Chronology, 1 October-30 November 1968, as retrieved from Assoc. of the Combined Action Program website.

21. 3rd CAG Command Chronology, 1-31 December 1968, as retrieved from Assoc. of the Combined Action Program website.

22. 4th CAG Command Chronology, 1-31 December 1968, as retrieved from Assoc. of the Combined Action Program website.

23. Jackson, *Yesterdays Are Forever,* p. 113.

24. Assoc. of the Combined Action Program website.

25. Assoc. of the Combined Action Program website; Hemingway, *Our War Was Different,* p. 6; "Fact Sheet on the Combined Action Force," III MAF, 31 March 1970.

26. Jackson, *Yesterdays Are Forever,* p. 113.

27. Assoc. of the Combined Action Program website; Jack Shulimson, *U.S. Marines in Vietnam . . . 1966,* HQMC, 1982, p. 239, in *Our War Was Different* by Hemingway, p. 6; "Fact Sheet on the Combined Action Force," III MAF, 31 March 1970.

28. 1st CAG Command Chronology, 1-31 December 1968, and 4th CAG Command Chronology, 1-31 December 1968, as both retrieved from Assoc. of the Combined Action Program website.

29. III MAF Staff Letter, as quoted by *Wikipedia Encyclopedia,* s.v. "Combined Action Platoon"; Hemingway, *Our War Was Different,* p. 9.

30. Amazon.com product description, of *The Combined Action Platoons: The U.S. Marines' Other War in Vietnam,* by Michael E. Peterson (New York: Praeger, 1989).

31. *Publishers Weekly Review* at Amazon.com of *Our War Was Different,* by Al Hemingway (Annapolis, MD: Naval Inst. Press, 1994).

32. The Future Role of the Combined Action Program," by Major Michael Duane Weltsch USMC, thesis for U.S. Army's Cmd. and Gen. Staff College, 1991.

33. Ibid.

34. Poole, *Tequila Junction,* pp. 218, 219; Jack Shulimson, *U.S. Marines in Vietnam . . . 1966,* HQMC, 1982, p. 239, in *Our War Was Different* by Hemingway, p. 6.

35. "Fact Sheet on the Combined Action Force," III MAF, 31 March 1970.

36. Edward J. Drea, "Nomonhan: Japanese—Soviet Tactical Combat, 1939," *Leavenworth Papers No. 2* (Ft. Leavenworth, KS: Combat Studies Inst., U.S. Army's Cmd. & Gen. Staff College, 1981), p. 62; *Night Movements*, trans. and preface by C. Burnett (Tokyo: Imperial Japanese Army, 1913), reprint (Port Townsend, WA: Loompanics Unlimited, n.d.), pp. 70, 71.

37. Leinster, "The Two Wars of General Walt," pp. 83, 84.

38. Memorandum for the record from H.J. Poole.

39. Leinster, "The Two Wars of General Walt," pp. 83, 84; *Wikipedia Encyclopedia,* s.v. "Combined Action Platoon."
40. Leinster, "The Two Wars of General Walt," pp. 83, 84.
41. Ibid.
42. Maitland and McInerney, *Vietnam Experience,* p. 94.
43. Charles R. Smith, U.S. Marines in Vietnam . . . 1969, HQMC, 1988, p. 290, in *Our War Was Different* by Hemingway, p. 7.
44. Don Moser, "Their Mission Defend, Befriend," *Life,* 25 August 1967.
45. 3rd CAG Command Chronology, 1-31 December 1968, as retrieved from Assoc. of the Combined Action Program website.
46. 4th CAG Command Chronology, 1-31 December 1968, as retrieved from Assoc. of the Combined Action Program website.
47. Vietnam era Marine intelligence, infantry, and CAP veteran, in telephone conversations with author from 6-13 January 2012.
48. Ibid.
49. Ibid.
50. Multi-tour U.S. Army Special Forces veteran of the wars in Iraq and Afghanistan, in telephone conversations with author between September 2006 and late 2011.
51. Moser, "Their Mission Defend, Befriend."
52. "List of Killed in Action: Combined Action Program, 1965-1971."
53. Moser, "Their Mission Defend, Befriend."
54. Memorandum for the record by H.J. Poole.
55. "List of Killed in Action: Combined Action Program, 1965-1971."
56. *Wikipedia Encyclopedia,* s.v. "Combined Action Platoon."
57. "The Future Role of the Combined Action Program," by Weltsch, p. 104; Hemingway, *Our War Was Different,* p. 11; "Fact Sheet on the Combined Action Force," III MAF, 31 March 1970.
58. William C. Westmoreland, *A Soldier Reports* (New York: Da Capo Press, 1989), as quoted in *Wikipedia Encyclopedia,* s.v. "Combined Action Platoon."
59. Lewis W. Walt, *Strange War, Strange Strategy: A General's Report on the War in Vietnam* (New York: Funk and Wagnalls, 1970), p. 105, as quoted in *Wikipedia Encyclopedia,* s.v. "Combined Action Platoon."

Chapter 15: *The Belated End to Carlson's Research*

1. "From Makin to Bougainville," by Hoffman, photo annotation, p. 25.
2. Memorandum for the record from H.J. Poole.
3. Memorandum for the record from H.J. Poole.

Chapter 16: *Future War's Most Promising Model*

1. George B. Clark, Their Time in Hell: The 4th Marine Brigade at Belleau Wood (Pike, NH: The Brass Hat, 1996), pp. 44-66; "The Pacific," DVD, 10-part miniseries, 530 minutes, from Tom Hanks, Steven Spielberg, and Gary Goetzman, HBO and DreamWorks, n.d.

2. *Mao's Generals Remember Korea,* pp. 153-155.

3. Chesty Puller, as quoted in *Marine,* by Burke Davis (New York: Bantam Books, 1964), p. 390.

4. *Semper Fidelis,* Camp Lejeune Environmental Mgt. Div., p. 37.

5. "From Makin to Bougainville," by Hoffman, p. 5.

6. *Handbook on German Military Forces,* TM-E 30-451 (Washington, D.C.: U.S. War Dept, 1945), reprint (Baton Rouge, LA: LSU Press, 1990), p. 230; .*Handbook On U.S.S.R. Military Forces,* TM 30-340 (Washington, D.C.: U.S. War Dept., 1945), republished as *Soviet Tactical Doctrine in WWII,* with foreword by Shawn Caza (West Chester, OH: G.F. Nafziger, 1997), p. V-47; Poole, *The Tiger's Way,* pp. 148, 149.

7. Poole, *The Tiger's Way*, pp. 168-172.

8. Poole, *Global Warrior,* pp, 18-22.

9. "Why Did Armored Corps Fail in Lebanon," by Hanan Greenberg, Israeli News, 30 August 2006.

10. Gudmundsson, *Stormtroop Tactics,* pp. 146,147.

11. Timothy T. Lupfer, "The Dynamics of Doctrine: The Changes in German Tactical Doctrine during the First World War," *Leavenworth Papers No. 4* (Fort Leavenworth, KS: Combat Studies Inst., U.S. Army's Cmd. & Gen. Staff College, 1981), in MCI 7401, *Tactical Fundamentals,* 1st course in Warfighting Skills Program (Washington, D.C.: Marine Corps Inst., 1989), p. 43.

12. Memorandum for the record by H.J. Poole.

13. Ibid.

14. Col. David H. Hackworth U.S. Army (Ret.) and Julie Sherman, *About Face* (New York: Simon & Schuster, 1989), p. 594.

15. Gudmundsson, *Stormtroop Tactics,* p. 18.

16. Ibid., p. 147.

17. *Marine Rifle Company / Platoon,* FMFM 6-4 (Washington, D.C.: HQMC, 1978), p. 5.

18. Memorandum for the record by H.J. Poole.

19. Bermudez, *North Korean Special Forces,* p. 155.

20. *Inside North Korea: Three Decades of Duplicity* (Seoul: Inst. of Internal and External Affairs, 1975), p. 74, from Bermudez, *North Korean Special Forces,* p. 233.

Appendix A: *Extent of Rifleman Training*

1. *Marine Corps Ground Training in WWII,* by Kenneth W. Condit, Gerald Diamond, and Edwin T. Turnbladh (Washington, D.C.: Hist. Br., HQMC, 1956), p. 161; WWII Gyrene (www.ww2gyrene.org), s.v. "boot camp."
2. *Marine Corps Ground Training in WWII,* by Condit, Diamond, and Turnbladh, pp. 164, 165.
3. WWII Gyrene (www.ww2gyrene.org), s.v. "boot camp."
4. CG FMF in SDA ltr to CMC, 17Sep43, 1975-60-20-10, in *Marine Corps Ground Training in WWII,* by Condit, Diamond, and Turnbladh, p. 167.
5. *Marine Corps Ground Training in WWII,* by Condit, Diamond, and Turnbladh, p. 172; WWII Gyrene (www.ww2gyrene.org), s.v. "boot camp."
6. Dir P&P memo to CMC, 23Feb43, 1975-60-20-10, in *Marine Corps Ground Training in WWII,* by Condit, Diamond, and Turnbladh, p. 171.
7. Commemorative website at the following url: Http://greatestgeneration.tumblr.com/post/3528703327/knife-fight-training-at-marine-boot-camp-in-san-diego.
8. *Marine Corps Ground Training in WWII,* by Condit, Diamond, and Turnbladh, pp. 9-17.
9. Commemorative website at the following url: Http://ablecompany24.com/CAMPS/advancedtraining.html.
10. *Wikipedia Encyclopedia,* s.v. "Parris Island."
11. *Marine Corps Ground Training in WWII,* by Condit, Diamond, and Turnbladh, pp. 164.
12. "A Brief History of the United States Marine Corps in San Diego," by CW2 Mark J. Denger, California State Military Museum.
13. John C. Shivley, *The Last Lieutenant* (New York: New American Library, 2002), p. 38, in the following url: http://ablecompany24.com/CAMPS/advancedtraining.html.
14. Philip Emerson Wood, letter of December, 1942, in this url: http://ablecompany24.com/CAMPS/advancedtraining.html.
15. Commemorative website at the following url: Http://ablecompany24.com/CAMPS/advancedtraining.html.
16. *Semper Fidelis,* Camp Lejeune Environmental Mgt. Div., pp. 32-34.
17. Commemorative website at the following url: Http://ablecompany24.com/CAMPS/advancedtraining.html.
18. *Semper Fidelis,* Camp Lejeune Environmental Mgt. Div., p. 31.
19. *Fighting on Guadalcanal, FMFRP 12-110* (Washington, D.C. U.S.A. War Office, 1942), p. 25.
20. *Semper Fidelis,* Camp Lejeune Environmental Mgt. Div., p. 32.

21. Ibid.
22. Ibid., p. 34.
23. John Barry letter of 13 September 1943 (#64 from the list at http://www.jbww2.com/32.html), within the following url: http://ablecompany24.com/CAMPS/advancedtraining.html.
24. Ibid.
25. Ibid.
26. Eugene B. Sledge, *With the Old Breed* (New York: Ballantine Books, 2007), p. 19, in the following url: http://ablecompany24.com/CAMPS/advancedtraining.html.
27. Commemorative website at the following url: Http://ablecompany24.com/CAMPS/advancedtraining.html.
28. "Sands of Iwo Jima," videocassette, 109 min., Republic Pictures, 1988.
29. WWII Gyrene (www.ww2gyrene.org), s.v. "flamethrower."
30. "Gung Ho," Universal Studios.
31. Col. Merritt A. Edson, in *Fighting on Guadalcanal,* pp. 14-19.
32. "From Makin to Bougainville," by Hoffman, p. 23.
33. "Gung Ho," Universal Studios.
34. *Semper Fidelis: A Brief History of Onslow County, North Carolina, and of Camp Lejeune,* p. 59.
35. Ibid., p. 71.
36. Ibid., p. 80.
37. Memorandum for the record by H.J. Poole.
38. "Sands of Iwo Jima," Republic Pictures.

Glossary

3/1	3rd Battalion, 1st Marines	U.S. Marine infantry battalion.
1/3	1st Battalion, 3rd Marines	U.S. Marine infantry battalion.
2/3	2nd Battalion, 3rd Marines	U.S. Marine infantry battalion.
3/3	3rd Battalion, 3rd Marines	U.S. Marine infantry battalion.
1/4	1st Battalion, 4th Marines	U.S. Marine infantry battalion.
2/4	2nd Battalion, 4th Marines	U.S. Marine infantry battalion.
3/4	3rd Battalion, 4th Marines	U.S. Marine infantry battalion.
1/5	1st Battalion, 5th Marines	U.S. Marine infantry battalion.
1/9	1st Battalion, 9th Marines	U.S. Marine infantry battalion.
2/21	2nd Battalion, 21st Marines	U.S. Marine infantry battalion.
3/22	3rd Battalion, 22nd Marines	U.S. Marine infantry battalion.
2/29	2nd Battalion, 29th Marines	U.S. Marine infantry battalion.
3/29	3rd Battalion, 29th Marines	U.S. Marine infantry battalion.
A-4	U.S. aircraft designator	Douglas "Skyhawk," carrier-capable ground-attack jet
ACT	Advanced Combat Training	Additional infantry instruction
AK47	Communist weapon designator	North Vietnamese assault rifle
APD	Auxiliary Personnel [Transport] Destroyer	U.S Navy destroyer converted for carrying Marine Raiders

ARVN	Army of [the Republic] of Vietnam	South Vietnamese ground forces
B-40	Communist weapon designator	North Vietnamese variant of RPG-2
BAR	Browning Automatic Rifle	Heavy repeating rifle used in WWII
B.C.	Before Christ	Prior to the year zero
C-47	U.S. aircraft designator	"Skytrain" or "Dakota," developed from Douglas DC-3 transportation aircraft and then reconfigured to drop illumination flares
CAC	Combined Action Company	Administrative headquarters for several CAPs
CAG	Combined Action Group	Administrative headquarters for several CACs
CAP	Combined Action Platoon	Unit consisting of three PF squads, each containing one U.S. Marine fire team
CBS	Columbia Broadcasting System	U.S. TV network
CCF	Chinese Communist Forces	Another name for the PLA
CCRB	Course Curriculum Review Board	Panel to insure what taught comes from principal manuals
CIDG	Civilian Irregular Defense Group	Assemblage of Vietnamese militiamen
CO	Commanding Officer	Person in command of a unit
CP	Command Post	Place from which unit commander operates
CWO	Chief Warrant Officer	Senior member of intermediate level between enlisted and officer ranks

DA	Department of the Army	Pentagon's subsection for the Army
DHCB	Dong Ha Combat Base	U.S. installation at Dong Ha
DIA	Defense Intelligence Agency	U.S. enemy information bureau
DMZ	Demilitarized Zone	No-mans land between North and South Vietnam
E-5	Pay grade designator	Sergeant in the Marines
E-6	Pay grade designator	Staff Sergeant in the Marines
E-7	Pay grade designator	Gunnery Sergeant in the Marines
E-8	Pay grade designator	First Sergeant or Master Sergeant in the Marines
E-9	Pay grade designator	Sergeant Major or Master Gunnery Sergeant in the Marines
E&E	Escape and Evasion	Art of eluding a pursuer
ELO	Essential Learning Objective	Teaching goal
FAC	Forward Air Controller	He who controls airstrikes
FDC	Fire Direction Center	Where mortar tube settings computed on a plotting board
FMCR	Fleet Marine Corps Reserve	Where enlisted personnel, who have enough active-duty years to retire, go until reaching 30-year mark
FMFM	Fleet Marine Field Manual	Instructional pamphlet
4GW	Fourth Generation Warfare	War waged in four arenas at once—religious/psychological, economic, political, and martial

GI	Government issue	Colloquial term for U.S. military service member
HQMC	Headquarters Marine Corps	Staff sections through which Commandant manages the organization
ICT	Individual Combat Training	Infantryman instruction
IJA	Imperial Japanese Army	Nipponese ground forces
ITR	Infantry Training Regiment	Marine training command
ITS	Infantry Training School	Marine place of preparation for all junior enlisted jobs within infantry field
JCS	Joint Chiefs of Staff	Leaders of all U.S. service branches
KIA	Killed in Action	Those who expire in combat.
LAAW	Light Antitank Assault Weapon	M-72A2, mostly used for bunker busting in Vietnam
LAR	Light Armored Reconnaissance	Reconnoitering by lightly armed, wheeled personnel carriers
LCM-8	Landing Craft Medium	Small, front-loaded Navy cargo vessel
LP	Listening Post	Nighttime OP
LPO	Communist weapon designator	North Vietnamese flamethrower
LVT	Landing Vehicle Tracked	Marine amphibious tractor
LVTH	Landing Vehicle Tracked Howitzer	LVT with gun turret on top
LZ	Landing Zone	Helicopter touch-down area
M14	U.S. weapon designator	Main service rifle during early stages of Vietnam War

M16	U.S. weapon designator	Main service rifle during latter stages of Vietnam War
M-42	U.S. Army "Duster"	Twin 40mm guns on tank chassis, only used in ground fire role in Vietnam
M48	U.S. weapon designator	Medium Marine tank
M.A.	Master of Assault	WWII Marine infantryman's graduation diploma for advanced training
MAF	Marine Amphibious Force	Overall designation of Marines deployed to Vietnam
MARSOC	Marine Special Operations Command	Headquarters of all Marine special operators
MCRD	Marine Corps Recruit Depot	Marine boot camp
MEF	Marine Expeditionary Force	Overall designation of Marines's standby force
MILES	Multiple Integrated Laser Engagement System	Individually worn device for simulated casualty assessment, registers hit with continual beeping sound
MULE	U.S. vehicle designator	M274 Truck, Platform, Utility, 1/2 Ton, 4X4
MW	Maneuver Warfare	Way of fighting in which surprise takes precedence over firepower
NCO	Noncommissioned Officer	Junior enlisted leader, pay grades E-4 and E-5
NCOIC	NCO in Charge	Head NCO
NVA	North Vietnamese Army	U.S. foe in Vietnam
OIC	Officer in Charge	Head commissioned officer

OJT	On-the-Job Training	Instruction through actually doing something
ONTOS	U.S. weapon designator	Rifle, Multiple 106 mm, Self-propelled, M50
OP	Observation Post	Viewing station.
PF	Popular Forces	Local militiaman in Vietnam
PFC	Private First Class	Second-lowest enlisted rank in the U.S. military
PLA	People's Liberation Army	Parent of all Mainland Chinese Armed Forces
POW	Prisoner of War	Captured enemy combatant
PT	Physical (Fitness) Training	Group exercise in the military
RPD	Communist weapon designator	North Vietnamse automatic rifle with bipod mount
RPG	Rocket Propelled Grenade Weapon	North Vietnamese bazooka
SA-2	Communist weapon designator	North Vietnamese surface-to-air missile
SEABEE	Phonetic spelling of "construction battalion"	Navy builders of ground support facilities
2GW	Second Generation Warfare	Focus is on destroying enemy strongpoints and people
SF	Special Forces	U.S. Army special operators
SKS	Communist weapon designator	North Vietnamese rifle
SNCO	Staff Noncommissioned Officer	More senior enlisted leader, pay grades E-6 and above
SOI	School of Infantry	USMC grunt academy
TAOR	Tactical Area of Responsibility	A unit's assigned sector

3GW	Third Generation Warfare	Focus is on bypassing foe's strongpoints to more easily destroy his strategic assets
TNT	2,4,6-Trinitrotoluene	An early type of explosive
U.S.	United States	America
USMC	United States Marine Corps	America's amphibious force
UW	Unconventional Warfare	For infantrymen, E&E and fighting like a guerrilla
VC	Viet Cong	NVA-advised guerrillas in Vietnam
WIA	Wounded in Action	Injured in combat
WWI	World War I	First global conflict
WWII	World War II	Second global conflict
WWIII	World War III	Next global conflict
XO	Executive Officer	Second in command of a unit
YD	Military map reading acronym	Same as Grid Coordinate (GC), map location in relation to 1,000-meter longitudinal and latitudinal increments

Bibliography

U.S. Government Publications, Databases, and News Releases

Bougainville and the Northern Solomons. By Major John N. Rentz. "USMC Historical Monograph." Washington, D.C.: Historical Branch, Headquarters Marine Corps, 1946. As retrieved from url: www.ibiblio.org/hyperwar/USMC/USMC-M-NSols/USMC-M-NSol-2.html

"A Brief History of the 4th Marines." By James S. Santelli. *Marine Corps History Reference Pamphlet.* Washington, D.C.: Historical Division, Headquarters Marine Corps, 1970.

"A Brief History of the United States Marine Corps in San Diego." By CW2 Mark J. Denger. California State Military Museum. At this url: http://www.militarymuseum.org/SDMarines.html#15.

Campaigning. FMFM 1-1. Washington, D.C.: Headquarters Marine Corps, 1990.

"The Chosin Reservoir Campaign." By Lynn Montross and Captain Nicholas A. Canzona. *U.S. Marine Operations in Korea 1950-1953 Series.* Volume III. Washington, D.C.: Historical Branch, Headquarters Marine Corps, 1957.

Command Chronologies for 1st and 3rd Battalions, 4th Marines. U.S. Marine Corps History Division Vietnam War Documents Collection. The Vietnam Center and Archive, Texas Tech University. From urls: www.recordsofwar.com/vietnam/usmc/1stBn4thMarines.htm and www.recordsofwar.com/vietnam/usmc/3rdBn4thMarines.htm.

Drea, Edward J. "Nomonhan: Japanese—Soviet Tactical Combat, 1939." *Leavenworth Papers No. 2.* Ft. Leavenworth, KS: Combat Studies Institute, U.S. Army's Command and General Staff College, 1981.

"Fact Sheet on the Combined Action Force." III MAF, 31 March 1970. As retrieved from the unofficial website of the CAP Program.

Fighting on Guadalcanal. FMFRP 12-110. Washington, D.C.: U.S.A. War Office, 1942.

"The Final Campaign: Marines in the Victory on Okinawa." By Colonel Joseph H. Alexander. *Marines in WWII Commemorative Series.* Washington, D.C.: History and Museums Division, Headquarters Marine Corps, 1996.

"From Makin to Bougainville: Marine Raiders in the Pacific War." By Major Jon T. Hoffman. *Marines in WWII Commemorative Series.* Washington, D.C.: Marine Corps Historical Center, 1995.

"The Future Role of the Combined Action Program." By Major Michael Duane Weltsch USMC. Thesis for U.S. Army's Command and General Staff College, 1991.

The Guerrilla and How to Fight Him. FMFRP 19-9. Quantico, VA: Marine Corps Combat Development Command, 1990.

Handbook on German Military Forces. TM-E 30-451. Washington, D.C.: U.S. War Department, 1945. Reprint. Baton Rouge, LA: LSU Press, 1990.

Handbook on Japanese Military Forces. TM-E 30-480. Washington, D.C.: U.S. War Department, 1944. Reprint. Baton Rouge, LA: Louisiana State University Press, 1991.

Handbook on the Chinese Armed Forces. DDI-2680-32-76. Washington, D.C.: Defense Intelligence Agency, July 1976.

Handbook on the Chinese Communist Army. DA Pamphlet 30-51. Washington, D.C.: Headquarters Department of the Army, 7 December 1960.

Handbook on the Chinese People's Liberation Army. DDB-2680-32-84. Washington, D.C.: Defense Intelligence Agency, November 1984.

Handbook On U.S.S.R. Military Forces. TM 30-340. Washington, D.C.: U.S. War Department, 1945. Republished as *Soviet Tactical Doctrine in WWII,* with foreword by Shawn Caza. West Chester, OH: G.F. Nafziger, 1997.

Huber, Thomas M. "Japan's Battle for Okinawa, April - June 1945." *Leavenworth Papers No. 18.* Ft. Leavenworth, KS: Combat Studies Institute, U.S. Army's Command and General Staff College, 1990. As retrieved on 19 November 2011 from the following url: www.cgsc.edu/carl/resources/csi/Huber/Huber.asp#contents.

"Instances of Use of United States Armed Forces Abroad, 1798-2010." By Richard F. Grimmett. *Congressional Research Service Report R41677,* 10 March 2011.

Isolation of Rabaul. By Henry I. Shaw and Major Douglas T. Kane. *History of U.S. Marine Corps Operations in World War II Series.* Volume II. Washington, D.C.: Historical Branch, Headquarters Marine Corps, 1963. As retrieved from the following url: www.ibiblio.org/hyperwar/USMC/II/index.html#contents.

Iwo Jima: Amphibious Epic. Lieutenant Colonel Whitman S. Bartley. Washington, D.C.: Historical Branch, Headquarters Marine Corps, 1954.

Lupfer, Timothy T. "The Dynamics of Doctrine: The Changes in German Tactical Doctrine during the First World War." *Leavenworth Papers No. 4.* Fort Leavenworth, KS: Combat Studies Institute, U.S. Army's Command and General Staff College, 1981. As referenced in MCI 7401, *Tactical Fundamentals,* 1st Course in Warfighting Skills Program (Washington, D.C.: Marine Corps Institute, 1989), page 43.

"Malaysia: A Country Study." DA Pamphlet 550-45. *Area Handbook Series.* Washington, D.C.: Headquarters Department of the Army, 1984.

Malik, Mohan. *Dragon on Terrorism: Assessing China's Tactical Gains and Strategic Losses Post-September 11.* Carlisle, PA: Strategic Studies Institute, U. S. Army's War College, October 2002.

Marine Corps Ground Training in WWII. By Kenneth W. Condit, Gerald Diamond, and Edwin T. Turnbladh. Washington, D.C.: Historical Branch, G-3, Headquarters Marine Corps, 1956. Xerox of pages 7-31 and 158-175, from Museum at Marine Corps Recruit Depot Parris Island.

Marine Rifle Company / Platoon. FMFM 6-4. Washington, D.C.: Headquarters Marine Corps, 1978.

"The Marine War: III MAF in Vietnam, 1965-1971." By Jack Shulimson. Washington, D.C.: Marine Corps Historical Center, 1996. From url: www.vietnam.ttu.edu/events/1996_Symposium/96papers/marwar.htm

Marines in the Central Solomons. By Major John N. Rentz. "USMC Historical Monograph." Washington, D.C.: Historical Branch, Headquarters Marine Corps, 1952. As retrieved on 30 November 2011 from the following url: www.ibiblio.org/hyperwar/USMC/USMC-M-CSol/USMC-M-CSol-1.html

McMichael, Major Scott R. "The Chinese Communist Forces in Korea." *A Historical Perspective on Light Infantry.* Chapter 2. *Leavenworth Research Survey No. 6.* Fort Leavenworth, KS: Combat Studies Institute, U.S. Army's Command and General Staff College, 1987.

Night Movements. Translated and preface by C. Burnett. Tokyo: Imperial Japanese Army, 1913. Reprint. Port Townsend, WA: Loompanics Unlimited, n.d.

Official 1st Amtrac Battalion website. As retrieved from the following url: www.amtrac.org.

Official 1st Battalion, 4th Marines' website. As retrieved from this url: www.i-mef.usmc.mil/external/1stmardiv/1stmarregt/1-4/.

Official 4th Marines' website. As retrieved from the following url: www.marines.mil/unit/3rdmardiv/4thregiment/Pages/HomePage.aspx

Official 2nd Battalion, 4th Marines' website. As retried from this url: www.i-mef.usmc.mil/external/1stmardiv/5thmarregt/2-4/.
Official 3rd Battalion, 4th Marines' website. As retried from this url: www.i-mef.usmc.mil/external/1stmardiv/7thmarregt/3-4/.
Okinawa: The Last Battle. By Roy E. Appleman, James M. Burns, Russell A. Gugeler, and John Stevens. *United States Army in World War II Series*. Washington, D.C.: U.S. Army's Center of Military History, 2000. As retrieved on 30 November 2011 from the following url: www.history.army.mil/books/wwii/okinawa/index.htm#contents.
Okinawa: Victory in the Pacific. By Major Chas. S. Nichols, Jr., USMC, and Henry I. Shaw, Jr. "USMC Historical Monograph." Washington, D.C.: Historical Branch, Headquarters Marine Corps, 1955. As retrieved from the following url: www.ibiblio.org/hyperwar/USMC/USMC-M-Okinawa/index.html#index
The Recapture of Guam. By Major O.R. Lodge. "USMC Historical Monograph." Washington, D.C.: Historical Branch, Headquarters Marine Corps, 1954. As retrieved from the following url: www.ibiblio.org/hyperwar/USMC/USMC-M-Guam/index.html.
Semper Fidelis: A Brief History of Onslow County, North Carolina, and of Camp Lejeune. Document prepared by the Louis Berger Group Incorporated under contract with the U.S. Army's Corps of Engineers and with Lieutenant Colonel Lynn L. Kimball USMC (Ret.) as consulting historian. Camp Lejeune, NC: Environmental Management Division, 2006.
Tactics. FMFM 1-3. Washington, D.C.: Headquarters Marine Corps, 1991.
U.S. Marines in Vietnam: An Expanding War, 1966. By Jack Shulimson. Washington, D.C.: History and Museums Division, Headquarters Marine Corps, 1982.
U.S. Marines in Vietnam: Fighting the North Vietnamese 1967. By Major Gary Tefler, Lieutenant Colonel Lane Rogers, and V. Keith Fleming, Jr. Washington, D.C.: History and Museums Division, Headquarters Marine Corps, 1984.
U.S. Marines in Vietnam: High Mobility and Standdown 1969. By Charles R. Smith. Washington, D.C.: History and Museums Division, Headquarters Marine Corps, n.d.
U.S. Marines in Vietnam: The Defining Year 1968. By Jack Shulimson, Lieutenant Colonel Leonard A. Blaisol, Charles R. Smith, and Captain David A. Dawson. Washington, D.C.: History and Museums Division, Headquarters Marine Corps, 1997.
"The War in the Northern Provinces: 1966-68." By Lieutenant General Willard Pearson. *Vietnam Studies*. Washington, D.C.: Headquarters Department of the Army, 1975.
Warfighting. FMFM 1. Washington, D.C.: Headquarters Marine Corps, 1989.

Civilian Publications

Analytical Studies, Databases, and Websites

Alexander, Joseph H. *Edson's Raiders: 1st Marine Raider Battalion in World War II.* Annapolis, MD: Naval Institute Press, 2001.
Answers. As retrieved from its website, answers.com.
Association of the Combined Action Program website. As retrieved from this following url: http://www.cap-assoc.org/.
Association of 1st Battalion, 4th Marines' website. As retrieved from this url: http://1stbn4thmarines.com/.
Association of 4th Marines' website. As retrieved from the following url: www.marines.mil/unit/3rdmardiv/4thregiment/.../HomePage.aspx.
Association of 2nd Battalion, 4th Marines' website. As retrieved from this url: http://www.2ndbn4thmarines.com/.
Association of 3rd Battalion, 4th Marines' website. As retrieved from this url: http://thundering-third.org.
Association of U.S. Marine Raiders' website. As retrieved from this url: http://www.usmarineraiders.org/.
Association of 6th Marine Division website. As retrieve from the url: http://www.sixthmarinedivision.com.
Bermudez, Joseph S., Jr. *North Korean Special Forces.* Annapolis, MD: Naval Institute Press, 1998.
Carlson, Evans F. *Twin Stars of China: A Behind-the-Scenes Story of China's Valiant Struggle for Existence by a U. S. Marine who Lived and . . ."* N.p.: Dodd Mead, 1940. Excerpts as quoted in *Gunny G.'s Globe and Anchor,* s.v. "gung ho." As retrieved from the following url in August 2011: http://www.angelfire.com/ca/dickg/gungho.html.
China Page. As retrieved from its website, www.chinapage.com.
Chinh, Truong. *Primer for Revolt.* Introduction by Bernard B. Fall. New York: Praeger, 1963.
Clark, George B. *Their Time in Hell: The 4th Marine Brigade at Belleau Wood.* Pike, NH: The Brass Hat, 1996.
Commemorative website at the following url: http://bellsouthpwp.net/p/d/pdavison/memorial.html.
Daley, LaVarre. *United States Marine Corps Raiders: A Personal Account.* N.p.: Pal-Mit Industries, 2002.
Dan Marsh's Marine Raider Page. Created by former member of 4th Raider Battalion. As retrieved in November 2011 from its website, www.usmcraiders.com.
Davidson, Phillip B. *Vietnam at War—The History: 1946-1975.* New York: Oxford University Press, 1988.
Davis, Burke. *Marine.* New York: Bantam Books, 1964.
Dunnigan, James F. and Albert A. Nofi. *Dirty Little Secrets of the Vietnam War.* New York: Thomas Dunne Books, 1999.

The German Squad in Combat. Translated and edited by U.S. Military Intelligence Service. From a German manual. N.p., 1943. Republished as *German Squad Tactics in WWII*. By Matthew Gajkowski. West Chester, OH: Nafziger, 1995.

Giap, General Vo Nguyen. "Once Again We Will Win." As quoted in *The Military Art of People's War,* edited by Russel Stetler. New York: Monthly Review Press, 1970.

Gilbert, Ed. *U.S. Marine Corps Raider 1942-43*. London: Osprey Publishing, 2006.

Global Security. From its website, globalsecurity.org.

Gudmundsson, Bruce I. *Stormtroop Tactics—Innovation in the German Army 1914-1918*. New York: Praeger, 1989.

Hackworth, David H. and Julie Sherman. *About Face*. New York: Simon & Schuster, 1989.

Hemingway, Al. *Our War Was Different*. Annapolis, MD: Naval Institute Press, 1994.

Henderson, Wm. Darryl. *Cohesion: The Human Element in Combat*. Washington, D.C.: National Defense University Press, 1985.

Hoyt, Edwin P. *The Marine Raiders*. New York: Pocket Books, 1989.

Jackson, Richard D. *Yesterdays Are Forever: A Rite of Passage through the Marine Corps and Vietnam*. Galt, CA: Working Title Publishing, 2007.

Kim, Ashida. *The Invisible Ninja: Ancient Secrets of Surprise*. New York: Citadel Press, 1983.

Lanning, Michael Lee and Dan Cragg. *Inside the VC and the NVA: The Real Story of North Vietnam's Armed Forces*. New York: Ivy Books, 1992.

Lind, William S. *The Maneuver Warfare Handbook*. Boulder, CO: Westview Press, 1985.

Livingston, James E., Colin D. Heaton, and Anne-Marie Lewis. *Noble Warrior*. Minneapolis: Zenith Press, 2010.

Maitland, Terrence and Peter McInerney. *Vietnam Experience: A Contagion of War*. Newton, MA: Boston Publishing, 1968.

Mao's Generals Remember Korea. Translated and edited by Xiaobing Li, Allan R. Millett, and Bin Yu. Lawrence, KS: University Press of Kansas, 2001.

Mao Tse-tung: An Anthology of His Writings. Edited by Anne Fremantle. New York: Mentor, 1962.

Merriam-Webster Dictionary. As retrieved from its website, www.merriam-webster.com.

Merrill, Ray. *My Three Years in the Marine Corps*. Leawood, KS: Leathers Publishing, 2003.

Military History Online. As retrieved from its website, militaryhistoryonline.com.

Morning Sun (China). As retrieved from its website, morningsun.org.
Nolan, Keith William. *Operation Buffalo: USMC Fight for the DMZ* New York: Dell Publishing, 1991.
Nolan, Keith. *The Magnificent Bastards: The Joint Army-Marine Defense of Dong Ha, 1968*. New York: Ballantine, 2007.
Peterson, Michael E. *The Combined Action Platoons: The U.S. Marines' Other War in Vietnam*. New York: Praeger, 1989.
Phrases. As retrieved from its website, www.phrases.org.uk.
Poole, H. John. *Dragon Days: Time for "Unconventional" Tactics*. Emerald Isle, NC: Posterity Press, 2007.
Poole, H. John. *Global Warrior: Averting WWIII*. Emerald Isle, NC: Posterity Press, 2011.
Poole, H.J. *The Last Hundred Yards: The NCO's Contribution to Warfare*. Emerald Isle, NC: Posterity Press, 1997.
Poole, H. John. *One More Bridge to Cross: Lowering the Cost of War*. Emerald Isle, NC: Posterity Press, 1999.
Poole, H. John. *Phantom Soldier: The Enemy's Answer to U.S. Firepower*. Emerald Isle, NC: Posterity Press, 2001.
Poole, H. John. *Tequila Junction: 4th-Generation Counterinsurgency*. Emerald Isle, NC: Posterity Press, 2008.
Poole, H. John. *Terrorist Trail: Backtracking the Foreign Fighter*. Emerald Isle, NC: Posterity Press, 2006.
Poole, H. John. *The Tiger's Way: A U.S. Private's Best Chance for Survival*. Emerald Isle, NC: Posterity Press, 2003.
Ross, Bill D. *Iwo Jima—Legacy of Valor*. New York: Vintage Books, 1986.
Smith, George W. *Carlson's Raid: The Daring Marine Assault on Makin*. Novato, CA: Presidio Press, 2001.
Smith, Michael S. *Bloody Ridge: The Battle That Saved Guadalcanl*. Novato, CA: Presidio Press, 2000.
Soviet Combat Regulations of November 1942. Moscow: [Stalin], 1942. Republished as *Soviet Infantry Tactics in World War II: Red Army Infantry Tactics from Squad to Rifle Company from the Combat Regulations*. With translation, introduction, and notes by Charles C. Sharp. West Chester, OH: George Nafziger, 1998.
The Strategic Advantage: Sun Zi & Western Approaches to War. Edited by Cao Shan. Beijing: New World Press, 1997.
Sun Bin's Art of War: World's Greatest Military Treatise. Translated by Sui Yun. Singapore: Chung Printing, 1999.
Sun Tzu. *The Art of War*. Translated by Samuel B. Griffith. Foreword by B.H. Liddell Hart. New York: Oxford University Press, 1963.
Sun Tzu. *The Art of War*. Translated by Thomas Cleary. Boston, MA: Shambhala Publications, 1988.

Sun Tzu: The New Translation. By J.H. Huang. New York: William Morrow, 1993.

Sun Tzu's Art of War: The Modern Chinese Interpretation. By General Tao Hanzhang. Translated by Yuan Shibing. New York: Sterling Publishing, 1990.

Synopsis of *Killing Ground on Okinawa: The Battle of Sugar Loaf Hill.* By James J. Hallas. Annapolis, MD: Naval Institute Press, n.d. From Tom's Recommended Reading Roster. As retrieved from the url: www.once-an-eagle.com/docs/readingroster.html

36 Stratagems: Secret Art of War. Translated by Koh Kok Kiang and Liu Yi. Singapore: Asiapac Books, 1992.

Unofficial website of the CAP Program. As retrieved from this url: http://capmarine.com/index.htm.

West, Bing. *The Village.* New York: Pocket Books, 1972.

Wikipedia Encyclopedia. As retrieved from its website, wikipedia.org.

Wukovits, John. *American Commando.* New York: New American Library (Penguin) 2009.

Yahara, Col. Hiromichi Yahara. *The Battle for Okinawa.* Translated by Roger Pineau and Masatoshi Uehara. New York: John Wiley & Sons, 1995.

Young, Paul R. *First Recon—Second to None: A Marine Reconnaissance Battalion in Vietnam, 1967-68.* New York: Ivy Books, 1992.

Zich, Arthur and the editors of Time-Life Books. *The Rising Sun: World War II.* Alexandria, VA: Time-Life Books, 1977.

Videotapes, Movies, DVDs, TV Programs, Slide Shows, and Illustrations

"Gung Ho!: The Story of Carlson's Makin Island Raiders." Movie. 87 minutes. Universal Studios, 1943. Based on factual story by Lt. W.S. LeFrancois USMC. With Lt.Col. Evans Carlson USMCR as technical advisor.

"Heartbreak Ridge." Movie. 130 minutes. Directed and produced by Clint Eastwood. Warner Home Video, 1986.

"The Pacific." DVD. 10-part miniseries. 530 minutes. From Tom Hanks, Steven Spielberg, and Gary Goetzman. HBO and DreamWorks, n.d.

"Sands of Iwo Jima." Videocassette. 109 minutes. Republic Pictures, 1988.

"Victory in the Pacific," PBS's *American Experience.* NC Public TV, 1 April 2012.

Letters, E-Mail, and Direct Verbal Conversations

Former member of 3rd Raider Battalion and then 3/4. In conversations with author during October 2010, August 2011, and the Fall of 2011.

Guthrie, CWO4 Charles "Tag," A/1/4 member at Con Thien. In e-mails to the author between November 2011 and July 2012.

Multi-tour U.S. Army Special Forces veteran of wars in Iraq and Afghanistan. In telephone conversations with author between September 2006 and late 2011.

Vietnam era Marine intelligence, infantry, and CAP veteran. In telephone conversations with author during first half of 2012.

Newspaper, Magazine, Radio, and Website Articles

Carlson, Evans. As quoted in "Gung Ho," by Alfred F. Moe, *American Speech,* volume 42, number 1, February 1967, page 58. And originally from interview associated with "Carlson of the Raiders," by Don Burke, *Life,* 20 September 1943.

Cooling, Major Norman L. "Russia's 1994-96 Campaign for Chechnya: A Failure in Shaping the Battlespace." *Marine Corps Gazette,* October 2001.

Kitchens, Lieutenant Colonel Gregory H., USMCR. "Building the Team for Unit Excellence." *Marine Corps Gazette,* December 2003.

Lehrack, Otto. "Dai Do: The Strategic Battle for Dong Ha," *Leatherneck,* March 2009.

Leinster, Colin. "The Two Wars of General Walt." *Life,* 26 May 1967.

Lind, William S. "Fourth Generation Warfare's First Blow: A Quick Look." *Marine Corps Gazette,* November 2001.

McQuown, Max. "Learning from Dai Do." *Marine Corps Gazette,* April 1988.

Moser, Don. "Their Mission Defend, Befriend." *Life,* 25 August 1967. As retrieved from the following url: http://home.earthlink.net/~life_magazine_67/life_mag_008.htm.

Nolan, Keith William. "The Battle of Dai Do." *Leatherneck,* August 1994.

Rabinovich, Abraham. "Militants Seen As Able to Hit Tel Aviv." *Washington Times,* 18 July 2006.

"Some Interesting Facts about Korea: The Forgotten War." *DAV Magazine,* May/June 2000.

Taylor, Vic. "Hotel Company-Day Three." *Marine Corps Gazette,* April 2004.

Thomas, Lieutenant Colonel Timothy L. and Lester W. Grau. "Russian Lessons Learned from the Battles for Grozny." *Marine Corps Gazette,* April 2000.

Weise, William. "Memories of Dai Do." *Marine Corps Gazette,* September 1987.
Weise, William. "Memories of Dai Do [a Sequel]." *Marine Corps Gazette,* April 2004.
"What Was the Long March." By Kallie Szczepanski. *Asian History About.com.* As retrieved from the following url about 1 August 2011: http://asianhistory.about.com/od/asianhistoryfaqs/f/longmarch.htm.
"Why Did Armored Corps Fail in Lebanon." By Hanan Greenberg. Israeli News, 30 August 2006.

About the Author

After 28 years of commissioned and noncommissioned infantry service, John Poole retired from the United States Marine Corps in April 1993. While on active duty, he studied small-unit tactics for nine years: (1) six months at the Basic School in Quantico (1966); (2) seven months as a rifle platoon commander in Vietnam (1966-67); (3) three months as a rifle company commander at Camp Pendleton (1967); (4) five months as a regimental headquarters company (and camp) commander in Vietnam (1968); (5) eight months as a rifle company commander in Vietnam (1968-69); (6) five and a half years as an instructor with the Advanced Infantry Training Company (AITC) at Camp Lejeune (1986-92); and (7) one year as the Staff Noncommissioned Officer in Charge of the 3rd Marine Division Combat Squad Leaders Course (CSLC) on Okinawa (1992-93).

While at AITC, he developed, taught, and refined courses on maneuver warfare, land navigation, fire support coordination, call for fire, adjust fire, close air support, M203 grenade launcher, movement to contact, daylight attack, night attack, infiltration, defense, offensive Military Operations in Urban Terrain (MOUT), defensive MOUT, Nuclear/Biological/Chemical (NBC) defense, and leadership. While at CSLC, he further refined the same periods of instruction and developed others on patrolling.

He has completed all of the correspondence school requirements for the Marine Corps Command and Staff College, Naval War College (1,000-hour curriculum), and Marine Corps Warfighting Skills Program. He is a graduate of the Camp Lejeune Instructional Management Course, the 2nd Marine Division Skill Leaders in Advanced Marksmanship (SLAM) Course, and the East-Coast School of Infantry Platoon Sergeants' Course.

In the 18 years since retirement, John Poole has researched the small-unit tactics of other nations and written eleven other books: (1) *The Last Hundred Yards,* a squad combat study based on the consensus opinions of 1,200 NCOs and casualty statistics of AITC and CSLC field trials; (2) *One More Bridge to Cross*, a treatise on enemy proficiency at short range and how to match it; (3) *Phantom Soldier,* an in-depth look at the highly deceptive Asian style of war; (4) *The Tiger's Way,* the fighting styles of Eastern fire teams and soldiers; (5) *Tactics of the Crescent Moon,* insurgent procedures in Palestine, Chechnya, Afghanistan, and Iraq; (6) *Militant Tricks,* an honest appraisal of the so-far-undefeated *jihadist* method; (7) *Terrorist Trail,* tracing the *jihadists* in Iraq back to their home countries; (8) *Dragon Days,* an unconventional warfare technique manual; (9) *Tequila Junction,* how to fight narco-guerrillas; (10) *Homeland Siege,* confronting the 4GW assault by a foreign power's organized-crime proxies; and (11) *Expeditionary Eagles,* outmaneuvering the Taliban.

As of September 2010, John Poole had conducted multiday training sessions (on 4GW squad tactics) at 40 (mostly Marine) battalions, nine Marine schools, and seven special-operations units from all four U.S. service branches. Since 2000, he has done research in Mainland China (twice), North Korea, Vietnam, Cambodia, Thailand, India (twice), Pakistan (twice), Iran, Lebanon, Turkey, Egypt, Sudan, Tanzania, Venezuela, and Sri Lanka. Over the course of his lifetime, he has visited scores of other nations on all five continents. He tried to visit Lahore in the late Spring of 2011. The Pakistani visa request was not honored.

Between early tours in the Marine Corps (from 1969 to 1971), John Poole worked as a criminal investigator for the Illinois Bureau of Investigation (IBI). After attending the State Police Academy for several months in Springfield, he was assigned to the IBI's Chicago office. There, he worked mostly on general criminal and drug cases.

Name Index

A

B

C

D

E

F

G

H

I

J

K

R

S

T

U

V

W

X

No entries

Y

Z

No entries.